Armed Drones and Globalization in the Asymmetric War on Terror

This book is a critical exploration of the war on terror from the prism of armed drones and globalization. It is particularly focused on the United States' use of the drones, and the systemic dysfunctions that globalization has caused to international political economy and national security, creating backlash in which the desirability of globalization is not only increasingly questioned, but the resultant dissension about its desirability appears increasingly militating against the international consensus needed to fight the war on terror.

To underline the controversial nature of the "war on terror" and the pragmatic weapon (armed drones) fashioned for its prosecution, some of the elements of this controversy have been interrogated in this book. They include, amongst others, the doubt over whether the war should have been declared in the first place because terrorist attacks hardly meet the United Nations' casus belli—an armed attack. There are critics, as highlighted in this book, who believe that the "war on terror" is not an armed conflict properly so called, and, thus, remains only a "law enforcement issue".

The United States and all the states taking part in the war on terror are obligated to observe International Humanitarian Law (IHL). It is within this context of IHL that this book appraises the drone as a weapon of engagement, discussing such issues as "personality" and "signature" strikes as well as the implications of the deployment of spies as drone strikers rather than the Defence Department, the members of the U.S. armed forces. This book will be of value to researchers, academics, policymakers, professionals, and students in the fields of security studies, terrorism, the law of armed conflict, international humanitarian law, and international politics.

Professor Fred Aja Agwu is the Head of the Division of International Law and Organization at the Nigerian Institute of International Affairs (NIIA), Lagos, Nigeria.

Routledge Research in the Law of Armed Conflict

Available titles in this series include:

Islamic Law and the Law of Armed Conflict
The Armed Conflict in Pakistan
Niaz Shah

Cluster Munitions and International Law
Disarmament with a Human Face?
Alexander Breitegger

Accountability for Violations of International Humanitarian Law
Essays in Honour of Tim McCormack
Jadranka Petrovic

Humanization of Arms Control
Paving the Way for a World free of Nuclear Weapons
Daniel Rietiker

Armed Drones and Globalization in the Asymmetric War on Terror
Challenges for the Law of Armed Conflict and Global Political Economy
Fred Aja Agwu

Forthcoming titles in this series include:

International Law and Drone Strikes in Pakistan
The Legal and Socio-Political Aspects
Sikander Ahmed Shah

Islam and Warfare
Context and Compatibility with International Law
Onder Bakircioglu

The Concept of Military Objectives in International Law and Targeting Practice
Agnieszka Jachec-Neale

Cosmopolitan Ethics and Law on Autonomous Weapons in Modern Warfare
Ozlem Ulgen

Armed Drones and Globalization in the Asymmetric War on Terror

Challenges for the Law of Armed Conflict and Global Political Economy

Fred Aja Agwu

Routledge
Taylor & Francis Group
LONDON AND NEW YORK

First published 2018 by Routledge

2 Park Square, Milton Park, Abingdon, Oxfordshire OX14 4RN
52 Vanderbilt Avenue, New York, NY 10017

Routledge is an imprint of the Taylor & Francis Group, an informa business

First issued in paperback 2020

Library of Congress Cataloging-in-Publication Data
Names: Agwu, Fred, author.
Title: Armed drones and globalization in the asymmetric war on terror : challenges for the law of armed conflict and global political economy / Fred Aja Agwu.
Description: New York : Routledge, 2018. | Series: Routledge research in the law of armed conflict | Includes bibliographical references and index.
Identifiers: LCCN 2017040078 | ISBN 9781138566934 (hardback) | ISBN 9781351342582 (webpdf) | ISBN 9781351342568 (mobipocket) | ISBN 9781351342575 (epub)
Subjects: LCSH: Uninhabited combat aerial vehicles (International law) | Uninhabited combat aerial vehicles (International law)—United States. | Targeted killing—Government policy—United States. | War (International law) | War on Terror, 2001–2009. | Terrorism—Prevention—Law and legislation. | Globalization.
Classification: LCC KZ6687 .A39 2018 | DDC 341.6/3—dc23
LC record available at https://lccn.loc.gov/2017040078

ISBN: 978-1-138-56693-4 (hbk)
ISBN: 978-0-367-59365-0 (pbk)

Typeset in Galliard
by Apex CoVantage, LLC

Be they nation-states or non-state actors, this book is in furtherance of the message in the north garden at the United Nations Headquarters in New York, expressed in the bronze statute by the Soviet sculptor, Evgeny Vuchetich, that envisions and symbolizes when "we shall beat our Swords into Plowshares".

Contents

Acronyms

AARMS	Academic & Applied Research in Military Science
ACSRT	African Centre for the Study and Research on Terrorism
AJIL	*American Journal of International Law*
AMU	Arab Mahgreb Union
AMISON	African Union Mission in Somalia
APT	ASEAN Plus Three
AQAP	Al-Qaeda in the Arabian Peninsula
AQC	Al-Qaeda Central
AQEA	Al-Qaeda East Africa
AQIM	Al-Qaeda in the Islamic Maghreb
ARF	ASEAN Regional Forum
ASEAN	Association of South East Asian Nations
AUMF	Authorization for the Use of Military Force
AWS	Autonomous Weapon System
CENTCOM	Central Command (United States)
CIA	Central Intelligence Agency
COIN	Counter-insurgency
CNN	Cable News Network
CVE	Countering Violent Extremism
ECOWAS	Economic Community of West African States
ECtHR	European Court of Human Rights
FATA	Federally Administered Tribal Areas (Pakistan)
GPS	Global Public Square
GPS	Global Positioning System
ICBMs	Inter-Continental Ballistic Missiles
ICC	International Criminal Court
ICRC	International Committee of the Red Cross
ICSR	International Center for the Study of Radicalization
ICTY	International Criminal Tribunal for the former Yugoslavia
IEDs	Improvised Explosive Devices
IHL	International Humanitarian Law
IMT	International Military Tribunal
ISIS	Islamic State of Iraq and Syria

ISIL	Islamic State of Iraq and Levant
JSOC	Joint Special Operations Command
LaWS	Laser Weapon System
MALE	Medium-Altitude Long Endurance (armed drone)
MAOB	Massive Air Ordinance Blast
MJTF	Multinational Joint Task Force
MTCR	Missile Technology Control Regime (1987)
NASA	National Aeronautical and Space Agency
NATO	North Atlantic Treaty Organization
NCEF	National Christian Elders Forum
OLC	Office of Legal Counsel (State Department)
POW	Prisoner of War
P.5	Permanent 5 (members of the UN Security Council)
RAN CoE	Radicalization Awareness Network Center of Excellence
RCEP	Regional Comprehensive Economic Partnership
SCC	Shanghai Cooperation Council
SLAR	Side-Looking Airborne Radar
THAAD	Terminal High-Altitude Area Defence
TPP	Trans-Pacific Partnership
UAVs	Unmanned Aerial Vehicles
UMS	Unmanned Systems
UNGA	United Nations General Assembly
UNHCR	United Nations High Commission for Refugees
WoT	War on Terror

Preface

The central argument in this book is that armed drones and globalization play quixotic roles in the war on terror (WoT). Both are at the same time harmful and beneficial in the prosecution of the war. In the case of armed drones, it must be recalled that there have always been, at every historical juncture in the development of the law of armed conflict, serious problems in the adoption of legitimate means and methods of warfare. In this era of the asymmetric war on terror, these problems have been exacerbated by the emergence of armed drones as new weapons. Human ingenuity in technological invention and application has once again proved to be far ahead of the development of the law of armed conflict. Without prejudice to the efforts in the Martens Clause (including the associated efforts by legal publicists and the drafters of the various Hague Conventions up to the four Geneva Conventions and the Additional Protocols) to preempt the use of obnoxious methods and means of warfare to violate the principles of humanity, the emergence of insurgent terrorists that do not set stock by the rules engagement as well as the armed drones used to counter them have increasingly disrupted settled expectations in the conduct of the conflict.

Drone strikes have become increasingly controversial by the day. In this controversial nature, armed drones have become proximate to nuclear weapons in terms of ambiguity as weapons of war. This same ambiguity is also presented by globalization. Thus, and this is reinforcing the central proposition of this book, although armed drones and globalization were supposed to leverage the war on terror, they have become quixotic tools for the exacerbation of this infernal conflict. Whereas armed drones are supposed to ensure a pin-prick isolation and liquidation of terrorists without much collateral damage, these weapons have rather in most cases exacerbated these humanitarian tragedies, especially in the case of signature strikes; thus, orchestrating what critics call "a terrorism industrial complex". This complex is created by the "blowback" consequences.

The same goes for globalization. Whereas the technologically shrunken world and the attendant global village were supposed to mean prosperity for all nations and peoples, the inherent distortions in the globalizing world have meant that mass poverty and inequality have caused many nations and peoples to take up the cudgel against globalization, both in the developed and developing nations. Brexit is quite illustrative. Migration, which is a major component of globalization, has become stigmatized on account of its capacity to disperse terrorists, cause cultural contamination, and put pressure on public services, amongst other alleged complications. The consequence is that an otherwise globalizing world is witnessing a widespread relapse into nationalism and what *The Economist* calls "protectionism and nativism"; this situation has the danger of the world being deprived of the requisite general community coalescence that is required to tackle or prosecute the "war on terror". The situation in Syria is quite illustrative.

Again, in addition to being controversial weapons that cause complications for humanitarian principles in the war on terror, armed drones also pose serious challenges to the principles of self-defence, the observation of the rule of restricting battles to the frontlines, ethics of warfare, and chivalry in warfare, amongst others. These complications are direr with the prospect of the introduction of Autonomous Weapons Systems (AWS), which are robotic machines that lack the capacity for distinction and proportionality required in every armed combat. So, the "war on terror" may be raging today, but one of the most controversial realities surrounding it is that it is not yet fully regulated by international law. As a result of this situation, the "war" remains an intriguing one for the student of the law of armed conflict in particular and international law in general.

This book is a critical exploration of some of the objective scholarly perspectives on the war on terror, from the prism of armed drones and globalization. It is particularly focused on the United States' use of the drones, and the systemic dysfunctions that globalization has caused to international political economy and national security, creating some backlashes in which the desirability of globalization is not only increasingly questioned, the resultant dissension about its desirability appears increasingly militating against the international consensus needed to fight the war on terror. To underline the controversial nature of the "war on terror" and the pragmatic weapon (armed drones) fashioned for its prosecution, some of the elements of this controversy have been interrogated in this book; and they include, amongst others, first, the doubt over whether the war should have been declared in the first place because terrorist attacks hardly meet the United Nations' *casus belli*—an armed attack. There are critics, as highlighted in this book, who believe that the "war on terror" is not an armed conflict properly so called, and, thus, remains only a "law enforcement issue".

The second element is the armed drones' paradoxical narrative: a new species of weapon that is both a mixture of facts and fiction, fictionalized by the likes of Richard Clarke and Andrew Niccol, amongst others, to illustrate the fact that it is both today's weapon as well as the weapon of the future. Today's armed drone as an implement of warfare is a de facto implement, being (like the nuclear weapon) under no specific conventional law or treaty regulations. Hence, even when, like the nuclear weapon, its legality is ambiguous, its deployment in the war on terror remains legitimate as a pragmatic tool of self-defence against enemies that themselves do not play by the rules of engagement. But what is of more serious concern is not so much the issue of the legality of the armed drone as it is of the international humanitarian anxiety that its use occasions. Some of the scholarly positions explored in this book believe that the United States is violating international law in the application of the armed drone; but the position of this book is that this is hardly true because there is no law to be violated to the extent that the law of armed conflict does not regulate the use of armed drones; neither does it regulate terrorist insurgencies. And because the law did not envisage the "war on terror", it simply does not regulate it.

What the United States and all the states taking part in the war on terror are obligated to observe (courtesy the Martens Clause and Article 3 common to the Geneva Conventions) is International Humanitarian Law (IHL). So, it is within this context of IHL that this book appraises the drone as a weapon of engagement, discussing such issues as "personality" and "signature" strikes as well as the implications of the deployment of spies (the CIA as an intelligence agency) as drone strikers rather the Defence Department, the members of the U.S. armed forces. This contradiction reinforces the double or Janus-faced nature of the war on terror (a duel straddling between law enforcement and an armed conflict). If the war on terror were to be characterized solely as law enforcement, only a spy agency like the CIA can partake in its prosecution because the members of the armed forces would stand disqualified by the law; but if it were termed an armed conflict properly so called, its prosecution would remain the exclusive preserve of the members of the armed forces as combatants, while a spy agency like the CIA would be off it. Unfortunately, the status of this "war" remains contentious and unresolved.

This book also explores the characterization of this "war" as a "global war" on terror by the George W. Bush administration; vis-à-vis the cautions attitude of the Obama administration to that conceptual inclination. It, however, notes that this characterization implicitly touches the question of battlefields or frontlines (the battlespace) as well as the geographical spread of the conflict. But although there may be contestations over whether or not the "war on terror" is war properly so-called, what is evident is that this conflict is an asymmetric duel in which the so-called weaker opponent thrives because of, as the authorities explored in this book clearly highlight, (1) the existence of bigotry, warped, or extremist ideologies; (2) the existence of sanctuaries in permissive environments that are receptive and supportive; (3) the easy access to weapons; and (4) the increasing situations where active and functional intelligence seem not only to be diminishing but sometimes overwhelmed by the masterminds of terrorism.

Against the foregoing, this book sums up that in the armed drone and the "war on terror", the main protagonist, the United States, is confronted with a "grey area" in the environment of armed conflict. This "grey area" is a challenge that the Law of Armed Conflict must confront and resolve in order to streamline the use of armed drones vis-à-vis international law. This is the same way that the contradictions in globalization must be confronted and resolves in order to end or lessen its propensity to create and spread animosities that make individuals and groups susceptible to employing terrorist means to fight back. Nevertheless, it is not every work that is obliged to be dialectical in terms of proffering an alternative pathway or solutions. However, dialectical analyses are sometimes inevitable; so inevitable that it is, thus, difficult or impossible to escape them.

Hence, in the spirit of dialectics, I have tried, in the final chapter, to be part of the suggestion of ways to successfully prosecute the war on terror. But like Patrick Chabal and Jean-Pascal Dalox observed in their *Africa Works*, at page 163, this book is more of "a diagnosis" of the problem, a prognosis rather than a solution. The book is more of a prognosis than a guide to finding all the solutions to the problem. It does not have such overweening ambition or pretention to prescribing the solution to the entire problems. Rather, it draws attention to the challenges, the serious predicaments in the deployment or use of armed drones as well as other challenges to the successful prosecution of "the war on terror", like the challenges posed by the tendency to allow the contradictions in globalization to continue to fester; or even to retreat from globalization. So, this book ultimately leaves the task of proffering far-reaching solutions to the global policy establishment, the professionals, and the technical/scientific as well as socio-political and further legal researches in the Law of Armed Conflict and Globalization.

I must express my immense debt of gratitude to Dr. Micah Zenko of the United States Council on Foreign Relations for his contributions, directly and indirectly, in the making of this book. Although I had started the work before meeting Micah in May 2014 in New York, during a Council of Councils meeting, I must confess that his presentation during that meeting, alongside Dr. Marcel Dickow of the German Institute for International and Security Affairs, offered me some new vistas and tremendous insight. Over one year later in December 2015 when I was scrounging for additional relevant literature, I wrote Micah and he gave me some inestimable leads. Micah, I thank you. The researching of this book took place when there was unprecedented dearth of academic materials in the Library of the Nigerian Institute of International Affairs (NIIA), with the Institute at the cusp of failing to renew its e-library facilities, and with its computers down owing to disuse and power challenges. It was Mrs. Pamela Ogwuazor-Momah, one of the Senior Librarians in the Institute that came to my rescue, pressing her personal laptop to service. Pamela, I thank you too.

For several days while researching this book, I was at the Library of the United States Information Service (USIS) in Lagos. Those visits enabled me to access vital literature, including some of the most recent academic journal that had entries on the subject matter of this book. For his unstinting assistance at USIS, I especially thank Messers Abudu Kester. I thank my publishers too. I do not know everybody in Rutledge by name and, thus, cannot mention each and every one of them here, more so because of spatial constraints. But I must nonetheless not fail to thank Brianna Ascher for the hard work she put in to make this book a reality. I must also appreciate her colleague, Mary Del Plato, for her contributions. Like every other member of the Routledge team that I was privileged to work directly with, I must thank Lisa Salonen for her glorious endeavours, and, of course, the copy editor in the team, for doing nice work.

Finally, I will like to thank the members of my family, my wife and children, for their kind support. And while I give all the credit to all those that directly and indirectly assisted in the making of this book, I hereby indemnify all of them from the shortcomings that may be found in it. So, I take full responsibility for whatever failings, real or perceived, that might be found in the book.

Professor Fred Aja Agwu, PhD
NIIA, Lagos
ajaagwu@yahoo.com
July 2017

1 Introduction

Asymmetric Warfare: A Terminological Simplification

Geometrically speaking, asymmetry denotes inequality. It is asymmetrical when the sides in a shape, pattern, or relationship are unequal.[1] Asymmetric relationships are sometimes detonative of congenital or irreversible inequality, like in filial relationships, which can be captured in the imagery, "John is the father of Bill", a filial relationship between a father and a son.[2] Asymmetry pervades the physical and social realities of nature. In contemporary security environments, for example, although the nature and threat of inter-state armed conflicts remain unchangeable, real and omnipresent, what has really changed about armed conflicts today is in their physiognomy, the emergence of asymmetric conflicts, defined by the entrance of non-state actors—the sub-national insurgent groups.[3] Thus, "an asymmetric conflict typically involves two actors, one "strong" and one "weak".[4] It is characterized, as Robert Sloane put it, quoting Robin Geiss, by "significant inequality in arms, disparate distribution of military strength and technological capability in a given conflict".[5]

So, being intrinsically characterized by "power disparities", asymmetric warfare has always been a combat that is historically "a logical choice for a weaker military opponent".[6] However, asymmetric engagements manifest an uncanny situation in which the strength of the so-called weaker opponent "is paradoxically rooted in its own weakness", a paradox that is reflected in the Chinese leader,

1 See Paul Proctor (1978, ed.), *Longman Dictionary of Contemporary English*, Paper Edition, England, Longman Group Limited. pp. 52, 474.
2 See Robert L. Barnhart (1974, ed.), *The World Book Dictionary*, Vol. 1, A–K, Chicago, Doubleday & Company Inc. pp. 131, 783.
3 Ibid., p. 6.
4 See Giuseppe Caforio (2013), "Officer and Commander in Asymmetric Warfare Operations", *Journal of Defence Resources Management*, Vol. 4, No. 1(6), p. 25, note 1.
5 See Robert D. Sloane (2011), "New Battlefields/Old Laws: Shaping a Legal Environment for Counterinsurgency", Proceedings of the Annual Meeting (American Society of International Law), Vol. 105, March 23–26, p. 371.
6 See Stephen C. Small (2000), "Small Arms and Asymmetric Threats", *Military Review*, November–December, No. 6, p. 34.

Mao Zedong's submission "that the insurgent is like a fish that swims in the ocean of the people",[7] the people here are, metaphorically, a shield for the insurgent to evade square and direct targeting. It is in the sense of this people connection, the fact of insurgents hiding in the civilian population, that in asymmetric warfare, terrorism is an adjunct; thus, firmly presenting a situation in which "a militarily weak force uses limited resources to offset the strengths of a more powerful military force".[8]

The implication of the terrorism genre of warfare being asymmetry is that it is also basically of a low-intensity nature.[9] And being a low-intensity conflict means that this form of warfare does not entail direct confrontation; for the army keeps on stalking "another illusory" or elusive enemy, thus, making nonsense of its predilection and dependence on conventional "mechanization and advanced technology".[10] Although highly mechanized or technology-driven weapons have led to such anti-terror brands of warfare as "electronic warfare", "precision-guided weapons warfare", and "information warfare",[11] the terrorists as adjunct categories in asymmetric conflicts have largely remained resilient. It is in this resilience that asymmetric warfare remains a nightmare that challenges the foundation of conventional "doctrinal development and force structure"[12] in every military organization; so much so that, before 9/11 and their entanglement with counter-terrorism operations, that is, after the bitter experiences of the United States (in Vietnam) and France (in Southeast Asia), both countries and, indeed, every other country's conventional military, viscerally detest the likelihood or possibility of future involvement in wars of asymmetric nature, be it counter-insurgency or counter-terrorism.[13]

As a matter of fact, in Vietnam, although for the insurgents, there were actually "some rhyme or reason" behind their (the North Vietnamese and the Viet Cong[14]) guerilla/terrorist tactics, they, indeed, made a mess of the conventional, the doctrinal, and the force structure known to the United States' military. The doctrinal and force structure known to countries are predicated on "conventional battles", defined in part as "combat between forces several hundreds of meters apart, whose observation is generally unimpeded by all objects".[15] In conventional mode of combat, "technology offers much promise" as it makes it possible

7 Loc. Cit.
8 Ibid., pp. 33–34.
9 See Daniel S. Challis (1987), "Counterinsurgency Success in Malaya", *Military Review*, February, No. 2, p. 56.
10 See Thomas J. Kuster Jr. (1987), "Dealing with the Insurgency Spectre", *Military Review*, No. 2, p. 21.
11 See Stephen C. Small (2000), "Small Arms and Asymmetric Threats" . . ., p. 33, op. cit.
12 See Daniel S. Challis (1987), "Counterinsurgency Success in Malaya" . . ., p. 56, op. cit.
13 Loc. Cit; see also Thomas J. Kuster Jr. (1987), "Dealing with the Insurgency Spectre". . ., p. 21, op. cit.
14 See Michael Maclear (1981), *Vietnam: The Ten Thousand Day War*, England, Thames Methuen, p. 368.
15 See Stephen C. Small (2000), "Small Arms and Asymmetric Threats" . . ., p. 35, op. cit.

for the battle to be "dominated by the combatant whose weapon can hit the enemy without the enemy being able to hit back".[16] It is this technological superiority that countries possess and use to their maximum advantage "when weapon sights and improved munitions take their toll on less technologically sophisticated opponents"[17]—the guerillas, insurgents, and terrorists who consequently avoid conventional combats.

In asymmetric warfare, the insurgents embark on a shifty strategy; in which they implicate the enemy in ground wars, but avoid engagements that would allow that enemy "to draw on its technical superiority".[18] Because it is in the character of guerilla warfare/terrorism that it is not patterned towards any conventional doctrine, groups like the Viet Cong "were not pursuing any military victory" but keen in causing doctrinal disorientation to the Americans.[19] Michael Maclear vividly presents an American soldier's frustrating description of the hit and run tactics of the non-conventional Viet Cong:

> It was hit and miss. Like hunting a humming bird. You would get to one village; nothing there. Another village—and nothing there. The enemy, the humming-bird that we were after, was just buzzing around. You secure a village, you search it, and you leave, and the village reverts to the enemy.[20]

The U.S. military were, thus, "operating against an enemy they seldom saw"; so much so that they became paranoid and "the minute they got beyond their very, very tightly circumscribed circle of familiarity, it was a foreign, alien—in the sense of 'other'—world".[21] In fact, "the military mission became to inflict casualties and the primary reason for existence became to minimize your own casualties"; and in this reflex for survival, "blowing things up, burning huts" in "frustration of being ignorant and not knowing where the enemy was"[22] became the order of the day. And so, the Americans became so frightened or embedded in fear that "in some cases, it led to outlets of violence against the population in general".[23]

This was the kind of situation that Stephen Small had in mind when he wrote that "as evidenced by the Vietnam War, military responses [to asymmetric conflicts] devolved in ham-handed affairs conducted in close proximity to civilian settlements", and that these are "solutions in the postmodern age [that] lead only to morally pyrrhic victories".[24] Ham-handed military responses to asymmetric

16 Loc. Cit.
17 Loc. Cit.
18 See Sheila Macrine (2016), "The Psychology of Radicalization", *The Counter Terrorist*, June–July, p. 12.
19 See Michael Maclear (1981), *Vietnam: The Ten Thousand Day War*. . ., p. 368, op. cit.
20 Loc. Cit.
21 Ibid., p. 381.
22 Ibid., p. 380.
23 Ibid., p. 381.
24 See Stephen C. Small (2000), "Small Arms and Asymmetric Threats" . . ., p. 34, op. cit. Parentheses mine.

warfare lead to pyrrhic victories because the proximity to civilian settlements means that these military operations take place in urban terrains; even though "since ancient times, urban combat has been brutal", resulting in an inability to minimize collateral damage.[25] The arbitrary firepower implicit in ham-handed military operations in urban terrains makes it pretty difficult if not impossible to sort out the enemy combatants from noncombatants, both in the heat of the operations as well as "in the wake of the damage done".[26]

Materially, the duel between David and Goliath was not only a classical case of an asymmetric (even though a direct confrontation) warfare, it was also a confrontation between low tech and high tech; for while the Philistines had mastered the art of iron forging against which the Israelites had no chance, the latter only possessed "hard-edge blades", the stuff that bronze weapons are made of.[27] In this biblical duel, David stayed out of the range of the fearsome sword of the Philistine giant, deploying his tactical surprise of pulling out his sling and felling the Philistine while still being taunted by the giant.[28] So, whereas "symmetric warfare has been identified as two opposing adversaries disposing of armed forces that are similar in all aspects such as force structure, doctrine, asset, and have comparable tactical, operational and strategic objectives"; "asymmetric warfare—as opposed to symmetric warfare—means that the opposing party is unable or unwilling to wage the war with comparable force, and has different political and military objectives than its adversary".[29]

It is in this lack of the capacity for conventional force comparable to the nation-state that terrorist insurgent resort to under-hand or crude tactics like attacking civilians, using crude or dirty weapons, refusing to wear appropriate or identifiable insignia, refusing to bear arms openly and, of course, refusing to conduct operations according to the rules of armed conflict. And unlike the Nigerian Governor Kashim Shettima of Borno State who averred that the Boko Haram's attacks on "soft targets are signs of the terrorists' weakness and their desperation to tell their terror co-travelers around the world that they are not yet finished";[30] the attacks on soft targets are actually no weakness on the part of the terrorists but rather their inherent strength, the modus operandi that helps them offset their inability to engage in conventional battles.

Terrorists' attack on soft targets is, therefore, a paradox to the extent that it is strength in their otherwise weakness. It is essentially because of the evasive and criminal nature of the operations of terrorists that drones (both armed and

25 Ibid., pp. 34–35.
26 Ibid., p. 34.
27 See Josef Joffe in "Asymmetric Warfare: Since David Fought Goliath, the Weak Have Been Able to Vanquish the Strong", *Time* (New York), September 24, 2001, p. 47.
28 Loc. Cit.
29 See Bordas Maria (2014), "Current Issues of International Law in Regulating Counter-Insurgency and Counter-Terrorism", *AARMS*, Vol. 13. No. 4, p. 571.
30 See Kashim Shettima in "Boko Haram: Reasons Military Must Spare Nobody", *The Nation* (Lagos), Wednesday, February 15, 2017, back page.

unarmed intelligence-oriented ones) have been devised to take them out from their hovels or safe havens without, at least, theoretically speaking, risking hitting the "host" state or incurring unacceptable collateral damage. This is principally what makes the use of drones in asymmetric warfare (whether counter-insurgency or counter-terrorism) very attractive. Like drug cartels and other transnational criminal threats, terrorism is part of the "nonparadigmatic" groups eluding existing taxonomies in armed conflicts that have continued to proliferate owing partly to the fact that the foreign policy of interventionism (by the West) often provokes ethical responsibilities and resentments.[31]

Terrorists—who can erupt in forms ranging from asymmetric "combatants" to pure criminals—are elusive and difficult to eradicate with conventional forces.[32] In the terrorist brand of asymmetric conflict/warfare, the nation-state is between the devil and the deep blue sea in the choice of using either conventional or "unconventional" weapons. This is because in the absence of conventional combats and the futility or ineffectiveness of "conventional" weapons, the application of electronic warfare against terrorists (through precision-guided munitions like smart bombs or armed drones), has the danger of destroying unintended targets and leading to unacceptable collateral damage that fuels the rage of the terrorists, causing "blowbacks"—the tendency for the terrorists (in their deeply ingrained memory of hurt intermixed with their traditional motivation) to seize such mistakes as justifications for increased violence.[33] Unfortunately, the "low-collateral-damage munitions" and the nonlethal-capability-small arms, though essential for combating terrorism with little or no unintended consequences or collateral damage,[34] has proved ineffective for reining in the terrorism genre of asymmetric warfare.

Forms of Asymmetric Warfare

Different forms of armed conflicts are representative of asymmetric warfare in the sense of such armed conflicts being entirely unconventional warfare in nature or sharing the same ingredients or characteristics of irregularity. These varied forms (designated with different phraseology) include "insurgency, irregular warfare, unconventional warfare, revolutionary warfare, guerrilla warfare, terrorism", etc.[35] Asymmetric warfare of all forms share the same similarities: these include, "committing terrorist attacks, pursuing radical aims, and intimidating civilians, etc.".[36] Although asymmetric warfare can be traced back to the biblical duel between David and Goliath, and although it had existed throughout human

31 See Stephen C. Small (2000), "Small Arms and Asymmetric Threats" . . ., p. 35, op. cit.
32 Ibid., p. 36.
33 Ibid., p. 35.
34 Ibid., p. 36.
35 See Bordas Maria (2014), "Current Issues of International Law in Regulating Counter-Insurgency and Counter-Terrorism" . . ., p. 572, op. cit.
36 Loc. Cit.

history, it was not until the end of the Second World War that the phenomenon became accentuated, so much so that conventional warfare has become an exception while asymmetric warfare has become the rule.[37] Until now, the situation had been the other way round.

There are additional two categories of classification of symmetric warfare—the classification in fact and in law. These categories include "factual asymmetry", which Robin Geiss referred to earlier as characterized by significant inequality in arms, a disparate distribution of military strength and technological capability in a given conflict, and "legal asymmetry", in which one belligerent in the conflict "enjoys less or even no status under the traditional law of war".[38] The implication of "legal asymmetry" will be dealt with in due course here under the rubric of drones in International Humanitarian Law (IHL). It is because of the combination of these two attributes (factual and legal asymmetry) that asymmetric conflicts have the consequences of (1) eviscerating the idea of a distinct battlefield; (2) blurring the distinction between civilian and military objects; and (3) redefining what qualifies as military advantage.[39]

Unique Features of Asymmetric Warfare

Asymmetric conflicts eviscerate the idea of a battlefield and blur the distinction between civilian and military objects; which was why in his declaration of the war against terrorists, the United States President George W. Bush spoke about the global war on terror in terms of the battlefields being the entire world. It is because asymmetric conflicts blur the distinction between civilians and military objects that, in Afghanistan, civilian casualties were very high in 2010; for the Taliban, in what some analyst described as "lawfare", adopted the tactics of deliberately exploiting the rules in adopting civilian garb to render themselves, at least temporarily, illegitimate targets.[40]

Asymmetric conflicts also redefine what qualifies as military advantage, explaining why in the Gaza war of 2008–2009, Israel was not trying to retake territory, as in some old wars; rather, in the absence of this kind of conventional military objective, it focused simply on attempting to kill or capture as many of the enemy (rocketing southern Israeli cities) as it could, thus, making the whole thing, according to some opinions, quite counterproductive.[41] As distinct from unconventional or asymmetric warfare (especially the war on terror variant), conventional military advantage, as it were, aims to take territory, except in a war of self-defence that aims to return the situation to the status quo ante; aside from a situation of permanent aggression that may call for an occupation

37 Loc. Cit.
38 See Robert D. Sloane (2011), "New Battlefields/Old Laws . . .", p. 371, op. cit.
39 Ibid., p. 372.
40 Loc. Cit.
41 Loc. Cit.

of territory.[42] Some of these issues will be returned to and clarified shortly in due course, especially while discussing issues like the use of armed drones in self-defence, asymmetric conflicts in vanishing frontlines, and IHL in asymmetric conflicts (the terrorist campaigns variety), etc.

But it is important to clarify that one of the unique features of asymmetric warfare is that it is not amenable to the same variables that determine victory in conventional warfare, variables like strength, resoluteness, initiative, and luck.[43] In other words, it is not usually the strongest that prevails because asymmetric warfare has its own special rules, "different from those of the conventional war".[44] However, even though both the insurgent and the counter-insurgent operate in one space and time, most of the rules "applicable to one side do not work for the other"; for instance, "in a fight between a fly and a lion, the fly cannot deliver a knockout blow and the lion cannot fly".[45] In the war on terror, the terrorist can be denominated into a fly that can fly by dint of its hit and run strategy; but the nation-state is the lion than cannot fly; even though it can deliver its knockout blow with its armed drones.

Why Drones in Asymmetric Warfare?

Because it is not absolute lawlessness, warfare is defined by rules of engagement. But since it is a hostile intercourse between belligerents as national groups or between a national and a sub-national group(s), the outbreak of war (the moment the law of peace ceases) and the attainment of belligerent status are both attended by the application of the law of armed conflict by all the parties.[46] Unfortunately, these rules are only applicable in conventional warfare. Unconventional or asymmetric warfare, especially at the level of counter-terrorism, is another kettle of fish. By dint of its unconventional nature, the parties to asymmetric warfare hardly play by the rules; this is why the sub-national groups as terrorists can use such dirty weapons as the Improvised Explosive Devices (IEDs), while national groups like the United States can use armed drones for targeted killings. Although the use of these weapons in conventional warfare cannot be absolutely discounted, drones are unusual weapons of war that are forged as an instrument to achieve an unusual objective of targeted killing in an unusual warfare—asymmetric warfare.

At the moment, and as far as targeted killings in the war on terror go, drones are fashioned to deal with unusual actors in unusual armed conflicts. When he

42 See Fred Aja Agwu (2005), *United Nations System, State Practice and the Jurisprudence of the Use of Force*, Lagos, Malthouse Press Ltd., p. 79.
43 See David Galula (1964), *Counter-Insurgency Warfare: Theory and Practice*, New York, London, Frederick A. Praeger Publishers, pp. x–xi.
44 Ibid., p. xi.
45 Loc. Cit.
46 See Julius Stone (1954), *Legal Control of International Conflict: A Treatise on the Dynamics of Disputes and War-Law*, Sydney, Maitland Publications Pvt. Ltd., pp. 304–305.

spoke on the U.S. counter-terrorism policy at the National Defense University, President Obama provided the "context that the United States has taken lethal, targeted action against the al-Qaeda and its associated forces, using remotely piloted aircraft commonly referred to as drones".[47] According to the U.S. President, despite the United States' "strong preference for the detention and prosecution of terrorists, sometimes this approach is foreclosed" because:

> Al Qaeda and its affiliates try to gain a foothold in some of the most distant and unforgiving places on Earth. They take refuge in remote tribal regions. They hide in caves and walled compounds. . . In some places—such as parts of Somalia and Yemen—the state has only the most tenuous reach into the territory. In other cases, the state lacks the capacity or will to take action. It is also not possible for America to simply deploy a team of Special Forces to capture every terrorist. And even when such an approach may be possible, there are places where it would pose profound risks to our troops and local civilians—where a terrorist compound cannot be breached without triggering a firefight with surrounding tribal communities that pose no threat to us, or when putting U.S. boots on the ground may trigger a major international crisis.[48]

What President Obama underlined hereis that the capriciousness in the modus operandi of the terrorists—their evasiveness—creates the possibility of confrontation with the territorial state in circumstances that incur innocent civilian casualties; and that this situation unavoidably makes the resort to armed drones an imperative. But the question may be asked, what about Osama bin Laden; was he not a terrorist and yet not killed with armed drones? President Obama explained that Osama bin Laden being successfully taken out through a Special Forces operation was only a matter of luck, even though it was also a testament to the meticulous planning and professionalism of Special Forces too. According to him:

> . . . our operation in Pakistan against Osama bin Laden cannot be the norm. The risks in that case were enormous; the likelihood of capture, although our preference, was remote given the certainty of resistance; the fact that we did not find ourselves confronted with civilian casualties, or embroiled in an extended firefight, was a testament to the meticulous planning and professionalism of our Special Forces—but also depended on some luck. And even then, the cost to our relationship with Pakistan—and the backlash among the Pakistani public over encroachment on their territory—was so severe that we are just now beginning to rebuild this important partnership.[49]

47 See the "Full Transcript of President Obama's Speech on Counterterrorism Policy" at the National Defense University, Fort McNair, available at http://news.yahoo.com/full-transcript-president-obama-speech-counter-terrorism-policy-18 . . . (last visited on May 24, 2013).

48 Loc. Cit.

49 Loc. Cit.

This intervention by President Obama clearly encapsulates the obvious circumstances that make the United States' application of drone strikes in the war on terror quite inevitable. In sum, the risks are not just that the United States will in the absence of armed drones, lose or jeopardize the safety of its troops and incur casualties among the civilian populace when Special Forces are sent in, there is also the danger of ruffling diplomatic feathers as was the case in Pakistan when American Special Forces upended the rules governing self-defence against predatory individuals by breaching the territorial integrity of that country to kill Osama bin Laden. Apart from the benefits that the use of armed drones gives to the United States, there are, nevertheless, some downsides—like the risk of creating new enemies, the ambiguous legality of the strikes in international law, the question of accountability, and the question of ethics or morality—all of which President Obama also acknowledged in his counter-terrorism policy speech under reference.[50] This book examines these and other downsides in the use of armed drones in the war on terror, including its implications for international humanitarian law as well as chivalrous considerations.

50 Loc. Cit.

2 Insurgency and Terrorism as Forms of Asymmetric Warfare

Insurgency

From the North Atlantic Treaty Organization's (NATO) conceptualization, an insurgency is "the actions of an organized, often ideologically motivated, group or movement that seeks to effect or prevent political change of a governing authority within a region, focused on persuading or coercing the population through the use of violence and subversion".[1] Some Western nations (like the United States and France) may have been relentlessly frustrated and hence prone to agonizing over the phenomenon of insurgency because it renders many of their mechanized and advanced weapon technologies as well as their doctrinal developments and conventional force structures useless;[2] but they, nevertheless, sometimes find in insurgency a useful tool of international relations. This functional aspect of insurgency can be appreciated within the context of the two separate approaches to it: "backing the government in their fight against insurgency (as in Afghanistan), and backing the insurgents in their fight against the government (as in Libya[3]).

Even in Afghanistan, the United States and NATO made enormous use of the insurgency of the Northern Alliance to facilitate their dominance over the Taliban.[4] So, Washington may have made a pastime out of the vilification of insurgency, but it has at the same time, proved to be a useful tool in the vanquishing of the Taliban in Afghanistan, and Muammar Gaddafi of Libya, suggesting that insurgency is after all not entirely of a nuisance value. As a form of asymmetric warfare, an insurgency tries "to control one of the territories of the state. . .; occasionally respects the law of war . . . [because] insurgents do not

1 See Vlasta Zekulic, Ana Zuzic, and Adam Piskulic (2014), "Support to Insurgency and Counterinsurgency Operations", *AARMS*, Vol. 13, No. 1, p. 185.

2 See Thomas J. Kuster Jr. (1987), "Dealing with the Insurgency Spectre" . . ., p. 21, op. cit; see also Daniel S. Challis (1987), "Counterinsurgency Success in Malaya" . . ., p. 56, op. cit.

3 See Vlasta Zekulic, Ana Zuzic, and Adam Piskulic (2014), "Support to Insurgency and Counterinsurgency Operations" . . ., p. 183, op. cit.

4 See Fred Aja Agwu (2009), *National Interest, International Law and Our Shared Destiny*, Ibadan, Spectrum Books Ltd., pp. 127–126.

necessarily attack civilians".[5] However, "insurgent groups use not only guerrilla warfare, but often commit terrorist attacks . . ., nuanced by organized crimes".[6] In fact, it is not just that insurgents often commit terrorist attacks, the reality is that since the end of the Cold War—and with the emergence of insurgent terrorist groups like the Taliban, the ISIS, the Al-Shabab, and the Boko Haram, amongst others—insurgents now routinely engage in terrorist acts as a matter of rule (modus operandi) rather than exception. The terrorist activities of today's insurgents have been such that the "war on terror" as declared by the United States is now practically waged both in regional and global terms, having also been joined by the entire West in the various coalitions in Afghanistan, Iraq, and Syria.

Other attributes of insurgency include being (1) an organized movement of a group that leads to a protracted violent conflict; (2) a group that aims to weaken the control and legitimacy of an established order, overthrow the constituted government, and fundamentally change the socio-political order of the state; (3) a group that uses means such as subversion, armed conflict, sustained violence, social disruption, and sundry political actions to achieve their aims; and (4) a group with an aim that is rooted in the claim of autonomy or independence "for an ethnic minority, a more democratic government, or political and economic rights to a social class".[7] And as a genre that is not "warfare in the classic sense of armies fighting armies on a common battlefield",[8] insurgency has been present, especially since the advent of anti-colonial wars of the 20th century.[9]

The Objective of Insurgency

As an anti-colonial tool, insurgency as a form of asymmetric warfare was "an organized movement aimed at the overthrow of constituted government through [the] use of subversion and armed conflict"[10]—subversion here being the "interlocking systems of actions, political, economic, psychological and military, a form of revolutionary tactic that guerrillas apply" in the pursuit of political change.[11] Thus, from the anti-colonial context (especially from the Mao Tse-tung point of view), asymmetric conflict of the insurgency genre is "a formal doctrine that guides a weaker political force to accomplish its goals", as in "the desire of

5 See Bordas Maria (2014), "Current Issues of International Law in Regulating Counter-Insurgency and Counter-Terrorism" . . ., p. 573, op. cit. Brackets mine.

6 Loc. Cit.

7 Ibid., pp. 572–573.

8 See Michael T. Klare and Peter Kornbluh (1988), *Low Intensity Warfare: Counterinsurgency, Proinsurgency and Antiterrorism in the Eighties*, New York, Pantheon Books, p. 4.

9 See Teodor Frunzeti (2013), "Asymmetric, Unconventional and Hybrid Actions in 21st Century Warfare", *Strategic Impact*, No. 1, p. 8; see also Jake Diliberto (2014), "The New War Frontier: Understanding Modern Insurgency and the Syrian Civil War through the Iraq Insurgencies during 2006–2009", Paper for (2014 APSA Annual Conference) (Unpublished).

10 See Jake Diliberto (2014), "The New War Frontier . . .", op. cit. Brackets mine.

11 Loc. Cit.

indigenous people [or] group to pursue their own political interests to independently govern their society" by political revolt, employing the strategy of guerrilla warfare.[12]

The guerrilla movement or insurgency as a form of asymmetric warfare is exemplified by "the Jewish revolts against the Roman Empire, the French and Spanish Guerrilla Campaigns, Mao Tse-tung's People's Revolutions, and the French and British Campaigns within the Middle East and African Maghreb".[13] Outside the context of anti-colonial movements, insurgency has also been employed within post-colonial states by marginalized and disaffected groups seeking for self-determination or the right to be freed from the yolk of a new or larger political entity.

Between Traditional and Modern Terrorist Insurgencies

The anti-colonial uprisings in the East African nation of Kenya by Jomo Kenyatta's Mau Mau movement as well as Amílcar Cabral's PAIGC (Partido Africano da Independência da Guiné e Cabo Verde, or the Portuguese for African Party for the Independence of Guinea and Cape Verde) in the West African nation of Guinea-Bissau also count among the notable insurgencies that qualified as asymmetric armed conflicts of the 20th century. Another way of comprehending or interpreting the foregoing is to say that until recent times, insurgency had been almost the exclusive engagement of "Third World revolutionary movements and governments".[14] But the anti-colonial insurgencies could be better categorized as traditional insurgencies, having possessed tools that ranged from banditry, partisan uprising, to rudimentary guerrilla warfare, being at that time viscerally incapable of conducting campaigns at the rate or speed of modern terrorist insurgencies.[15]

In contrast, modern insurgencies are represented by the 21st century asymmetric warfare, "waged almost exclusively by non-state actors"—like Islamic terrorism, degenerate guerrillas, transnational criminal organizations, narco-terrorists, and other violent irrational entities.[16] One of the defining characteristics of terrorist insurgents is that they do not engage in pitched battles. All of them make virtue of asymmetry. As stated earlier, they—like the al-Qaeda—engage in a shifty strategy, in which they lure their adversary into ground wars, while avoiding engagements that would allow the military to draw on its technical superiority.[17] It must, however, be noted that narco-terrorists and transnational criminal organizations are at the periphery of modern terrorist insurgencies.

12 Loc. Cit.

13 Loc. Cit.

14 See Michael T. Klare and Peter Kornbluh (1988), *Low Intensity Warfare . . .*, p. 3, op. cit.

15 See Jake Diliberto (2014), "The New War Frontier . . .", op. cit.

16 See Teodor Frunzeti (2013), "Asymmetric, Unconventional and Hybrid Actions . . .", p. 8, op. cit.

17 See Sheila Macrine (2016), "The Psychology of Radicalization" . . ., p. 12, op. cit.

As pointed out earlier, the mainstream and organized actors in the 21st-century international terrorist insurgency are the radical militant Islamic extremists like the al-Qaeda, the Taliban, and the ISIS. The al-Qaeda is a global network because it possesses franchises in many regions of the world—like the Al-Qaeda in the Arabian Peninsula (AQAP), the Jabhat al-Nusra Front (an al-Qaeda franchise in Syria fighting the Assad regime, which later changed its name to Jabhat Fatah al-Sham [JFS, or Front for the Conquest of the Levant[18]]); and the Al-Shabab and the Boko Haram as al-Qaeda franchises in Somalia and Nigeria respectively. The al-Shabab is the al-Qaeda franchise that constitutes the Al-Qaeda East Africa (AQEA), which was initially led by the slain Fazul Mohamed—later replaced by Sheikh Ahmed Iman Ali.[19] However, with its "military surge in Syria and Iraq in 2013 and 2014", the ISIS or Daesh had "taken operational command and leadership of the global jihadist movement, eclipsing Al Qaeda Central (AQC), which attacked the US homeland on September 11, 2001"—having acquired control of "a sectarian army numbering more than thirty thousand combatants, in part through an amalgamation of local armed insurgencies in Iraq and Syria, and foreign recruits".[20]

The Boko Haram itself (sufficiently notorious in its own right after acquiring "global infamy for its 2014 kidnapping of 276 school girls" amongst other atrocities[21]) is a franchise of the ISIS; but its invincibility was challenged with the coming into office of Nigeria's President Buhari, who, supported by the Mano River Basin countries and the international community, energized the regional Multinational Joint Task Force (MJTF)[22] to debilitate and decimate, if not completely route the terror group—reportedly sending some of its rank and file straggling behind the theaters of combat.[23] By February 2017, Jeffrey Feltman, the UN Under-Secretary-General for political Affairs, had reportedly told the Security Council during the "Secretary-General's Fourth Report on the threat the group poses to international peace and security" that the Boko Haram had been "plagued by financial difficulties and an internal power struggle" that had split it into two factions.[24]

18 See "Syria's Ceasefire: A Risky Bargain", *The Economist*, September 17, 2016, p. 16; and "Al-Qaeda: The Other Jihadist State", *The Economist*, September 17, 2016, p. 54.

19 See Ngala Chome in "Portrait of an Insurgent", *New African*, April 2016, pp. 48–50.

20 See Fawaz A. Gerges (2016), *ISIS: A History*, New Jersey, Princeton University Press, p. 1.

21 See "No Major Link between Islamic State, Boko Haram—US Officials", *Daily Trust* (Abuja), Friday, June 10, 2016, p. 4.

22 See Fred Aja Agwu (2016), *Nations among Nations: Uneven Statehood, Hegemony and Instrumentalism in International Relations*, Ibadan, HEBN Publishers Plc., pp. 489–530.

23 Nigerian troops, with the assistance of vigilante groups in Borno State reportedly arrested high-profile members of the Boko Haram sect along the Biu-Damboa road fleeing to Birnin Kebi in Kebbi State, which was the rear of the theater of engagement in Sambisa Forest; see Karl Tsokar and Njadvara Musa in "Is Terrorists Name al-Barnawi as New Leader of Boko Haram", *The Guardian* (Lagos), Thursday, August 4, 2016, p. 6.

24 See "Boko Haram Is Broke, UN Envoy Tells Security Council", *Vanguard* (Lagos), Thursday, February 9, 2017, p. 4.

The report also had it that even though the Boko Haram as an "ISIL-affiliate" was still striving "to spread its influence and commit terrorist acts beyond Nigeria", some of its efforts were "directed and facilitated by ISIL personnel, while others were enabled by ISIL providing guidance or assistance or were inspired through its propaganda".[25] Although U.S. officials reportedly claimed that there was "no major link between Islamic State, Boko Haram";[26] there was no doubt that a critical and, indeed, crucial link existed between the two groups, the ISIS having at a point in time engineered the factionalization by purportedly naming Abu Musab al-Barnawi (former spokesman for the Boko Haram) as the successor to Abubakar Shekau.[27]

In any case, the existence of "no major link" was, however, not tantamount to the existence of no link at all; it could, perhaps, only mean that the link was minor, not major. This was because the U.S. officials' declaration under reference was made amid the Boko Haram's pledge of allegiance to the ISIS about a year earlier; but more importantly, the Boko Haram struck in Niger Republic (about the time the U.S. officials were disavowing any major link between the two groups) and reportedly "claimed the attack in the name of Islamic State—West Africa Province", an evident attestation to the fact that it is a franchise of the Syria-based ISIS.[28] And not long afterwards, the Nigerian State Security Service (DSS) reportedly burst an ISIS training cell in Kano State (Nigeria) and hauled some five suspects from Kogi State (Nigeria).[29]

The ISIS's naming of al-Barnawi as a successor to Shekau was to be indicative of not only a link between it and the Boko Haram, but also a split in the ranks of the Nigerian terror group; for no sooner was the announcement of al-Barnawi as leader made than Shekau emerged to disavow it and insist that he was still the leader of the deadly group.[30] But the Boko Haram was not just a clear franchise of the ISIS, its open declaration of allegiance to the ISIS was seen as "a branding exercise designed to boost its international jihadi credentials, attract recruits and appeal to the IS leadership for assistance".[31] The Boko Haram's bandying about of its "international jihadi credentials" before the ISIS was to prove that they were also the same kindred in "sacred terrorism"—the ISIS being putatively a "sacred terror" organization,[32] a euphemism for having a religious motivation or millenarian

25 Loc. Cit.
26 See "No Major Link between Islamic State, Boko Haram—US Officials" . . ., p. 4, op. cit; see also "U.S. Says No Major Link between Islamic State, Boko Haram", *The Guardian* (Lagos), Friday, June 10, 2016, p. 4.
27 See Karl Tsokar and Njadvara Musa in "Is Terrorists Name al-Barnawi. . .", p. 1, op. cit.
28 See "No Major Link between Islamic State, Boko Haram—US Officials" . . ., p. 4, op. cit.
29 See "DSS Busts ISIS Training Cell in Kano", *Leadership* (Abuja), Friday, June 10, 2016, p. 56.
30 See Karls Tsokar, Nkechi Onyedika-Ugoeze, and Kanayo Umeh in "Split in Boko Haram Terror Group as Shekau Reappears", *The Guardian* (Lagos), Friday, August 5, 2016, p. 1.
31 See "No Major Link between Islamic State, Boko Haram—US Officials". . ., p. 4, op. cit.
32 See Thomas P. M. Barnett (2004), *The Pentagon's New Map: War and Peace in the Twenty-First Century*, New York, G. P. Putman's Sons, pp. 43–44.

conviction. The religious colouration of modern terrorism is so profound that in its recognition as such, Sam Harris wrote in the *Washington Times* that:

> It is time we admitted that we are not at war with "terrorism". We are at war with Islam. This is not to say that we are at war with all Muslims, but we are absolutely at war with the vision of life that is prescribed to all Muslims in the Koran. The only reason Muslim fundamentalism is a threat to us is because the fundamentals of Islam are a threat to us. Every American should read the Koran and discover the relentlessness with which non-Muslims are vilified in its pages. The idea that Islam is a "peaceful religion hijacked by extremists" is a dangerous fantasy—and it is now a particularly dangerous fantasy for Muslims to indulge.[33]

The indictment of the Islamic religion (rightly or wrongly) in the terrorism controversy was such that after some reports suggested that all the terrorists involved in the attack at a Dhaka restaurant (in which 20 people were killed) were highly educated and belonged to rich families, the Bangladeshi author, Taslima Nasreen, rubbished the argument that it was poverty that made people terrorists; arguing, in addition, that Bangladesh had been a major contributor to global terror and that it was time people stopped saying that Islam was a religion of peace.[34] Islamic extremists of the hue of ISIS are not only violent, they have a "medieval prescriptions for life";[35] so much so that they are dreaded by fellow moderate Muslims. This could be gleaned from what happened on August 12, 2016, when Syrians shaved and lifted veils to celebrate their liberation from the Islamic State in Manbij.[36]

In fact, a man was observed cutting the beard of a civilian who was evacuated with others by the Syria Democratic Forces (SDF) fighters from an Islamic State–controlled neighbourhood of Manbij, in Aleppo Governorate.[37] In addition, victory signs were flashed as the man's beard was cut and a woman smoked a cigarette, while another set fire to a niqab as civilians embraced soldiers in celebration after being evacuated by the Syria Democratic Forces (SDF) from the Islamic State-controlled neighbourhood. Evidently, as solution to the problem of extremism and radicalization in Islam, it is obvious that the Islamic religion, like Christianity, needs some renaissance, an "Islamic reformation";[38] and, perhaps, some influence of this age of enlightenment.

33 See John L. Esposito and Dalia Mogahed (2007), *Who Speaks for Islam? What a Billion Muslims Really Think*, New York, Gallup Press Inc., pp. 72–73.

34 See "Stop Saying Islam Is a Religion of Peace: Taslima Nasreen", available at www.yahoo.com/news/stop-saying-islam-religion-peace-143200315.html (last visited on July 4, 2016).

35 See Reuters/Rodi Said, "Syrians Shave and Lift Veils to Celebrate Liberation from Islamic State in Manbij", available at www.yahoo.com/news/syrians-shave-lift-veils-celebrate-163656562.html?nhp=1 (last visited on August 16, 2016).

36 Loc. Cit.

37 Loc. Cit.

38 See Hisham al-Zoubeir, "Islamic Reformation or Islamic Renaissance?", available at www.livingislam.org/l/dch2_e.html (last visited on August 15, 2016).

It has been argued that Islam shares its fundamentalist or extremist streak with Christianity, including "the message of Revelation", which "Muhammad, like St. John, wrote at the dictation of an angel, and death on earth, as well as the second death [as] the plenty for refusal of the angelic message".[39] However, "after the failure of the hopes and expectations [of the Second Coming of the Saviour] for the year 1000 [including of course the year 2000], Christian fundamentalists have to be a bit cautious".[40] But the most important factor in the significant abatement or receding of Christian fundamentalism is the experience of the Reformation of the 16th century, and the Enlightenment of the 17th and 18th centuries;[41] Islam on the other hand has not experienced any reformation, neither has it been ostensibly influenced by the age of Enlightenment.

Apart from the Protestant Movement challenging the orthodoxy of Catholicism, "the Enlightenment affected countries that had embraced the Reformation more deeply than the Counter-Reformation countries", so much so that "up to the second half of the twentieth century, adherents of the papacy could regard the Enlightenment with some complacency, seeing it as a terminal disease of Protestantism and, as such, a merciful manifestation of the inscrutability of Devine Providence".[42] But Catholicism was itself not exonerated or spared from the influence of the age of Enlightenment. By the last quarter of the 19th century or thereabout, the "rot" of the Enlightenment values "had set in in the Vatican's own backyard", so much so that among the faithful, around 1975, "it became apparent that the *Magisterium*—the supreme authority of the papacy in matters of faith and morals—was no longer working, even among those Catholics with the greatest traditional reputation for obedience to the leader of the Church".[43]

Although the Enlightenment attacked many orthodoxies, but "for the Catholic Church as an institution, there was no field of morals that was more sensitive and significant than human sexuality and reproduction"; but, with the Enlightenment, many of the Catholic faithful began to, for instance, question or "disobey the instructions contained in *Mater et Magistra* (1960), *Humanae Vitae* (1968), and other papal and Episcopal documents"—to manifest disobedience to papal encyclicals in matters of sexuality and reproductive ethics, like in the use of contraception methods of family planning.[44] Sticking to Enlightenment values in defiance of the Church's "total prohibition of recourse by the faithful to artificial means of contraception", an otherwise "unequivocal and peremptory teaching of their Church",[45] and embarking on this defiance in the face of

39 See Conor Cruise O'Brien (1994), *On the Eve of the Millennium: The Future of Democracy through an Age of Unreason*, New York, The Free Press, p. 10. Brackets mine.
40 Loc. Cit. Brackets mine.
41 Ibid., p. 12.
42 Loc. Cit.
43 Ibid., pp. 12–13.
44 Ibid., pp. 13–15.
45 Ibid., p. 13.

"the teeth of peremptory orders to the contrary" are all with no thanks to the Enlightenment.[46]

It has equally been argued that some of the Catholic faithful might have even embarked on this defiance without "poring over the works of Locke and Montesquieu, of Voltaire and Diderot and d'Alembert" (some of the literature on the Enlightenment), and that they acquired the dissent "through the wider Protestant and post-Protestant environment of the British Isles and of North America"; or, indeed, made the "rational decisions, based on their understanding of their own personal situation, as to what would be best for their own happiness on earth as married people, and for the happiness of their children".[47] Thus, according to O'Brien:

> The Enlightenment we need [in Islam as in Christianity] is one that is aware of the dark, especially the dark in ourselves. An Enlightenment that is on guard against hubris. An Enlightenment that is aware that there is far more evidence extant in favour of the Christian doctrine of Original Sin than of Rousseau's doctrine of Original Virtue. An Enlightenment that respects the religious imagination, but not the claim of some religious to know what God wants from us and to have the duty to enforce that knowledge.[48]

Unfortunately, however—and this is according to Hisham al-Zoubeir—as far as matters of Reformation and/or, indeed, Enlightenment are concerned:

> As of now, the evidence for a successful exercise in this area seems to be somewhat lacking; Muslims have yet to be convinced their faith requires a reformation, in light of the violence and death that so characterized the Christian Reformation. Nor do they appear to be particularly impressed when the strongest calls for reform come from quarters that do not appear to have the integrity of Islam as a primary motivation.[49]

But the said Islamic terrorism is actually the handiwork of the millenarian terrorists that (repudiated by the mainstream currents in the Islamic faith) are considered as marginal or peripheral groups in the Islamic faith. Thus, all acts of terrorism are attributed to this "terrorist minority" in Islam;[50] and as the argument suggestively goes, it is, indeed, this minority (further "minoritized" by the fact that it is not all Sunnis that are supportive of the al-Qaeda and later, ISIS fundamentalism and jihad) that wages the contemporary terrorist campaigns that roil or convulses the entire world. But to what extent is the so-called minority a minority? Although radicalism and the ideal of jihad are a common denominator

46 Ibid., p. 14.
47 Loc. Cit.
48 Ibid., p. 30. Brackets mine.
49 See Hisham al-Zoubeir, "Islamic Reformation or Islamic Renaissance?" . . ., op. cit.
50 See John L. Esposito and Dalia Mogahed (2007), *Who Speaks for Islam?* . . ., p. ix, op. cit.

of both Sunni and Shiite Islam; essentially, the ideology from where this conception of the "terrorist minority" in Islam obtains is in Wahhabism, a Saudi Arabian deeply conservative Islamic group who, in its strict form of Islam, has "some points in common political Islam".[51] Be it the al-Qaeda or the ISIS, the groups' "spiritual roots lie with Wahhabism, a fundamentalist branch of Sunni Islam more than two centuries old".[52]

As a matter of fact, "Wahhabism received an influential boost through its adoption by the House of Saud in the 18th century; when King Abdulaziz Al-Saud founded the modern nation of Saudi Arabia in 1932 and consolidated control of Islam's two most holy cities—Mecca and Medina".[53] Thereupon, "Wahhabism reaped the benefits", having been adopted as a state religion by one of the richest nations on earth; "which then goes to spend billions of dollars exporting this puritanical form of Islam to the rest of the world".[54] Thus, although the Sunnis (who are Wahhabists) are a minority in Saudi Arabia, but their displacement from power by the American-led invasion of the country resulted in a serious backlash and the ISIS insurgency because of the serious support they receive, if not directly from Saudi Arabia, but from the entire Sunni/Wahhabist establishment in the region.

Nevertheless, as a movement/political thought, political Islam itself is inherently embedded in the character of Islam, a religion that naturally seeks "to overthrow secular states and replace them with Islamic theocracies".[55] However, it is only sects like the Hamas and the Muslim Brotherhood that have the ultimate goal of creating nation-states that are predicated on Islamic law and values.[56] On its part (and like the al-Qaeda), the ISIS is not nationalistic, for it rather views the nation-state as a man-made and sinful contraption that should be done away with and replaced with the Caliphate where identity would not be ethnic, where everyone would be known by the Muslim identity.[57] So, for particularly (the Sunni) Islamic jihadist, "the past—especially the life of [Prophet] Muhammad—is programmatic and provides a template for how to establish a religious political order".[58]

51 See Noah Feldman (2003), *After Jihad: America and the Struggle for Islamic Democracy*, New York, Farrar, Straus and Giroux, p. 47.

52 See "Apocalypse Now: The Islamic State Has a Brutal Vision for the Future That Fuels Their War against the World", published in a special *Newsweek* edition, "Killing ISIS: America's All-Out Assault on a Global Threat", 2016 (undated), p. 12.

53 Loc. Cit.

54 Loc. Cit.

55 See William McCant (undated), "Understanding Islam and Islamism", in Enrich Marquardt and Christopher Heffelfinger (undated, ed.); *Terrorism & Political Islam: Origin, Ideologies, and Methods: A Counterterrorism Textbook*, 2nd Edition, West Point, New York, Combating Terrorism Center, Department of Social Sciences, U.S. Military Academy, p. 29.

56 See "Apocalypse Now . . .", p. 13, op. cit.

57 Loc. Cit.

58 See William McCant (undated), "Understanding Islam and Islamism", in Enrich Marquardt and Christopher Heffelfinger (undated, ed.); *Terrorism & Political Islam: Origin, Ideologies, and Methods* . . ., p. 29, op. cit. Brackets mine.

When Prophet Muhammad began disseminating the revelations he received from angel Gabriel (which his followers termed to be literally the word of God), he and his followers were met with hostilities from those who thought he was trying to upset the apple-cart (or undermine the status quo)—the system of worship of their tribal gods that brought pilgrimage trade upon which revenue was tied.[59] To survive the threats, the Prophet invited his followers "to swear an oath of loyalty . . . to him that required them to defend him and other Muslims if they were attacked", a pledge that transcended tribal loyalties and changed "the basis of social relations in Arabia from kinship to religion: [as] fighting was to be used to protect the community of believers rather than one's kin" or tribe.[60] This was how identity shifted ethnic or tribal loyalties to that of belief and non-belief.[61] This Islamic philosophy of using its belief system to also form the basis of socio-cultural and political identity as well as national cohesion (even to the point of transcending ethnic or tribal loyalties) was what informed Somalia's vulnerability to the extremist al-Shabaab terrorist organization; for when the state of Somalia collapsed in 1992 partly because of clan differences, the people were exploited by the al-Shabaab terrorist group's use of Islam as an alternative identity to their fractious clans in nation-building.[62]

Thus, "since Muhammad was creating a new community (umma) that superseded tribal loyalties, he needed laws to regulate its behavior",[63] which was very important because of the pattern of the evolvement of the Arabian social system at that time. Because of the inhospitable desert nature of their environment, which could not support agriculture and the establishment of cities, the Arabs were "spread out and clustered into small groups of families; with no King to make laws and enforce them through an army".[64] What this meant was that when Islam emerged, it did not meet any "fixed laws enforced by a state".[65] Unlike Christianity that emerged "in a society governed by both Roman law and Jewish law", Islam and Jewish religions "emerged from tribal societies where there was no state, which meant that a state (the Ottoman Empire) had to be created to govern a large religious community".[66]

This accounts for the inherent political nature of Islam; and "like the Hebrew Bible, the Qur'an sanctions the use of violence in the service of religion, which naturally follows from the melding of religion and politics".[67] This is particularly

59 Ibid., p. 31.
60 Loc. Cit.
61 See "Apocalypse Now. . ., p. 13, op. cit.
62 This is the position of Jeffery Gentleman, the *New York Times* correspondent for Africa, while fielding questions from Fareed Zakaria in the latter's GPS programme on CNN, monitored in Lagos (Nigeria) on Sunday, May 28, 2017, between 8pm to 9pm local time.
63 See William McCant (undated), "Understanding Islam and Islamism", in Enrich Marquardt and Christopher Heffelfinger (undated, ed.); *Terrorism & Political Islam: Origin, Ideologies, and Methods*, . . ., p. 32, op. cit.
64 Ibid., p. 29.
65 Ibid., p. 32.
66 Loc. Cit.
67 Loc. Cit.

why the ISIS's "propaganda machine focuses on linking its actions with the struggle of the prophet Muhammad and his immediate successors as they conquered much of the Arabian peninsula in the 7th century, reasoning that the Islamic empires of later centuries (represented by the modern Arab states) possess greater wealth and power but make little or no recourse to pristine Islamic practices.[68] In other words, the ISIS believes that even though these post-Ottoman Empire Arab states were magnificent, they were unfortunately "too worldly, with caliphs even drinking wine".[69] Consequently, the "ISIS wants to establish its ideological purity by going back to the earliest days of Islam".[70]

But although political Islam (whether of the Hamas, the Muslim Brotherhood, or the ISIS variety) is inherent in the nature of the religion itself, its resurgence in modern times ensued with the writings of a Pakistani journalist and politician, Abdul A'la Mawdudi, which began to be published in Egypt in 1951 and was focused on the seizure of state power in the belief that "if you really want to root out corruption now so widespread on God's earth, stand up and fight against corrupt rule; take power and use it on God's behalf" [as] "it is useless to think you can change things by preaching alone".[71] It is the thinking by Arab nationalists (particularly following the failure of Arab nationalism to defeat Israel) "that an Islamic state was a real possibility" and that it was their bounden "duty to execute the infidel who was ruling their state".[72]

Having been, thus, persuaded to assassinate Anwar Sadat (declaring him worse than a bad Muslim) because of Egypt's 1978 peace deal with Israel, this movement propagating political Islam was to be later bolstered by "Arab Afghans (and with Osama bin Laden, "Afghans" only in that they had fought [the Soviets] in Afghanistan)"[73] in its "belief that the Prophet and his followers are the most important models for crafting a religiously proper life".[74] Indeed, it was within this context of political Islam's conviction about the irreplaceable place of religion in the making of a good political society that some analysts have sought to explain the "Arab Spring"—the argument that whereas the Middle East dictators consolidated political power, that fixation with political power facilitated socio-economic decline, paving the way for the re-emergence or reinvigoration of political Islam as an alternative approach to the destruction of corruption and facilitating nation-building or national development.[75]

68 See "Apocalypse Now . . .", 2016 (undated), p. 13, op. cit.
69 Loc. Cit.
70 Loc. Cit.
71 See Mahmood Mamdani (2004), *Good Muslim, Bad Muslim: America, the Cold War, and the Roots of Terror*, New York, Pantheon Books, CODESRIA Book Series, pp. 53–54.
72 See Noah Feldman (2003), *After Jihad* . . ., p. 46, op. cit.
73 Loc. Cit. Brackets mine.
74 Ibid., p. 47.
75 This is, for instance, the view of Fareed Zakaria, anchorman of the Global Public Square (GPS) programme to mark the 9/11 15th anniversary, Cable News Network (CNN), monitored in Lagos (Nigeria) on Sunday, September 11, 2016, 3pm–4pm, local time.

The idea of the terrorist organizations being in the minority is also promoted by the parting of ways between the Saudis and political Islam strictly so called; that is, the fact that although both Wahhabism and political Islam share the belief that the Prophet and his followers' 7th-century practices are the most important models of proper life, Saudi Arabian courts still apply Islamic law while its "form of government derives from traditional tribal rule, updated and fitted to monarchy".[76] In this frame, the deeply conservative Wahhabists mind religious affairs and the courts while "the Saudi rulers had to pressure Wahhabi scholars just to allow modern conveniences like cars into the Kingdom"; but on its part, political Islam while laying claim to religious fervor, "is forward-looking and eminently modern in its insistence on science, propaganda, technology, and engagement with the world", a "freelancing" that "Saudi Wahhabism found . . . unnerving".[77]

Moreover, whereas strict political Islam believes that about anyone can wage jihad (which is why Osama bin Laden and his al-Qaeda network began the enterprise), "the Saudis thought that the decision to wage jihad lay with the ruler, not the individual believer", rejecting "the idea that small groups could go around declaring rulers to be infidels and killing them [like Osama bin Laden, the ISIS, or those that earlier on assassinated Anwar Sadat]".[78] This is where the Wahhabists broke rank with the Saudi rulers and essentially became the "practitioners of [strict] political Islam", with the Saudi support only implicit.[79] Sometimes, the acquiescence of Saudi rulers to political Islam is only for the "geostrategic interests to keep the Iranians at bay", the reason of building a "regional balance of power with Iran" since the latter (Iran) is reputedly exporting or "supporting Shiite Hezbollah in Lebanon", a situation that compels the Saudis to support the Sunni brands of political Islam".[80]

It will be recalled that there are deep-seated differences between Sunni Islam and Shiite Islam. From the account of the differences as rendered by Elaine Sciolino, Iran is fighting a 7th-century battle in the 21st century.[81] It will be recalled too, that doctrine wise, as Sciolino previously put it, "Iran's leaders haven't figured out what Islamic message to rely on in their struggle to build a modern society"; for while "some insist on the strict version of Islam as they believe it was at its creation", some "others want to interpret Islam to fit the modern era", all "colored by the Messianic nature of Shiite Islam, which predominates in Iran, but which is in the minority in the rest of the Muslim world".[82] But essentially, the major difference between the Sunni and Shiite Muslims, the reason "the Shiites split from the mainstream Sunnis", arose from a conflict over

76 See Noah Feldman (2003), *After Jihad . . .*, p. 47, op. cit
77 Loc. Cit.
78 Loc. Cit. Brackets mine.
79 Loc. Cit.
80 Loc. Cit.
81 See Elaine Sciolino (2000), *Persian Mirrors: The Elusive Face of Iran*, New York, The Free Press, p. 38.
82 Loc. Cit.

the succession to Prophet Mohammed "as Islam's political and spiritual leader when he died in A.D. 632".[83]

Whereas the Sunnis,, whose name comes from the Arabic word for "tradition" argue that the leader should be selected in the pre-Islamic way: through consensus among the community's elders; . . . a minority believed that Ali, the Prophet's pious first cousin and son-in-law, should replace him because that's what Mohammed decreed";

thus, "earning these dissidents what in Arabic is known as Shiites or partisans of Ali".[84] To further intensify the conflict, in A.D. 661, "Ali was stabbed to death while praying in Kufa, in Iraq"; and "nearly twenty years later, Ali's followers, led by his son, Hosein, rebelled against the ruling hierarchy".[85] And even though "Hosein had been forewarned of his martyrdom in a vision", he still defiantly "set out for Kufa" where "the forces of the Sunni Caliph Yazid stopped him on the sun-scorched plain of Karbala" and "during a ten-day battle, Hosein was stabbed to death as he held a sword in one hand and a Koran in the other".[86]

During the battle too, "his male relatives and their supporters were shot with arrows and cut into pieces" and "their severed heads were brought to Yazid in Damascus" as the Sunni caliph continue to reign.[87] So, "for Shiites, the death of Hosein is the seminal event in their history; and because few Shiites came to Hosein's aid during the battle, their successors were left with both the burden of Sunni oppression and a permanent guilt complex"[88] that accounts for the "bad blood" between the Sunnis and the Shiites to this day. In fact, martyrdom and guilt have come to become one of the pillars of Shiite Islam.[89] The Shiites pillars of Islam also include the recognition of "twelve historic Imams or rightful spiritual rulers"; among them is an infant (the twelfth) Imam that supposedly "disappeared" in a cave in A.D. 874, believed not to be dead but somehow hidden and will return one day as the Redeemer who will create the perfect and godly society; and, without intending any parallel with the messianic infant twelfth Imam, there is Imam Ayatollah Khomeini.[90]

But be the foregoing as it may, it must be noted that in political Islam, the fingerprint of the Wahhabis is more pronounced than that of the Saudi rulers. Indeed, the Wahhabi militant fundamentalism is as much a threat to the United States and other nations of the world as it is to the Saudi regime (rulers). So, the question is how come, despite the fact that the Sunnis generally subscribe to the practice of Islam according to the 7th-century standards of Prophet Muhammad, it is not that all Sunnis that are sympathetic to the ISIS, which is also propagating

83 Loc. Cit.
84 Loc. Cit.
85 Loc. Cit.
86 Loc. Cit.
87 Loc. Cit.
88 Loc. Cit.
89 Loc. Cit.
90 Ibid., pp. 38–39.

the 7th-century standards? This is where politics comes in, the belief by many Muslims of the Sunni persuasion that political Islam is a movement created by the West, and this is to the extent that political Islam is not necessarily an Islamic movement, but a movement in resistance to the West's imperialist activities in the Middle East, like the Sykes-Picot lines in the sand.

It is the hypes of Wahhabism and political Islam that amplify what Sam Harris referred to above as "the relentlessness with which non-Muslims are vilified" in the pages of the Koran.[91] Political Islam proved irresistible to Wahhabism because as the "followers of the strict and austere Wahhabi creed . . . begun by Abdul Wahab (1703–1792)", it is "a movement to cleanse the Arab Bedouin from the influence of "Sufism, the trend of mystical Islam, which originated in Central Asia and Persia", and which "build their faith on prayer, contemplation, dances, music and sessions of physical shaking or whirling in a permanent quest for truth".[92] In addition to its jihad against corruption and infidels, Wahhabism considered the rituals of Sufism (critiqued for creating "an inner spiritual space within man that the outsider cannot penetrate", and the fundamentals of which "was to pierce the veils of human sense which shut man off from the Devine . . .") as totally unacceptable.[93] Curiously, although the ISIS

> is an organization best defined as Sunni fundamentalist and violently eschews mystic movements like the Sufi and the Shia, [it] ironically displays this same Sufi and Shia tendencies—[such as] claiming to go beyond the [Koran] text and to possess unique insight that allows for an exclusive interpretation of the text.[94]

Wahhabism and Salafism, the latter (Salafists) being the followers of Wahhabism in Afghanistan, are the opponents of Sufism and traditional or tribal-based practices.[95] Thus, part of Wahhabi/Salafist jihad is the doctrine of "al-wala'wal-bara (loyalty to Islam and Muslims disavowal of non-Muslims", the latter being the legitimate targets of violent attacks[96] In fact, what really underlines the minority status of these terrorists is that, as Ngala Chome pointed out, "recent Salafist preachers (unlike the earlier Salafists) reject mainstream society as impure and call for cleansing through violence".[97] But their minority status appears not to be a handicap as, though a lean organization, it still wages asymmetric warfare (terrorist campaigns) in very determined and stubborn manner, subjecting society to an unwarranted shifty conflict and hemorrhage.[98]

91 See John L. Esposito and Dalia Mogahed (2007), *Who Speaks for Islam?* . . ., p. 72, op. cit.
92 See Ahmed Rashid (2000), *Taliban: The Power of Militant Islam in Afghanistan and Beyond*, London and New York, I.B. Tauris, p. 84.
93 Loc. Cit.
94 See "Apocalypse Now . . .", p. 13, op. cit. Parentheses mine.
95 See Ahmed Rashid (2000), *Taliban* . . ., p. 85, op. cit.
96 See Ngala Chome in "Portrait of an Insurgent" . . ., p. 48, op. cit.
97 Ibid., pp. 49–50.
98 Ibid., p. 50.

But this sentiment about the fewness of the radical Muslims that adhere to militancy and terrorism does not go unchallenged. Bernard Lewis, for instance, opines that although these terrorists are in the minority (because many or, perhaps, most Muslims regard their "doctrine of jihad", their extremist and terrorist tendencies as a "grotesque travesty of the nature of Islam"[99]); the fact, nevertheless, is that whereas "terrorism requires only a few", "the West must defend itself by whatever means will be effective".[100] Apart from the place of the dynamics of globalization in the making of terrorism, in making the dispossessed and disconnected to be predisposed to the messages of militant extremism, the right of response by the West, apparently with whatever means possible, is one of the main problematiques that this book engages—understanding the dilemma the West faces in the bid to defend itself against this minority but highly dangerous group by whatever means at its disposal, including using the armed drones that sometimes orchestrate unacceptable collateral damage. This matter will be revisited in due course in the fuller discourses in this book.

Differentiating Counterinsurgency From Counterterrorism

It is important to reiterate the fact that, although asymmetric warfare could be dated way back to the biblical duel between David and Goliath, as far as the 20th and 21st centuries experiences of this unconventional phenomenon are concerned, the revolutionary insurgency of the Mao Tse-Tung era, the insurgency of the Viet Cong in Vietnam, "the 1948–60 British-Malay struggle against a determined communist insurgency",[101] the anti-colonial movements of the sort that Amílcar Cabral and other African nationalist icons fought, the war on terror against the escapades of the al-Qaeda, ISIS, Taliban and the Northern Alliance in Afghanistan; and the Boko Haram in Nigeria are archetypal or truly representative. And although an insurgent can become a terrorist, a terrorist can also become an insurgent; but because terrorism is, nevertheless, intrinsically different from insurgency, the approaches to these two varieties of asymmetric warfare differ.

In other words, irrespective of the 20th and 21st centuries fusion of insurgency and terrorism as forms of asymmetric warfare, the approaches to solving them tend to differ; hence, the terminological incidence of counter-insurgency as distinct from counter-terrorism. But despite this reality, some popular literature still tend to denominate or conflate counter-insurgency with counter-terrorism; with one, for instance, stating that "counterinsurgency

99 See Bernard Lewis (2003), *The Crisis of Islam: Holy War and Unholy Terror*, New York, The Modern Library, p. xxxii.

100 Loc. Cit.

101 See Thomas J. Kuster Jr. (1987), "Dealing with the Insurgency Spectre" . . ., p. 21, op. cit; see also Daniel S. Challis (1987), "Counterinsurgency Success in Malaya" . . ., p. 56, op. cit.

(COIN) encompasses all those military, paramilitary, economic, psychological and civil actions which government takes for defeating an insurgency".[102] However, the fact is that whereas counter-insurgency is strictly a military affair, counter-terrorism (even though sometimes used interchangeably with counter-insurgency in popular literature[103]) strictly so called, on the other hand, is a more conciliatory humanitarian strategy that is used to engage insurgency because of the failure of the application of direct military engagements in dealing with the problem.[104]

Thus, counter-terrorism is a complex political, socio-economic, and humanitarian engagement that minimizes the military component in the idea that it is "an integrated set of military, political, economic and social measures that attempts to resolve the underlying causes" of terrorist insurgency.[105] It is essentially because of the futility of counter-insurgency strictly so called (being replete with an aggressive military solution to terrorism that orchestrates the local population's sympathy and the phenomenon of "blowback") that a de-emphasis on aggressive military operations and the enlistment of the socio-economic, political, and the psychological approach in counter-terrorism is resorted to by the authorities. This is why counter-terrorism is also often called "a win the population strategy".[106] With aggressive military tactics, the population can only be further alienated rather than conciliated and won over.

Terrorism

Arising from its definitional problem, it is a fact that "terrorism has often been classified according to ideology or belief-system of its perpetrator—hence nationalist/separatist terrorism, left-wing terrorism, right-wing terrorism [like nationalists or white supremacists in the United States], religious terrorism, single-issue terrorism and so on".[107] Alex Schmid, for instance, has four ideological classifications of terrorism, which, according to him, were introduced by David C, Rapoport and come in waves: the Anarchist Wave (1870–1920s); the Nationalist Wave (1920s–1960s); the New Left/Marxist Wave (from the 1960s to the 1980s); and the Religious Wave (from the late 1970s to today and beyond).[108] At the extreme of this ideological characterization of terrorism is the British

102 See Vlasta Zekulic, Ana Zuzic, and Adam Piskulic (2014), "Support to Insurgency and Counterinsurgency Operations" . . ., p. 187, op. cit.

103 Loc. Cit; see also Bordas Maria (2014), "Current Issues of International Law in Regulating Counter-Insurgency and Counter-Terrorism" . . ., p. 586, op. cit.

104 Loc. Cit.

105 Loc. Cit.

106 Loc. Cit.

107 See Anthony Richards (2015), "From Terrorism to 'Radicalization' to 'Extremism': Counterterrorism Imperative or Loss of Focus", *International Affairs*, Vol. 91, No. 2, p. 375.

108 See Alex P. Schmid (2016), "Research on Radicalization: Topics and Themes", *Perspectives on Terrorism*, Vol. 10, No. 3, June, p. 26.

conception of the extremist or radical/terrorism as "vocal or active opposition to fundamental British values, including democracy, the rule of law, individual liberty and mutual respect and tolerance of different faiths and beliefs".[109]

It is in this ideological context that—in addition to the al-Qaeda, the ISIS, and the religious ideology that drives them—radical nationalist or separatist groups like the Irish Republican Army (IRA) and the Basque separatist organization ETA in Spain could also be labeled as terrorist organizations.[110] Nevertheless, in this ideological characterization of terrorism (with the attendant "increase in political, religious and ideological violence across the globe" and its "terrorism-related fatalities since 9/11 . . .), the four terrorist groups mainly [held] responsible for these deaths include Islamic State (IS) in Iraq and Syria, Boko Haram in Nigeria, the Taliban in Afghanistan, and the al-Qaeda in various parts of the world", amongst others.[111] These are Salafist/Wahabbist terrorist organizations whose international network is held together by the ideological sentiment that "the dismal conditions in which Sunni Muslims in Africa, the Middle East, and Southeast Asia persist"; and that they are particularly "supporting helpless Muslims in Syria and Iraq".[112]

But in the West in particular, this ideological colouration of terrorism has essentially shaped in some quarters, the response to the problem, including the formulation in Europe and the United States, of de-radicalization and counter-terrorism policies that are often self-defeatist because they lead to more terror.[113] Below, under the rubric of radicalization as a weapon of terrorism, an attempt is made to clarify the fact that the stigmatization or linking of certain religious ideologies, including the so-called extremist but allegedly non-violent ones, either by willful misinterpretation, distortion and/or adaptation, paradoxically conduces to terrorism. The blanket characterization of ideologies as terrorist in nature, and hence indiscriminately stigmatizing them, has the unfortunate consequence of creating disaffection and strengthening the clash of civilization narrative, which often makes those who would otherwise be the dissuaders of the terrorists to be part of the problem.

So, cast in the mould of an ideological phenomenon, terrorism becomes a very hard war to be won. As an ideology that is spreading round the world, the war on terror becomes a fight against an ideology that can only be won when there

109 See Anthony Richards (2015), "From Terrorism to 'Radicalization' to 'Extremism' . . .", p. 376, op. cit; see also Akimi Scarcella, Ruairi Page, and Vivek Furtado (2016), "Terrorism, Radicalization, Extremism, Authoritarianism and Fundamentalism: A Systematic Review of the Quality and Psychometric Properties of Assessments", *PLoS ONE* (Public Library of Science), DOI: 10, 1371/journal.pone.0166947, December 21, p. 2.

110 See Anthony Richards (2015), "From Terrorism to 'Radicalization' to 'Extremism' . . .", pp. 373–374, op. cit.

111 See Akimi Scarcella, Ruairi Page, and Vivek Furtado (2016), "Terrorism, Radicalization, Extremism, Authoritarianism and Fundamentalism . . .", p. 2, op. cit.

112 See Michael Weiss and Hassan Hassan (2015), *ISIS: Inside the Army of Terror*, New York, Regan Arts, p. xi.

113 See Alex P. Schmid (2016), "Research on Radicalization . . .", p. 26, op. cit.

is a generational shift away from the attractiveness of that ideology; when a new generation rejects that extremist ideology. This is why President Trump stands contradicted when, in hiking the U.S. defence spending by $54 billion in his 2018 proposed budget, he boasted that his action was to enable America to start winning wars again.[114] But the war on terror is not amenable to an easy win as was the case with the Cold War that was equally ideological. This is because terrorism (in addition to being contentiously ideological in the question of whether or not it is as a result of a clash of civilization) is also millenarian in nature; that is, in seeking martyrdom, the terrorist does not quite admit of earthly compromise or placation.

But although terrorism is quite different from those political struggles in the developing and underdeveloped world that morph into the sort of revolutionary insurgencies and anti-colonial battles, which the likes of Mao Tse-tung and Amílcar Cabral fought in Asia and Africa respectively, the West, according to Kalundi Serumaga, in its long-standing habit of "deploying the terrorist label to suit imperialist ends", still persists in creating definitional dilemmas for terrorism here by conflating it with political struggles, especially in the context of the colonized and "third world" where "terrorism remained an all-encompassing term, throwing together warlords, secessionists, radical Islamic clerics, leftist dissidents and common thugs".[115] Hence in this context, there is this irony that in some of the developing and underdeveloped nations, "yesterday terrorist is often today's liberation hero—and possibly tomorrow's autocrats".[116] It is also within this context of the politicization of terrorism that it can be assumed that:

> Technically, many African countries have had terrorists as their Presidents. Nelson Mandela, Samora Machel, Silva Kiir, Joachim Chissano, Jomo Kenyatta, Houri Boumediene, Yoweri Museveni, Paul Kagame, Meles Zenawi, Joseph Kabila, Pierre Nkurunziza, and Robert Mugabe have all come to power by the fact of having been members of organizations that used armed violence to achieve political ends. Some, like Kenyatta, Mugabe and Mandela were even officially branded terrorists by the powers opposed to them at the time.[117]

In other parts of the world outside Africa, Menachem Begin was once declared wanted by the police in British Palestine following his being "a prime suspect in the blowing up of the King David Hotel in Jerusalem, in which 91 people, including a UN mediator (and 12 Jewish people) died"; but Begin was later to

114 See "Trump Hikes Defence Spending", *The Nation* (Lagos), Tuesday, February 28, 2017, p. 47.

115 See Kalundi Serumaga in "Terrorism in Africa Is No Longer Somebody Else's War", *New African*, April 2016, p. 35.

116 Loc. Cit; see also Fred Aja Agwu (2007), *World Peace through World Law: The Dilemma of the United Nations Security Council*, Ibadan, University Press Plc., pp. 185–191.

117 See Kalundi Serumaga in "Terrorism in Africa . . .", p. 35, op. cit.

become Israel's Prime Minister and negotiate with Egypt's President Anwar Sadat at Camp David.[118] In fact, Vladimir I. Lenin, the leader of the Russian Bolshevik Revolution, was labeled a terrorist—comparable to Osama bin Laden—who, as Thomas Barnett put it, "like Osama bin Laden, Lenin also dreamed of taking vast swath of the planet offline, creating a kind of alternative universe where our rules [Western rules] didn't apply, where our money found no purchase, and where our power had no reach"; and like bin Laden, Lenin taught adherents that their 'way of life' was endangered".[119]

However, although it is sometimes the case that political dissidents morph into terrorists (especially as seen with those in the struggle for self-determination in the Middle East); there is, nevertheless, no doubt that political dissidents do not necessarily at all times transform into outright terrorists. But like political dissidents, and even though terrorists act irrationally with attacks on innocent civilians and other soft targets, these terrorists, whether localized or international, have "specific grievances" against the system—"be it an oppressive regime, the 'hegemonic' United States, or the 'polluting' forces of globalization".[120] In fact, even a critique of U.S. President Clinton's perceived tardiness in taking action against terrorists, especially in the alleged loss of Osama bin Laden when a window of opportunity to kill him existed in the Fall of 1998,[121] attributed that reluctance to act not only to the fact that President Clinton "wanted a guaranteed hit or nothing at all" from a conclusive intelligence,[122] but also to the President's ideological persuasion "that most terrorists were misunderstood, [even though they] had legitimate grievances and could be appeased".[123]

But the controversy over who the terrorist really is (or is not), is inherent in the attempt by imperialism or the powerful Western nations on the one hand to reduce the issue to a question of power relations (the strong branding the weak as terrorist); and the attempt on the other hand by those that use violent means to pursue their socio-political or economic objective to deny the terrorist label, even when they patently aggress civilian and otherwise protected places or objects in armed conflicts. The politicization of the definition of terrorism has been at the heart of the disagreement between the Western powers and the rest of the world, especially the Afro-Asian and Arab countries.[124] For many years, the United Nations weighed in to resolve this dispute over the definition of terrorism, but all seeming agreements have "fallen victim to debates about what represents legitimate resistance, and where the limits are on the use of violence, especially in cases

118 Ibid., p. 37.

119 See Thomas P. M. Barnett (2004), *The Pentagon's New Map . . .*, p. 45, op. cit.

120 Ibid., p. 84.

121 See Robert "Buzz" Patterson (2003), *Dereliction of Duty: The Eyewitness Account of How Bill Clinton Compromised America's National Security*, Washington, D.C., Regnery Publishing Inc., p. 129.

122 Ibid., p. 130.

123 Ibid., p. 131. Brackets mine.

124 See Fred Aja Agwu (2007), *World Peace through World Law . . .*, p. 199, op. cit.

which some might designate as national liberation struggles"; thus, leaving the entire exercise with "no arbiter in the form of an accepted text".[125]

However, what really resolves this controversy is the question of who the object or target of this violent pursuit is. When the target of violence is deliberately, massively, and exclusively civilian or non-military in nature, the charge of terrorism can hardly be denied, no matter the depth of the righteousness of their grievances. Madeleine Albright poignantly made this point when she lamented that there are many autocratic governments that seek to establish clarity in the definition of terrorism where none exists; and that they do this by "smearing political opponents as 'terrorists' whether or not that description applies".[126] Although the characterization of terrorism may have some political colouration, the essential or primary consideration in characterizing the traditional terrorist is in this penchant to attack soft targets like civilian populations. And although the Turkish government consider the separatist Kurdistan Workers Party (PKK) as a terrorist organization; some few minutes into the New Year of 2017 when a lone terrorist struck an Istanbul (Turkey) nightclub, killing some 39 revelers and leaving several others wounded, some convictions were that it was the handiwork of the ISIS rather than the PKK.[127]

The aforementioned conclusion derived from the fact that, unlike the PKK that are said to restrict their targets to the military and police institutions/installation, the ISIS had established notoriety for attacking soft or civilian targets.[128] Although in less than 24 hours, the ISIS predictably took responsibility for the Istanbul nightclub attack,[129] it did not, however, prevent the Turkish government from regarding the PKK as a terrorist organization, whether or not its sole targets were not civilians but military and police installations. But Madeleine Albright resolves the controversy along the line of acknowledging the inviolability of civilians or non-military objects in her submission that "to admit that many situations are unclear is not to say that clarity of responsibility is impossible to sort out", irrespective of the grievance: be it by the millenarian al-Qaeda, the secular anti colonial nationalist, an ultra-nationalist or a group aspiring for a revolutionary change of government.[130] Hence, according to her:

> When someone places a bomb in the federal building in Oklahoma City, or sends poison through the mails, or opens fire on people praying in a mosque,

125 See Rosemary Foot (2005), "Collateral Damage: Human Rights Consequences of Counterterrorist Action in the Asia-Pacific", *International Affairs*, Vol. 81, No. 2, March, p. 421.

126 See Madeleine Albright (2003), *Madam Secretary: A Memoir*, New York, Miramax Books, p. 479.

127 This, for instance, was the view expressed by Robert Baer, a former CIA operative while fielding questions from Rosemary Church on CNN, January 2, 2017, monitored in Lagos (Nigeria) at 7am local time.

128 Loc. Cit.

129 CNN Newsroom, monitored in Lagos (Nigeria) on Tuesday, January 3, 2017, at 8pm.

130 See Madeleine Albright (2003), *Madam Secretary* . . ., p. 479, op. cit.

> or turns a vegetable market into a scene of carnage, or flies an airplane into an office building, the moral issues are simple. It does not matter how angry, desperate or demoralized a person might be. There is no political, historical, religious, economic, or ideological justification for willfully murdering innocent people.[131]

The millenarian al-Qaeda and their associated forces in the ISIS do all of what Albright mentions. And the degeneracy of contemporary terrorist insurgents is inherent in the fact that, unlike in the past when terrorists "wanted a lot of people watching and not a lot of people dead", today's terrorists "want a lot of people dead and even more people crippled by fear and grief".[132] It is probably because of the vulnerability of civilians and the attendant heavy casualty that in the wake of the January 1, 2017 Istanbul (Turkey) nightclub attack under reference, Pope Francis, in his New Year address at St. Peter's Square in Rome, said that terrorism is a plague in which the "stain of blood" covers "the world with a shadow of fear and a sense of loss".[133] But unlike the modern-day millenarian terrorists that make a fetish of the targeting of civilians, the African anti-colonial fighters that imperialism framed as terrorists never attacked civilians in a coordinated way, including the use of suicide bombing.

And what again set them apart from the millenarian terrorists is that their goal was exclusively political and once achieved, they dropped their armed struggle. The millenarian terrorists are inclined to waging a permanent armed struggle to achieve martyrdom because their aim of a global caliphate or making the rest of humanity to accept their ways of life is totally unrealistic and non-feasible. But without this politicization, the contestations about the meaning of terrorism becomes an exercise in sterility, for the modern-day terrorist insurgents remain the millenarian groups whose precursors were the al-Qaeda that have now also morphed into the ISIS, the Al-Shabab, and the Boko Haram—many of them also having emerged on account of continued material or political frustrations.

This is to the extent that terrorist insurgents typically possess, at the incipient stage, identifiable socio-political and economic agendas or earthly goals (like the aspiration for self-determination), the lack of attainment of which drives them to millenarian terrorists: those that, out of disgruntlement with earthly political situations, become fatalistic, averse to any political agenda, and now turn their allegiance, not to any institution or geopolitical expression on earth, but to a higher authority in heaven.[134] Thus, although the millenarian subsequently supersedes the political or material,[135] but in agential and structural terms, the millenarian

131 Ibid., pp. 479–480.

132 See Sheila Macrine (2016), "The Psychology of Radicalization" . . ., p. 9, op. cit.

133 See "Terrorism Casts Bloodstain over the World, Says Pope", *The Nation* (Lagos), January 2, 2017, p. 6.

134 See Fred Aja Agwu (2009), *National Interest, International Law* . . ., p. 126, note 146, op. cit.

135 See Fred Aja Agwu (2013), *Themes and Perspectives on Africa's International Relations*, Ibadan, University Press Plc., pp. 273–281.

consciousness issues from the frustration over the plain failure to attain the political or material objects.

It was against this background that political Islam and Wahhabism/Salafism erupted in the wake of the Palestinian resistance and Arab nationalism's failure to roll back the state of Israel in the 1967 six-day war, its subsequent loss of faith in the ability of the Arab States to seize back the occupied West Bank and Gaza Strip, and its loss of faith in the Yasser Arafat leadership and the ability of the intifada movement to regain the lost lands and achieve the Palestinian state, thus, feeling let down by the secular approaches and now resorting to Islamic radicalism through the Hamas, the millenarian agenda that employs the vehicle of radical Islamism in the perpetration of suicide terrorism.[136] It is also believed that in Somalia:

> Religious belief had little, if anything at all, to do with this. In fact, it was the failure of the essentially secular warlords to bring an end to their conflicts that gave rise to the religious interventions that also then armed themselves.[137]

It was for this same loss of faith in secular institutions—expressed in the failed prebendal relationship between the members of the Boko Haram (*Jamaatu Ahlil Sunna Lidawati wal Jihad*) and the politicians in northern Nigeria (who used to recruit, pay, and use them for electoral purposes); the Janus-faced or structural ambiguity in the Nigerian 1999 Constitution (which in the same breath asserted the country's secularity in section 10 while allowing for an appeal sharia court in section 275); and even at an individual level, the extrajudicial killing of their leader, Mohammed Yusuf, in 2009—that drove the Boko Haram sect into the millenarian stance of denouncing Western education as evil, believing (in the characteristic Wahhabi/Salafist rejection of mainstream societal practices[138]) that it was only an Islamic state (for groups like Hamas and the Muslim Brotherhood; unlike the ISIS that is anti-nationalism and believes in the creation of a Caliphate[139]) that is governed by sharia law that can guarantee people jobs and good or ostensible means of livelihood, and resultantly leading the sect to adopt the terrorist tactics of the al-Qaeda and ISIS.[140]

Like the al-Shabaab, the Boko Haram was to be subsequently taken over by co-religionists from outside who have a broader agenda.[141] Kalundi Serumaga paints a very interesting picture of how African governments suffer self-inflicted

136 See Fred Aja Agwu (2009), *National Interest, International Law* . . ., p. 126, note 146, op. cit.

137 See Kalundi Serumaga in "Terrorism in Africa . . .", p. 37, op. cit.

138 See Ngala Chome in "Portrait of an Insurgent" . . ., pp. 48–50, op. cit.

139 See "Apocalypse Now . . .", p. 13, op. cit.

140 See Animasawun Gbemisola Abdul-Jelil (2016), "Agential and Structural Explanations of Radical Islamism in Northern Nigeria in the Fourth Republic", *Nigerian Army Journal*, Vol. 1, No. 1, February.

141 See Kalundi Serumaga in "Terrorism in Africa . . .", p. 37, op. cit.

terrorist challenges in the bid to fight the malaise. For him, Africa has particularly been put on the spot by modern terrorist insurgencies because its governments' prioritization of the war on terror over and above every other thing has led to the emergence of "the security state in Africa" with the resultant near state of emergencies everywhere, eroding all manner of freedoms over the entire landscape.[142] Consistent with this security state that emerges under the guise of the war on terror, and like imperialist powers, African "governments often tailor definitions of terrorists to fit their own political end", which then lead them to the resort to extrajudicial abuses, human rights violations, arbitrary arrests, illegal detentions, disappearances, renditions, and extrajudicial killings.[143]

When, with the active acquiescence of the West, the Algerian military annulled that country's democratic elections in 1992, sparking off "a vicious and bloody war between the Islamists and the army, and in which the Islamists deployed terrorist tactics", this "state security" arose when, as "the essential strategy of the army, its leadership of *eradicateurs*, and the secret intelligence service, the *Department du Renseignement et de la Securite* (DRS)" infiltrated the GIA, the armed group of the Islamists—*Front Islamique du Salut* (FIS).[144] The result of this was that the army and the DRS went on a killing spree, so much so that "it was difficult to know who was killing who" as "many of the worst civilian massacres and other atrocities had been committed by army units and the DRS masquerading as Islamists".[145] In fact, "the DRS became the real power in Algeria, a state-within-a-state"; with its Director-General, Mohammed "Toufik" Mediene, wielding "power through an elaborate patronage system that co-opted the political and business elite, providing the DRS access to both political and business rents".[146]

The passage of draconian laws (arising from these emergency powers) also gives rise to "the rise of conflict economies" and the opportunism of the national armies fighting the insurgents; the sort of military opportunism and high-handedness that in turn leads to its own peculiar "blowback", the very terrorist pathologies the governments are struggling with: "militant radicalization of swathes of the population, especially the youth in politically marginalized regions" or populations; and the "exposure of their own populations to militant attacks".[147] The malaise of security agencies' excesses arising from the syndrome of the "security state" was seen first-hand in Nigeria when Mohammed Yusuf of the Boko Haram became a victim of an extrajudicial tactic that allegedly fueled the Boko Haram insurgency.

In the same vein, Nigeria's President Muhammadu Buhari was also reported to have threatened that his government would give pipeline vandals the Boko

142 Ibid., p. 36.
143 Loc. Cit.
144 See Jeremy Keenan in "How Terror Came to the Sahel", *New African*, April 2016, p. 57.
145 Loc. Cit.
146 Loc. Cit.
147 Kalundi Serumaga in "Terrorism in Africa . . .", p. 36, op. cit.

Haram treatment,[148] a euphemism for the application of heavy-handed military tactic, the sort that was used to roll the Boko Haram insurgents out of many northeast Nigerian cities into their notorious redoubt at Sambisa Forest; from where the sect was also besieged and its Camp Zero later captured by the Nigerian military. This approach—the rise of excesses or heavy-handedness owing to the emergence of the "security state" and the unilateral labeling of groups as terrorists to suit political purposes—from Kalundi Serumaga's perspective, only exacerbates the terrorism pathologies on the African continent, especially (in agential terms) from the materialistic motivational basis.

Even though Nigeria's President Buhari claimed to have defanged the Boko Haram by rolling it back and dominating its camp zero fortress in Sambisa Forest, the sect remained resilient—to the dismal of the ever-skeptical United States and Transparent International.[149] It continued to severely challenge the Nigerian state almost to the status of a failed state; not just on account of challenging the state's monopoly of force, but also on the account of the Nigerian government having "little or no control over a significant part of its territory".[150] And like in all failed states, the Boko Haram was able to find haven in northern Nigeria because (as demonstrated by the existence of the *almajiri* system) the state had substantially retreated from the socio-economic lives of most people, giving the Islamists the opportunity to create not just an alternative space, but, indeed, an alternative magnetic space where the impoverished and disconnected in the society also retreated and became vulnerable to radicalization.

The ascendance of Islamist terrorism is what happens—as in the Middle East with the ISIS, the al-Nusra, and other terrorist organizations—when "religion is achieving political functions because political institutions are not able to do

148 President Buhari was quoted to have said to the members of the Nigerian community in Beijing (China) as follows, "the government is still being dared, but those who are sensible should have learnt a lesson. Those who are mad, let them continue in their madness. I am aware that in the last two weeks, the national grid collapsed a number of times. I hope this message will reach the vandals and saboteurs who are blowing up pipelines and installations. We will deal with them the way we dealt with Boko Haram"; see Kelvin Ebiri, Hendrix Oliomogbe, Alemma-Ozioruwa Aliu, Gbenga Salau, and Julius Osahun in "Pipeline Vandals: Niger Deltans Warn Buhari on Tactics; Say B'Haram War Strategy Won't Work; It's a Ploy to Emasculate Region", *The Guardian* (Lagos), April 17, 2016, pp. 1–2.

149 The United States' "Country Report on Terrorism 2016" as well as Transparency International's Report of the same year accused the federal government of deceit, that it lied in its claim to have defeated the Boko Haram, citing corruption and Nigeria's security agencies' animosity and refusal to share intelligence as factors militating against success in the war against the terrorist sect; see "Boko Haram: US, TI Reports Confirm FG's Deceit", *Vanguard* (Lagos), Thursday, August 3, 2017, p. 11. In fact, there is no love lost between the United States and Nigeria's military and other security agencies in the fight against the Boko Haram; see Fred Aja Agwu (2016), *Nations among Nations*. . ., pp. 490, 595–597, op. cit.

150 See John Campbell (2011), *Nigeria: Dancing on the Brink*, New York, Rowman & Littlefield Publishers Inc., p. 139.

that", the state having failed and retreated.[151] As seen in the Middle East, this apparently reinforces the primacy of the political and socio-economic rather than the so-called sacred or millenarian motivation in terrorism because the "ISIS would not have done as well as it has if it were not for the breakdown of state institutions in Syria and Iraq" because of "decades of dictatorship, failed governance and development, and abject poverty"—all of which were made worse by "foreign intervention and the Palestinian tragedy, and which led to "rising sectarianism".[152] In Nigeria, state failure and attendant retreat reinforced the Boko Haram when it exacerbated the soft security threat that climate change posed, creating a cesspool of displaced farmers and herdsmen who, due to the loss of the vital means of their socio-economic sustenance to desertification, became vulnerable to instrumentalization by the Islamists as they drifted to southern Nigeria, attacking, kidnapping, and killing unsuspecting locals in the guise of searching for pasture for their cattle.

Although the Buhari government claimed to have decimated the Boko Haram, when some retired military Generals (Joshua Dongonyaro, Zamani Lekwot, T. Y. Danjuma, etc.) met under the auspices of the National Christian Elders Forum (NCEF), on the state of the nation, they expressed anxiety about the subsisting use of herdsmen to advance the Boko Haram agenda, lamenting that "a group of people not voted by the citizens wrest control of governance from duly elected government officials . . . sponsoring grazing reserves for herdsmen across the nation"; instead of, in the absence of the international practice of ranching, giving Sambisa Forest to the herdsmen.[153] The NCEF reasoned that "the real problem with the country is that Jihad has been launched in Nigeria and Islamists . . . interfering with governance", using the "Boko Haram and herdsmen as violent jihad".[154] In fact, the apprehension that the Boko Haram menace in Nigeria may be exacerbated grew when Morocco, located in the Mahgreb and ipso facto known to have been infested with the AQIM, applied for the membership of the Economic Community of West African States (ECOWAS) with all its baggage of being a quarrelsome country that had destabilized the Arab Mahgreb Union (AMU) where it belongs in geophysical terms.[155]

The kingdom of Morocco in the ECOWAS would clearly make the West African sub-region another magnetic space for the Middle East–based AQIM. Thus, AQIM will effectively reinforce its relationship with the Boko Haram in Nigeria, exploit and convert the ECOWAS Protocol on freedom of movement

151 The thought of Professor Badie, Director of the International Relations Programme at Political Sciences School of Paris as analyzed by Tobia Princewill in "Humiliation in African Context", *Vanguard* (Lagos), Friday, July 21, 2017, p. 40.

152 See Fawaz A. Gerges (2016), *ISIS: A History* . . ., p. 289, op. cit.

153 See Sam Eyoboka in "Avert Another War, Danjuma, Dongonyaro, Lekwot, Others Warn", *Vanguard* (Lagos), Friday, July 14, 2017, pp. 1, 5.

154 Ibid., p. 5.

155 See Owei Lakemfa in "When the Goat Claims Same Paternity with the Sheep", *Vanguard* (Lagos), June 23, 2017, p. 31.

of people, goods and services, to (like the Fulani herdsmen across the region had exploited and converted it to a Protocol on "freedom of movement of cows"[156]) a Protocol on free movement of AQIM and Boko Haram terrorists. This is the extent to which the security anxieties (in hard or military terms and soft in terms of climate change and porous borders) in West African and Nigeria in particular can also be germane to the growth and spread of terrorism in the sub-region. It must be reiterated that although the result may not be equivalent to David slaying Goliath, terrorism is an asymmetric response that can be very hurtful.

Terrorism and the Impoverished/Disconnected

Although cumulatively, contemporary international terrorism has its political and millenarian roots in such issues as the liquidation of the Ottoman empire by European imperialism (the ancient grievance against the Sykes and Picot line in the sand[157]), "the Palestinian-Israeli conflict, conditions in Iraq, Afghanistan and Pakistan, and the future of Kashmir and Indo-Pakistani relations",[158] there is no doubt that it also has a materialistic dimension; and it is at the level of this materialistic dimension that terrorism feeds fat from the impoverished and the disconnected. It explains why many of those that have been vulnerable to recruitment in the terrorist networks have mainly been the disposed and disconnected in the society. In northern Nigeria, although not territorially defined, the *almajiris*, the "traditional Islamic school pupil/student",[159] constitute this category of impoverished and disconnected group that is very vulnerable to recruitment by terrorist groups. Though not exactly the same, the *almajiri* is an institution that is comparable to the *madrasa* in the Muslim societies of especially the Middle East. The *almajiri* "is the face of the monumental failure of the northern Muslim community to find a point where traditional method of teaching young Muslim elements of their faith will be isolated from its structural limitations and political indifference".[160]

The *almajiri* system is built on the belief of both the parents of the pupils/students and their society/faith that the youth of these pupils/students be "sacrificed virtually in rags, hunger and exposure to damaging social tendencies [as] a useful investment for [an] adult and next life".[161] Hence, the *almajiri* is an

156 See Omeiza Ajayi in "Nigeria's Problems Started with Awo's Introduction of Tribal Politics", *Vanguard* (Lagos), Monday, June 26, 2017, p. 43.

157 See "The War within: Europe and America Made Mistakes, But the Misery of the Arab World Is Caused Mainly by Its Own Failures", *The Economist*, May 14, 2016, p. 7.

158 See Martha Crenshaw (2009), "Terrorism as an International Security Problem", in Jeffrey H. Norwitz (2009, ed.); *Pirates, Terrorists, and Warlords: The History, Influence, and Future of Armed Groups around the World*, New York, Skyhorse Publishing, p. 401.

159 See Hakeem Baba-Ahmed in "Lawwali, almajiri", *Daily Trust* (Abuja), Friday, May 6, 2016, back page.

160 Loc. Cit.

161 Loc. Cit. Parentheses mine.

epitome of social privation.[162] In northern Nigeria, the *almajiri* has been so weather-bitten that

> sentiments and signs of weakness have been erased from his countenance and replaced by an unapologetic posture that tolerates an existence at the mercy and compassion of strangers, and an acceptance that his life has been designed by parents and teachers along lines of a long tradition.[163]

The *almajiri* consists of millions of children that stay behind and get "tied down by a strong and stubborn value system that was neither threatened nor cajoled by the state" in an environment where, paradoxically, millions of other children "join the scramble for a future anchored around western values and systems".[164] In these circumstances where the *almajiris* are consigned to the life of "begging and wretched existence . . . as the hallmark of Islamic education",[165] they become vulnerable and easily instrumentalized by those extremists whose distorted narrative of Islam espouses violence.

In al-Qaeda in East Africa (AQEA), the al-Shabaab leader, Sheikh Ahmed Iman Ali, found very willing followers "in Nairobi's Majengo neighbourhood, an old slum settlement historically dominated by Muslims" because he "provided financial assistance to poor Muslims for burials, medical bills, school fees for needy students" and "reined in prostitution".[166] Thus, it is habitual for the terrorists not only to seek to insert themselves inside local conflicts (that is, exploit the people's disaffection), they also exploit the "abominable marginalization" of the oppressed lot, as has happened amongst the indigenes of this Kenyan coast.[167] It is, therefore, evident that even though religious belief may be a factor in radicalization, it does not thrive in isolation, as economic, dislocation, immiseration, and disconnection from society also contribute in equal measure to the making of the naïve mind, or the delusion that makes this radicalization very easy; explaining why, for instance, the *almajiris* of northern Nigeria would be part of many riots in Kaduna or even form the bulk of the foot soldiers in the Boko Haram insurgency.

Like the *almajiri* in northern Nigeria and the Majengo neighbourhood in Nairobi (Kenya), like Molenbeek in Brussels (Belgium), all impoverished and disconnected communities, whose inhabitants are marginalized and ostensibly drained of any sense of having a stake of any form in the society. The poverty in neighbourhoods like the foregoing generates so much sense of alienation and disconnectedness that the people there are not only inclined but also sympathetic and want to shelter terrorists. Hence, when the "jihadists who carried out

162 Loc. Cit.
163 Loc. Cit.
164 Loc. Cit.
165 Loc. Cit.
166 See Ngala Chome in "Portrait of an Insurgent" . . ., pp. 48–50, op. cit.
167 See Kalundi Serumaga in "Terrorism in Africa . . .", p. 37, op. cit.

the terrorist attacks on Paris fled that city, they melted into an underground of sympathetic neighbours in a Muslim ghetto at the very heart of Europe—the Molenbeek neighbourhood in Brussels".[168]

In Europe, most of the arrested ISIS's local cells operatives (like Nicolas Moreau in France, for instance) were people that had returned from fighting in Iraq and Syria to inflict death and destruction on the homeland, people who had been petty criminals, disillusioned with life and converted to Islam in prison.[169] They were the disconnected and oppressed; and, as it were, terrorism in Brussels has revealed the self-evident truth, if not trite knowledge, that alienation and stigmatization breeds radicalization.[170] There is a "divisive rhetoric" in Belgium in which "Belgians of a different colour, no matter how long they have lived in the country and regardless of whether or not they were born in Belgium are referred to as . . . allochtoon (from foreign soil)".[171]

The situation had been such that the so-called individuals "from foreign soil", even when they speak well with flawless Flemish, such flawlessness was often complimented as being too good "for an allochtoon"; and this was emblematic of the "unwillingness to accept that non-white Belgians have as much right to the nation as their Caucasian countrymen".[172] This discrimination and stigmatization is further worsened by alienation of the non-white immigrant population at the level of employments. Without regard to qualification, an immigrant had reportedly recalled "going to an employment office once to register and being told, without being asked for my qualifications, that there was an opening for a cleaner and I could start immediately".[173] For this and probably other reasons, Molenbeek (Brussels) the denizens of which has a huge immigrant population, "has a huge unemployment problem and therefore a lot of idle hands, which gained its notoriety way before it became linked with jihadists".[174]

This is not to talk about Belgium's police that is reportedly all-white and, as such, is not only insular, but also bereft of bonding or mutual trust with the immigrant ethno-religious population; a police in which the proposal for diversification in terms of the absorption of ethnic and religious minorities was allegedly resisted. This is a Belgium in which, educationally, there is "a teaching body that is mostly monolithic (white Belgians, often from Christian homes . . .) . . ., blind to the needs of students who are unlike them"; and where not much effort is made to "wrest control of the narrative of what Islam

168 See Karl Vick in "What Terrorists Acting Alone Says about the Loyalty of U.S. Muslims", *Time* (New York), October 3, 2016, p. 7.

169 See "Is in Europe: The Race to the Death", *The Guardian* (Lagos), Friday, March 25, 2016, p. 18.

170 See "In the Shadow of Terror", *New African*, May 2016, pp. 70–71.

171 Ibid., p. 71.

172 Loc. Cit.

173 Loc. Cit.

174 Loc. Cit.

is from those who propagate terror".[175] These dynamics of the Belgian society are, therefore, clearly oblivious of the truism that "one who feels part of a community does not seek to destroy it".[176]

Hence, in Molenbeek, the immigrants-dominated neighbourhood of Brussels, radicalization and terrorism are rife since "the devil finds work for idle hands" because of the marginal employment of the local and, of course, the under-policing of the community; for as it were, "even after the Paris attacks, Molenbeek got only 50 extra police officers" in a police force that is dominated by Caucasians and non-whites under-represented.[177] This reality is a strong factor in the creation of the sense of rejection and resentment that conduce to radicalization. In fact, in another part of Europe (France to be precise) where some immigrants are not treated in a very hospitable manner; Nicolas Moreau, as aforementioned, reportedly confessed to interrogators that "he couldn't stand the 'injustice' and couldn't see any future in this country [France]".[178] It was because of the sympathetic inclination of the marginalized and alienated in the Molenbeek neighbourhood in Brussels to terrorists that "the most wanted man in Europe hid out for four months before he was finally discovered blocks from his family home".[179]

Compare this to Ahmad Khan Rahami, the master-mind of the September 17, 2016 explosion in Manhattan's (New York) Chelsea neighbourhood (that injured about 29 people) as well as an earlier detonation the same day in New Jersey who was immediately given away by an informant who summoned the police after discovering him "huddling against the elements" asleep in the vestibule of a tavern in Linden, New Jersey.[180] It was believed that Rahami, like Tamerlan Tsarnaev (the Boston Marathon bomber) was all alone, failed to find sanctuary, slept in the street and was arrested after just 50 hours at large not only because the terrorist was "in a country newly transfixed by terrorism" and alert with "surveillance cameras, instant forensics and a coordinated security apparatus", but also because he struck a population that is "striking for its aspiration and assimilation", the assimilation of immigrants of all orientations, including Muslims.[181] Incidentally, it was the same September 17 that Rahami struck that another lone wolf, a Somali immigrant that was promptly killed at the scene, carried out a knife attack that wounded 10 people in St. Cloud, Minn., an attack that ISIS took credit for.[182]

But as part of the war on terror in the wake of the surge in the "lone wolf" syndrome and other fanatical Islam-inspired (especially ISIS) attacks, some European countries have become involved in Islamic education with the requisite dose of

175 Loc. Cit.
176 Loc. Cit.
177 Loc. Cit.
178 See Kalundi Serumaga in "Terrorism in Africa . . .", p. 37, op. cit.
179 See Karl Vick in "What Terrorists Acting . . .", pp. 7–8, op. cit.
180 Ibid., p. 7.
181 Ibid., p. 8.
182 Loc. Cit.

civics courses in their countries.[183] Some of these countries have tried to shift ground and confront their long history of settled ideals regarding the relationship between the state and religion.[184] In the United Kingdom, for instance, "children imbibe a British Islamic culture with an emphasis or stress on interfaith relations and obedience to British laws, such that traditions like British royal events are celebrated keenly"; in Belgium, despite being credited as a "Catholic Kingdom", the state now includes Islam among the religions for which it conducts civics courses, and in the bid to cultivate a peculiar brand of "Belgian Islam", now has a Muslim body ("led by a well-connected Moroccan") advising it; and in France too, the state is also confronting "its own history and long-settled deals regarding the state's relationship" with religions, now introducing some changes in the regime or practice of *laicite* (secularism) that was instituted in 1905 in order "to replace foreign financing of mosques with national resources".[185]

The Notoriety of the Modern Terrorist

The notoriety of the modern terrorist derives essentially from the fact that the terrorist does not observe any restraint; neither does the terrorist have any sense of proportion or discrimination between the "guilty" and the innocent. It is, therefore, worth reinstating here that it is only when terrorism is not politicized with individuals in innocuous nationalist struggles (individuals that do not pose any form of threats to innocent civilians) being denominated or characterized as terrorists that the definitional contentions over the issue might be surmounted. But this does not also discount the fact that the nationalist involved in liberation struggles does not sometime morph into the secular or millenarian terrorist that mobilize the socio-politically disconnected and economically disposed to wreak havoc on soft targets, especially the civilian members of society. However, it is only when the politicization of terrorism in this regard ceases that the debate about who the terrorist is would become totally uncalled for and, indeed, all the more very sterile.[186]

Thus, terrorist operations can be limited to the efforts of that small group that uses "fear and disruption in an attempt to control the actions of a larger entity".[187] However, because the characterization of terrorism is not quantitatively determined in terms of number, it is the profundity of the havoc it causes on the innocent civilian population and other soft targets like public infrastructure that

183 See "Islamic Education in Europe: Faith of Our Fathers", *The Economist*, August 20, 2016, p. 45.
184 Loc. Cit.
185 Ibid., pp. 45–46.
186 See Fred Aja Agwu (2013), *Themes and Perspectives*. . ., pp. 237–245, op. cit; see also Fred Aja Agwu (2007), *World Peace through World Law* . . ., pp. 185–191, op. cit.
187 See David L. Bongard and William R. Schilling (2002), "Terrorist Operations in Nontraditional Warfare", in William R. Schilling (2002, ed.); *Nontraditional Warfare: Twenty-First Century Threats and Responses*, Washington, D.C., Brassey's Inc., p. 54.

matters. Thus, the point is made that the terrorists might be few, but the larger entity they terrorize also have the right to device whatever means to defend itself; even though there is equally the pragmatic need to adhere to the minimum level of decency at the level of humanitarian considerations by restricting these means and methods of responses to terrorist attacks to what is accepted by human civilization; otherwise, the terrorist would succeed in dragging humanity away from its cherished values, into the lowest level of indignity conceivable.

But this, as will be seen in due course, has been very difficult because the "terrorists rely on concealment and subterfuge for success"; they function in secret, wearing no uniform and generally move or mingle with the general population without attracting attention to themselves.[188] Sometimes, "their cause may be viewed with sympathy by a portion of the population", some of whom can be recruited for logistical support, or as new members.[189] It is because "terrorist insurgents" sometimes enjoy the sympathy of the local population that counter-insurgency as observed above is also acclaimed as "a win the population strategy". As a matter of operational routine, "terrorists rarely strike directly at their enemy's military strength"; as they have honed the strategy of bombings, assassinations, robberies, poisoning and "other acts of violence against symbolic targets designed to disrupt the social, political, and economic structure of their enemies".[190] Highlighting the terrorists' penchant for soft targets, Bordas Maria harped on the fact that "terrorists use violence and threats against the population, property, places of public use, public transportation system, infrastructural and other facilities in order to reach a general fear in the society"; and, as opposed to insurgents, "trigger psychological effects" and "intimidation" that could force the government to overreact.[191]

And emphasizing the notoriety of terrorist organizations, Bordas Maria also goes further to write that "terrorist groups are clandestine agents increasingly on a transnational level".[192] But drawing attention to the similarities and distinction between terrorists and insurgents, Bordas Maria wrote further that:

> Both of the insurgents and terrorists use violence acts, have political aims . . . [However, while] terrorist groups, on the other hand, are often also well organized, and tend to escalate the violent conflict . . .; insurgent groups . . . try to control one of the territories of the state, while terrorists normally do not; insurgents occasionally respect the law of war, but terrorists never; insurgents try to have the support of the population, while it is not important for terrorists; insurgents do not necessarily attack civilians, but it is the rule for terrorists.[193]

188 Loc. Cit.

189 Loc. Cit.

190 Loc. Cit.

191 See Bordas Maria (2014), "Current Issues of International Law in Regulating Counter-Insurgency and Counter-Terrorism" . . ., p. 573, op. cit.

192 Loc. Cit.

193 Loc. Cit. Brackets mine.

Thus, according to Bordas Maria, "in order to make a distinction between insurgency and terrorism, the most important point of view is as to whether they commit common crimes or use lawful armed force".[194] The infamy in terrorism inheres in the fact that "when insurgents seriously violate international law, for example attack civilians, civilian objects, kill prisoners, etc., they evidently cannot be considered as lawful combatants"[195] but outright terrorists. It is the attack on soft targets, especially the civilian population that distinguishes the traditional insurgent from the terrorist. However, although the distinction between the insurgent and the terrorist was largely valid in the past, some of these comparisons (similarities and distinctions) do not hold totally true today with the advent of ambidextrous groups like the Taliban, the ISIS, the Al-Shabab, and the Boko Haram; all of them are insurgent groups that also excel as terrorists.

The implication is that with this unprecedented fusion of insurgency with terrorism (that is, the emergence of the terrorist insurgent), territories are now sought and held by terrorists; and some terrorist organizations now enjoy the massive support of parts of populations, especially in Wahabbist or Salafist societies (like the Sunnis in Iraq/Syria; and the Boko Haram in northeast Nigeria). It is, indeed, in this morphing of insurgency into terrorism that has resulted in such paradoxical terminology as the "terrorist insurgent" who, although enjoys the support of the local civilian populations in some places, nevertheless, now also attacks civilians. The onset of the terrorist insurgents has since been attended by anxiety in many security circles; and this has been evident in the frustration by military officers in the Western world that have had to endure the blight of this affliction in many areas of their engagement with these terrorists.

Hence, P. H. Liotta used the befitting apothegm to illustrate the frustrations that attend terrorist campaigns when he quoted Martin van Creveld as remarking (with respect to the unconventional tactics of the terrorists) that "a ghost is stalking the corridors of general staffs and defence departments all over the developed world—the fear of military impotence, even irrelevance" in the face of insurgents; while also quoting a military officer lamenting in 1964 to journalists in Southeast Asia about this transformation of war, regretting that "if only the little bastards would just come out . . . and fight like men, we'd cream them".[196] Unfortunately, it is in the character of the terrorist campaigns aspect of asymmetric warfare that this ghost keeps stalking the corridors of general staffs and defence departments all over the developed world, engendering the fear of military impotence and even irrelevance despite the sophisticated armaments of the armies of these developed nations; and that these little bastards never come out and fight like men, of course, knowing full well that not being well resourced like conventional armies, they would easily be creamed off.

194 Ibid., p. 574.

195 Loc. Cit. Brackets mine.

196 See P. H. Liotta (2009), "Takin' It to the Streets: Hydra Networks, Chaos Strategies, and the 'New' Asymmetry", in Jeffrey H. Norwitz (2009, ed.); *Pirates, Terrorists, and Warlords* . . ., pp. 414, op. cit.

The Ambidexterity of the Modern Terrorist

But there is a clear recognition that insurgency has since fused with terrorism. It was for reasons of this fusion that a Czarist Russian minister, a very exalted servant of the Romanov, was credited to have said that terrorism "may be totally senseless, but it is a poisonous, indeed, horrifying idea that seeks to draw power from impotence".[197] That Czarist Russian minister was actually talking about the phenomenon of insurgency that has adopted terrorist campaigns. Yet, as seen earlier, insurgency (when not involved in terrorist campaigns) is not at that point necessarily coterminous with terrorism. The only thing that an insurgency shares with terrorism when it is not into terrorist campaigns is the fact of belonging to the genre of asymmetric warfare; and as all asymmetric wars go, they are defined by the idea that the strong party can be bested by refusing to meet it in an open battle.[198] In polemology, therefore, insurgency is a genre of conflict, while terrorism is an instrument or tactic that insurgents adopt for engendering intimidating fear and apprehension.

The Islamic State of Iraq and Syria (ISIS), for instance, is an insurgent group that applies two strategies, one conventional (as in when the group engages Iraqi, Syrian or the Arab multinational forces in a pitched conventional battle), and the other terrorist bombings or campaigns, using Improvised Explosive Devices (IEDs). The same applies to other insurgency groups like the Al-Shabab in Somalia, and the Boko Haram in Nigeria, etc. There may be the temptation to offhandedly dismiss the Al-Shabab and Boko Haram as downright terrorist organizations comparable to the al-Qaeda and devoid of any iota of insurgency comparable to the ISIS or even the Niger Delta militants.[199] On the contrary, the Al-Shabab and the Boko Haram are also consummate insurgent groups with ambidextrous capabilities, having combined their engagement of the nation-state in insurgencies with terrorist campaigns, the Al-Shabab taking on the rump of the Somali army as well as African Union forces and seizing territories in Somalia while the Boko Haram takes on the Nigerian military and later the Multinational Joint Task Force (MNJTF) in pitched battles and taking territories in the north-east region of Nigeria. This is in addition to the Boko Haram's dare-devilbombing campaigns.

Thus, a full-fledged insurgency is characteristically ambidextrous in its approach to warfare; that is, it is possessed of the dual capability for both conventional actions and terrorist campaigns. It, therefore, stands to reason that every insurgent is a potential terrorist, but not every terrorist (particularly the lone wolves) is or could be an insurgent. It is the terrorist campaigns that insurgents adopt (using such "dirty weapons" as the Improvised Explosive Devices)

197 See Josef Joffe in "Asymmetric Warfare . . .", p. 47, op. cit.

198 Loc. Cit.

199 For a detailed analysis of insurgency and how it applies to the Niger Delta militants, see Fred Aja Agwu (2011), *From Rebellion, Insurgency to Belligerency: The Niger Delta Oil War in International Law*, Ibadan, University Press Plc., pp. 1–13, 57–68.

that consistently fuel the conceptual confusion of the insurgent with the terrorist. This confusion sometimes engineers the impression that, between the two, pragmatically and conceptually, there is a distinction without a difference. This, however, is not the case; for insurgency and terrorism, in definitional and pragmatic terms, are two different categories of asymmetric engagements in armed conflicts.

However, this book sometimes takes liberty in using insurgency and terrorism interchangeably wherever compelled to do so; and this is largely not only because of the ambidextrous capability of the insurgent, but also because terrorism cannot be defeated without first defeating insurgency. This interchangeable application of both concepts is particularly compelling because, according to Bordas Maria:

> After having analyzed the differences, it should be clear that we couldn't identify any insurgent or terrorist group that would have only terrorist or insurgent characteristics. . . . [T]here are no clear insurgent or terrorist groups in practical reality, but non-state armed troops having more or less features of insurgency, terrorism or organized crime.[200]

As observed earlier, insurgency and terrorism all fall into the broad genre of asymmetric armed conflict, a strategy that has a biblical progeny, having been invented and honed in the asymmetric duel between David and Goliath.[201] However, the new asymmetric warfare is represented in the terrorist campaigns of the al-Qaeda, the ISIS, and the Boko Haram. It is the preferred strategy of these insurgents whenever they lose territory or want to demonstrate their seriousness by showing the capacity for threat and destruction in far-flung places like the United States on as seen on 9/11. The terrorist campaigns of the al-Qaeda (the only group that do not have territory but enjoy sanctuaries or safe haven in territories taken by the Taliban and the ISIS, etc.), the ISIS, the Al-Shabab, and the Boko Haram also extend to sponsoring some elements that are intoxicated or deranged by their toxic ideology of hate into operating as loners; these are the "lone wolf militants" that the insurgents inspire.[202]

The Phenomenon of Domestic/Homegrown Terrorism

The al-Qaeda terrorist network and the ISIS are typically representative of today's most vicious and modern international or transnational terrorism.[203] Modern terrorism has basically been internationalized, manifesting itself in

200 See Bordas Maria (2014), "Current Issues of International Law in Regulating Counter-Insurgency and Counter-Terrorism" . . ., p. 574, op. cit.
201 See Josef Joffe in "Asymmetric Warfare . . .", p. 47, op. cit.
202 See "ISIS Explodes", *Time* (New York), November 30–December 7, 2015, p. 24.
203 See Thomas P. M. Barnett (2004), *The Pentagon's New Map* . . ., p. 91, op. cit.

transnational conspiracies that lead to aircraft hijacking and the kidnapping and murder of diplomats, etc.[204] For instance, the international nature of the Boko Haram as a terrorist organization essentially derives from its terrorist activities that not only straddle all the Lake Chad Basin countries of Nigeria, Cameroun, Chad and Niger Republic, but also in the group's pledging of allegiance to the ISIS, carrying out attacks in the name of the Islamic State (its so-called West African Province), and flaunting its international jihadi credentials to continue to woo the ISIS in Syria.[205] In fact, the internationalization of the Boko Haram terror was further confirmed when the Nigerian State Security Services busted an ISIS training cell in Kano, Nigeria, and arresting suspects that were reportedly transiting "to Libya, Morocco and other places with ISIS presence".[206]

However, despite the trans-border nature of international terrorism, it still has a domestic dimension, which is essentially the local franchises that were largely inspired from abroad; that is, the extremist religious lone wolves as well as the secular lone wolves,[207] whose zealotry and self-righteous indignation had been goaded into extreme homicidal resolutions: the likes of Timothy McVeigh and the Norwegian Anders Behring Breivik.[208] Although international or transnational in nature, "all terrorism is ultimately local: it occurs within states".[209] The al-Qaeda operatives, for instance, "cut their teeth on Afghanistan's internal violence".[210] But the homegrown terrorism phenomenon is therefore partly a consequence of the foreign policies of the Western nations, especially the United States and the UK, whose intervention in Iraq "under false pretexts was widely viewed as an attack on a Muslim country in immigrant circles", angering "many young Muslims in Western Europe, making some of them susceptible to recruitment efforts of Islamist terrorist organizations".[211]

Apart from those angered Muslims who are resident in the West and had never been to the Middle East, the phenomenon of homegrown terrorism also emerged from among the immigrant Diaspora communities.[212] Although the term foreign fighters had come "to mean Western Muslims travelling to Iraq and Syria", there is now "the issue of returning fighters", men and women who after fighting for the al-Qaeda or ISIS, return to menace the Western

204 See Fred Aja Agwu (2007), *World Peace through World Law . . .*, p. 198, op. cit.
205 See "No Major Link between Islamic State, Boko Haram—US Officials". . ., p. 4, op. cit.
206 See "DSS Busts ISIS Training Cell in Kano". . ., p. 56, op. cit.
207 See Anthony Richards (2015), "From Terrorism to 'Radicalization' to 'Extremism' . . .", p. 373, op. cit.
208 See Wole Soyinka (2004, 2005), *Climate of Fear: The Quest for Dignity in a Dehumanized World*, New York, Random House, pp. 117–118, 125–126; see also *Saturday Mirror* (Lagos), August 25, 2012, p. 55.
209 See Thomas P. M. Barnett (2004), *The Pentagon's New Map . . .*, p. 84, op. cit.
210 Ibid., p. 93.
211 See Alex P. Schmid (2016), "Research on Radicalization . . .", p. 26, op. cit.
212 Loc. Cit.

nations as lone wolves as exemplified by the attack in Belgium.[213] This was "on March 22, 2016, when a cell of Belgian Islamists—most of whom had spent time in Syria—detonated bombs at Brussels Airport and on the city's metro, killing 32 people".[214] In "an April 2016 report", the International Center for Counter-Terrorism in the Hague "estimated that about 30% of the total 4,294 Europeans who had fought with ISIS and other extremist groups had returned".[215]

The phenomenon of domestic or homegrown terrorists has, by Alex Schmid's reckoning, shifted "the public discussion away from Western meddling in the Muslim world to Islamist meddling with Muslim youth in the West in the form of radicalization and recruitment", using the social media, the "mosques and other recruitment hot spots such as prisons".[216] So, apart from the terrorist scourge in the internecine wars within the Middle East, the Western nations are now domestically in the league of the most heavily targeted in the tangled network of these terrorist campaigns by modern 21st-century insurgencies. The mayhem inherent in this internal or homegrown terrorism is wrought by both those radicalized in the social media and the immigrant Diaspora, not only in the United States and other Western nations, but also in many other countries around the world. This is one of the reasons for the backlash against globalization to the extent that it involved migration and the influx of refugees. As will be seen later in this book, it is one of the reasons for U.S. President Donald Trump's travel ban against the seven Muslim-dominant nations of Syria, Iran, Iraq, Libya, Yemen, Sudan, and Somalia.

In the United States, these internal terror threats are also represented by secular terrorists like Theodore Kaczynski and Timothy McVeigh, amongst others.[217] But the homegrown terror that plagues the United States (residents inspired in the social media) are the mainly "sacred terrorists" that were inspired by the ISIS, the lone wolves (Syed Farook and his wife, Tashfeen Malik) that struck at San Bernardino, and Saddique Mateen, the 29-year-old Afghanistan-American that killed 49 people in a rampage on Sunday, June 12, 2016 at the Pulse gay nightclub in Orlando, Florida.[218] President Barack Obama himself had admitted that:

> . . . we face a real threat from radicalized individuals here in the United States. Whether it's a shooter at a Sikh Temple in Wisconsin; a plane flying

213 See Charlotte McDonald-Gibson in "The Former Neo-Nazi Helping Returning ISIS Fighters Let Go Hate", *Time* (New York), February 27–March 6, 2017, p. 36.

214 Loc. Cit.

215 Loc. Cit.

216 See Alex P. Schmid (2016), "Research on Radicalization . . .", p. 26, op. cit.

217 See David L. Bongard and William R. Schilling (2002), "Terrorist Operations in Nontraditional Warfare", in William R. Schilling (2002, ed.); *Nontraditional Warfare* . . ., p. 62, op. cit

218 See "Orlando Shooter Omar Mateen's Father: I Don't Forgive Him", *The Nation* (Lagos), June 14, 2016, p. 44. For more incidents of some of these secular and "sacred" massacres in the United States, see also "40 Years of Massacres", *Time* (New York), June 27, 2016, pp. 32–33.

> into a building in Texas; or the extremist who killed 168 people at the Federal Building in Oklahoma City—America has confronted many forms of violent extremism in our time. Deranged or alienated individuals—often U.S. citizens or legal residents—can do enormous damage, particularly when inspired by larger notions of violent jihad. That pull towards extremism appears to have led to the shooting at Fort Hood, and the bombing of the Boston Marathon.[219]

The internal terrorism in the United States may be real, but this does not exclude the fact that America's greatest anxiety in the menace of terrorism comes from outside its borders, especially the al-Qaeda and its "associated forces", the Islamic extremists from the Middle East. It is the Middle East terror that primarily and directly menaces as well as inspires the American lone wolves. Most of the cases of America's domestic terror that President Obama outlined were masterminded by individuals that were inspired by the Middle East Islamic extremists, the sworn enemies of America, out to harm the country's interests and citizens wherever they may be found in the world, at home or abroad. The way to understand and deal with this problem was one of the major campaign issues in the United States 2016 Presidential election, with the candidates on the two major sides of the partisan divide—the Republican and the Democratic Parties—recognizing it as a veritable booby-trap that could make or mar their chances of winning the White House.

Donald Trump, then the Republican Party's presidential candidate nominee, fell into this booby-trap when he was seen "demonizing Muslims and playing right into the hands of ISIS" with "his proposal to ban 1.5 billion Muslims from even coming to our country [the United States]".[220] It is true that American leaders and elite have a superlative conception of their country. It was in this superlative mode that the Democratic Party's presidential candidate nominee, Hillary Clinton, declared as follows: "I believe with all my heart that America is an exceptional country—that we're still, in Lincoln's words, the last, best hope of earth. We are not a country that cowers behind walls. We lead with purpose, and we prevail".[221]

But it is equally true that this manner of bragging does not seem to be sufficient or enough to attract to the United States, the degree of vicious and unprecedented terror that is witnessed today, and which was not in existence until recently. There is really something to the hostility and viciousness that the radical

219 See the "Full Transcript of President Obama's Speech on Counterterrorism Policy" . . ., op. cit.

220 This was part of the U.S. Democratic Party's presidential candidate nominee's (Hillary Clinton) campaign speech in San Diego on Thursday, June 2, 2016; see "Hillary Clinton Speaks about National Security on Thursday in San Diego", available at www.marketwatch.com/story/text-of-hillary-clintons-speech-on-national-security-2016-06-02?siteid=rss&rss=1 (last visited on Friday, June 3, 2016).

221 Loc. Cit; see also Fred Aja Agwu (2016), *Nations among Nations* . . ., pp. 30–33, op. cit.

Islamists of the Middle East in particular extend to the United States. So, because the evidence abounds, as will be seen in due course, it is beyond the hypothetical to impute a combination of cultural differences, the United States foreign policy (and, indeed, the foreign policy of many Western nations), and historical circumstances to the problem.

3 The War on Terror (WoT)

The 9/11 Antecedents in the WoT

When terrorism was strictly a phenomenon that was basically engaged in by disgruntled individuals or groups against soft targets (comprising the civilian population and public infrastructures) with casualties and sundry damage not usually enormous, and with the sole intention being to instill fear and force state authorities to the negotiation table with the ultimate aim of offering concessions, it was basically treated as a law enforcement issue that did not necessitate the declaration of war and the application of the armed forces. But ever since terrorism transcended, seeking maximum impact and grabbing global attention and at times utilizing the enlistment of pure military strategies to seek to kill and destroy in vast scales without seeking negotiations, and even taking territories to boot, the attitude to the phenomenon changed. And although September 11 (9/11), 2001 was practically the watershed, terror attacks against the United States did not start with 9/11; neither did heavy-handed reactions by Washington against terrorists start with 9/11.

The only difference that 9/11 made was to usher in Washington's "formal" declaration of the war on terror, now combining law enforcement strategy with a heightened enlistment of the armed forces. Before 9/11, Washington had used its armed forces in prosecuting the war on terror without a formal declaration as happened during the George W. Bush presidency. This pre-9/11 war-like response had cut across U.S. Republican and Democratic governments. When on October 8, 1985, under the Republican President Ronald Reagan, "a group of Palestinian terrorists seized the Italian luxury liner *Achille Lauro* off the coast of Alexandria, Egypt, . . . seeking the release of Palestinian prisoners held by Israel", and in the course of which they killed an American, "sixty-nine-year-old Leon Klinghoffer", members of the U.S. First Special Forces Operational Detachment-Delta (Delta Force) quickly set up operations at Sigonella Naval Air Station in Sicily for the potential interdiction and seizure of the ship.[1]

Although the terrorists left the ship under a safe haven provided by Egypt two days later and boarded an Egyptian airliner, bound for the sanctity of Tunisia

1 See Robert "Buzz" Patterson (2003), *Dereliction of Duty . . .*, p. 132, op. cit.

on October 11, the U.S. Navy F-14 jets intercepted the airliner and forced it to land at Sigonella where members of the Delta Force surrounded the jet and took the terrorists into captivity.[2] There was also the instance of the La Belle Discotheque bombing in West Berlin the next year on April 5, 1986, which killed one American soldier and wounded more than 200, of which at least 60 were U.S. servicemen.[3] In response after pinpointing "Libya as the perpetrator", the United States on April 15 launched "airstrikes at the heart of Libya", using "fifteen U.S. Navy A-6 and A-7 attack jets" to hit military targets in Benghazi;[4] but notwithstanding the effort to restrict the attack to military targets, President Gaddafi's compound was also reportedly hit.

Under the Democratic regime of President Bill Clinton, and in response to the al-Qaeda's bombings of the United States embassies in Kenya and Tanzania on August 1, 1998, Washington also ordered "synchronized airstrikes in Afghanistan and Sudan" against camps suspected to be hosting Osama bin Laden's terrorist organization;[5] including, perhaps inadvertently, the Sheifa chemical plant on the outskirt of Khartoum. These, amongst other instances, were emblematic of the fact that the United States had actually been conducting the war on terror long before 9/11: 9/11 was just the most significant moment in the war because the enormity of the al-Qaeda's strikes in New York and Washington D.C. spurred Washington to formally take on the group and, later, all identified terrorist organizations with a global reach, especially those posing a threat to the United States and its allies.

The 9/11 Attacks

The September 11, 2001 (9/11) terrorist attacks on the United States happened at a time when, with the end of the Cold War, America was gloating over having "weathered every war [as] every war has come to an end"; particularly with the collapse of the Berlin Wall, when the successive American governments and the citizenry thought that a new dawn of democracy had taken hold abroad, and a decade of peace and prosperity roaring at home in their country.[6] As President Barack Obama put it:

> For a moment, it seemed the 21st century would be a tranquil time. Then, on September 11th 2001, we were shaken out of complacency. Thousands were taken from us . . . This was a different kind of war. No armies came to our shores, and our military was not the principal target. Instead, a group of terrorists came to kill as many civilians as they could.[7]

2 Ibid., pp. 132–133.
3 Ibid., p. 133.
4 Loc. Cit.
5 Ibid., pp. 180–181.
6 See the "Full Transcript of President Obama's Speech on Counterterrorism Policy" . . ., op. cit.
7 Loc. Cit.

Another perspective by William Banks is that, on 9/11, a band of al-Qaeda-linked terrorist operatives "commandeered four separate but coordinated aircraft in pursuit of preselected targets" in the United States:

> Two of the planes struck in New York City at the World Trade Center, causing both towers to collapse, killing approximately 3,000 persons . . . A third plane was flown directly into the Pentagon in Arlington, Virginia, where 189 persons died, including all who were on board the plane. The fourth plane crashed in Stony Creek Township, Pennsylvania, apparently after passengers overpowered the terrorists, preventing the aircraft from being used as a missile towards its unknown target. All forty-five persons aboard were killed in the crash.[8]

But "within hours . . . the hijackers had been linked to Al Qaeda and Usama bin Laden",[9] a terrorist organization that was sheltered in Afghanistan by the Taliban regime locked in a vicious insurgency with the Northern Alliance. The 9/11 attacks triggered a host of dramatic security impulses in the United States that changed, not just the country's relations with the rest of the world, but also the configuration of international security consciousness as a whole—the declaration of the war on terror; military intervention in Afghanistan to defeat the Taliban regime and destroy the al-Qaeda at its base; the 2003 preemptive war in Iraq; fundamental organizational reforms of security at home, including the establishment of the Department of Homeland Security; and, internationally, the conferment of a top priority on anti-terrorism, with the United Nations, NATO, and the European Union following suit to immediately "develop counterterrorism policies based on international cooperation", and with NATO invoking "its collective defense provision for the first time".[10]

Ostensibly, the terrorists (hijackers) were goaded by Osama bin Laden and his henchmen in the al-Qaeda movement's declaration of jihad and fatwa on the United States and its allies.[11] In that call for jihad because of the grievances that bin Laden essayed out in his videotape of October 7, 2001, he, along with other al-Qaeda henchmen, invoked what was termed "the unanimous opinion of the ulema throughout centuries that when enemies attack the Muslim lands, Jihad becomes a personal duty of every Muslim"; adding this call for jihad to a fatwa that declared that

> to kill Americans and their allies, both civil and military, is an individual duty of every Muslim who is able, in any country where this is possible, until the Aqsa mosque [in Jerusalem] and the Haram mosque [in Mecca] are freed

8 See William C. Banks (2005), "The Predator", in Volker C. Franke (2005, ed.); *Terrorism and Peacekeeping: New Security Challenges*, Westport, CT, London, Praeger, pp. 143–144.

9 Ibid., p. 144.

10 See Martha Crenshaw (2009), "Terrorism as an International Security Problem", in Jeffrey H. Norwitz (2009, ed.); *Pirates, Terrorists, and Warlords* . . ., p. 401, op. cit.

11 See Bernard Lewis (2003), *The Crisis of Islam* . . ., p. xxvi, op. cit.

from their grip, and until their armies, shattered and broken-winged, depart from all lands of Islam, incapable of threatening any Muslim.[12]

The document on this declaration of jihad and pronouncement of fatwa on the United States and its allies further showed that the al-Qaeda henchmen, after citing some Qur'an verses, said:

> By God's leave, we call on every Muslim who believes in God and hopes for reward to obey God's command to kill the Americans and plunder their possessions wherever he finds them and whenever he can. Likewise we call on all Muslim ulema and leaders and youth and soldiers to launch attacks against the armies of the American devils and against those who are allied with them from among the helpers of Satan.[13]

Although religiously motivated terrorism had long existed, this declaration of jihad and pronouncement of fatwa was clearly the first time a terrorist organization (the al-Qaeda) would come clean and unambiguously reinvent itself, showing, indeed, that "sacred terror" was a real let-motif in terrorist campaigns—for all the while, many terrorist movements had been posturing as secular, political, and ideological movements, sublimating that religious motivation in order to accommodate their sponsors.[14] It was probably because of the al-Qaeda's declaration of jihad and the pronouncement of fatwa against the United States and its allies that, both before and after 9/11, Washington has been repeatedly dealing with a complex terrorist threat. As Carafano and Rosenzweig observed:

> The full extent of the terrorist threat to America is not fully known. We do not even know how many terrorist operatives are in the United States. . . The U.S. State Department has a list of over 100,000 names world-wide of suspected terrorists or people with contact to terrorists. Before its camps in Afghanistan were shut down, al-Qaeda trained at least 70,000 people—and possibly tens of thousands more. Al-Qaeda-linked Jemaah Islamiyah in Indonesia is estimated to have 3,000 members across Southeast Asia and is still growing. Although the estimates of the number of al-Qaeda members, al-Qaeda wannabes, al-Qaeda look-alikes, and sons and daughters of al-Qaeda in the United States have varied since 9/11, the figure provided by the government in recent, supposedly confidential, briefings to policy-makers is about 5,000. This estimate may include those who are engaged in fundraising for terrorist organizations and others who were trained in some fashion to engage in a future attack, whether or not they are actively engaged in a terrorist cell.[15]

12 Ibid., pp. xxvi–xxvii.
13 Ibid., p. xxvii.
14 See Thomas P. M. Barnett (2004), *The Pentagon's New Map* . . ., pp. 43–44, op. cit.
15 See James Jay Carafano and Paul Rosenzweig (2005), *Winning the Long War: Lessons from the Cold War for Defeating Terrorism and Preserving Freedom*, Washington, D.C., Heritage Books, pp. 91–92.

The implication of this horrifying picture is that "no one can say with certainty how many terrorists are in the United States", even when more beyond the estimation of Washington may be coming, for "[m]ore than 500 million people [are] admitted into the United States [annually], of which 330 million are non-citizens".[16] And Carafano and Rosenzweig explained further, although many of these people pose no risk to the United States, "but hidden in their vast numbers are people we do have to worry about".[17] It was this scary scenario that prompted Thomas Barnett to express the view that America has the responsibility to step "up to the challenge of defining this new global security rule set, or we will see those rules established by people who dream of a very different tomorrow".[18] But despite America's frontline position in the war on terror, it remains at risk of sustained attacks.

This situation is pathetic because the successive American administrations (including American allies) have always made the comprehensive strategic decision of being in the vanguard of the movement for an enduring peace in the Middle East, the type of peace that will accommodate the interest of all the parties, both the Israelis and the Palestinians. It was for the need to ensure this comprehensive strategy that, according to the John Chilcot Report, Sir Christopher Meyer, the British Ambassador to the United States, wrote to Tony Blair (then British Prime Minister) that U.S. President George W. Bush was committing a strategic blunder in the Middle East by exclusively focusing on the invasion of Iraq and the overthrow of Saddam Hussein without factoring in the tackling of the Arab-Israeli conflict.[19]

The Caliphate: Why Terror Is After America and Its Allies

The United States' relations with the Middle East and the Muslim world in general is a controversial subject at all times; in which a division exists between those that peddle the notion that the United States is impartially in favour of, especially, the state of Israel, and those that think that Washington has always pursued peace in the region and had never been patently or inordinately pro-Israel. To the latter, that is, those that believe that America is not against the Arab world or Islam, belong Daniel Benjamin and Steven Simon, who argued that granted the fact that the United States' support for Israel has frequently put it at odds with the Muslim world over the years; but this notwithstanding:

> . . . the U.S. has sent its military into action three times in the last decade in part, at least, to protect Muslims. In the Gulf War, the U.S. and its allies

16 Ibid., p. 92.
17 Loc. Cit.
18 See Thomas P. M. Barnett (2004), *The Pentagon's New Map* . . ., p. 46, op. cit.
19 See Kurt Eichenwald in "The War on Error: A Damning Report from Britain Details Everything Bush Didn't Know before He Invaded Iraq, and When He Didn't Know It", *Newsweek*, August 5, 2016, p. 19.

> liberated Kuwait from Iraqi occupation and safeguarded Saudi Arabia from invasion. In the Balkans, America led NATO to stop Serb aggression and ended genocidal killing of Muslims in Bosnia and Kosovo.[20]

Unfortunately, as will be seen soon, part of the grouse of the al-Qaeda (and later the ISIS) in targeting the United States and its allies, is the U.S. presence in the Middle East region, particularly Washington's continued blocking of their dream of a Caliphate equivalent to the Ottoman Empire; even though it can also be essentially argued, as American apologists like Benjamin and Simon aforementioned would argue, that U.S. presence is to safeguard the region from itself, from its bellicose leaders like Saddam Hussein. Admittedly, the United States has a serious "strategic cooperation" with Israel; yet, it was not all of Israel's military actions in the region that have been supported by the United States, like the Israeli's 1981 preemptive bombing of Saddam Hussein's Osiraq nuclear reactor.[21]

In any case, this "strategic cooperation had a slow start", as the United States and Israel were not always on the same page in many defence matters, like the exchange or trade in advanced weapons technologies (the Israelis were ahead in unmanned aerial vehicles, and air-to-ground guided smart bombs, amongst others[22]), and even military exercises, amongst others.[23] Thus, it is not absolutely true that the United States obliges Israel unconditionally at all times, especially in also implicitly including Israel in the implementation of the U.S. Congress' "Comprehensive Anti-Apartheid Act of 1987" that prohibited military cooperation with South Africa, since there was a dark hint Israel could be sending arms to South Africa in violation of a United Nations' embargo.[24]

But why is terror particularly against the United States, especially the terrorists of Middle East origin, from the Taliban-hosted al-Qaeda to the ISIS; and now, their franchises around the world, including the homegrown ones, the lone wolves that these terrorist organizations inspired to strike within the borders of the United States. The West, particularly America, is not the only sufferers of terror attacks because terrorism has grown to be a global affliction, with even Africa developing homegrown ones; but the Western world, especially the United States, is terror's prime target. The question posed in the sub-heading is real and not rhetorical, for it is one question that is not only asked by Western politicians, but also the ordinary folk in that society. Although the entire Western nations are in the crosshairs of Islamic extremists from the Middle East and elsewhere around

20 See Daniel Benjamin and Steven Simon in "Islam's War of Words", *Time* (New York), November 12, 2001, p. 35.

21 See Richard A. Clarke (2004), *Against All Enemies: Inside America's War on Terror*, New York, Free Press, pp. 43–44.

22 Ibid., pp. 44–45.

23 Ibid., pp. 45–46.

24 Ibid., p. 44.

the world, the United States leads the pack in this unenviable position of being heaped with opprobrium and targeted by the fundamentalists.

If the sub-heading question must be pointedly answered, it can be said that the West and, especially America, face the terrorist threats from the Middle East radicals because of reasons that range from the economic, the political, to the religious—the latter of which involves the fact that these Middle East extremists and militants have fundamentally perverted the teaching of Islam and inflamed passions against those they call unbelievers, thus framing societal values and religious differences in terms of the clash of civilization.[25] Meanwhile, these are differences, the divergences in religion and societal values that should otherwise be a source of humanity's strength in its immense or far-flung diversity. Today, part of the war on terror is the reversal of this toxic narrative of the extremists and militants that there is a clash of civilization.

This clash of civilization narrative is not helped by the wide perception that the West slights the Arab World, especially with the alleged United States' support of Israel, one time support of the Shah of Iran, and the Operation Desert Storm of 1991 that evicted Iraq from Kuwait, all of which "reinforced the belief of the Middle East radical elements that the United States is anti-Arab and anti-Muslim".[26] Osama bin Laden, in his videotape of October 7, 2001 (shortly after 9/11), spoke about the "humiliation and disgrace" that Islam had suffered for "more than eighty years";[27] apparently alluding to the 1918 defeat of the last of the great Muslim empires—the Ottoman sultanate—by Anglo-French imperialism, a defeat in which its capital, Constantinople, was occupied and its sovereign held captive and "partitioned between the victorious British and French Empires".[28] The defeat and partition of the Ottoman Empire dealt a big blow to the ascendancy of the Sunni Islamic group, its control and subjugation of other religious group in the region.

Historically, "the whole Levant is a multi-ethnic, multi-religious area that can't easily be separated into ethnic-based nation states".[29] It has been inhabited by "groups possessing in some cases, bitterly opposed beliefs living cheek by jowl"; and which created "a tumultuous region all-too-often characterized by violence and oppression". The importance of the defunct Ottoman Empire was that, "for centuries, the tension between these various ethnicities and religious groups—Arabs and Kurds, Shiite and Sunni, to name a few—were kept to a manageable simmer by the Levant's preeminent power"—the Ottoman

25 See David L. Bongard and William R. Schilling (2002), "Terrorist Operations in Nontraditional Warfare", in William R. Schilling (2002, ed.); *Nontraditional Warfare* . . ., p. 58, op. cit.

26 Loc. Cit.

27 See Bernard Lewis (2003), *The Crisis of Islam* . . ., p. xv, op. cit.

28 Ibid., pp. xvi.

29 See "Lines in the Sand: Who's Responsible for the Current Conflict in Syria? Some Say It's Mapmakers", published in a special *Newsweek* edition, "Killing ISIS: America's All-Out Assault on a Global Threat", 2016 (undated), p. 17.

Empire.[30] But the ascendancy of the Ottoman Empire, and the early calm associated with it, came with a cost that was only favourable to the Sunni and disadvantageous "to those in the empire who didn't share the ruling dynasty's Sunni Muslim faith".[31] Hence, these non-Sunni faiths paid for their freedom and rights—"the groups of Christians, Jews and non-Sunni Muslims found themselves organized in groups called millets, which had to pay special taxes to continue practicing their faith".[32]

One of the most severe disadvantages was that the Ottoman Empire "barred non-Muslims from testifying against Muslims in court"; but despite the flaws of the Ottoman Empire, "the millet system granted [the] various religious communities a large degree of autonomy, allowing them to elect their own leaders and administer their own justice regarding religious matters".[33] Thus, although the Ottoman Empire kept the peace, it remained "imperfect and, by the standards of modern liberal democracies, [a] grossly unfair system [that was] marred by the occasional outburst of violence between various religious communities (particularly Christians and Jews)" until "the victorious powers of World War I shattered" the Empire "and established between them, a new order for the Middle East" by partitioning it amongst themselves.[34]

The partition was in the controversial Sir Mark Sykes (for the British) and Francois Georges-Picot (for the French) line on the map of the Levant (also called the Sykes and Picot line in the sand), which had in May 1916 (at the height of the First World War), carved up the Ottoman Empire.[35] With the Sykes-Picot lines in the sand, "much of what is now modern-day Syria fell under French domination, including all of Lebanon; while Britain assumed either direct or indirect control of vast swaths of Mesopotamia (including Iraq) and the rest of Syria".[36] Whereas "the French gave political preference to Christians [who under the Ottoman had to pay their way to the right or freedom to worship and organize their leadership] in Lebanon"; "in Baghdad, the British empowered a Sunni minority to rule over a majority Shiite populace".[37] It was evidently the arbitrary nature of the Sykes and Picot line that has caused so much chaos and confusion in the Middle East, "stranding" the Kurds in Iraq, Syria, and Turkey by denying them an independent nation of their own.[38]

It was as a result of the Sykes-Picot lines that "religious and ethnic groups imbued with a strong sense of nationalism found themselves bound together in states where privilege and rights were doled out by a handful of elites".[39] As it

30 Loc. Cit.
31 Loc. Cit.
32 Loc. Cit.
33 Loc. Cit. Brackets mine.
34 Ibid., pp. 17–18.
35 See "The War within . . .", p. 7, op. cit.
36 See "Lines in the Sand . . .", p. 19, op. cit.
37 Loc. Cit. Brackets mine.
38 See "The War within . . .", p. 7, op. cit.
39 See "Lines in the Sand . . .", p. 19, op. cit.

were, "intermittent armed conflict became a way of life as different groups jockeyed for power, with peace usually coming with the price of brutal, repressive dictatorship such as Saddam Hussein's Iraq or Bashar al-Assad's Syria"—dictators that acted "like little Ottoman sultans" because "they held together this mosaic [of religious and ethnic communities] through authoritarianism and fear".[40] Thus, the Sykes and Picot line entrained so much mess in the region—"a century of imperial betrayal and Arab resentment; instability and coups; wars; displacement, occupation and failed peacemaking in Palestine; and almost everywhere, oppression, radicalism and terrorism".[41]

So, one of the consequences of the Sykes and Picot line is that the "Arab states are suffering a legitimacy crisis".[42] The United States–led invasion of Iraq did not help matters because as soon as authoritarian leaders like Saddam Hussein were removed, "the nationalist passions among the various communities" exploded.[43] For instance, "Saddam Hussein had basically consolidated Sunni power [in Iraq] through the military and the Ba'ath Party", but that invasion "eliminated both those institutions of Sunni domination and thrust a civil war" on American hands.[44] Instead of the invasion ushering in a new age of freedom and equality for the Middle East, Washington "unleashed a sectarian violence between the Sunni and the Shiites",[45] creating the aperture for the emergence of ISIS. Under the Ottoman Empire, the Sunni with their kinship with Wahhabism called the shot in the Levant, even up to the post-Ottoman Arab states like Iraq. The American invasion and disempowerment of the Sunni and the restoration of the Shiites accounted for why the ISIS is basically a Sunni partisan organization. And although the Sunnis are in the minority in Iraq, the effectiveness of their ability to fight back under the ISIS platform was only made possible by the support they got from their fellow Sunnis, who are in the majority or mainstream Islam.

But unlike the Hamas and the Muslim Brotherhood, the ISIS (like the al-Qaeda) is an anti-nationalist group[46] that is averse to the existence of those nation-states (like Iraq and Syria) that resulted from the Sykes-Picot lines. So, "despite declaring themselves the Islamic State, actual statecraft is considered anathema to their existence" because ISIS considers "divisions such as nationality, ethnicity or race [as] man-made and sinful".[47] The ISIS dreams of the return or reinvention of the Ottoman Empire, a "dream of a utopia where nothing separates individuals [particularly Muslims] except for belief and non-belief"; a goal in which it does not just want to take over Iraq and Syria but also "to wipe them off the map as an important step toward creating their united paradise"—the

40 Loc. Cit.
41 See "The War within . . .", p. 7, op. cit.
42 Loc. Cit.
43 See "Lines in the Sand . . .", , p. 19, op. cit.
44 Loc. Cit.
45 Loc. Cit.
46 See "Apocalypse Now . . .", p. 13, op. cit.
47 Loc. Cit.

Caliphate.[48] The ISIS's dream of the Caliphate (which it shares with the al-Qaeda) also extends to uniting the whole of "humanity under its banner of belief".[49]

And having not "got over the fall of the Ottoman Empire", the terrorists are trapped in the spasm of all kinds of "ideologies—Arabism, Islamism and now jihad"; all these exist in the throes of the collapsing Arab states and the reversion to ethnic and religious identities in the wake of the Arab Spring, seeking "some greater statehood beyond the frontiers left by the colonizers" (the British and the French in the Sykes and Picot lines).[50] It is in this context of seeking to avenge the loss of the Ottoman Empire (the Caliphate) that the name al-Qaeda was derived from the Arabic word, "the foundation or base, as in the foundation of a building".[51] In other words, the al-Qaeda movement was the foundation, "the first piece, the necessary base for the edifice that would be a global theocracy, the great Caliphate";[52] the new Caliphate that Osama bin Laden wanted to establish in vengeance against the loss of the Ottoman Empire—that old or last Muslim Caliphate.

But instead of making it a futuristic venture the way that the al-Qaeda did, the ISIS emerged on the horizon and realized the Caliphate by dramatically declaring it on June 29, 2014. Unfortunately, the ISIS's Caliphate was not as permissive and protective of minority rights in the Levant as was the Ottoman Empire. While the Ottoman Empire was permissive of minority rights through the millet system, the Caliphate that the ISIS proclaimed in the Levant brutalized the minorities, inflicting genocide on the Yazidis[53] and expelling Christians from its areas of control.[54] Like its predecessor—the al-Qaeda—the ISIS exclusively appropriated the Levant with a sense of entitlement, escalating the exodus of Christians from that region, an exodus that dates back in time to decades as a result of violence, persecution, and a lack of economic opportunities.[55] In fact, in northern Iraq in particular, ISIS's militants forced the exodus of Christians by destroying churches, libraries and monuments, all in the bid to wipe out any trace of some of the places considered Christian areas.[56]

Before the advent of the ISIS, and apparently referring to when the United Nations' coalition evicted Saddam Hussein from Kuwait, Osama bin Laden and his extremist group had nursed grouses over the coalition of the Western world's

48 Loc. Cit.

49 Ibid., p. 11.

50 See "The War within . . .", p. 7, op. cit. Brackets mine.

51 See Richard A. Clarke (2004), *Against All Enemies* . . ., p. 148, op. cit.

52 Loc. Cit.

53 See "Looking for Justice: Once Helpless Women Captives of ISIS Seek Revenge on the Islamic State from the Frontlines", in a special *Newsweek* edition, "Killing ISIS: America's All-Out Assault on a Global Threat", 2016 (undated), pp. 88–89.

54 See "Paradise Lost: ISIS's Campaign of Violence Is Driving the Last Christians from the Holy Land", in a special *Newsweek* edition, "Killing ISIS: America's All-Out Assault on a Global Threat", 2016 (undated), pp. 52–57.

55 Ibid., p. 52.

56 Ibid., p. 54.

(led by the United States) occupation of "the lands of Islam, from where they threatened Muslims";[57] they were equally grieved about that occupation advancing "the perceived American bias in favor of Israel",[58] and offending the fact that "Caliph Umar decreed that Jews and Christians should be removed from all but the southern and eastern fringes of Arabia, in fulfillment of an injunction of the Prophet uttered on his deathbed: Let there not be two religions in Arabia".[59] With the killing of Osama bin Laden by the United States in 2011, his son, Hamza bin Laden, has since vowed revenge, not just for his father's death, but also "for those who defended Islam".[60]

In the terrorists' characteristic way of making the most of cyberspace, an audio message that was posted online (as reported by the *Times of India*) had Hamza threatening the United States thus: "We will continue striking you and targeting you in your country and abroad in response to your oppression of the people of Palestine, Afghanistan, Syria, Iraq, Yemen, Somalia and the rest of the Muslim lands that did not survive your oppression".[61] This is the kind of propaganda that Sadiq Khan, the first Muslim Mayor of London, had in mind when he said that all that radical Islam and its avant-garde hate preachers do is to say the untruth that the West hate Islam, thus, inspiring attacks also on those Muslims they perceive to be Western, even though it is absolutely possible to be liberal and Western as well as be mainstream Muslim.[62] But the fact that the extremists also attack fellow Muslims in itself tasks the theory of the clash of civilization when explaining the rise and continued surge of Islamic terrorism.

To underline the "sacred" (religious) motive in the mission of this new face of the resurgent al-Qaeda, Hamza—reportedly in his mid-20s and who was also reportedly "at his father's side in Afghanistan before the 9/11 attacks and [had] spent time with him in Pakistan after the U.S.-led invasion pushed much of al-Qaeda's senior leadership there"—further stated in his threat that "as for the revenge of the Islamic nation for Sheikh Osama . . ., it is not revenge for Osama the person but it is revenge for those who defended Islam".[63] The long and short of this prejudicial disposition of the Middle East radical elements against not just the United States but also the entire Western world is the strengthening of the so-called notion of the clash of civilization, in which the West has become literally besieged by the radicals, extremists, and militants who inspire

57 See Bernard Lewis (2003), *The Crisis of Islam* . . ., p. xxvii, op. cit.

58 Ibid., p. xxviii.

59 Ibid., p. xxix.

60 See "Bin Laden's Son Threatens to Avenge Father's Assassination", *The Punch* (Lagos), Monday, July 11, 2016, p. 10; see also "Bin Laden's Son Threatens to Avenge for Father's Assassination", *Vanguard* (Lagos), Monday, July 11, 2016, p. 37.

61 See "Bin Laden's Son Threatens to Avenge Father's Assassination" . . ., p. 10, op. cit.

62 Sadiq Khan on Fareed Zakaria's Global Public Square (GPS) programme to mark the 9/11 15th anniversary, Cable News Network (CNN), monitored in Lagos (Nigeria) on Sunday, September 11, 2016, 3pm–4pm, local time, op. cit.

63 See "Bin Laden's Son Threatens to Avenge Father's Assassination" . . ., p. 10, op. cit.

terrorist campaigns almost everywhere in the world, especially in those nations and regions where the Islamic and non-Islamic world meet or interface—places like "Nigeria, Sudan, Bosnia, Macedonia, Chechnya, Sinkiang, Kashmir, Timor, Mindanao, et cetera".[64]

The Middle East terror groups are not only against the United States and the West as a whole for what they consider the latter's prejudicial policies against the Muslim world, they are also against individuals they perceive as such. For instance, Kofi Annan, while the Secretary-General of the United Nations, confirmed that the "al-Qaeda had long before named me [Kofi Annan] as one of their targets for my role in what it saw as the dismemberment of Indonesia, Asia's largest Muslim nation, following the independence of East Timor".[65] It was for the same reason that Sergio Vieira de Mello, the United Nations Special Representative in Iraq, was also targeted, leading to his death on August 19, 2003, when "a massive [al-Qaeda] bomb . . . struck the UN headquarters in Baghdad, resulting in many casualties", including Sergio and 22 UN officers.[66]

So, the foregoing attempts to answer the question of why the al-Qaeda and the other Middle East militants are after the United States and its allies—what they seem to have done wrong to deserve this level of hostility from these Islamic extremists and militants; that is, what the crime of the United States is in order to warrant the anti-Americanism that is so rife in the Middle East. As now evident, the answer to this question has some roots in history. It is history that assists in unraveling this "mystery". But although this is an objective attempt at finding an answer to the question of why terror is after the United States and the West in general, it is important to equally emphasize that the grouse of these extremists and militants is actually beyond the al-Qaeda's perception of the humiliation of Muslims in the destruction of the Ottoman Empire. The anger against the United States is equally rooted in recent historical developments—the dynamics of the "defunct" Cold War.

The U.S. President Obama may have crooned earlier about the end of the Cold War and how America had weathered all wars, but the fact remains that the Cold War still resonated in the present war on terror. As Stephen Small and Thomas Barnett variously put it, "although the specter of the big one [nuclear war] has faded in the post-Cold War world, the reality of smaller-scale contingencies [in terrorist attacks] has exploded";[67] even though "the Pentagon is showing all the right signs of taking this grand challenge as seriously as they took the nuclear age that preceded it".[68] The September 11 attacks and the consequent

64 See Bernard Lewis (2003), *The Crisis of Islam* . . ., p. 92, op. cit.

65 See Kofi Annan (2012), *Interventions: A Life in War and Peace*, New York, The Penguin Press, pp. 315–316. Brackets mine.

66 Ibid., p. 318. Brackets mine.

67 See Stephen C. Small (2000), "Small Arms and Asymmetric Threats" . . ., p. 32, op. cit. Parentheses mine.

68 See Thomas P. M. Barnett (2004), *The Pentagon's New Map* . . ., pp. 44–45, op. cit.

war on terror are actually the result of how the United States prosecuted the Cold War, the decision to extend its obsessive confrontation with the Soviet Union to the insertion of its military influence in the Persian Gulf.[69]

America's extension of its military to the Persian Gulf region happened under the Presidencies of Ronald Reagan and George H.W. Bush.[70] Apparently, Washington does not have any blame for this policy because it was ostensibly acting true to real-politic, both in terms of its economic interest and the need to balance the geopolitical equation with the Soviet Union. The 1974 Arab oil boycott of the United States had pressed home the importance of the Persian Gulf resources.[71] What the Arab oil embargo did was to heighten and make the United States develop a skin-deep sensitivity to its interests and events generally in the Middle East region. It was, therefore, with shock that Washington apprehended the 1979 Iranian revolution in which the Shah of Iran (a friend and ally of Washington) was dethroned by Islamic radicals.[72]

Matters were not helped by the coincidental invasion of the region (Afghanistan) by the Soviet Union in December (Christmas Day) of that year, 1979; thus forcing the United States to weigh in as a counterpoise, a decision that saw it fighting multiple wars in the region while confronting the fall-out of those wars (Middle East terrorism) at home.[73] When talking about the Cold War provenance of the ongoing war on terror, Richard Clarke draws some parallels between the two phenomena as follows:

> Both conflicts raged globally, with regional wars, secret sleeper cells, and competing ideologies. The two struggles also threatened the horrific destruction of our cities by weapons of mass destruction [although in the Cold War we knew the enemy actually had thousands of nuclear weapons]. Our opponents in both vowed to seek the imposition of their form of government and way of life on all nations.[74]

It is certainly in this light that the U.S. Cold War policy doubtlessly contributed tremendously to international terrorism, especially the Middle East–oriented terrorists. But then, why does this terror also seek to destroy American allies? The reason is obvious. International alliances are a critical component of American power; and Secretary Hillary Clinton affirmed this much during one of her presidential campaign outings in the declaration that:

> America's network of allies is part of what makes us exceptional. And our allies deliver for us every day. Our armed forces fight terrorists together; our

69 See Richard A. Clarke (2004), *Against All Enemies*. . ., p. 35, op. cit.
70 Loc. Cit.
71 Ibid., p. 36.
72 Loc. Cit.
73 Loc. Cit.
74 Ibid., p. 37.

> diplomats work side by side. Allies provide staging areas for our military, so we can respond quickly to events on the other side of the world. And they share intelligence that helps us identify and defuse potential threats . . . When I was Secretary of State, we worked closely with our allies Japan and South Korea to respond to this threat, including by creating a missile defense system that stands ready to shoot down a North Korean warhead, should its leaders ever be reckless enough to launch one at us. . . . That's the power of allies. And it's the legacy of American troops who fought and died to secure those bonds, because they knew we were safer with friends and partners.[75]

American allies are Washington's systemic foreign policy structures; hence, terrorists also focus on the destruction of the alliance in order to deter it from lending itself as an instrument of American power. As the Chilcot report later revealed, it was for the sake of the transatlantic alliance, especially in NATO, that the British, despite their misgivings about America's "harebrained scheme" for the 2003 invasion of Iraq, lent themselves to that controversial intervention.[76] When the British government began building a new nuclear reactor at Hinkley Point, it could tolerate the French company, EDF, financing most of the project apparently because of the bond of the NATO alliance; but as soon as Theresa May became the British Prime Minister in 2016, she put the project on hold because of security concerns over China's role; China, being not in any alliance (especially military alliance) with the British, was also reportedly providing some of the funding.[77]

Thus, alliances are significant factors in the behaviour of nations and determine how non-members, including non-state actors/entities like terrorist organizations, react to members. This is the reason it cannot be doubted that the terrorist attack of June 28, 2016 on Turkey, Istanbul's international airport was on account of Turkey being not just an American ally (even though geographically proximate to the Middle East) but was also offering Washington an airbase for the conduct of military airstrikes against Daesh, as the ISIS terror group is pejoratively called.[78] And it is not only terrorists that are deeply envious and desirous of destroying American allies; as Secretary Clinton also said, "now Moscow and Beijing are deeply envious of our alliances around the world, because they have nothing to match them".[79]

It is, therefore, significative of the value of the NATO alliance to American power that when a snafu ensued between the United States and Turkey in the

75 See "Hillary Clinton Speaks about National Security on Thursday in San Diego" . . ., op. cit.

76 See Kurt Eichenwald in "The War on Error . . .", pp. 16–20, op. cit.

77 See "The World This Week", *The Economist*, August 6, 2016, p. 5.

78 See Jared Malsin in "With Another Civilian Attack, ISIS's War on Turkey Intensifies", *Time* (New York), July 11–18, 2016, pp. 16–17. In response, Turkey's President Recep Tayyip Erdogan urged global unity, reiterating that "there is no difference between Istanbul, Ankara and Berlin, Izmir and Chicago or Antalya and Rome", Ibid., p. 6.

79 See "Hillary Clinton Speaks about National Security on Thursday in San Diego" . . ., op. cit.

wake of a failed coup in the latter, the Turkish President, Recep Tayyip Erdogan, began "thumping his nose at the West";[80] the result of which was a sense of unease, not only in Washington but also in the entire community of the NATO alliance. The NATO matters in the war on terror because Turkey had been critically useful to the U.S. war on terror, especially in Washington's fight against the ISIS—if nothing else, Turkey could disrupt the ISIS using it as a conveyor belt for the fighters and "sleepers" (terrorist cells) it was sending from the Middle East region to different Western nations.[81] These ISIS fighters first went to Turkey, where they got fake passports—some do "plastic surgery in Turkey in order to be unrecognized"—and then they "slip out individually via varying routes to the West".[82]

When, in August 2016, Turkish forces entered Syria, that move was ignored by Washington even though the objective was not only to combat the ISIS, but also to enable Ankara to "prevent the Syrian Kurdish People's Protection Units (the militia known as YPG) from setting up an [independent] enclave on the Syrian border with Turkey".[83] Such an independent or sovereign entity for the Kurds in Syria is considered to be capable of further firing the zeal of the Kurdish separatist movement in Turkey. Just as Turkey seemed to be using the issues of immigration and refugees as aces against the EU; it was also (in addition to its anger with the United States for sheltering Gulen) using its role in reining in the ISIS as an ace too against Washington. This was also beside Ankara's concern (if not anger) that the United States was arming the PKK (known in Syria as the YPG and in Iraq as the Persmega) that it regards as terrorists and would not like to have an independent and sovereign state.

Turkey, Iran, Iraq, and even Syria do not want an independent homeland for the Kurds.[84] Turkey's arbitrary intervention in the civil war in Syria (just as it did in Iraq) was a complicated move because, being antagonistic to the Kurds, it put the United States in a diplomatic bind since both Turkey and the Kurds were supposed to be allies of Washington in the war on terror. And despite Iraq's protestations against Turkey's incursion, the United States clearly (albeit tacitly) acquiesced, and this acquiescence was expedient, if only "Turkey shuts down its border—as it appears to have done so far—and stops turning a blind eye to ISIS fighters and weaponry slipping in and out of Syria", an action that would constitute "a win for the anti-ISIS coalition".[85] Turkey's bulwark utility against the ISIS is part of its relevance in the NATO alliance, and in the U.S. war on terror.

80 See Ian Bremmer in "Turkey and Russia Get Closer—and Worry the West", *Time* (New York), August 22, 2016, p. 8.
81 See Bill Powell, Mahmoud Shikh Ibrahim, Jack Moore, and Mirren Gidda in "The New ISIS Crisis", *Newsweek*, October 21, 2016, p. 31.
82 Loc. Cit.
83 Ibid., pp. 31–32. Brackets mine.
84 See Janine di Gionanni and Sophia Slater in "Abandoned Issues: Will the Battle of Mosul Lead to an Independent Iraqi Kurdistan? Or Another American Betrayal?", *Newsweek*, November 4, 2016, p. 16.
85 See Bill Powell, Mahmoud Shikh Ibrahim, Jack Moore, and Mirren Gidda in "The New ISIS Crisis" . . ., p. 32, op. cit.

It is also why the ISIS would not spare Turkey, should the opportunity to strike Ankara present itself any time anywhere.

It is a testament to the importance of U.S. allies that it was no boon, as a presidential candidate, Donald Trump, consistently made threats "to renege on the U.S. commitment to protect allies under attack",[86] telling the *New York Times* on one occasion that the United States would only come to the aid of allies if they "fulfilled their obligations to us"—[87] allies he implicitly called a bunch of spongers or freeloaders. Domestically and internationally, therefore, the apologists of the U.S. tradition of building and depending on its alliances were truly apprehensive about Trump doing business and being soft with Putin in the name of friendship because it would give the unpredictable Putin more room to disrupt the cohesion of the NATO alliance, such as what he attempted with Turkey after the failed coup in that country; or as China did in bringing Turkey into the Shanghai Cooperation Council (SCC).[88]

As he departed the White House, President Obama implicitly said this much as he harped on the value of the United States' alliance in fighting the ISIS. He declared thus:

> So let's be vigilant, but not afraid. ISIL will try to kill innocent people. But they cannot defeat America unless we betray our Constitution and our principles in the fight. Rivals like Russia or China cannot match our influence around the world—unless we give up what we stand for, and turn ourselves into just another big country that bullies smaller neighbors.[89]

And as *The Economists* wrote, if President Trump walks away from American allies because he thinks that they are freeloaders who fail to pay for the security they receive, then regional and global problems will certainly become harder to solve.[90] Indeed, both regionally and globally, terrorism will severely fester and become harder to be unilaterally solved by any country. The al-Qaeda and ISIS terrorists, for instance, see the United States and its allies as obstructionists to their jihadist ambitions, especially their dreams of restoring the Caliphate. This is exactly why the terrorists are after the United States and its allies. But President Trump himself in his inauguration speech did not go back on his anti-American allies campaign gimmicks; neither did he disappoint those who feared that he was going to abandon American allies. In one instance, the newly sworn-in President

86 See "Europeans Cooling on NATO", *Time* (New York), September 5, 2016, p. 7.

87 See "United States May Abandon NATO Protection", *The Guardian* (Lagos), Friday, July 22, 2016, p. 53.

88 See Onyekachi Wambu in "The Old Silk Road and a New World Order", *New African*, August–September 2016, p. 98.

89 See "Full Text of President Obama's Farewell Speech" in Chicago on January 10, 2017, available at www.wsj.com/amp/articles/BL-WB-67205?responsive=y (last visited on January 11, 2017).

90 See "The New Nationalism: With His Call to Put 'America First', Donald Trump Is the Latest Recruit to a Dangerous Nationalism", *The Economist*, November 19–25, 2016, p. 9.

Trump was unequivocal about abandoning American allies. Listen to President Trump:

> For many decades, we've . . . subsidized the armies of other countries while allowing for the very sad depletion of our military. We've defended other nations' borders, while refusing to defend our own, and spent trillions and trillions of dollars overseas while America's infrastructure has fallen into disrepair and decay [and the] strength and confidence of our country has dissipated over the horizon. . . . From this day, a new vision will govern our land. From this day, it's going to be America first. . . . We will seek friendship and goodwill with the other nations of the world, but we do so with the understanding that it is the right of all nations to put their own interests first.[91]

But in another instance in the same inaugural speech, President Trump said that "we will reinforce old alliances and form new ones and unite the civilized world against radical Islamic terrorism, which we will eradicate completely from the face of the earth".[92] But although President Trump's inaugural speech was replete with cloven-hoof and self-contradictory statements, he has certainly not been true to his mantra of "from this day forward, it's going to be only America first". Not when, as will be seen later in this book, he had moved against Assad in Syria for his alleged use of chemical weapons against his own people, deployed a missile defence system to South Korea against the threat from North Korea, and contemplated about sending more troops into Afghanistan as well as increasing American military advisors in Somalia. With some of these policies, President Trump is being faithful to American allies and enhancing the prospect of continued coherence among them in the war on terror.

America's Declaration of WoT

> Freedom and democracy are under attack. . . . Our war on terror begins with Al-Qaeda, but it does not end there. It will not end until every terrorist group of global reach has been found, stopped and defeated; . . . we will make no distinction between terrorists who committed these acts and those who harbor them.
>
> (President George W. Bush)[93]

91 See "Full Text of President Donald Trump's Inauguration Speech", available at http://abcnews.go.com/Politics/full-text-president-donald-trumps-inauguration-speech/story?id=44915821 (last visited on Wednesday, January 25, 2017). Brackets mine.

92 Loc. Cit.

93 Quote reproduced in snippets by William C. Banks (2005), "The Predator", in Volker C. Franke (2005, ed.); *Terrorism and Peacekeeping* . . ., p. 144, op. cit.

The scourge of terrorism springs essentially from the scourge of insurgency. But if counter-insurgency can defeat insurgency, it is obvious that it cannot defeat terrorism; hence, the counter-terrorism onslaught by the United States in the "war on terror" (WoT) that Washington declared against the al-Qaeda in the wake of the September 11, 2001 (9/11) attacks. The above epigram embodies the statements made by President George W. Bush at two different occasions; one, during his visit to the destroyed World Trade Center site (New York), the day after September 11, 2001 that the terrorists struck; and the other on September 20, 2001 in his address to the joint session of Congress. These two separate statements practically represent the declaration of the war on terror (WoT) by the United States.

It is important to note that despite the determined bid to cast this "war" as a clash of civilization by Osama bin Laden, President W. Bush emphasized in the aftermath of this declaration that the United States was waging a war against terrorism, not against Islam.[94] This was to be later reiterated by President Obama when he declared that although the ideology of extremism is fueled by those who propagate the belief "that Islam is in conflict with the United States and the West . . . this ideology is based on a lie, for the United States is not at war with Islam".[95] Earlier on September 14, 2001, a joint Resolution by the U.S. Congress had authorized President Bush to use "all necessary and appropriate force" against "persons he determines planned, authorized, committed, or aided the terrorist attacks of September 11", a Resolution that William Banks described as possessing "sweeping authority" that "is not time-limited; nor does it have a geographic constraint"; a Resolution that did not also narrow the President in "his discretion on choice of target . . . in any way, so long as the target is connected to September 11".[96]

Hence, whereas the epigram in the exordium of this chapter (President Bush's statement during his visit to the ruins of the World Trade center and his address to the joint session of Congress) practically epitomizes President Bush's declaration of war (the "war on terror"), the September 14 Resolution was a war resolution that provided the President the ideological basis to characterize it as a global war (rightly so because the al-Qaeda had declared the war in a global proportion, having enjoined its members to kill Americans and their allies in any country and wherever possible[97]) that increasingly justified the application of the armed drones.

Thus, Washington's declaration of the WoT was primarily against the al-Qaeda; but, since then, terrorism has literally blossomed and fought back from different parts of the world with the emergence of more terrorist groups like the Al-Shabab

94 See John L. Esposito and Dalia Mogahed (2007), *Who Speaks for Islam?* . . ., p. ix, op. cit.
95 See the "Full Transcript of President Obama's Speech on Counterterrorism Policy" . . ., op. cit.
96 See William C. Banks (2005), "The Predator", in Volker C. Franke (2005, ed.); *Terrorism and Peacekeeping* . . ., p. 150, op. cit.
97 See Bernard Lewis (2003), *The Crisis of Islam* . . ., p. xxvii, op. cit.

from Somalia, the ISIS from Syria and Iraq, and the Boko Haram from Nigeria. The growth and increased capacity of terrorism to fight back was reinforced by the emergence of the ISIS, a transnational terrorist entity that had a knack for online radicalization and inspiration of lone-wolf attacks.[98] Even in Southeast Asia that was hitherto believed to have cultivated some bulwarks against militant Islamism through the peaceful and tolerant nature of its people's own Islamic faith as well as "the relative incompetence of local jihadists",[99] terrorism had also fought back, first, in the year immediately following 9/11, when the "members of Jemaah Islamiya (JI), dedicated to establishing a South-East Asian caliphate, were behind the bombing in 2002 of a Bali nightclub that killed more than 200" people.[100]

The emergence of the ISIS saw a wide spate of radicalization of Muslims in the Southeast Asian nations of Indonesia, Malaysia, Singapore, Philippine, and Thailand, many of which has witnessed terrorist attacks after many of their citizens (as many as 600, including women and children, by some estimates) that joined and fought for ISIS returned home.[101] In fact, in Indonesian, it was Bahrun Naim (head of a Southeast Asian unit fighting with the ISIS in Syria and Iraq) that planned the bombing of Starbucks (a Western target) and a traffic police post in central Jakarta from Syria.[102] Some sort of resurgence in attacks has also been experienced on the part of the Taliban. These are not only symptomatic of the dangers of radicalization, they are also indicative of the widespread nature of the phenomenon of terrorism, which makes it imperative that the United States approaches the war against terror as declared by it from a multilateral rather than a unilateral standpoint.

Third World War in Piecemeal

If the war on terror could be described as a world war, it was principally because the al-Qaeda itself had a priori practically declared a world war in its call for jihad and pronouncement of fatwa on the United States and its allies, calling on every Muslim who is able, and in any country where possible, to kill Americans and their allies.[103] In the wake of 9/11 when the United States responded with a declaration of the war on terror, Richard Clarke drew a parallel between the "defunct" Cold War and the war on terror, one of the ingredients in the paralleling of the two wars being that "both conflicts raged globally, with regional wars, secret sleeper cells and competing ideologies".[104] The point here is that in the

98 See "Singapore: The Eastern Fringe of the Muslim World Worries about Islamic State's Influence", *The Economist*, January 23, 2016, p. 44.
99 Ibid., p. 43.
100 Ibid., p. 44.
101 Ibid., pp. 43–44.
102 Ibid., p. 43.
103 See Bernard Lewis (2003), *The Crisis of Islam* . . ., p. xxvii, op. cit
104 See Richard A. Clarke (2004), *Against All Enemies* . . ., p. 37, op. cit.

wake of 9/11, and following the U.S. declaration of the war on terror, there was an escalation or upsurge in terrorists' attacks around the world as the terrorists practically fought back.

As President Obama noted, "from Yemen to Iraq, from Somalia to North Africa, the threat today is more diffuse, with Al-Qaeda affiliate in the Arabian Peninsula—AQAP—the most active in plotting against our homeland".[105] But it is not only the United States' homeland that the al-Qaeda posed a threat. Europe had also effectively come within the crosshairs of these terrorists. In this war, Africa was originally thought to be merely "caught in the crossfire", a "victim of violent action intended by the terrorists for the United States" on the one hand, and also "a victim of violent action taken by the United States and intended for the terrorists".[106] But this is not so any more. Africa is no longer just in the crosshairs in the violent "global contest between militant jihadism and Western powers"; and it is no longer an innocent bystander in other people's war; it is also no longer a collateral damage that is merely contending with the disruptions of a "foreign war" fought on its soil.[107]

Rather, deriving from the al-Qaeda' millenarian objective of seeking to build a global Caliphate, Africa now has its own homegrown terrorists that recognize and target Africans as enemies. In fact, the threat agents had even gone beyond the al-Qaeda to now include the ISIS and the associated terrorist organizations and their "secret sleeper cells". In Africa, too, the regional manifestation of terrorist attacks range from the AQIM straddling North Africa and the Sahel, to the Jamaat Ahl as-Sunnah lid-Da'wah wa'I-jihad (the Boko Haram) terrorizing the Lake Chad Basin countries of Nigeria, Chad, Niger, and Cameroon; and the Harakat al-Shabaab al-mujahideen that terrorize both the Horn of Africa (Somalia) and East African nations of Kenya and Uganda, with a determination to carry the battle to Ethiopia and beyond in that neighbourhood.[108] But the global dimension and severity of terror in the wake of 9/11 were such that after the November 13, 2015 Paris attacks, Pope Francis described the phenomenon as a "Third World War in piecemeal".[109] This description by the Pontiff was not without reason.

105 See the "Full Transcript of President Obama's Speech on Counterterrorism Policy" . . ., op. cit.

106 See Ali A. Mazrui, Seifudein Adem, and Abdul Samed Bemath (2008, ed.), *The Politics of War and the Culture of Violence: North-South-Essays*, Trenton, NJ, Asmara, Eritrea, Africa World Press Inc., p. 139; see also See Fred Aja Agwu (2016), *Nations among Nations* . . ., p. 522, op. cit.

107 See Kalundi Serumaga in "Terrorism in Africa . . .", pp. 34–35, op. cit.

108 Ibid., p. 35.

109 When asked whether he believed these horrific attacks were amounting to a third world war, the Pope responded, saying that he believes they are "a piece" of a "piecemeal World War III". The Pope also said, "I am moved and I am shaken", a terrifying thought that suggested that Pope Francis was as stirred by the incident as anyone else; see "Pope Francis Speaks Out & Calls Paris Attacks Part of Third World War", available at http://hollywoodlife.com/2015/11/14/pope-francis-paris-attacks-third-world-war-piece-terror/ (last visited on January 22, 2016).

Before 9/11, the war on terror in a formal and deliberately declared form did not exist; the fight against the malaise was muted and had not been as widespread as it became after 9/11. In fact, as William Banks asserts, "it has often been said that the September 11 terrorist attacks changed everything", and that to those cataclysmic attacks, "the United States clearly reacted by changing long-standing tenets of counterterrorism strategy".[110] Part of the change was that "where law enforcement and intelligence gathering were the primary instruments of U.S. policy against terrorism outside any designated battlefield, after September 11, a formal war was not only declared, the concept of theater of war itself was shelved in the war on terrorism".[111] In the war on terrorism, targets were broadened beyond Osama bin Laden and his close circles and extended beyond the boundaries of Afghanistan[112] to Iraq, Yemen, and now Syria. This dramatic territorial expansion in the war on terror is part of the reasons why it is denied any notion of battlefields, frontlines or formal theaters of war.

Beyond the conventional practice of confronting enemies on the battlefields, the United States, particularly because of the unconventional modus operandi of the terrorists themselves, and even though there was a ban in political assassination ("enshrined in an executive order first by President Gerald Ford and unchanged since President Reagan's iteration in 1981"[113]), began to permit the explicit targeting of individuals with lethal force (the practice of targeted killings); the alternative of which would be the highly controversial "snatch and kill" operations conducted by squads of commandos, and which risked igniting local feuds in the territory of its allied nations like Yemen.[114] With the U.S. moving beyond the battlefields in the war on terror, Special Forces evolved; and the evolving Special Forces roles and missions found "the military carrying out covert operations much the same way that the CIA has traditionally done, an overlap that was questioned by critics.[115]

The whole notion of battlefields, war theaters, or frontlines will be discussed later in this book; but suffice it to say that even though bereft of battlefields, the war on terror as formally or consciously declared by the United States, was practically fought in many regions of the world: against the Taliban in Afghanistan, the ISIS in Syria, Iraq, and Libya; the al-Qaeda (also all over the places the group had developed franchises or cells); the Al-Shabab in Somalia and Kenya; and the Boko Haram in Nigeria, amongst other places that international terrorism had developed or taken root. Eurasia and Asia were also not left out, for Russia, China, including even India all battle terrorism in one way or the other. Even when the Russian President Putin took sides in Syria with the Assad regime, he was also pretentiously fighting terrorism. In all of this, the United States was initially more fixated on the al-Qaeda; but now, with the al-Qaeda focused on

110 See William C. Banks (2005), "The Predator", in Volker C. Franke (2005, ed.); *Terrorism and Peacekeeping* . . ., p. 146, op. cit.
111 Loc. Cit.
112 Ibid., p. 147.
113 Ibid., p. 149.
114 Ibid., pp. 146–147.
115 Ibid., p. 148.

"fighting insurgencies in Muslim-majority countries" like Syria and had "not in recent years sought to launch mass-casualty attacks in the West",[116] the ISIS has risen as a formidable terrorist group that Washington is mortally afraid of, and, thus, more determined to combat; more so, as Fareed Zakaria said, the ISIS has risen as an idea that inspires people around the world.[117]

But this is not to sing the *Nunc Dimittis* for the al-Qaeda. At the moment, the "al-Qaeda also has more resources at its disposal today than ever, and more geographic reach; . . . running its largest training camp ever—in, of all places, Afghanistan".[118] What with the resurgence of the Taliban in Afghanistan, "with the Taliban ascendant on the battlefield and Al-Qaeda still joined at the hip with once and perhaps future rulers there"[119]? What observers predict may happen is that there may be some unintended consequences in Syria that may make the al-Qaeda rethink its not planning attacks in the West at the moment: Russia's intervention in Syria, supported by Iran and the Hezbollah, can frustrate the agenda of the al-Qaeda and the ISIS to depose President Bashar al-Assad and, hence, make the al-Qaeda begin to turn attention on the West with its new-found resources and "geographic reach".[120] In this case, the possibility of using Syria as a launching pad, just as it did with the Taliban-controlled Afghanistan, is still an option for the al-Qaeda.[121] Until this happens, the resources and attention in the West have gone to the fight against ISIS.[122]

The Making of the ISIS Fixation

> In the Islamic State's brief few years of existence, they've managed to make an indelible and gruesome impression on the American psyche through a campaign of constant carnage. The only organization guaranteed to elicit more hatred, fear and disgust in the average American, and they had to murder 3,000 Americans to achieve that level of infamy. ISIS, by contrast, hasn't coordinated any attacks on the homeland (though their ideology of hate has inspired many shootings), but the group still manages to take its place alongside Nazis and the Ku Klux Klan as shorthand for "bad guys". That ISIS provokes strong emotions in Americans is understandable.
>
> (*Newsweek* special edition on "Killing ISIS", 2016, undated, p. 10)

116 See Bill Powell, Mahmoud Shikh Ibrahim, Jack Moore, and Mirren Gidda in "The New ISIS Crisis" . . ., p. 32, op. cit.

117 Fareed Zakaria, the GPS anchorman, talking to Becky Anderson in her Connect the World programme on CNN, monitored in Lagos (Nigeria) on Sunday, September 11, 2016, at 4pm, local time.

118 See Bill Powell, Mahmoud Shikh Ibrahim, Jack Moore, and Mirren Gidda in "The New ISIS Crisis" . . ., p. 33, op. cit.

119 Loc. Cit.

120 Loc. Cit.

121 Loc. Cit.

122 Loc. Cit.

Like in its inadvertent creation of the al-Qaeda, the fact that the United States is the creator of the ISIS is well documented.[123] Both the al-Qaeda and ISIS are in part, the consequences of Washington's power projection in the Middle East.[124] They both "undeniably cut into [the] share of the Jihad market".[125] Since 9/11 and its aftermath (that is; the death of Osama bin Laden), the al-Qaeda may have paled into insignificance in comparison with the ISIS—what with bin Laden's "second-in-command, Ayman al-Zawahiri, . . . said to be a doddering, uncharismatic bean counter"—but the al-Qaeda is still alive and kicking; since it is undeniable that under Zawahiri's stewardship, the terror organization "grew its largest paramilitary force ever—in Syria alone, Jabhat Fateh al-Sham has 10,000 fighters loyal to it"; and it has also slowly but surely expanded its footprints globally, in the Levant (Greater Syria) region, the Indian subcontinent and West and North Africa.[126] Perhaps, about the only things that prevented the al-Qaeda from joining forces with the ISIS was "doctrinal and strategic differences—as well as big egos"; and these differences do not appear set to change any time soon, which means that the al-Qaeda and ISIS are far from joining forces.[127]

The al-Qaeda and the ISIS were both the creations of Washington's foreign policy gone awry. Even when, for partisan political reasons, Jeb Bush, a younger brother to President George W. Bush, tended to insinuate that (an insinuation that was a Republican mantra during the 2016 Presidential primaries,[128] and reiterated by Donald Trump during his presidential debate with Hillary Clinton) it was President Obama's alleged precipitate withdrawal from Iraq that created the lacuna that the ISIS emerged and filled, he was instantly contradicted by the self-evident truth that President George W. Bush created ISIS in the first place with his invasion of Iraq.[129] The huge foreign policy catastrophe in the invasion of Iraq was captured by Kofi Annan, former Secretary-General of the United Nations, thus:

> The shattering damage done by the US-led invasion of Iraq was of course not limited to the loss of 22 UN officers on August 19, 2003. In the course of the decade following the invasion, an estimated 115,000 Iraqi civilians died in the ensuing anarchy and civil war; more than 10,000 coalition soldiers were killed or wounded; some 4 million people were made refugees

123 See, for instance, Jonathan Broder in "Made in America? How the Origins of the Islamic State May Lie in Washington, D.C.", *Newsweek*, June 12, 2015, published in a special *Newsweek* edition, "Killing ISIS: America's All-Out Assault on a Global Threat", 2016 (undated), pp. 22–25; see also Fred Aja Agwu (2016), *Nations among Nations*. . ., pp. 30–36, op. cit.

124 Fred Aja Agwu (2016), *Nations among Nations*. . ., pp. 33–39, op. cit.

125 See Bill Powell, Mahmoud Shikh Ibrahim, Jack Moore, and Mirren Gidda in "The New ISIS Crisis" . . ., p. 32, op. cit. Brackets mine.

126 Loc. Cit.

127 Loc. Cit.

128 See Jonathan Broder in "Made in America? . . .", p. 24, op. cit.

129 Ibid., p. 22.

> or were internally displaced; social, economic, and environmental devastation; the standing of the United Nations as an institution and an agent of global security gravely harmed; the promise of multilateralism so ardently sought in the aftermath of the end of Communism blighted; the Middle East peace process set back another decade or more; the vital priority of creating a stable Afghanistan unable to foster terror and instability blithely discarded; Al-Qaeda strengthened rather than weakened; Sunni-Shia differences in the Arab world transformed into a murderous schism; the vital and noble principle of humanitarian intervention tainted by its association with aggression and domination; and last, the global standing of the United States, a founding member of the United Nations and long-standing pillar of international order, tarnished by identification with the worst of the abuses, tragedies, and chaos that war brings in its wake.[130]

It was the exacerbated Sunni-Shia differences in the Arab world that Kofi Annan adverted to above as having been transformed into a "murderous schism" by the invasion of Iraq that the ISIS was part of. As Kurt Eichenwald wrote in *Newsweek*:

> To this day, the world grapples with the consequences of this military folly of former President George W. Bush, which sparked a conflagration that has spread across the Middle East and contributed mightily to the creation of ISIS—the Islamic State extremist group filled with members of former Iraqi dictator Saddam Hussein's military and Baath Party.[131]

Eichenwald wrote this in an analysis of President George W. Bush's "largest strategic blunder in American history: the 2003 invasion of Iraq to destroy Weapons of Mass Destruction (WMD) that didn't exist"; and in the context of "a damning report [the Chilcot Report, named after its chairman, Sir John Chilcot] [that] details everything Bush didn't know before he invaded Iraq, and when he didn't know it".[132]

There actually was nothing like President Obama precipitately withdrawing from Iraq because although his predecessor, President Bush, "negotiated an agreement which was approved by the Iraqi parliament, giving U.S. forces permission to remain in the country until 2011, along with immunity from arrest and prosecution", that status of forces agreement proved temporary.[133] It was temporary because when President Obama assumed office and "began negotiating a similar accord", with the goal of leaving behind some 5,000 American soldiers to "train the Iraqis and help with counterterrorism", the negotiation did not go well because

> not only did Muqtada al-sadr, the fiercely anti-American Shiite cleric, threaten to unleash his militia on any remaining U.S. troops, but the new

130 See Kofi Annan (2012), *Interventions*. . ., p. 318, op. cit.
131 See Kurt Eichenwald in "The War on Error . . .", p. 16, op. cit.
132 Loc. Cit. Parentheses mine.
133 See Jonathan Broder in "Made in America? . . .", p. 23, op. cit.

> government of Iraqi Prime Minister Nouri al-maliki was forced to acknowledge that most Iraqis wanted the occupation to end.[134]

What ultimately led to the rejection of that status of forces agreement was not only because of the fact that Iraq had (by the time Obama became President) become a parliamentary democracy where a parliamentary approval was required,[135] it was also because of the nationalist outburst that dreaded the fact that "having foreign troops in your country is . . . an unnatural act", and that "giving them legal immunity is . . . even more unnatural".[136] But Prime Minister Nouri al-Maliki did not help matters either with his domestic policy of intensifying sectarian tensions, which "antagonized the long-suffering and disillusioned population" and "marginalized sentiments of national unity".[137] In addition, the fact that the Prime Minister Nouri al-Maliki (a Shiite) decided to recklessly upend the fragile sectarian balance in Iraq had also undermined whatever benefit that the surge under President Bush had achieved in terms of stabilizing that country; for not only did the Sunnis that fled across the border into Syria join the al-Nusra Front, the perception that Syrian President Assad was "supported by Iran" had led Sunni officials and other wealthy patrons in Turkey and the Persian Gulf Emirates to begin "funneling money and weapons to the rebels", who they saw as the "defenders of the Sunni heartland against Iranian Shiite proxies".[138]

This was essentially how not only Iraq but also Syria got engulfed in the conflagration. The situation, therefore, did not warrant solely laying the blame on the doorsteps of President Obama, as some political partisans are wont to. As it were, "the Iraqi sectarian divides, which ISIS exploited, run deep and were not susceptible to permanent remedy by [U.S.] troops at their height, let alone by 5,000 trainers under Iraqi restraints" that was contemplated in the botched status of forces agreement.[139] In fact, confirming the George W. Bush administration's strategic blunder in Iraq, Scott McClellan, the Press Secretary to that administration, confessed that although "as Press Secretary, I spent countless hours defending the administration from the podium in the White House briefing room . . ., I have since come to realize that some of them were badly misguided";[140] for "history appears poised to confirm what most Americans today have decided—that the decision to invade Iraq was a serious strategic blunder".[141] Although the Chilcot Report "shows the President believed Saddam possessed WMD", but it was equally of the view that Bush "and his administration were irresponsible

134 Loc. Cit.
135 Ibid., p. 24.
136 Ibid., pp. 23–24.
137 See Fawaz A. Gerges (2016), *ISIS: A History* . . ., p. 109, op. cit.
138 See Jonathan Broder in "Made in America? . . .", p. 24, op. cit.
139 Loc. Cit.
140 See Scott McClellan (2008), *What Happened: Inside the Bush White House and Washington's Culture of Deception*, New York, Public Affairs, p. x.
141 Ibid., p. xiii.

in their use of the intelligence that led them to that conclusion"; so much so that "by summer of 2001, as the CIA sent reports to the White House about an impending Al-Qaeda attack [that eventually happened on September 11, 2001] on U.S. soil, the administration turned more of its attention to Iraq".[142]

In being enamoured of Iraq, the then National Security Adviser, Condoleezza Rice, while testifying before the 9/11 Commission, said that in the pursuit of Osama bin Laden and the al-Qaeda, President George W. Bush had become "tired of swatting flies".[143] When the matter was pursued further with her by Senator Bob Kerrey (who felt that it was only once under the Presidency of Bill Clinton that the United States swatted flies on August 20, 1998, an obvious reference to the cruise missiles attacks on Afghanistan and Sudan in the wake of the simultaneous bombing of U.S. embassies in the East African countries of Kenya and Tanzania), Rice replied that what she meant by the swatting of flies was "the disruptions" of the al-Qaeda network abroad that the CIA was embarking upon, going after "bad guys" like Abu Zubaydah.[144] It was also because of this fixation on the "axis of evil", particularly on Iraq, that the Bush Presidency was distracted by Iraq and the missile defence,[145] distracted in "debating the fine points of the ABM Treaty . . ., looking up at the sky for the fighter cover".[146]

Before his administration's invasion of Iraq, President W. Bush had earlier in his State of the Union speech on January 29, 2002, "proclaimed that Iran, North Korea, and Iraq made up an "axis of evil" seeking WMD and involved in terrorism worldwide".[147] Having—by the proclamation that these states are the "axis of evil" (implying that war was inevitable); and "not thinking geopolitically but instead focusing on the single goal of overthrowing Saddam"—President George W. Bush acquired the reputation of a cowboy that could hardly be "trusted on war plans", ignoring all entreaties and warning by American allies like the United Kingdom that in taking on Iraq alone without tackling the paramount issue of the Arab-Israeli conflict, "we could find ourselves bombing Iraq and losing the Gulf".[148]

But the President George W. Bush administration had become irrevocably committed to the invasion of Iraq; and according to the British Ambassador to the United States, Sir Christopher Meyer, Bush was saying "in effect that destroying Saddam is a crusade against evil to be undertaken by God's chosen nation . . ."[149] This invocation of the crusade metaphor as well as the messianic

142 See Kurt Eichenwald in "The War on Error . . .", p. 18, op. cit.
143 See "Condoleezza Rice Testifies before 9/11 Commission", available at http://edition.cnn.com/2004/US/04/08/Rice.testifies/ (last visited on August 12, 2016).
144 Loc. Cit.
145 See Condoleezza Rice (2011), *No Higher Honor: A Memoir of My Years in Washington*, New York, Crown Publishers, p. 260.
146 See Richard A. Clarke (2004), *Against All Enemies* . . ., p. 26, op. cit.
147 See Kurt Eichenwald in "The War on Error . . .", p. 19, op. cit.
148 Loc. Cit.
149 Loc. Cit.

appeal in the notion of America as the "God's chosen nation" was all suggestive of the existence of a clash of civilization; they were the sort of images and metaphors that defined the post-9/11 toxic language that inescapably played into the hands of the Middle East fanatics that were propagating the narrative/ideology of a clash of civilization as the raison d'être for their invidious terrorism campaigns against the United States and its allies. At least, by dint of the diplomatic dispatches, reports or submissions by the British Ambassador to the United States, Christopher Meyer, it was evident that "the Bush administration was adrift",[150] that the American plan was "a hare-brained scheme" in the sense that "the Bush administration . . . was not taking serious action to address problems, and [that] there was no strategic concept for a military plan".[151]

Hence, although the British Prime Minister Tony Blair took the risk of gambling on the side of the United States by joining in the invasion of Iraq, British officials were (behind closed doors) dismissive of "the Bush plan to impose a democratic government on Iraq as perilous, given that the country had no experience with such a political system and was in a region where the concept was almost anathema".[152] Even when—because it "was beyond US capabilities"—the British counseled the need for "a UN umbrella", the "need for U.N. participation in administering a new Iraqi government" (the "post-Saddam Iraq"), "the Americans batted away the suggestions of the British".[153] Rather, "the Pentagon was building its day-after strategy on unsupported assertions that Western military forces would be greeted as liberators", a "naïve belief" that "reflected a fundamental lack of understanding of the Middle East—[which is that that] enemies of the West and Sunni supporters of Saddam would not disappear".[154]

This gross underestimation of the realities in the Middle East was not helped by the fact that in the post-Saddam Iraq, just like in the post-Taliban Afghanistan before it,[155] "there was plenty of attention paid to which corporations would get to profit from the Iraq reconstruction, while the humanitarian needs after Saddam's fall were given far less thought".[156] In Afghanistan, many Non-Governmental Organizations (NGOs) had practically "descended" on Kabul and skimmed off the entire foreign aid meant for the post-war reconstruction of that country.[157] In fact, the use of these NGOs "magnified and exacerbated" the

150 Loc. Cit.
151 Ibid., p. 20. Brackets mine.
152 Loc. Cit.
153 Loc. Cit.
154 Loc. Cit.
155 See Daron Acemoglu and James A. Robinson (2012), *Why Nations Fail: The Origins of Power, Prosperity, and Poverty*, New York, Crown Business, pp. 450–452.
156 See Kurt Eichenwald in "The War on Error . . .", p. 18, op. cit.
157 These NGOs and the representatives of the U.S. government poured into the country with their private jets in pursuit of their own agendas, deploying much of the aid money into the service of bureaucrats ("to chauffeur and chaperone them around, paying them multiples of . . . salaries"), including "to commission an airline to shuttle around UN and other international officials" whereas the public infrastructure (schools and other public services

challenges associated with foreign aid, highlighting the following contradictions: one, that donors "hijack foreign aid to pursue their own security objectives rather than those which would help the poorest"; two, that the cost of the budget for the war on terror now gobbles up the aid budget; and three, that "major donors are failing to coordinate aid through existing multilateral institutions, choosing instead to create their own new mechanisms [the NGOs] and pursue their own priorities".[158]

So, in Iraq as in Afghanistan, the absence of "the rapid establishment of security and repair of infrastructure, particularly the electric grid", heightened the enormous danger of getting pulled into the resultant quagmire, the sectarian civil war that engulfed the post-Saddam Iraq, which was later aggravated by the emergence of the ISIS.[159] And so, the post-Saddam Hussein Iraq became an apotheosis of the stark warning that was issued by a British intelligence: that "a poorly handled invasion, without proper, realistic preparation for the aftermath, would prompt a flood of Muslims joining extremist groups, followed by years of attacks".[160] This was exactly what happened in Iraq; and the flood of Muslims joining the extremist groups was further heightened by the incident of "blowback", the attraction to join that was caused by the real or perceived humanitarian catastrophe that the application of armed drones for the targeted killing of the extremists had caused.

And as if to aggravate this not inconsiderable strategic faux-pas, the Bush administration laid the template for the hasty exit of American troops from Iraq. It was this hasty exit of American troops that created the vacuum that conduced to the formation of ISIS, a vacuum that would have been forestalled, had the Iraqi government in the wake of the Obama administration agreed to grant the United States a status of forces agreement (despite the force's inherent deficiencies) to enable the retaining of some American troops in Iraq for security purposes.[161] The consequence was that Saddam was "replaced by a swarm of terrorists who would see the Western occupation of Iraq as a battle against Islam".[162] This was irrespective of the fact that ideologically, according to the Joint Intelligence Committee of the British Cabinet Office on November 28, 2001, Saddam was poles apart from the Sunni extremist network that was linked to Osama bin Laden.[163]

Many of these terrorists, including the lone wolves, apparently believed that the United States were at war with Islam, a belief that took hold when the United

---

for the development of democratic and inclusive institutions necessary for the restoration of law and order) in Afghanistan remained in tatters; see Daron Acemoglu and James A. Robinson (2012), *Why Nations Fail*. . ., p. 451, op. cit.

158 See Ngaire Woods (2005), "The Shifting Politics of Foreign Aid", *International Affairs*, Vol. 81, No. 2, March, p. 393.

159 See Kurt Eichenwald in "The War on Error . . .", p. 20, op. cit.

160 Loc. Cit.

161 See Fred Aja Agwu (2016), *Nations among Nations*. . ., pp. 35–37, op. cit

162 See Kurt Eichenwald in "The War on Error . . .", p. 20, op. cit.

163 Ibid., p. 19.

States, after dispatching the Taliban regime in Afghanistan that was sheltering Osama bin Laden and his al-Qaeda network, invaded Iraq, another Muslim country that "was uninvolved in the Sept. 11 attacks".[164] This is the sense in which the ranks of the ISIS were not only populated by Sunni Islamic extremists, but also by "members of former Iraqi dictator Saddam Hussein's military and Baath Party" faithful[165] that were displaced from the elitist privileges they enjoyed under Saddam by the American-led invasion. According to Fawaz Gerges:

> The de-Baathification and dismantling of the army, on which tens of thousands of Arab Sunnis, if not more, depended for income, angered the Sunni community at large. The move cause large portions of not only soldiers but also former government officials, civil servants, doctors, professors, and teachers to be dismissed from their positions. Under the former [Baath Party] regime, party membership was generally a prerequisite for employment.[166]

So, apart from U.S. President Bush's bungling of the Iraqi invasion and post-invasion dispensation, the rise of the ISIS in Iraq was brought about "largely in reaction to the strident sectarian leadership of former Prime Minister Nouri al-Maliki"; who, "once the U.S. bugged out in 2009, set about purging Sunnis from the military and senior positions in the Iraqi government".[167]

The ISIS, therefore, was fundamentally a product of the "sectarian chaos" that descended on Iraq upon the exit of the United States and the emergence of Prime Minister Nouri al-Maliki.[168] But the Bush administration actually shares the responsibility for the rise of ISIS almost in proportional terms with the Iraqi Shiite-dominated government because the foundation of Prime Minister Nouri al-Maliki's sectarian government was laid by the United States foreign policy. It was the same was that American foreign policy led to the emergence of the al-Shabaab terrorist organization in Somalia that it led to the emergence of ISIS in Iraq and beyond with President Bush's pro-Shiite post-invasion policy. In Somalia, as indicated earlier, the Somali nation turned to the al-Shabaab when the United States slammed the door on its face following the "Black Hawk Down" (the Somali Syndrome); and being a country that had been ripped down at the middle by clan divisions, it turned to the Islamic religious identity as expounded by the al-Shabba in order to forge a common and unifying identity.[169]

164 See Karl Vick in "What Terrorists Acting . . .", p. 8, op. cit.

165 See Kurt Eichenwald in "The War on Error . . .", p. 16, op. cit.

166 See Fawaz A. Gerges (2016), *ISIS: A History* . . ., pp. 109–110, op. cit.

167 See Bill Powell, Mahmoud Shikh Ibrahim, Jack Moore, and Mirren Gidda in "The New ISIS Crisis" . . ., p. 32, op. cit.

168 Loc. Cit.

169 This is the position of Jeffery Gentleman, the *New York Times* correspondent for Africa, while fielding questions from Fareed Zakaria in the latter's GPS programme on CNN, monitored in Lagos (Nigeria) on Sunday, May 28, 2017, between 8pm to 9pm local time, op. cit.

It was in this same way that the Bush administration slammed the door on the face of the Sunnis by adopting the "vengeance of the victors" policy; in which, after bypassing the United Nations' mandate for the invasion and ignoring "the idea of trying Saddam under international law, or in a court with a broader legitimacy", he "put Saddam's fate in the hands of the new Iraqi government, dominated by Shiites and Kurdish politicians who had been victims of his [Saddam's] reign".[170] Consequently, the trial of Saddam was not only seen as a farce by the Iraqi Sunnis and the wider Arab world, "Washington disbanded the Iraqi Army, fired 50,000 bureaucrats and shut down the government-owned enterprises that employed most Iraqis"—in effect, disbanding the Iraqi state and "leaving a deep security vacuum, administrative chaos and soaring unemployment".[171]

The U.S. Iraq sectarian policy was founded on the ideology that "Baathism equaled fascism"; such that "every school teacher who joined the Baath Party to get a job was seen as a closet Nazi", while state-owned enterprises were seen as bad—a sectarian policy that turned out to be "less nation-building than they were nation-busting".[172] Instead of building a national Army, the U.S. post-invasion sectarian policy in Iraq built forces that "were overwhelmingly Shiite and Kurdish, mostly drawn from militias with stronger loyalties to political parties than to the state"; and this sectarian dominance by the Shiites was read by the Sunnis, "not as just a regime change but a revolution in which they had become the new underclass".[173] This was the background of the Sunni rebellion, in which (not being good guys themselves) they channeled into the ISIS, the barbarity with which they had supported the al-Qaeda, determined to resist the United States and its protégé Shiite government in Baghdad.[174]

It was partly upon this scenario that the ISIS came to possess a very fierce fighting machine; for practically all the state apparatuses at the disposal of the dethroned and executed Saddam Hussein—"the former Iraqi Baathist intelligence and military officials" made up the ISIS's leadership under al-Baghdad.[175] This confirmed the ISIS as a product of political Islam, actuated by not only the delusion of pursuing "a sacred religious cause", but also a political cause. But in the war on terror, the United States is committed to the destruction of ISIS because this terrorist group combines territorial ambition in the Middle East with vicious far-reaching attacks around the world, for which it became more notorious, even more so than the al-Qaeda that it was an outgrowth of.

Now, the question is this: how specifically did the ISIS share a connection with the al-Qaeda? The simple connection between the two, as already

170 See Fareed Zakaria in "Vengeance of the Victors", *Newsweek*, January 8, 2007, p. 9. Brackets mine.
171 Loc. Cit.
172 Loc. Cit.
173 Loc. Cit.
174 Loc. Cit.
175 See Bill Powell, Mahmoud Shikh Ibrahim, Jack Moore, and Mirren Gidda in "The New ISIS Crisis" . . ., p. 32, op. cit.

stated earlier, is that the ISIS leadership grew out of the al-Qaeda. In early 2006, "Ibrahim Awwad Ibrahim al-Badri, who years later adopted the nom de guerre al-Baghdadi" (Abu Bakr al-Baghdadi) went through tutelage under Abu Musab al-Zarqawi, the Iraqi al-Qaeda offshoot leader.[176] It was a thing of immense surprise how al-Baghdadi came away from al-Zarqawi as such a fiery jihadist, given that Zarqawi was considered an insipid and lackluster personality that did not make impressions because he was not only poor and of lowly birth,

> he also was not a well educated man or even a great theologian, but just a Jordanian whose route toward radicalization started in his own country, against his own regime, a fact that resonated with many youths who had turned to Salafism in the Arab world and that facilitated his claim to be emulating the example of the Prophet Mohammed.[177]

By Fawaz Gerges' account, it was al-Zarqawi's "unlikely rise to the heart of the jihadist movement" that made him an "inspiring figure for wannabe jihadists from the poorest sections of Arab societies"; including the factor of "his Bedouin roots that provided him with cultural and ethnic ties in the Arab crescent"[178] as well as attraction to people like al-Baghdadi; but it was not until 2015 that al-Baghdadi, then 44 years of age, "transformed the break-away al-Qaeda group from a battlefield force operating in the chaos of Syria and Iraq into a transnational terrorist franchise killing civilians in more than a dozen countries around the world".[179] Earlier in 2013 and 2014, the ISIS under al-Baghdadi recorded a great military surge in its hunger for a territorial space that would constitute its Caliphate, surprising U.S. President Barack Obama that had derisively dismissed it as a "jayvee squad",[180] amateurish and of no consequence or "serious threat to America's regional allies or interests, and overwhelming the Iraqi security forces, "despite being trained by the United States and costing anywhere between $8 billion and $25 billion".[181]

Apart from overrunning "Iraqi, Syrian, and Kurdish security forces and rival Islamists as well", the ISIS had, by the end of 2014, "captured approximately a third of Syria and Iraqi territories", edging "closer to the Iraqi-Jordanian-Saudi Arabian frontiers" from where it "carried out spectacular suicide bombings and multiple deadly incursions into Lebanese territory, capturing dozens of Lebanese security forces and traumatizing a society already polarized along social and

176 See Massimo Calabresi in "The Terrorist Abu Bakr al-Baghdadi: The Head of ISIS Exports Extreme Violence and Radical Beliefs around the Globe", *Time* (New York), December 21, 2015, p. 57.

177 See Fawaz A. Gerges (2016), *ISIS: A History* . . ., p. 76, op. cit.

178 Loc. Cit.

179 See Massimo Calabresi in "The Terrorist Abu Bakr al-Baghdadi . . .", p. 56, op. cit.

180 See Michael Weiss and Hassan Hassan (2015), *ISIS* . . ., p. xii, op. cit.

181 See Fawaz A. Gerges (2016), *ISIS: A History* . . ., pp. 1–2, op. cit.

sectarian lines".[182] By the end of 2014, the ISIS had got its tentacles "spread to Egypt, Libya, Yemen, North Africa, Afghanistan, Nigeria, and beyond, exposing the fragility of the Arab state system and the existence of profound ideological and communal cleavages within Middle Eastern and Islamic societies".[183] Meanwhile in Syria, there is, different from Al-Baghdadi's more brutal ISIS, the new al-Qaeda that morphed into the reputedly less brutal Jabhat al-Nusra that does not share the same worldview with ISIS, the al-Nusra having developed a less ambitious agenda in planning to declare an Islamic Emirate, "one notch down from a Caliphate".[184]

As already stated earlier, it was because the al-Qaeda does not share the same worldview with the ISIS beyond the "jihad market"; indeed, because of the wider doctrinal and strategic differences—the conflict egos—that both the al-Qaeda and ISIS could not join forces and do not appear capable of doing so anytime soon.[185] Part of these differences in ego, doctrinal and strategic calculations prompted the al-Qaeda leadership to warn the ISIS against holding territories in the name of a Caliphate—advising it to choose a network to a Caliphate, for holding territories would be unsustainable against the inevitable Western onslaught that later came to pass.[186] But the ISIS chose the path to its territorial dream of a Caliphate. It fostered this Caliphate on not only the mainly Sunni cities in Iraq, but also in parts of Syria, and in Libya, "where it established an important foothold in the central coastal city of Sirte—demonstrating that it could take and hold territory far from Raqqa, its so-called capital in Syria".[187] On the whole, by June 29, 2014, when the group declared a Caliphate in the territory it controlled,[188] the ISIS controlled "at its peak, more than 20,000 square miles of territory and the allegiance of the populace residing within".[189]

But conscious of its handicap, the impossibility of sustaining "territorial holdings without possessing significant anti-aircraft weaponry to deter U.S. airstrikes", the ISIS proceeded to painstakingly construct "their version of the famous Cu Chi tunnels in Vietnam—tunnels outside of Saigon that, during the war there, gave North Vietnamese fighters freedom of movement, the ability to protect weapons and ammunition from heavy American bombardment and—critically—an escape route that ensured they would be able to move on to the next battlefield—". . . [an] intricate network of tunnels with rooms, toilets, medical facilities and enough food to sustain a long fight".[190] Apart from the ISIS's Caliphate

182 Ibid., pp. 2–3.
183 Ibid., p. 3.
184 See "Syria's Ceasefire . . .", p. 16, op. cit; and "Al-Qaeda: The Other Jihadist State" . . ., p. 53, op. cit.
185 See Bill Powell, Mahmoud Shikh Ibrahim, Jack Moore, and Mirren Gidda in "The New ISIS Crisis". . ., p. 32, op. cit.
186 Ibid., p. 30.
187 Ibid., p. 29.
188 See Jonathan Broder in "Made in America? . . .", op. cit.
189 See "Killing ISIS: America's All-Out Assault on a Global Threat". . ., p. 6, op. cit.
190 See Bill Powell, Mahmoud Shikh Ibrahim, Jack Moore, and Mirren Gidda in "The New ISIS Crisis". . ., p. 29, op. cit.

consisting of the territorial hold on mainly Sunni territories, including the network of tunnels that would enable them "fight to the death",[191] the possession of this territory—the Caliphate—also enable the terrorist organization to make money, having seized oil wells that helped it to have access to oil money in both Iraq and Syria, and to generate some income that it used to complement those it earned from extortions.[192]

Al-Baghdadi combined his ambitious territorial goal of an Islamic state in the Middle East with an elaborate "apocalyptic vision of a final battle between the forces of radical Islam and the West".[193] It was on the premise of this apocalyptic vision that in mid-2014, he "declared slavery to be the universal human condition" in which "Muslims are indentured to Allah, while nonbelievers are the rightful property of Muslims".[194] In persuading his adherents along extremist and fatalistic ideology, al-Baghdadi impressed it upon them that "the time of death for each man or woman is preordained, implying that all killings must be the will of Allah"; thus, paving the way for his lieutenants to advance this toxic and intoxicating ideology in the message to ISIS supporters everywhere that "if you can kill a disbelieving American or European . . . kill the disbeliever whether he is a civilian or military".[195]

However, as Calabresi wrote, "Muslims worldwide reject al-Baghdadi's call to death".[196] The ISIS may have "become the best-equipped and funded terrorist group in history"—[197] without prejudice to 9/11, it may have outdone the al-Qaeda, especially with its October 31, 2015 atrocious exploit in bringing down the St. Petersburg-bound Russian passenger Metro jet, causing the death of 224 people;[198] and masterminding the November 13, 2015 Paris attack—and commanded global headlines as the most dangerous terrorist group;[199] yet, the Boko Haram in Nigeria (according to the Global Terrorism Index report by the Institute for Economics and Peace released in late 2015) exceeded it in 2014 as the deadliest terrorist group, having been "responsible for 6,644 deaths" that year—"an increase of 317 percent from the previous year".[200]

This was opposed to ISIS's responsibility for 6,073 deaths within the same period the report covered.[201] Between the two groups, however, was responsibility for more than half (51%) of the deaths attributed to terrorism in 2014, the

191 Loc. Cit.
192 Ibid., p. 30.
193 See Massimo Calabresi in "The Terrorist Abu Bakr al-Baghdadi . . .", p. 57, op. cit.
194 Loc. Cit.
195 Loc. Cit.
196 Loc. Cit.
197 See Ian Bremmer in "Six Steps to Building an ISIS Strategy", *Time* (New York), December 14, 2015, p. 10.
198 See Massimo Calabresi in "The Terrorist Abu Bakr al-Baghdadi . . .", p. 56, op. cit.
199 See "Boko Haram Overtakes ISIS as World's Deadliest Terror Group, Report Says", *The Guardian* (Lagos), November 24, 2015, p. 9.
200 Loc. Cit.
201 Loc. Cit.

deadliest year of record for terror, the year that, internationally, deaths from terrorism experienced a dramatic rise, increasing by 80% from the previous year.[202] Nevertheless, the Boko Haram recognizes ISIS as a senior comrade in crime, even as a superior, a fact that could be explained by the Boko Haram pledging allegiance to ISIS in March 2015, the year after it had exceeded ISIS in brutality.[203] The 2014 and beyond aggravated brutality and increased deaths resulting from the terrorism of the ISIS and the Boko Haram were strong indications that the war on terror should be taken seriously.

Coalescing Against Terrorism

International terrorism is not a problem that can be unilaterally and effectively solved by one state, not matter its might. This is because terrorism is not only international in nature, each terror cell is not only reinforced from abroad; each is also self-sustaining. The import of this is that the defeat of any terror network in one country does not necessarily implies its defeat in another, for its continued existence in the latter will later reinvigorate the former that had been supposedly defeated. This is an eternal verity in the dynamics of international terrorism, and a lesson that the United States itself has learned the hard way, for when Washington thought that it had defeated the al-Qaeda with the dismantling of that terror network in the Taliban-controlled Afghanistan and the decapitation of its leadership with the death of Osama bin Laden, the ISIS showed its face. This is not to talk about the AQIM, the AQAP, the al-Shabaab, the al-Nusra, and the Boko Haram, etc.

Sometimes, contradictory and delusive sentiments are expressed to the effect that Africa can go it alone independent of the rest of the world, especially the West, in the prosecution of the "war on terror" despite the immense benefits in coalescing to achieve an enduring solution to the problem. It was in this context that "in the ongoing debate on global peace and security" as it concerns the "war on terror", the former Nigerian President Olusegun Obasanjo argued that "what must however be avoided is letting outsiders—the same Afro-pessimists, recently turned into Afro-euphorists—define the discourse"; and that "building on our long history that encompasses colonial violence, post colonial domination, and internal and externally generated insecurity, we have the capacity to discuss our security in far more holistic and nuanced ways", empowering "our institutions at the national, regional and continental levels to handle the new security challenges".[204] In the same vein, Kalundi Serumaga urged that "Africa must tackle 'terrorism', but must first develop her own discourse, on her own terms and based on her own experiences, to provide an African framework to understanding the challenge".[205]

202 Loc. Cit.
203 Loc. Cit.
204 See Olusegun Obasanjo in "Africa Rising: The Security Threat", *New African*, April 2016, p. 39.
205 See Kalundi Serumaga in "Terrorism in Africa . . .", p. 37, op. cit.

But contrary to these sentiments that Africa can go it alone, it is clearly not realistic for any nation or continent to delineate any discourse based on the so-called peculiar experience, or to defeat international terror in isolation. As far as peculiar experiences go, apart from the punitive war on terror in Africa (as illustrated in Algeria with the DRS aforementioned[206]) that unfortunately engineered the rise of the "state security" from the African governments' response (which on its own exacerbate the pathologies of terrorism[207]), African governments do not have any unique experience that is different from that of the rest of the international community; and, as such, cannot pretend to possess ground-breaking thoughts or original African frameworks for understanding and tackling the challenges. Paradoxically, the former Nigerian President Obasanjo also acknowledged the global character of the terrorist affliction. According to him, "due to globalization, terrorism in Africa cannot be viewed in isolation; it is clearly not just an African challenge"; for "when terrorists strike in Mali, Algeria or Chad, the victims are not just Africans"; and "when terrorism and insecurity disrupt the developmental process in many African countries, especially in resource-rich nations like Nigeria or Angola, those who pay the price include the foreign corporations that have invested in the dream of an Africa in the rise".[208]

About the only pragmatic approach inherent in the narrative that Africa should exclude outsiders in seeking solution to terror is in former President Obasanjo's insistence that "partnerships and cooperation with the rest of the world should arise from . . . internal cohesion", which must be understood to imply not only inter-African solidarity but also the empowering of national, regional, and continental institutions.[209] Internal cohesion through empowered and strong institutions is very critical because, at the moment, Africa in isolation cannot boast of any ostensible institution that can help it fight terror, jointly or severally, particularly the institutions of intelligence, surveillance, and communication as well as international or joint anti-terror data bases. About the most recent idea or weapon to deal with security challenges that Africa chose in recent times was the Tana High-Level Forum that the late Ethiopian Prime Minister Meles Zenawi evolved since 2012 along with several other African leaders to complement its more formal African Union structure.[210]

Named after the shores of Lake Tana where the Ethiopian city of Bahir Dar is located, the Tana High-Level Forum (chaired by former Nigerian President Obasanjo himself as at the April 16 to 17, 2016 meeting) as a complement for the formal AU meetings of the African Heads of State and Governments, comprises "members of the peace and security community in Africa" and "a diverse range of

206 See Jeremy Keenan in "How Terror Came to the Sahel" . . ., p. 57, op. cit.

207 See Kalundi Serumaga in "Terrorism in Africa . . .", p. 36, op. cit.

208 See Olusegun Obasanjo in "Africa Rising . . .", p. 39, op. cit.

209 Loc. Cit.

210 See Desmond Davies in "Tana Forum Leads the Way on Africa's Security, 16–17 April 2016, Bahir Dar, Ethiopia", *New African*, April 2016, p. 40.

personalities" from the academia and beyond.[211] An assemblage of some former African Heads of State and Governments as well as academics like "Professor Funmi Olonisakin, founding Director of the African Leadership Centre at King's College, London; and Professor Mahmood Mamdani of Makerere University, Uganda" (as the Forum Advisory Board members), the Tana Forum only "encourages frank, relevant and candid dialogue, which it believes is fundamental to resolving conflict and transforming societies in Africa".[212]

Reminiscent of the AU Summit, and although equally a form of coalescence, the Tana Forum, even when as it were, primed to bring "together participants from Africa and Europe",[213] is more or less like a "talk-shop". Although some heads of state are sometimes in attendance, it cannot equal coalescence at the strictly formal level of the nation-state where the real political will and resources to make a practical difference dwell. The power of coalescence in the war on terror can be immense, and with instantaneous results. Think about the rare consensus of the Finance Ministers of members of the United Nations Security Council (a chamber that was hitherto a byword of paralysis because of the veto-wielding members) and other stakeholders that, in addition to the coalition's targeting of ISIS's oil installations, led to the emasculation of the terrorist group's finances, such that it began to dramatically cut the pay cheque of its fighters and record deserters or stragglers.[214]

The war on terror as declared by the United States in the wake of 9/11 was originally to combat the al-Qaeda; but Washington has now been practically joined by the West writ-large, which has aligned with its (Washington's) joint-coalition with some Arab nations to ramp up the air campaigns against the ISIS in Syria and Iraq. The point in a broad coalition is this wisdom aforementioned that no nation can singlehandedly defeat contemporary terrorism because of its international, amoebic, and Spirogyra formations. With its emergence and growth in daring-do and impunity, combating the ISIS, much more than the al-Qaeda (and also due largely to its viciousness) became the orbit or focus of this international war on terrorism, the group having exceeded the al-Qaeda in brutality, both in the Middle East and across many countries in Europe, North America, and Africa; in fact, the viciousness of the ISIS is expressed in Africa through its Boko Haram proxy.

The menace of ISIS was so huge that the United States declared that its actions against the Yazidis and other minority groups in Iraq and Syria constitute genocide.[215] The U.S. Secretary of State, John Kerry, had said that "ISIS

211 Ibid., p. 41.

212 Loc. Cit.

213 Loc. Cit.

214 See Mark Thompson in "War on ISIS Update: Two Steps Forward, One Step Back", *Time* (New York), February 22–29, 2016, p. 13.

215 See "U.S. Declares ISIS Action in Iraq, Syria Genocide", *The Guardian* (Lagos), Friday, March 18, 2016, p. 35.

is responsible for genocide against groups in areas under its control, including Yazidis, Christians and Shiite Muslims"; that this terrorist group trapped the Yazidis, killed them, enslaved thousands of Yazidi women and girls, "selling them at auction, raping them at will and destroying the communities in which they had lived for countless generations"; and that ISIS had equally executed Christians "solely for their faith" and also "forced Christian women and girls into slavery".[216] Without the intervention of the U.S. and Arab-led coalitions, according to Kerry, this abominable slaughter and general maltreatment of the people would have continued and more slaughter perpetrated.[217] The U.S. global coalition approach to the war on terror was actually a template upon which Nigeria was instructed in the employment of the regional coalition of the Lake Chad Basin Countries that led to the reinvigoration of the Multinational Joint Task Force (MJTF) and, later, the country's membership of the Islamic Coalition Against Terrorism, a 34-, largely Muslim, nation framework that was spearheaded by Saudi Arabia.[218]

Nigeria's reported membership of the Saudi-led anti-terror organization had caused some rumpus, with *The Guardian* (Lagos) editorializing that President Buhari ought to have "tabled such a sensitive matter before the National Assembly" (even when the Nigerian Constitution only recognizes domestication and not National Assembly approval before the country can enter into a treaty); that against the background of Nigeria's antecedent of secretly joining the Organization of Islamic Countries (OIC) under the military as well as the Christian/Muslims and Shiite/Sunni divides within the country, this particular move was tantamount to taking Nigeria into another form of Islamic organization, warning that "the cold war between Saudi Arabia and Iran even in diplomatic engagements need not be brought into Nigeria".[219] Although Nigeria's Minister of Foreign Affairs, Geoffrey Onyeama, debunked the notion[220] (contrary to the reported President Buhari's acknowledgement in *AlJazeera* of joining the organization[221]) that the country had signed any document for membership; he, however, recognized the fact that "the issue of terrorism is a serious one and we all have to work together".[222]

Nigeria's determination to go ahead with the international coalitions against terror, despite the many currents of its domestic contradictions is an indication of the potency of the policy of coalescing against the international menace. And amid the speculations that the Nigerian military were using South African mercenaries

216 Loc. Cit.
217 Loc. Cit.
218 See Olalekan Adetayo in "Nigeria, Part of Saudi's Anti-Terror Islamic Coalition—Buhari", *The Punch* (Lagos), Monday, March 7, 2016, p. 8.
219 See "Nigeria and the Islamic Coalition against Terror", *The Guardian* (Lagos), Editorial of Sunday, March 20, 2016, p. 12.
220 See Bridget Chiedu Onochie in "Nigeria Has Not Signed any Document on Islamic Alliance against Terrorism, Says Onyeama", *The Guardian* (Lagos), Friday, March 25, 2016, p. 3.
221 See "Nigeria and the Islamic Coalition against Terror" . . ., p. 12, op. cit.
222 See Bridget Chiedu Onochie in "Nigeria Has Not Signed any Document on Islamic Alliance against Terrorism, Says Onyeama" . . ., p. 3, op. cit.

in the fight against the Boko Haram,[223] the Buhari Presidency decidedly courted South Africa to enable the latter to lend the expertise of its military towards the success of Nigeria's counter-insurgency efforts, a closer bilateral cooperation that led to the South African President Jacob Zuma promising during a two-day visit to Nigeria in March 2016 that his government would return Nigeria's money, seized under President Jonathan when Nigerian officials tried to use it to procure arms and ammunition in the South African black market.[224] For Nigeria and Africa in general, a global or regional coalition against terrorism is inescapable because, in the light of the regional nature of this threat, and the utterly weak and incoherent national responses of the constituent nations, banding or acting together becomes quite inevitable.[225]

Again, for Africa, a global or regional coalescence approach had been further imposed by the fact that earlier "in 1992 in Dakar, the OAU passed a resolution pledging to coordinate the fight against extremism and terrorism among member states"; it had also pledged its commitment to playing its own part or role in combating international terrorism; and after 9/11 (in September 2002), it had "established the African Centre for the Study and Research on Terrorism (ACSRT), all of which inevitably "opened the door for member states to partner with the West in its counter-terrorism initiatives on the continent".[226] Although a red flag had been raised and fears entertained that the partnerships with the West had "fuelled jihadist insurgency on the continent",[227] but it was obvious that the international coalescence approach, be it regionally within Africa, or in partnership with the West, was a viable way to go; especially when individually, the typical African state is weak and lacks the strategic coherence to tackle this problem of terror. The benefit of this coalescence had been seen in the confrontation and rolling back of the Tuareg and al-Qaeda insurgency in northern Mali;[228] and in the Lake Chad Basin Commission's multinational force rolling back the Boko Haram in Nigeria and the entire sub-region.[229]

Characterizing the WoT: From Bush to Zedong and Huntington

The war on terror, with its compelling need for a coalition to tackle the ubiquitous and highly evasive terrorists, is a complex one; complex, not just because (with the exception of when the ISIS emerged and took hold of enormous

223 See Fred Aja Agwu (2016), *Nations among Nations* . . ., pp. 927–928, op. cit.

224 See Mohammed Abubakar, Terhemba Daka, Adeyemi Adepetun, and Uchenna Eze in "How MTN's Inaction Fuelled B'Haram Insurgency, by Buhari . . . S'Africa Will Return Confiscated Money", *The Guardian* (Lagos), Wednesday, March 9, 2016, pp. 1, 8.

225 See Kalundi Serumaga in "Terrorism in Africa . . .", p. 35, op. cit.

226 Loc. Cit.

227 Loc. Cit.

228 See Fred Aja Agwu (2013), *Themes and Perspectives* . . ., pp. 634–638, op. cit.

229 See Fred Aja Agwu (2016), *Nations among Nations* . . ., pp. 489–530, op. cit.

territories in Iraq and Syria) it is not exactly territorial in the sense of possessing definite battlefields—that is, in the sense of the terrorists taking up or possessing definite territories from where they can openly operate and be appropriately engaged—but also in the sense of skeptics believing that the United States is actually waging the war for purposes of securing its access to oil and other strategic interests. An insurgency that has morphed into terrorism does not take place in a typical war environment but "prevalently among the civilian population where the aggressors are often intermingled and disguised".[230] It is the terrorist's capacity to embed in the civilian population that is responsible for his elusiveness. The leader of ISIS, Abu Bakr al-Baghdadi, was an elusive target that was "moving constantly, often multiple times in 24-hour circle", not just because he rarely used communication that could be monitored, but also because he hid "mostly among sympathetic civilians in familiar desert villages, rather than with fighters in their barracks in urban areas where combat also took place.[231] Thus, terrorists are in archetypal conformity with Mao Zedong's prescription or thesis that insurgents must be like fish in water.[232] Dressed in street clothes, the terrorists often blend in and become indistinguishable from civilians.[233] The consequence of this is that operationally, fighting takes place in the presence of civilians, and the defence of civilians becomes part of the objectives that are pursued.[234]

But the attitude of the local population in the theater of the terrorists' operations is very decisive with respect to the outcome of the terrorists' plans or the counter-terrorism itself. The local population often exerts pressure on the insurgent terrorists and vice versa; whiles the behaviour of the counter-insurgency or counter-terrorism forces (the way and manner they conduct operations) can make or mar the "war" efforts in terms of the people being distrustful, hostile, or friendly.[235] It is this strategic importance of the civilian population in making or marring any counter-insurgency or counter-terrorism effort that makes it difficult if not absolutely impossible for any objective counter-terrorism approach to adopt the scorched-earth prescription of Samuel Huntington (in reaction to Mao Zedong) that the water be drained and the fish beached. This can only alienate and make the civilian population to align themselves with the terrorists.

Inevitably, however, the terrorist campaigns aspect of asymmetric conflicts "occur in the context of failed states"; that is, states that are characterized by weakness or non-existence of a central governments and their concomitant

230 See Giuseppe Caforio (2013), "Officer and Commander in Asymmetric Warfare Operations" . . ., p. 21, op. cit.

231 See "ISIS Leader, Baghdadi, Abandons Mosul to Field Commanders, US, Iraqi Sources Say", *Vanguard* (Lagos), Thursday, March 9, 2017, p. 42.

232 See Fred Aja Agwu (2011), *The Law of Armed Conflict and African Wars, Lagos*, Ibadan, MacMillan Nigeria Publishers Ltd., pp. 222–223.

233 See Giuseppe Caforio (2013), "Officer and Commander in Asymmetric Warfare Operations" . . ., p. 22, op. cit.

234 Ibid., p. 9.

235 Ibid., p. 13.

inability to control their territories.[236] And it is because terrorists embed in the civilian population that drones are used by the United States to take them out. Thus, the "WoT has many facets, with one being the use of drone attacks to target [the] leaders of Al-Qaeda and allied forces".[237] In fact, critics believe that one of the greatest problems in the "war on terror" is posed by the vagueness and broadness of the U.S. definition of the enemy it is fighting as "the Al-Qaeda, the Taliban and associated forces".[238] Another basic issue that makes the "war on terror" controversial is in its characterization, its ascribed scope, a war defined by President George W. Bush's administration as a global war; but this is a characterization that the President Obama's administration tended to dissociate itself from.[239]

Although this will receive a fuller exploration in the discourse later under the rubric of drones and the vanishing frontlines, it will be apposite to mention that, perhaps, the most benign interpretation that could be given to this global characterization of the war on terror is to say that it is waged beyond its immediate territorial confines in Africa and the Middle East (Iraq, Afghanistan, and Pakistan, for instance), extending to the attacks by the lone wolves in the West as well as the radicalization and recruitment of its "combatants" in cyber sphere. But exploring the distinction between the President Bush and Obama approaches, Jessica Stern believes that "many of Obama's counter-terrorism choices were framed as corrective responses to Bush's missteps", fully convinced that his "administration also had its own vision of how to combat the threat".[240]

President Obama's vision of how to win the war on terror is hinged on three platforms; first is his extensive use of drones; second is his extensive reliance on other governments to supply ground troops to fight the terror, and this is founded on his conviction that "if the United States cares more about the threat than the local authorities do, U.S. interventions are unlikely to succeed in the long run"; and third is President Obama's reliance on surveillance, especially electronic surveillance since the digital is far more widespread and vulnerable to exploitation, particularly since the former National Security Agency (NSA) contractor, Edward Snowden, in 2013, leaked enormous classified documents stored in digital form.[241]

The importance of surveillance lies in the fact that it limits collateral damage by providing intelligence; and it is also a potent instrument of tackling cyber terrorism and cyber war, two variants of terrorism that are even more deadly

236 Ibid., p. 10.

237 See Ahmad Nazir Warraich (2013), "The Use of Drones: Legal Grey Area?", *Strategic Studies*, Vol. 38, No. ¾, December, p. 65. Brackets mine.

238 Ibid., p. 75.

239 Ibid., p. 74.

240 See Jessica Stern (2015), "Obama and Terrorism: Like It or Not, the War Goes On", *Foreign Affairs*, Vol. 94, No. 5, September–October, p. 64.

241 Ibid., pp. 64–67.

than the conventional terrorist violence.[242] But irrespective of President Obama's commitment, the war on terror is also additionally plagued by the controversial incidence of armed drones as part of the means and methods of prosecuting the war (the drones' targets); and, of course, the United States' use of spies (the CIA) as part of the armed drones strikers, instead of exclusively using the Defence Department, the members of the armed forces.

Another problematic aspect or nature of the "war on terror" is the characteristics of the terrorists themselves: they are "illusive and cunning, difficult to track and impossible to eradicate".[243] The terrorists (the al-Qaeda, ISIS, Boko Haram, Al-Shabab, including the Taliban, amongst others) are not even deterred by the fact that they are facing the awesome powers of the United States and the sundry international coalitions, all of which were acting in response to the provocation of 9/11[244] and other acts of terror these terrorists had masterminded against Washington, its allies, and humanity in general. These 21st-century terrorist insurgents are, thus, more notoriously "dynamic"; they are "more connected and able to recruit from more sources than anything of the [traditional] Maoist era" insurgents; and (like the al-Qaeda, the ISIS, and the Boko Haram) modern insurgencies are more complex and capable of more indiscriminate violence.[245]

On November 13, 2015, Paris suffered an unprecedented terrorist attacks that left 130 people dead and more than 350 wounded; attacks in which Abdelhamid Abaaoud, a 28-year-old Belgian of Moroccan descent, led his ISIS-inspired group of an estimated nine terrorists to attack France's largest stadium, a crowded concert hall (the Bataclan concert hall), and a series of restaurants and cafes.[246] *The Economist* wrote (with respect to these attacks) that, "the terrorists shot anyone who strayed into their gun sights—ordinary mecs out for a gig, sharing a drink, or washing a football friendly".[247] These were ordinary civilians, men, women, children, and the aged, all ordinary folk that were normally not targets in any armed conflict; except, perhaps, in an asymmetric warfare of this nature, an insurgency that is combined with terrorist campaigns. Before the November 13 Paris attack, some suicide bombers linked to the same ISIS had also killed some 43 people in Lebanon; and in what *Time* magazine described as "a single grisly forth-night", the same ISIS used a bomb to destroy or bring down a Russian passenger jet over the Sinai region of Egypt.[248]

242 Ibid., pp. 66–67.

243 See Van Baldwin Carr (undated) in "Unmanned Aerial Vehicles: Examining the Safety, Security, Privacy and Regulatory Issues of Integration into US Airspace", p. 9, available at www.ncpa.org/pdfs/sp-Drones-long-paper.pdf (last visited on August 18, 2015).

244 Loc. Cit.

245 See Jake Diliberto (2014), "The New War Frontier . . .", op. cit.

246 See Missy Ryan, Emily Badger, and William Booth in "Nine Young Men and Their Paths to Terror in Paris", culled from the Washington Post and reproduced in *The Guardian* (Lagos), Friday, November 27, 2015, p. 48.

247 See "How to Fight Back: The Battle against the Islamic State Must Be Waged on Every Front", *The Economist*, November 21, 2015, p. 13.

248 Loc. Cit; see also "The Fight against ISIS", *Time* (New York), November 30–December 7, 2015, p. 3.

These are unpleasant scenarios that define asymmetric warfare; and underline the harrowing lack of any sense of proportionality or discrimination in it. At this level, insurgency intermeshes with terrorist movements, some of which have variants that are Millenarian in nature and, thus, implacably indisposed to earthly negotiations or placation.[249] The millenarians are a variant of terrorist insurgents that are "the killers in the street sheltering behind women and children", lone terrorists that are armed with girdles full of explosives and nails, and who cannot be deterred because they are determined to die so that they would go straight to Paradise.[250] In other words, these are people that are usually sworn to jihad and suicide; doing everything possible to "seduce and alienate the population in order to turn it against the government" or "remove a portion of the population that they cannot control".[251]

Whereas the Maoist-era type of insurgency's practice of embedding in the civilian population was rife during the Cold War era, it has, nevertheless, also infected modern insurgencies (modern insurgencies that are also capable of being dated that much back in history) and become more pronounced since the terrorist attack on the United States on September 11, 2001.[252] The 9/11 attacks were the classical cases of the application of terrorist campaigns, begun by the al-Qaeda insurgents in cahoots with the Taliban in Afghanistan. Since then, the threat by these sub-state groups has virtually dominated the intra and international security environment: more so because, with globalization, the negative impacts of their attacks have global reverberations.[253] But much more than the fact that globalization makes the attacks by modern terrorist insurgents "to have an effect on neighbouring states and even on other distant countries", the dominance of the global security environment by this asymmetric sub-state groups inheres in the statistical fact that "in 2011, there were 27 intrastate armed conflicts and only one interstate conflict".[254]

Although their resources (in terms of human, financial, and informational capacity) are much lower or leaner than those of the nation-state, modern terrorist insurgents continue to use improvised means of warfare to cause immeasurable human and material losses to both individual nation-states and the coalition of nation-states.[255] But reassuringly, the United States is indefatigably leading the rest of the world with an uncommon commitment in prosecuting the war on terror. However, doubts have continued to pervade around the world, including in Africa, that Washington is truly and honestly fighting terrorism and not

249 See Fred Aja Agwu (2013), *Themes and Perspectives . . .*, pp. 240–241, 262–263, op. cit; see also Fred Aja Agwu (2009), *National Interest, International Law . . .*, p. 126, note 146, op. cit.

250 See Josef Joffe in "Asymmetric Warfare . . .", p. 47, op. cit.

251 See Teodor Frunzeti (2013), "Asymmetric, Unconventional and Hybrid Actions . . .", p. 11, op. cit.

252 Ibid., p. 8.

253 Ibid., p. 6.

254 Loc. Cit.

255 Ibid., p. 9.

merely creating conditions that enable it to project power in the protection of its interests, especially its oil and strategic interests. Immediately after 9/11, there was a groundswell of global sympathy, solidarity, and consensus over the war on terror, so much so that Russian President Putin offered an unsolicited help to Washington soon after the terrorists struck on 9/11. In a telephone conversation in which Putin was informed that the United States had raised its alert, the Russian President showed an uncharacteristic or untypical understanding, informing, pronto, that in Russia, they had "canceled our exercises and brought our alert level down.[256]

Unfortunately, this "initial international consensus against terrorism [became] frayed in large part because [of] the war in Iraq".[257] The Iraqi invasion was built on the false premise of going after Weapons of Mass Destruction (WMD) that Saddam Hussein was believed to be capable of passing on to terrorists, but all that turned out to be a hoax. Rather, the President Bush Jr. was out to settle scores with Saddam and, perhaps, advance the oil/economic interest of the Bush family and the United States at large. The Iraqi invasion, thus, politicized the war on terror, destabilizing Iraq and setting off a civil and sectarian warfare between the Sunni and Shiite in particular, making Iraq "both a source of renewed motivation" for the recruitment of terrorists as well as "a training ground for al-Qaeda and related groups, particularly the al-Qaeda in Mesopotamia led by the late Abu Musab al-Zarqawi"[258]—the vicious ISIS. Recent historical realities also indicate that the United States and, indeed, the West writ-large had either contributed to the internal contradictions in Africa that are creative of terrorism, and that Washington was seduced by the lure of its economic interests to launch a preemptive war on terror in the continent, even long before the terror came in the form of the al-shabaab and the Boko Haram, amongst others.

To this end, the 1990s (especially 1992) and the early 2000s, were very critical or remarkable for the chain of events that led to Washington's active involvement in the war on terror in Africa, ostensibly for what, as Jeremy Keenan put it, has "to do with the US's energy crisis".[259] The year 1992 was when the secular Somalian warlords ultimately failed to maintain order, leading to state failure and disintegration in Somalia and the emergence of the Islamists who posed an infernal danger to oil and other shipping in the Gulf of Aden.[260] It was also in 1992 that "Algeria's military regime, with a "green light" from the West, annulled democratic elections", prompting the launching of terrorist campaigns by FIS and the beginning of the counter-terrorism operations of the DRS, the

256 See Condoleezza Rice (2011), *No Higher Honor* . . ., pp. 74–75, op. cit; see also Fred Aja Agwu (2016), *Nations among Nations* . . ., pp. 579–580, op. cit.

257 See Martha Crenshaw (2009), "Terrorism as an International Security Problem", in Jeffrey H. Norwitz (2009, ed.); *Pirates, Terrorists, and Warlords* . . ., p. 401, op. cit.

258 Loc. Cit.

259 See Jeremy Keenan in "How Terror Came to the Sahel" . . ., p. 57, op. cit.

260 See Kalundi Serumaga in "Terrorism in Africa . . .", p. 37, op. cit.

Algerian intelligence service.[261] The presumptively covert Western hand in the condonation of that elections annulment was France because, alongside other Western nations, the United States condemned the annulment, culminating in the imposition of sanctions (unlike its refusal to condemn al-Sisi many years later in Egypt[262]) and withholding of new and hi-tech weapons from the Algerian military and intelligence.[263]

It was the immense experience the DRS garnered from its counterterror operations in Algeria since 1992 that it lent to the United States as one of the defining indices of post-9/11; for the notorious DRS "provided the West with experience, information and access to terrorist networks" in that northwest region of Africa and beyond.[264] The benefit of condoning the elections annulment in Algeria in 1992 was beginning to be reaped bountifully. But more interesting was the fact that beyond the terrorism in Algeria, owing to that elections annulment, "Africa did not have much, if any, terrorism at that time".[265] It was the United States' ominous pulverization of the Taliban regime in Afghanistan and the scattering of the al-Qaeda all over the Maghreb and the Sahel region of Africa that led to the serious or aggravated onset of terrorism in Africa.[266] The situation was not helped either by the liquidation of the Muammar Gaddafi regime in Libya from where "weapons of all categories took flight in different directions . . ., especially in the Sahel".[267] Initially, it was a huge surprise how the attacks that came much later in 1998 on the United States' embassies in Nairobi and Dar es Salaam, and a Mombasa hotel in 2002 were to be a casus belli (with respect to the war on terror), having been considered far away from America's major oil resource regions.[268]

These regions were the Gulf of Aden (in terms of shipping) and the Gulf of Guinea, where prior to the shale revolution, and with the U.S. dependence on oil surpassing "the psychologically critical 50% level", the Dick Cheney Report (2001) estimated Washington would source its "25% oil imports by 2015".[269] It was this pre-shale revolution perception of America's deepening interest in the "African Oil Triangle" (the Gulf of Guinea) that generated the anxiety that led to the region's description by Theresa Whelan (U.S. Assistant Secretary of Defense for African Affairs) as an "ungoverned space" (or inadequately governed space),

261 See Jeremy Keenan in "How Terror Came to the Sahel" . . ., p. 57, op. cit.
262 See Fred Aja Agwu (2016), *Nations among Nations* . . ., pp. 379–388, op. cit.
263 See Jeremy Keenan in "How Terror Came to the Sahel" . . ., p. 57, op. cit.
264 Loc. Cit.
265 Loc. Cit.
266 Loc. Cit.
267 See Mohammed Abubakar, Valletta Malta, and Kamal Tayo Oropo in "Buhari Links Terrorism in Africa to Gaddafi's Fall: Canvasses Special Committee to Stem Tide, Says 12,000 Killed, Displaced in Nigeria", *The Guardian* (Lagos), Sunday, November 29, 2015, p. 3; see also Fred Aja Agwu (2013), *Themes and Perspectives* . . ., pp. 384, 390–392, op. cit.
268 See Jeremy Keenan in "How Terror Came to the Sahel" . . ., p. 57, op. cit.
269 Loc. Cit.

a pretext that in turn led to its designation as a frontline in the Global War on Terrorism (GWOT).[270] It is this sort of situation that has continued to create misgiving in the mind of many that the United States is actually honest with its ways in the war on terror.

The Audacity and Irrationality of Terrorist Insurgents

But again, the terrorists remain audacious. And this, in part, is basically because they lack adequate human, material, financial, and information resources, even when relentlessly desirous of fructifying their desire to inflict maximum damage on the psyche of the state and its population. It is also this situation that makes the modern terrorist insurgencies as militarized organizations to use the indirect actions of asymmetric warfare methods and procedures to compensate for their weaknesses.[271] They maximize the opportunities offered by a country's vulnerabilities, like the vulnerability of passengers in an airplane, while therein minimizing the victim country's overwhelming military firepower because all the cruise missiles in the world, for instance, cannot deal with foes that simply refuse to show up; those who cannot be captured and interrogated because they are consumed by the blaze that resulted from the explosions they set off, while their sponsors or "masters are hidden in the fog of anonymity",[272] either in distant territories or in cyberspace, a platform of the Internet. The idea behind this elusiveness (as in the David and Goliath gambit) is to devalue the best weapons of the enemy or stay out of reach of the enemy's superior might.[273]

Thus, these insurgents remain "incomprehensible, elusive and irrational" or even foolhardy in the methods they employ to inflict pains and seek to realize their goals or objectives.[274] Insurgents are elusive because although "not organized in military structure similar to that of a national army", they act individually or in small groups and seek fulfillment of concrete and tangible objectives that have great psychological impact on the civilian population.[275] Asymmetric warfare or insurgency and the concomitant counter-insurgency are, thus, a nightmare of epic proportion for every military organization, no matter how sophisticated in training and professionalism. Like in the Biblical David and Goliath confrontation, the insurgents use simple weapons like knives and box cutters

270 See Fred Aja Agwu (2009), *National Interest, International Law . . .*, pp. 228–230, note 146, op. cit.
271 See Teodor Frunzeti (2013), "Asymmetric, Unconventional and Hybrid Actions . . .", p. 10, op. cit.
272 See Josef Joffe in "Asymmetric Warfare . . .", p. 47, op. cit.
273 Loc. Cit.
274 Teodor Frunzeti (2013), "Asymmetric, Unconventional and Hybrid Actions . . .", p. 10, op. cit.
275 Loc. Cit.

and stay out of range.[276] Hence, the Israelis hardly achieve much against the assault rifle–wielding Palestinians in the latter's *intifadeh*, despite being armed with "Merkava tanks and F-16 attack planes"; since, as a "democratic" nation, it might be "loath to use 120-mm rounds or laser-guided bombs" against the Palestinian insurgents.[277]

But there is hardly anything that being democratic has to do with counter-insurgency because some democracies like the United States are known to have discarded democratic values in order to prosecute its counter-insurgency challenges in Fallujah (Iraq).[278] The United States used heavy hands in Fallujah, not deliberately, but because that option was imposed on it by the evasiveness or elusiveness of the insurgents, added to their terrorist campaigns. In fact, in Iraq under reference, General Stanley McChrystal, the veteran of the U.S. counter-insurgency in that country expressed his frustration with that asymmetric warfare thus:

> In the spring of 2003 we entered Iraq. What began as a heavily conventional military campaign to unseat the regime of Saddam Hussein had, by the fall of 2003, become a bitter, unconventional struggle against frustrated Sunnis who increasingly coalesced around a charismatic Jordanian extremist who had taken the name Abu Musad al Zarqawi. In the years that followed, we . . . found ourselves in a bitter fight that, in the beginning, was as confounding as it was bloody. The Task Force hadn't chosen to change; we were driven by necessity. Although lavishly resourced and exquisitely trained, we found ourselves losing to an enemy that, by traditional calculus, we should have dominated. Over time, we came to realize that more than our foe, we were actually struggling to cope with an environment that was fundamentally different from anything we'd planned or trained for. The speed and interdependence of events had produced new dynamics that threatened to overwhelm the time-honoured processes and culture we'd built.[279]

Frankly, asymmetric warfare does not defer to conventional dynamics, time-honoured processes and culture. It is no respecter of conventional planning, training or traditional calculus. And as General McChrystal confessed, in the asymmetric challenge of pursuing the Al-Qaeda in Iraq (AQI)—"a decentralized network that could move quickly, strike ruthlessly, then seemingly vanish into the local population"—the change that this unconventional warfare imposed on the U.S. military was the establishment of a taskforce that could "combine the agility,

276 See Josef Joffe in "Asymmetric Warfare . . .", p. 47, op. cit.

277 Loc. Cit.

278 See Janice Anderson, Anne William, and Vivian Head (2007), *War Crimes and Atrocities: Horrific Crimes Committed under the Guise of War*, London, Fatura, p. 502.

279 See Stanley McChrystal (2015), *Team of Teams: New Rules of Engagement for a Complex World*, New York, Portfolio/Penguin, p. 2.

adaptability, and cohesion of a small team with the power and resources of a giant organization", "a network that combined extremely transparent communication with decentralized decision-making".[280] This was the new approach that enabled the United States to face up to the unconventional challenge of the AQI, a typical modern or 21st-century insurgency.

Like the al-Qaeda network that simply "appeared and disappeared in a continuous manner"; and which cannot be vulnerable to direct actions, some parts of the population provide concrete, material, and moral support for the insurgents, which frequently execute combat actions and their elusiveness by hiding among the population.[281] It was for this reason that during the Vietnam war, Mao-Tse-tung (Mao Zedong) made the declaration that has already been cited earlier, that guerrillas must be as fish in water (that is, hide in the civilian population); but Samuel Huntington riposted that if insurgents should become like fish in water, the task of counter-insurgency must be to drain the water and isolate the fish.[282] The Mao Tse-tung/Samuel Huntington approach certainly spells catastrophe for the civilian population that must be destroyed to isolate the insurgents.

This is where the application of the armed drones becomes at least expedient, if only it can stave off the cataclysmic potentialities in the pursuit of terrorists in the midst of the civilian population. It is assumed that with its pin-prick precision, the armed drones can assist in saving the extreme measure of draining the water in order to beach the fish. But the question at issue here is this: is this objective being realized without any unacceptable collateral damage and the attendant consequences? Unfortunately, the expected precision from the drones seems to be a very tall order. The disastrous failings of the armed drones' capacity for precision, especially when embarking on signature strikes, have led to colossal civilian casualties and undesirable consequences too.

The Drone Solution and Inherent "Blowback"

How can terrorism be effectively combated in such a way that the state can at once defend itself and avoid the grisly humanitarian carnage that goes with acting with conventional weapons? When overwhelmed on 9/11 with the otherwise "malevolent airlines" used to slice the World Trade Towers, there was this sudden realization by the United States that there was "the need for a totally new defense technology".[283] In fact, some analysts even strongly felt that national

280 Ibid., the front blurb of the book.

281 See Teodor Frunzeti (2013), "Asymmetric, Unconventional and Hybrid Actions . . .", p. 10, op. cit.

282 See James E. Bond (1974), *The Rules of Riot: Internal Conflicts and the Law of War*, Princeton, NJ, Princeton University Press, p. 87; see also Fred Aja Agwu (2011), *The Law of Armed Conflict and African Wars*. . ., pp. 222–223, op. cit.

283 See Robert M. Oates (2002), *Permanent Peace: How to Stop Terrorism and War—Now and Forever*, Iowa, Institute of Science, Technology and Public Policy, p. 2.

defence "based on objective, physical science—on weaponry made largely of metal, using chemical, electronic, and nuclear technologies"[284] had failed in the face of stealth, "resolute and cunning terrorists willing to sacrifice their lives" to achieve devastating consequences.[285] Although this seeming fatalistic viewpoint did not propose the use of drones (of course, drones are objective and physical science-based weapons), it preferred to propose the psychic approach that it believed was "a systematic procedure" that would made "it possible to switch on peace as straightforwardly as we switch on the lights".[286]

This "subjective and consciousness-based" psychic power consists of "meditation technologies known and preserved for thousands of years in the timeless Vedic tradition of India".[287] Because all violence, both in terrorism and conventional war, originate from "social stress and tension, the fear and hostility between factions, nations, religions, and even competing civilizations", meditation by an individual or group "can calm down stress, tension, and hostility in that individual" or group.[288] The way this allegedly works, that is, the way that "the minds of people who are experts in meditation work is that when gathered together to meditate in one location" in a "transcendental meditation program", they can "calm down stress, tension, and hostility in the collective consciousness of the surrounding society", just like the broadcasting "radio stations radiate music through the underlying electromagnative field", by making use of a "subjective technology", "the most richly complex technological device ever created—the human brain", to "radiate harmony and peacefulness through an underlying field of consciousness".[289]

But the question that the proponent of using this Vedic tradition of India to solve terrorism and war fails to answer is why, despite the availability of this "subjective technology", there is still so much disharmony, violence, war, and terrorism in the Indian subcontinent, especially between the governments of India and Pakistan over the Kashmir region, and involving militant or terrorist organizations? So, this proposition is still at best a form of wishful thinking, idealism. This still makes the form of defence based on objective, physical science weapons (metal, chemical, electronic, nuclear technologies and, of course, the drone technology) the only objective and viable instrument for tackling terrorism and warfare, despite the unfortunate reality it embodies—the occurrence of the grisly scenario in humanitarian tragedies. Although a terrific weapon of war, drones are fairly precise weapons against the elusive terrorist, even though it introduces the preemptive strike tradition that modern international law abhors.

But it was actually to advance the task of avoiding any kind of grisly scenario in a confrontation between terrorism and counter-terrorism in a predominantly

284 Ibid., p. 3.
285 Ibid., pp. 1–2.
286 Ibid., p. 3.
287 Loc. Cit.
288 Ibid., p. 4.
289 Loc. Cit.

civilian setting that human creativity (the intractable ingenuity of man) resulted in the invention of armed drones, a technology that aims to confront and rein in the audacity of the terrorists by privileging the precise targeting of these destructive extremists in a mass of the civilian population with little or no harm to the civilian populace. Armed drones have allegedly come in to constitute a procedure that pointedly and rigorously ensures the targeting of the insurgents in such a way and manner that would minimize collateral civilian damage; even though this unfortunate collateral damage often occurs and leads to a "blowback"—that is, the motivation of those aggrieved by the collateral damage and loss of civilian lives to join the insurgents.[290] And this clan of the aggrieved that join the insurgents do so, more determined than ever to hit the United States where it hurts the most.

Even before the introduction of drones in the war on terror, the United States was doing the much it could to avoid needless collateral damage and the resultant blowback. For instance, in the fall of 1998, when a window of opportunity existed to kill Osama bin Laden,[291] President Clinton hesitated to strike because although there was the seeming reality that "the intelligence sources were conclusive", the president was more concerned about avoiding unwholesome collateral damage and the consequent blowback; hence, he insisted on "a guaranteed hit or nothing at all".[292] In fact, before he was eventually felled (killed) in a hellfire of missiles from a drone strike in August 2009, and also arising from the situation in which the majority of drone strikes had missed their targets, killing civilians in 2006 alone at an estimated ratio of 687 civilians to only 14 al-Qaeda leaders, the Pakistani Taliban chieftain, Baitullah Mehsud, had often boasted that because of its tendency to miss its targets and inflict some casualties on the civilian population, every drone attack by the United States often brought him three or four additional suicide bombers.[293]

This is the context of the persuasion that drone strikes actually foster international terrorism because they indirectly increase the number of militants.[294] From Afghanistan, through Iraq, to Israel with the Hezbollah in the 2006 war, findings have shown that the exposure of the local population to civilian casualties could cause "the insurgents over the long run to have a revenge mindset that resulted in greater recruitment of insurgents".[295] In fact, as Colonel Gross said, in the Counterinsurgency Operations Manual, the assumption that if you kill ten of the

290 See Sam Roggeveen (2014) in "Proliferation of Unmanned Aerial Vehicles: The Future of Drones", A Panelist Paper at the (2014 Council of Councils Annual Conference Panelist Papers), May 11–13.

291 See Robert "Buzz" Patterson (2003), *Dereliction of Duty . . .*, p. 129, op. cit.

292 Ibid., p. 130.

293 See Fred Aja Agwu (2011), *The Law of Armed Conflict and African Wars . . .*, p. 64, op. cit.

294 See Micah Zenko (2013), "Reforming U.S. Drone Strike Policies", Council on Foreign Relations Center for Preventive Action, *Council Special Report No. 65*, January, pp. 10.

295 See Robert D. Sloane (2011), "New Battlefields/Old Laws . . .", p. 373, op. cit.

enemy, you will have fewer than ten left is quite illusory because in the context of exposing the casualties to the local populace, you might end up creating more insurgents.[296] Thus, a counter-insurgency operation that kills five insurgents can be counterproductive if as a consequence, it serves to recruit 50 more insurgents or terrorists.[297]

U.S. General McChrystal was clearer in the presentation of the problem as he differentiated between the insurgents and ordinary civilians, arguing, by implication, that it is the casualties amongst the civilians that multiplies the insurgents/terrorists. Robert Sloane cited General McChrystal thus:

> In conventional warfare in Afghanistan, from a conventional standpoint, the killing of two insurgents in a group of ten leaves eight remaining; but if civilian casualties are incurred as a consequence, then ten minus two is not equal to eight; rather, ten minus two is equal to twenty.[298]

It is against this background that Robert Oates pointed out that "experience in the Middle East have shown that killing terrorists (and, inevitably, innocent civilians) only creates more terrorists"; as "Islamic terrorists will be recruiting young men to a life of terrorism against America with tales of a heartless, faceless [using armed drones], seemingly endless bombing of an entire Islamic nation".[299] As it were, the certain terrorist reprisals for this bombing will only embody the central religious principle of "*as you sow, so shall you reap*", replicated in the law of physics that states that "every action has an equal and opposite reaction" and heightening the "vicious cycle of terrorism" with all its "heartless attacks and vengeful retaliations".[300] This is also what Col. Lawrence Wilkerson of the United States army described as the creation of a "terrorist industrial complex".[301]

It was in the context of this "blowback" that in Yemen, for instance, in 2010, the Obama administration described al-Qaeda in the Arabian Peninsula (AQAP) as encompassing "several hundred al-Qaeda members"; but by July 2012, AQAP members had risen to "a few thousand members".[302] However, the evidence that U.S. drone strikes create "blowback"—the situation "whereby killing suspected militants or civilians leads to the marked radicalization of local populations that join or sympathize with al-Qaeda or affiliated organizations"—is reputed to vary widely.[303] Blowback, in any case, has not been the only contradiction associated

296 Ibid., pp. 372–373.
297 Loc. Cit.
298 Loc. Cit.
299 See Robert M. Oates (2002), *Permanent Peace . . .*, p. 2, op. cit.
300 Ibid., pp. 2–3.
301 Col. Lawrence Wilkerson expressed this view in an *Aljazeera* documentary entitled *Drone*, monitored in Lagos (Nigeria) on Monday, August 22, 2016, between 9pm and 10pm local time.
302 See Micah Zenko (2013), "Reforming U.S. Drone Strike Policies" . . ., p. 10, op. cit.
303 Loc. Cit.

with drone strikes. In Pakistan, the continuation of drone strikes had exposed the fault lines between the country's military and its democratically elected parliament that in April 2012 demanded "an immediate cessation of drone attacks inside the territorial borders of Pakistan",[304] obviously because of the failure of the weapons as a precision instrument, and, of course, because of the consequent high level of civilian casualties.

Between March and May 2007 alone, more than 130 Afghan civilians were killed by U.S., and its allies', drone strikes, causing a situation in which "even among those predisposed to support the West, the mounting loss of life" was engendering anger, an anger that undermined any gain that might come as a result of killing some of the al-Qaeda henchmen.[305] This is not to talk about the fact that the al-Qaeda leadership is promptly regenerated immediately it is destroyed by any of the surgical drone strikes. In other words, irrespective of the fact that a drone strike is characterized as "a model of surgical counterterrorism", insurgents are also "adaptable beasts", with which if you "remove one vital organ . . . another will regenerate".[306] It was the death in June 2006 through armed drone strikes of the notorious Abu Musab al-Zarqawi, and also in May 2010 when the United States killed the only two men above Abu Bakr al-Baghdadi (the founding leader of the ISIS) that the latter (al-Baghdadi) "emerged as emir"[307] and even became more vicious in ISIS than his predecessors in the al-Qaeda.

It was for the reasons of the complications in the use of armed drones that Josef Joffe considered that "states have to think last about pinpoint precision weapons and concentrate first on myriad other means" or tools at their disposal for the catching of terrorist insurgents, what in "spy-speak" is known as "human intelligence": the infiltration of the ranks of the terrorists, including their bases in Afghanistan or Waziristan (Pakistan) and teaching the intelligence officials and soldiers to speak the local language of the enemy, be it Arabic or any other relevant language.[308] In confirmation of the truism that the hitting of innocent civilians by drones often triggers the recruitment of more terrorists, Faisal Shahzad, the Pakistani American that tried to detonate a bomb at Times Square in New York in 2010 confessed during his court case that his actions were justified because "when the drones hit, they don't see children".[309]

In fact, in also underlining the fact that "drone strikes could inspire terrorist strikes on U.S. soil", Jessica Stern made the point that "Faisal Shahzad who tried and failed to detonate a bomb in New York City's Time Square in 2010

304 Ibid., p. 11.
305 See Romesh Ratnesar in "Life after Death: The Struggle against Jihadists Won't Be Won Just by Killing Their Leaders", *Time* (New York), May 28, 2007, p. 13.
306 Loc. Cit.
307 See Massimo Calabresi in "The Terrorist Abu Bakr al-Baghdadi . . .", p. 57, op. cit.
308 See Josef Joffe in "Asymmetric Warfare . . .", p. 47, op. cit.
309 See Geert-Jan Alexander Knoops (2012), "Legal, Political and Ethical Dimensions of Drone Warfare under International Law: A Preliminary Survey", *International Criminal Law Review*, Vol. 12, p. 716.

reportedly claimed he acted to avenge a 2009 drone strike that killed Baitullah Meshud, the leader of the Pakistani Taliban".[310] It was actually acknowledged by Alexander Knoops that this is the extent that drone attacks can serve as a recruitment tool for the al-Qaeda and other terrorists and or insurgents.[311] Indeed, as Jessica Stern put it, "the use of drones to target suspected al-Qaeda operatives in Yemen has been correlated with a rapid growth in membership in the group's Yemen-based affiliate".[312] It is also in this context of blowbacks that Robert Sloane thinks that the United States should "try to rebalance the proportionality test in lethal targeting that's been used by U.S. forces and by other forces as well"; that is, "refocusing military operations from an enemy-centric viewpoint to a civilian population-centric viewpoint" because it is an exogenous incentive to reduce civilian casualties.[313]

With its capacity to create "blowbacks", armed drones' strikes are agent provocateurs, the same unsavory role that terrorist insurgents also play in asymmetric conflicts. As agent provocateurs that not only target civilians with a view to demoralizing the state authorities, terrorist "combatants" locate in awkward neighbourhoods and hence deploy from densely populated civilian areas in such a way that a military response from the state would result in civilian casualties and cause the "blowback" under reference; and not only forcing the recruitment of "new enlistees from the outraged civilian population", but also stoking an "outcry from certain sectors of the international community".[314]

This is the stock in trade of the Hamas in Gaza, the West Bank, and Lebanon; and it has provoked Israel in incurring heavy civilian casualties in trying to respond to their missile attacks on Israeli cities The unavoidable civilian casualties and the attendant "blowback" are some of the controversial points in the use of drones in counter-terrorism as a form of asymmetric armed conflict. Drones belong in the category of the modern and highly challenging appliances of warfare that can bypass the belligerents and strike at targets or objects behind the enemy line, including, inadvertently, civilians.[315] Still, insurgents are irrational, not only because they oppose or are "pitched" against a numerically and technologically superior enemy in the nation-state; they also do not care about the civilian victims of their action, be it in their area of "jurisdiction" or in the territory of their enemy.[316] But for the sake of humanity; that is, instead of the Huntington-style

310 See Jessica Stern (2015), "Obama and Terrorism . . .", p. 65, op. cit.

311 See Geert-Jan Alexander Knoops (2012), "Legal, Political and Ethical Dimensions of Drone Warfare under International Law. . .", p. 716, op. cit.

312 See Jessica Stern (2015), "Obama and Terrorism . . .", p. 65, op. cit.

313 See Robert D. Sloane (2011), "New Battlefields/Old Laws . . .", p. 373, op. cit.

314 See Samuel Estreicher (2012), "Privileging Asymmetric Warfare (Part III)?: The Intentional Killing of Civilians under International Humanitarian Law", *Chicago Journal of International Law*, Vol. 12, No. 2, p. 591.

315 See Fred Aja Agwu (2011), *The Law of Armed Conflict and African Wars*. . ., pp. 30–31, op. cit.

316 See Teodor Frunzeti (2013), "Asymmetric, Unconventional and Hybrid Actions . . .", p. 9, op. cit.

invasion and destruction of an entire city in pursuit of insurgents (as happened in the Iraqi city of Fallujah[317]), drones often come in handy for the identification and liquidation of the insurgents without incurring serious humanitarian issues.

The Anomaly of Terrorists as Combatants

It is an anomaly or a misnomer of some sort to deploy such terminologies as "belligerency", "combatancy", or even "pitched battle" in the analysis of terrorist campaigns–related asymmetric warfare. This is because, being not conventional in character, the sub-national or non-state entities involved in this kind of conflict are not, vis-à-vis the opponents, "separated by a linear front", and the distinction between civilian and military targets are not respected.[318] Insurgents do not constitute a regular "armed force" as distinct from a "peaceful populace".[319] They are not combatants in the strict sense of "organized armed forces, groups and units which are under a command responsible to that Party for the conduct of its subordinates . . .".[320]

Being sometimes not a cohesive unit but rather disparate and independent cells located in different countries, insurgents of the terrorist hue are also "not subject to an internal disciplinary system which, *inter alia*, shall enforce compliance with the rules of international law applicable in armed conflicts".[321] Thus, they are not ever irregular forces—levees *en masse*, or volunteers—known to international law in the sense of (1) those commanded by a person responsible for his subordinates, (2) those that have a fixed distinctive sign recognizable at a distance, (3) those that carry arms openly, and (4) those that conduct their operations in accordance with the laws and customs of war.[322] Insurgents of the terrorist variety are at best unprivileged and unprotected combatants to the extent that they could face punishment, including the death sentence where applicable, after a trial by a well-constituted court/jury.[323]

317 See Janice Anderson, Anne William, and Vivian Head (2007), *War Crimes and Atrocities*. . ., p. 502, op. cit.

318 See Teodor Frunzeti (2013), "Asymmetric, Unconventional and Hybrid Actions . . .", p. 10, op. cit.

319 See Fred Aja Agwu (2011), *The Law of Armed Conflict and African Wars*. . ., pp. 30–31, op. cit.

320 Loc. Cit; see Article 43 of Protocol 1, Additional to the Geneva Conventions, August–September, 1977.

321 See Article 43 of Protocol 1, Additional to the Geneva Conventions, August–September, 1977.

322 See Fred Aja Agwu (2011), *The Law of Armed Conflict and African Wars*. . ., p. 32, op. cit.

323 Ibid., p. 33.

4 Dirty/Nightmarish Weapon Platforms in WoT

The Improvised Explosive Devices (IEDs)

> For every move we make, the enemy makes three . . . The enemy changes techniques, tactics and procedures every two to three weeks.
>
> (Brigadier General Joe Ramirez Jr.)[1]

It is in the nature of insurgency/terrorism and counter-insurgency/counter-terrorism that the parties to it—be they nation-states or non-state entities (national or sub-national groups)—are compelled to deploy dirty, illicit, or dubious weapons that unavoidably constitute a serious concern, not just to themselves as "combatants", but also to the civilian population as bystanders. This assertion is true of the use of IEDs by terrorists, and the use of armed drones by the nation-state; so far mainly by the United States. Like the IEDs, the armed drone is a dirty weapon to the extent that it is not a conventional weapon; and also to the extent that it is at the same time capable of both targeted and indiscriminate killings. A weapon is dirty, illicit, or dubious when (prohibited or un-prohibited, regulated or unregulated) "the military benefits of their use can never be proportionate to the suffering they cause".[2] Thus, terrorism is often defined by the modus operandi of the terrorist; that is, in terms of the weapons terrorists deploy.

It is in the foregoing contexts of being defined by the type of weapon they use, like in being "armed with box cutters and contaminated envelopes" of anthrax, that Robert Oates wrote that "terrorism amounts to unknown people attacking unknown targets with unknown weapons at unknown times", thus, referring to terrorists as sociopaths that attack the defenceless, civilized world.[3] Beyond terrorists, unacceptable weapons are also used by the state. These are weapons

1 Brigadier General Joe Ramirez Jr., as quoted by Bobby Ghosh in "The Enemy's New Tools", *Time* (New York), June 25, 2007, p. 34.
2 See Michael Byers (2005), *War Law: Understanding International Law and Armed Conflict*, New York, Grove Press, p. 124.
3 See Robert M. Oates (2002), *Permanent Peace . . .*, pp. 1–2, op. cit.

that do not discriminate between civilians and combatants, weapons that cause superfluous injuries or sufferings before sure death: comprising, amongst others, explosive or expanding ("dum-dum") bullets, booby-traps, blinding laser, nerve and mustard gas, nuclear and biological weapons.[4] There are also chemical weapons, barrel bombs, and cluster munitions, the sort that Bashar al-Assad allegedly uses to counter the rebel fighters, the ISIS, and the al-Nusra in Syria.[5]

As far as this reality of dirty and nightmarish weapons goes, drones and Improvised Explosive Devices (IEDs)—though included—are, however, not the only source of concern. Cyberspace or internet platforms are also a problem because they create strength and offer the insurgents an opportunity to even upend or narrow the gap in the asymmetric relationship between them and the nation-state. With respect to IEDs, the epigrammatic lamentation at the beginning of this chapter was that of Brigadier General Joe Ramirez Jr.; then, the deputy commanding general of the Combined Arms Training Center at the Fort Leavenworth, Kansas. Like Ramirez Jr., General Stanley McChrystal (as seen earlier) had also agonized over the unexpected transmutation of the war in Iraq from the conventional into a dispiriting insurgency in which the insurgents began to use IEDs, amongst other unconventional tactics, to nullify all the conventional or traditional strategies the U.S. military knew and had planned.

Yet, it is often taken for granted that the conflicts between the state and sub-state entities or insurgents are asymmetric in nature. But one pragmatic question that must be asked here, and, of course, with an answer proffered, is this, in the face of IEDs and virtual or cyberspace, what is really asymmetric about the so-called asymmetric conflict between insurgents and the nation-state? Although the asymmetric imagery in all of this can convey the notion of an irreversible "inequality", practical experience seems to suggest otherwise; that is, the insurgents are really giving the nation-state a run for its money. Otherwise, the nation-state in all the known theaters of engagement across the world, be it in the Chechen Province of Russia, the Middle East, or the northeast region of Nigeria, would have long walloped the insurgents and cruised home to victory. The fact that this has not easily happened is a testament to the fact that although the nation-state has a conventional superior firepower, the insurgents have continued to be an unceasing nuisance.

Thus, the relationship between a nation-state and a sub-nation-state can be theoretically asymmetrical, but this asymmetry can be erased in the real world, especially in the world of the weak nation-state; as, for instance, a sub-national group like the Islamic State of Iraq, Syria, and the Levant (ISIS, ISIL), an

4 See Michael Byers (2005), *War Law . . .*, pp. 124–125, op. cit.

5 See Peter Schwartzstein in "Syria Superbugs: Bashar al-Assad's War in Syria Could Produce Something Far More Deadly Than ISIS, the End of Antibiotics", *Newsweek*, September 23, 2016, pp. 18–21.

umbrella organization of Sunni insurgency group controlled by the al-Qaeda,[6] have proved to be a nightmare to the state of Iraq and Syria; and even the U.S.- and Arab nations–led multinational force that confront them. This is also true of the Boko Haram in Nigeria. In fact, in the Iraqi conflict in particular, it was by dint of the use of IEDs that the ISIS significantly humbled American power (the way the Taliban also did in Afghanistan), ostensibly Vietnamizing the wars in the sense of creating a quagmire in these places for superpower Washington. The characteristic American "Old Testament warfare, applied with overwhelming force and done with quickly"[7] has been practically neutralized in these places.

Whereas the U.S. army is trained to fight in conventional or traditional warfare, insurgency "is an interlocking system of political, economic, psychological and military actions" that tend to doom the Americans to failure despite their overwhelming firepower.[8] In Iraq, the IED industry has dozens of bomb factories; and the only metric that mattered to the operators of the industry is the number of American casualties, having killed at least 230 American service personnel in April and May 2007; just after the start of the "President Bush's surge strategy to quell the bloody Shiite-Sunni war".[9] The insurgents are "an increasingly sophisticated and tenacious enemy" that unleash "a flurry of new or rarely used tactics and innovations designed to maximize the death toll" amongst American forces.[10] They gird for battle against American forces in Baghdad and beyond, hiding lots of IEDs and car bombs, and rapidly deploying ahead in strategic areas, including fully built neighbourhoods, conscious of the fact that "once the Americans were fully deployed, it would be hard to move bombs around".[11]

It was truly by dint of the IEDs that in both Afghanistan and Iraq, the insurgents have brought wars to the streets.[12] In urban setting of Iraq, for instance, these insurgents have creatively undermined "the U.S. military's high-tech tools" because the urban terrain suits "the militants' low cunning", using IEDs.[13] As part of the insurgents' "cataclysmic showdown" with American forces in Iraq, IEDs are buried in garbage dumps (which can defeat devices meant to locate the bombs) in the streets of Baghdad, while "discarded refrigerators on the curb could be packed with explosives; so much so that "every parked car is potentially

6 See Bobby Ghosh in "The Enemy's New Tools" . . ., pp. 31–32, op. cit.
7 See P. H. Liotta (2009), "Takin' It to the Streets: Hydra Networks, Chaos Strategies, and the 'New' Asymmetry", in Jeffrey H. Norwitz (2009, ed.); *Pirates, Terrorists, and Warlords* . . ., p. 414, op. cit.
8 Loc. Cit.
9 See Bobby Ghosh in "The Enemy's New Tools" . . ., p. 32, op. cit.
10 Loc. Cit.
11 Loc. Cit.
12 See P. H. Liotta (2009), "Takin' It to the Streets: Hydra Networks, Chaos Strategies, and the 'New' Asymmetry", in Jeffrey H. Norwitz (2009, ed.); *Pirates, Terrorists, and Warlords* . . ., p. 414, op. cit.
13 See Bobby Ghosh in "The Enemy's New Tools" . . ., p. 33, op. cit.

a vehicle-borne IED (military jargon for a car bomb)".[14] IEDs are also buried in loose rubbles and stacked with human feces to foreclose any inclination to inquire or investigate it too closely; and they are also hidden in human cadavers to booby-trap American soldiers, who, inclined, especially to retrieve the bodies of fallen colleagues, fall victim when the explosives are detonated.[15]

The detonation of these dirty bombs is usually accomplished by the insurgents, using remote-control devices made from primitive tools—"soldering irons, old printed circuit boards, discarded TV remotes and other bits of electronic detritus".[16] Instruments of death are, thus, fashioned from crude implements such as these: including "turning an old toy walkie-talkie into a trigger for an explosion 90 meters away or programming a washing machine timer to set off an IED two hours later".[17] Bombs are also buried deep in the dirt tracks on the outskirts of Baghdad used by American patrol teams; and, in the cities, they are "planted in sewers and irrigation culverts" so that "their concrete lining would direct most of the force of the explosion upwards—enough to turn an Abrams tank into an airplane".[18] Although, there were reportedly no reports that an Abrams tank had been taken out by IEDs since the onset of the insurgency, there were, however, "anecdotal evidence" that deeply buried bombs have devastating effects on other heavily armoured American vehicles.[19]

In fact, hundreds of huge IEDs are known to be more destructive than the armour-piercing bombs that the United States believes are smuggled into Iraq from Iran.[20] As very potent roadside bombs, IEDs are reckoned with to have accounted for roughly 80% of American deaths in Iraq.[21] The United States has often been pushed to respond to the havocs wrecked by this sort of dirty weapon by deploying heavy or "ham-handed" tactics; but this has often (and this is unfortunate) resulted in heavy casualties amongst the civilian population since hostilities in asymmetric warfare is historically "conducted in close proximity to civilian settlements".[22] It is in the context of this ham-handedness and the resultant collateral damage that "blowbacks" cannot be exclusive to the use of armed drones. Any weapon, whether conventional or unconventional, that creates the impression of ham-handedness, especially with some high collateral damage, can also alienate the local population and draw some sympathy to the insurgents/terrorists; even though these insurgents/terrorists also use the IEDs to wreak havoc on the civilian populace too.

14 Ibid.
15 Loc. Cit.
16 Ibid., p. 31.
17 Loc. Cit.
18 Ibid., pp. 32–33.
19 Ibid., p. 33.
20 Ibid., p. 32.
21 Loc. Cit.
22 See Stephen C. Small (2000), "Small Arms and Asymmetric Threats" . . ., p. 34, op. cit.

Cyberspace

As dirty weapons go, the IEDs are not the only one of its kind as far as obnoxiousness is concerned. Cyberspace/internet as an avenue for online recruitment and radicalization of terrorists is also an illicit platform to the extent that jihadists use it for "agitation and propaganda, intelligence collection and dissemination, communication, training, indoctrination, identity shaping, community building and crime".[23] Apart from economic contradictions, it is in cyberspace that globalization also lends itself as an instrument for the exacerbation of terrorism. With cyberspace in the globalizing world, the Caliphate that ISIS seeks may no longer be strictly territorial but also exist in the digital sense with the terror group's loss of territory.

And as an arena for "deploying a new asymmetric weapon"—a new asymmetric weapon in the sense that "influence operations [particularly radicalization as a sort of influence] takes place in cyberspace"[24]—cyberspace enables operations on multiple levels: communications channel, facilitation of information storage and retrieval; and, perhaps, more importantly, people can "live, play and find companionship in the internet; communities form on the internet and loyalties emerge, often created by a common perceived enemy or through hatred for other communities, societies and cultures".[25]

This explains why any serious national security consideration must take the world of cyber security very seriously as a zone of cooperation.[26] In the operations of terrorists/jihadists, their community in cyberspace "has taken on aspects of a nation called the Virtual Umma";[27] and this is in this context of using the cyberspace to facilitate storage and retrieval of information, that Al-Awki, though dead from the United States drone strikes long ago, still influences the Virtual Umma greatly as his toxic messages still remain in cyberspace, inspiring terrorists against the United States, from the Boston Marathon bombers, to the San Bernardino shooters, and Omar Mateen, the Orlando gay nightclub shooter without anybody being able as at yet to take the messages down. In fact, this is the context that Michael Hayden (U.S. former Director of the National Security

23 See A. Aaron Weisburd (undated), "Jihadist Use of Internet and Implications for Counterterrorism Efforts", in Enrich Marquardt and Christopher Heffelfinger (undated, ed.); *Terrorism & Political Islam: Origin, Ideologies, and Methods* . . ., p. 397, op. cit.

24 See Massimo Calabresi in "The Trouble Maker: Putin Is Now Donald Trump's Problem", *Time* (New York), January 16, 2017, p. 20, Brackets mine.

25 See A. Aaron Weisburd (undated), "Jihadist Use of Internet and Implications for Counterterrorism Efforts", in Enrich Marquardt and Christopher Heffelfinger (undated, ed.); *Terrorism & Political Islam: Origin, Ideologies, and Methods* . . ., p. 397, op. cit.

26 See Admiral James Stavridis in "The U.S. Should Form a Closer Military Alliance with Israel", *Time* (New York), January 16, 2017, p. 16.

27 See A. Aaron Weisburd (undated), "Jihadist Use of Internet and Implications for Counterterrorism Efforts", in Enrich Marquardt and Christopher Heffelfinger (undated, ed.); *Terrorism & Political Islam: Origin, Ideologies, and Methods* . . ., p. 397, op. cit.

Agency and the CIA) referred to cyberspace as "cyber weapons", indeed, "special weapons".[28]

As a weapon, cyberspace is also a domain; and just like the other three domains (Land, Sea, Air, and Space), it has its own peculiar characteristics, and some of these characteristics include the fact that it is not only "inherently global" and "inherently strategic", it is also "characterized by great speed and great maneuverability", so much so that "it favors the offense".[29] Just as in the domain or operational environment of the air force, the prevalent concern is "air dominance and air superiority", in the domain of cyberspace, the dominant concern is about "information dominance and information superiority"; in which, according to Hayden, the United States (and, indeed, any other sophisticated power) seeks "to use it for our purposes when we want to, and deny its use to others when we choose to".[30] It is this capacity of a nation to use the cyberspace for whatever purposes it chooses and to deny its use to others whenever it chooses that sums up the concept of the cyberspace domain and cyberspace dominance.[31]

But here again, it becomes, indeed, pretty difficult to measure symmetry and asymmetry in insurgency and counter-insurgency because insurgents/terrorists have also moved into cyberspace (and with war being both a condition and a contention[32]) where the success or otherwise of the "combatants" is neither a function of the available resources nor the number of men engaged in the conflict. Success in cyberspace conflict is rather more of a function of skill, being technologically savvy or dexterous, either in the positive or negative or destructive sense. In fact, it has been remarked that "ISIS's command of the online battlefield rests on its use of social media to attract and indoctrinate", and that "this is the dark side of globalization".[33] On Thursday, June 16, 2016, the Federal Government of Nigeria raised an alarm, alerting Nigerians on the existence of a new mobile application (APP) that was developed by the ISIS "for propagating jihad to children".[34]

The Nigerian Minister of Information and Culture, Lai Mohammed, reportedly explained that "the mobile application, tagged 'Huroof' (Arabic alphabet or letters), is to be used by [the] group to teach children the Arabic alphabets

28 See Michael V. Hayden (2016), *Playing to the Edge: American Intelligence in the Age of Terror*, New York, Penguin Press, p. 147.

29 Ibid., p. 128.

30 Loc. Cit.

31 Ibid., p. 129.

32 See Fred Aja Agwu (2005), *United Nations System, State Practice and the Jurisprudence of the Use of Force . . .*, pp. 25–33, op. cit.

33 See David Von Drehle in "Beating ISIS: The War against the Terror Group Requires the Kind of Leadership That Has Gone Missing", *Time* (New York), November 30–December 7, 2015, p. 26.

34 See "Govt. Raises the Alarm on ISIS' Indoctrination of Children", *The Guardian* (Lagos), Friday, June 17, 2016, p. 11.

with the aid of guns, military tanks and cannons".[35] In fact, the ISIS' "nimble social media campaign resonates" with its followers and sympathizers around the world.[36] This explains why it has been able to build support bases and "staked its black flag in parts of Afghanistan, Algeria, Egypt, Libya, Nigeria, Pakistan, Russia, Saudi Arabia and Yemen"; with U.S. intelligence fearing that Bangladesh, Indonesia, Somalia, and Tunisia might be next in the execution of their global strategy of expanding their affiliations and motivating people to kill their fellow citizens.[37] Apart from being the domain for recruitment and radicalization of extremists, cyberspace conflicts (the attacks therein) happen to blunt the capacity for information warfare that has since been "considerably facilitated by the revolution in information and communication technologies"[38] that are now deployed by both the state and non-state actors seeking to use or control the local population that is key to asymmetric warfare.[39]

The cyberspace has made the notion of territorial sanctuary or safe haven for insurgents very outdated. The 9/11 attacks in the United States was a defining moment that facilitated this transition or change of bases (safe havens) for the al-Qaeda and many insurgents from the territorial (the so-called ungoverned space) to the cyberspace. As soon as 9/11 happened, the United States invaded Afghanistan and by December 7, 2001, had routed or overthrown the Taliban regime in Afghanistan with the attendant disruption of the al-Qaeda infrastructure in that country.[40] In fact, "the loss of that sanctuary was a major setback—a strategic defeat—[for the al-Qaeda] and the embryonic global insurgency it was facilitating from that Afghan base".[41] It was while faced with this challenge of loss of territory that the al-Qaeda began seeking to innovate and adapt; it hence replicated what it had lost in Afghanistan in the internet. That is, it employed "the Internet to establish in cyberspace a virtual sanctuary from which to carry out many of the activities they had initiated from their Afghan base in 1996–2001".[42]

Prominent amongst these activities is the attracting and radicalization on line of its members or jihadists in small groups.[43] Cyberspace makes the terrorists to be increasingly evasive, particularly because they now communicate electronically with increased encryption of their messages.[44] And with sanctuaries now

35 Loc. Cit. Brackets mine.
36 See Mark Thompson in "War on ISIS Update . . .", p. 13, op. cit.
37 Loc. Cit.
38 See Teodor Frunzeti (2013), "Asymmetric, Unconventional and Hybrid Actions . . .", p. 9, op. cit.
39 Ibid., p. 10.
40 See Richard Shultz (2009), "Virtual Sanctuary Enables Global Insurgency", in Jeffrey H. Norwitz (2009, ed.); *Pirates, Terrorists, and Warlords* . . ., p. 425, op. cit.
41 Loc. Cit. Brackets mine.
42 Loc. Cit.
43 See "How to Fight Back . . .", p. 13, op. cit.
44 Loc. Cit; see also Haley Sweetl and Edwards in "Encryption: Can Silicon Valley Help", *Time* (New York), November 30–December 7, 2015, p. 31.

in cyberspace, it is beginning to be clear that it may be unnecessary for victim countries to lob cruise missiles in suspected insurgents' training camps in the so-called ungoverned or inadequately governed territories as did the United States in Afghanistan and Sudan in the wake of the Dar es Salam and Nairobi twin or simultaneous bombing of American embassies.[45] The consequence of this reality, as *The Economist* put it, is that "counter-terrorism strategies that worked before may prove less effective" against groups like ISIS that have cultivated and honed their deployment of cyberspace to consummate their terrorist activities.[46]

Cyberspace, like weak states, is a boon to terrorism. The United States policy strategies on counter-terrorism seriously reckon with the fact that weak states are vulnerable to terrorism.[47] This explains why, in Indonesia, for instance, support and the joining of ISIS was done without the government's capacity to act, being, in any case, not considered illegal; and in Malaysia, the government itself "thoroughly politicized Islam, leaving little room for dissent from its harshest rules",[48] thus creating an environment of extremism and terrorism. Terrorist havens like the Niger Delta (as did the United States Deputy Assistant Secretary of Defence for African Affairs, Theresa Whelan, and U.S. General James Jones (testifying before the Senate Armed Services Committee), are often described as "ungoverned spaces".[49] Similarly, *The Economist* also believes that Southeast Asia is a region that "offers plenty of remote areas outside state control in which militants can hide [like the Philippine island of Mindanao and southern Thailand]".[50]

The logic of "ungoverned spaces" is that they are breeding grounds and convenient abodes from where terrorists stage their attacks. But with cyberspace, this theory of "ungoverned spaces" has extended beyond territorial spaces like Waziristan and many failed and/or collapsed and, thus, ineffectively governed nations around the world. For one, as developed and effectively mapped out with the GPS technology as it is, the United States is not an (and does not have any) "ungoverned space", yet terrorists are bred and plan their operations from within this very powerful and fully governed country, the San Bernardino (Calif.) attacks in December 2015, amongst others, being very instructive. Thus, cyberspace is the quintessential ungoverned space that is used as an intractable haven for terrorists. For one, according to Michael Hayden, there is lacking, "a Lockean social contract in the cyber domain", thus making the place "an almost purely Hobbesian universe, a universe where Hobbes' description of ungoverned life as 'poor, nasty, brutish and short' really applies".[51] This explains why "web extremism" persists and the operators of the various social media sites have been unable

45 See Josef Joffe in "Asymmetric Warfare . . .", p. 47, op. cit.
46 See "Singapore . . .", p. 44, op. cit.
47 See Fred Aja Agwu (2009), *National Interest, International Law* . . ., pp. 237–238, op. cit.
48 See "Singapore . . .", p. 44, op. cit.
49 See Fred Aja Agwu (2009), *National Interest, International Law* . . ., p. 230, op. cit.
50 See "Singapore . . .", p. 44, op. cit. Brackets mine.
51 See Michael V. Hayden (2016), *Playing to the Edge* . . ., p. 132, op. cit.

to take down or tackle this genre of extremism.[52] This has resulted in a new kind of metastasized threat on the social media.[53]

Despite the efforts of many European countries (in the wake of the surge in the al-Qaeda and ISIS-inspired attacks) "to institute a more secular-oriented Islamic culture in their various countries, the human links with Pakistan through satellite television and online learning" was a big drag that has continued to militate against this effort.[54] And web extremism in particular thrives because cyberspace is hugely unregulated, which has led to the incidence and rise of "the digital madrassa".[55] The digital madrassa is exemplified by the Sirat-ul-Mustaqeen, "a madrassa in a run-down part of Rawalpindi in the Pakistani Punjab" whose teachers work round-the-clock "to spread the message of Islam".[56] At the close of work when its pupils are home in bed, the "teachers use Skype to connect to homes in Britain, France, Norway and Sweden, where teenagers attempt to read the unfamiliar Arabic script of the Koran"; online sessions that many European parents find "more convenient than after-school classes at the local mosque".[57]

This digital approach to Islamic education may have seemed convenient for these European parents but the "digital madrassa is also a convenient tool in the hands of "web extremists" to recruit and radicalize a generation of adherents. This is more so when these "online Koranic academies" can easily be distorted, perverted, and put to inappropriate use because they "range from one-man affairs to institutions more like call-centers, with IT managers and teachers working shift"[58] possibly for purposes of retaining clients, and in the process of which some extremists seeking "to return to the perceived purity of seventh-century Islam . . . in some respects similar to the Wahhabism of Saudi Arabia"[59] may take control of the religious instruction. This is not only a probability, it is a possibility that has often turned into a reality, leading to the epidemic of radicalized youths that have embraced the ideology of the al-Qaeda and the ISIS, along with these groups' affiliates like the al-Nusra and the Boko Haram.

Like the toxic message of the late American-born al-Qaeda henchman, Al-Awlaki, that lingers in cyberspace and continue to radicalize and win adherents to the radical Islam and militancy he espoused, Nigeria's President Mohammadu

52 This is an argument by one of the interlocutors in an *Aljazeera* documentary entitled *Drone*, monitored in Lagos (Nigeria) on Monday, August 22, 2016, between 9pm and 10pm local time, op. cit.

53 Anne Marie Slaughter talking to Fareed Zakaria on GPS programme during the 15th anniversary of 9/11, CNN, monitored in Lagos (Nigeria) on September 11, 2016, 3pm–4pm local time.

54 See "Islamic Education in Europe . . .", p. 45, op. cit.

55 See "World-Wide Mullahs: The Rise of the Digital Madrassa", *The Economist*, August 20, 2016, p. 46.

56 Loc. Cit.

57 Loc. Cit.

58 Loc. Cit.

59 Loc. Cit.

Buhari, once reportedly confessed that "despite the damage done so far to the capacity of the insurgents [the Boko Haram], their warped ideologies still linger through personal contacts [in the] social media".[60] Meanwhile, as Nigeria signed a Memorandum of Understanding (MoU) with Huawei Technologies, the Secretary to the government, Babachir Lawal, confessed that the much the country had successfully done in prosecuting its counter-insurgency was with the aid of Information and Communication Technology (ICT) that enables the navigation of cyberspace.[61] This, however, is not to suggest that, to the terrorist, the cyberspace is a substitute for territory. Territory is still very critical to the continued functioning of insurgents, especially in the mounting of terrorism campaigns. This is why the ISIS strongly holds onto and defends Mosul in Iraq and Raqqa in Syria.

And as *The Economist* contends, it uses these territories to raise money, attract, train, and coordinate thousands of its terrorists; in addition, the fact is that "for as long as it controls its would-be capital, Raqqa, and the Iraqi city of Mosul", the ISIS would remain "a symbolic 'homeland' for radical Muslims".[62] For these and many more reasons, terrorists strive to keep territories, even in uninhabited territories like the Sambisa Forest in northeast Nigeria, the Rafin Sanyi Forest in Kaduna State (north central Nigeria), and the Bagoma Forest in Niger State (Nigeria), the latter two of which also play host to bandits and kidnappers.[63] Territories that are controlled by terrorists or territories that offer them havens are often termed "ungoverned" by the West and used as a ploy or ideological justification for intervention. So, the fact that the ISIS continued the defence of its territories (withstanding the world's superpowers: the U.S.-led coalition and Russia) was a source of potent inspiration to its adherents and the entire world of extremism and jihad.[64]

But the West and, of course, the whole world of counter-insurgency was determined to deny the ISIS the territories it held because these territories offered it the oxygen for self-sustenance. Since the Iraqi government, supported by the United States, ramped up the military operations in October/November 2016, which led to the crumbling of the Caliphate, the contraction and loss of territory by the ISIS, that territorial loss of Tikrit, Erbil, Ramadi, Fallujah, and Mosul, amongst other Iraqi cities (what *Newsweek* described as the "rubble-izing" of Sunni cities in Iraq and Syria), severely hurt and disrupted the terrorist organization by decreasing "the

60 See Mohammed Abubakar, Karis Tsokar, and Kelvin Ebiri in "Washington Cautions against Excessive Force on Extremists", *The Guardian* (Lagos), Wednesday, August 24, 2016, p. 6. Parentheses mine.

61 See Karis Tsokar in "FG Links Success in Counter-Insurgency, Anti-Graft Crusade to ICT", *The Guardian* (Lagos), Wednesday, August 24, 2016, p. 4.

62 See "How to Fight Back . . .", p. 14, op. cit. Brackets mine.

63 See Maryam Ahmadu-Suka, "Birnin Gwari Bandits Return with a Vengeance", *Daily Trust* (Abuja), Saturday, October 29, 2016, p. 15.

64 See "How to Fight Back . . .", p. 14, op. cit.

flow of foreign fighters attracted to the group".[65] Apart from this loss of territories bringing about the decrease of the ISIS's "ability to pull off significant attacks", thus, damaging and eroding the prestige that attended fighting for it,[66] the terrorist group also suffered "the loss of "face" associated with battlefield defeats".[67]

As "the Iraqi government, backed by U.S. airpower and special operations forces", and supported by the Kurdish peshmerga, methodically retook the Iraqi Sunni heartland cities aforementioned and rolled back if not diminished or extinguished the territories held by the Caliphate, it clearly became unfashionable to fight for the ISIS in the absence of that territorial space.[68] Hence, "the flow of foreign fighters going" to the Caliphate dwindled; and instead of the $500 a month paid to fighters (with a gift of a cell phone and a car) after taking Mosul, ISIS began to conscript "locals for $50 a month"—but even at that, it had "fallen three months behind . . . in paying even that amount".[69] The foregoing illustrates the enduring importance of territory over cyberspace in the activities of terrorists. The acquisition of territory (which is enabled by the existence of chaos) provides a backbone for terrorist insurgency. However, the existence of cyberspace provides some form of atonement to terrorist insurgents, for terrorists can create a terrorism beachhead there whenever they lose territory. For instance, the ISIS is feared to be capable, in the event of its loss of a physical Caliphate, of realizing a cyber-caliphate where it can retreat to continue its radicalization of vulnerable individuals and the sending of lone wolves to Europe, the United States, Asia, and, of course, other Middle East countries.[70]

But another illustration of the importance of territory to terrorist insurgency was recorded in the wake of the institutional collapse in Yemen as "military forces backed by a Saudi Arabia-led coalition" battled "the Houthi rebels who seized much of the country in 2014 and 2015"; thus, prompting the Al-Qaeda in the Arabian Peninsula (AQAP) to benefit "from the security vacuum created by the Yemen's . . . civil war" by gathering some territory that made it to begin to plot to attack the United States homeland again.[71] Yemen had descended into or assumed the character of the West's so-called ungoverned space—its ideological ploy for unilateral intervention. As the largest threat to the West, AQAP's acquisition of territory in civil war-stricken Yemen was particularly enabled by the fact

65 See Bill Powell, Mahmoud Shikh Ibrahim, Jack Moore, and Mirren Gidda in "The New ISIS Crisis" . . ., p. 30, op. cit.

66 Loc. Cit.

67 Ibid., p. 32.

68 Ibid., p. 28.

69 Loc. Cit.

70 This is the perspective of Fareed Zakaria in his GPS programme, CNN, February 26, 2017, monitored in Lagos, Nigeria, from 9pm–10pm, local time.

71 See Jared Malsin in "Al-Qaeda Is Gathering Strength as Yemen Burns", *Time* (New York), February 20, 2017, p. 9.

that the "U.S. shifted resources to the fight against ISIS in 2014–2015" in Iraq and Syria.[72]

But apparently the only snag in driving the ISIS out of the territories it holds is the paradox that "modern armies are good at driving jihadists off territory, even if they are bad in rebuilding countries afterwards".[73] This has been witnessed in Afghanistan and in Iraq; the latter (Iraq) of which, in the bid to drive not out just Saddam Hussein but also the al-Qaeda, the United States virtually destroyed the Iraqi State and was unable to rebuild it. This partly led to the rise of the ISIS. Later in 2016, in the second liberation of Iraqi Sunni territories from the ISIS, another snag was created. The reclamation of the territory that was taken by the ISIS created the situation in which, with that loss of territory or its Caliphate, the ISIS treacherously morphed into a network, looking more like the al-Qaeda, recruiting fighters that flow back into the West, fighters with tremendous skills in using car bombs and "weaponized chemical stuff",[74] and fighters that constitute "more than 300 sleepers" from the Middle East region to different Western nations.[75]

However, there still exists, some remnant of hopes that "the loss of territory will diminish ISIS's ability to pull off high-profile, mass-casualty attacks—just as Al-Qaeda's loss of its sanctuary in Afghanistan after 9/11 did".[76] As a matter of fact, the top leadership of the al-Qaeda had told al-Baghdadi (leader of the ISIS) that it was easier to maintain a network.[77] The al-Qaeda leadership had warned Baghdadi against the folly in instantly creating and trying to maintain a physical Caliphate because it would be unsustainable, and trite to say that the West would descend on it and destroy it.[78] So, even though AQAP had taken territory in Yemen and even launched offensives in "towns in the southern Abyan province", it had relied heavily on its networks for far-flung attacks, like "the 2015 attack on the offices of *Charlie Hebdo* in Paris" and the increasing "intent on striking Americans in the U.S., with [its leader, Qassim] al-Rimi urging followers to "burn the land beneath their [Americans] feet".[79]

Radicalism/Radicalization

The weaponization of radicalism and radicalization by terrorists is an integral part of terrorist insurgency. It is this instrument of terror that is behind Emily Feldman's catastrophic prediction that "ISIS's Caliphate may be crumbling, but

72 Loc. Cit.

73 See "How to Fight Back . . .", p. 14, op. cit.

74 See Bill Powell, Mahmoud Shikh Ibrahim, Jack Moore, and Mirren Gidda in "The New ISIS Crisis" . . ., pp. 30–31, op. cit.

75 Ibid., p. 31.

76 Ibid., p. 30.

77 Loc. Cit.

78 Loc. Cit.

79 See Jared Malsin in "Al-Qaeda Is Gathering Strength as Yemen Burns" . . ., p. 9, op. cit. Parentheses mine.

the thousands of children it has brainwashed could terrorize us for years".[80] The ISIS, like other terrorist groups, had "devoted extensive resources to the indoctrination of children in its territory", swiftly and methodically forcing its curriculum on schools and luring children to its training camps with gifts and propaganda videos—including the children of its supposed Yazidi and Christian enemies—brainwashing and sending them off to battle as soldiers and suicide bombers.[81] It is by dint of this indoctrination that the adherents of ISIS deem it fun to go to jihad, having been steeled in the radical interpretation of Islamic law.[82]

As a distinctive weapon category, radicalization thrives on the development of a "hatred mantra" that "positions the enemy as less than human", committing the individual or group to a radical "way of life and dedication to the cause, perceived or actual".[83] Through radicalization, people "forgo peaceful forms of protest and instead, opt to become terrorists and attempt mass-murders".[84] Whether or not with the madrassas in or outside the domains of cyberspace, radicalism and its derivative, radicalization, are very dangerous and destructive weapons in the hands of the terrorist. All terrorist organizations employ radicalism and radicalization in plying their nefarious trade—from the al-Qaeda, the ISIS, the AQIM, the al-Shabaab, and the Boko Haram.

Although extremism and radicalization are related, conceptually, a distinction can be drawn between them along the line of the British conception of extremism as a "vocal or active opposition to fundamental values, including democracy, the rule of law, individual liberty, and mutual respect and tolerance of different faiths and beliefs"; while on its part, radicalization is "the process by which an individual or group comes to adopt increasingly extreme political, social or religious ideals and aspirations that either 1) reject or undermine the status quo or 2) reject or undermine contemporary ideas and expressions of freedom of choice".[85]

So, radicalization itself is, a priori, a Siamese twin with radicalism in the sense of it being a derivative of radicalism, a process by which a person is imbued or adopts the extremist or radical mindset, the belief in radicalism.[86] Radicalization is a process of "socialization to extremism" that manifests itself in acts of terrorism.[87] For groups like the al-Qaeda and the ISIS, radicalization is a process through which they impart in their followers their notion or claim that they are

80 See Emily Feldman in "And a Child Shall Lead Them", *Newsweek*, July 14, 2017, p. 24.
81 Loc. Cit.
82 Loc. Cit.
83 See Sheila Macrine (2016), "The Psychology of Radicalization" . . ., p. 14, op. cit.
84 Loc. Cit.
85 See Akimi Scarcella, Ruairi Page, and Vivek Furtado (2016), "Terrorism, Radicalization, Extremism, Authoritarianism and Fundamentalism . . .", p. 2, op. cit.
86 See Asta Maskaliunaite (2015), "Exploring the Theories of Radicalization", *International Studies: Interdisciplinary Political and Cultural Journal*, Vol. 17, No. 1, pp. 9, 12.
87 See Alex P. Schmid (2016), "Research on Radicalization . . .", pp. 26–27, op. cit.

"acting on behalf of Islam".[88] Radicalization is therefore an instrument used by terrorists to sell their cause; and they do this through a twisted interpretation of fact, tailored for the acquisition of legitimacy for their cause.[89] Nevertheless, because as a disposition radicalism can be progressive or retrogressive, there is some whiff of controversy about the end of radicalization, that is, the end to which it serves.

Thus, it is the same way that there is "lament that there is no unified and universally accepted definition of terrorism"—which brings about a major obstacle in the efforts to tackle—that there is also lament about the lack of consensus on the end that radicalization serves.[90] In progressive terms, radicalization can be a pathway to a positive end; that is, a sensitization that imbues people with the right consciousness or awareness. As far as it concerns terrorism, radicalization is retrogressive to the extent that it is "socialization to extremism which manifests itself in terrorism"; a "process of adopting an extremist belief system, including willingness to support or use violence as a method to effect social change"; the "process by which a person comes to support terrorism and forms of extremism leading to terrorism".[91] In this context, people are radicalized to use terrorism in pursuit of their cause, be it a nationalist/separatist cause, or a religious cause, the former represented by African nationalist or decolonization movements and the European left-wing organizations like ETA, the PKK, and the Basque, while the latter is represented by groups like the al-Qaeda and the ISIS, amongst others.[92]

Through radicalization, very vulnerable people are brainwashed or sensitized by extremist ideologies of either secular or religious movements to attack state symbols (like the police and soldiers as is the case with the Kurd's resistance group—the PKK) in Turkey—also known in Syria as the YPG and in Iraq as the Persmega; or attack the civilian population, as is the case with the al-Qaeda and the ISIS.[93] Hence, as "a pathway to terrorism, [a] gradual slide into extremism, fundamentalism, or even more generally, a movement towards justifying violence and finally personally engaging in it", radicalization is also the "development of beliefs, feelings and actions in support of any group or cause in a conflict"; indeed, it is "what goes on before the bomb goes off",[94] the "Black Box which contains the riddle of 'what goes on before the bomb goes off", a phrase formulated by Peter Neumann of the London-based International Center for the study of Radicalization (ICSR).[95]

88 See Anthony Richards (2015), "From Terrorism to 'Radicalization' to 'Extremism' . . .", p. 372, op. cit.

89 See Fred Aja Agwu (2016), *Nations among Nations* . . ., p. 563, op. cit.

90 See Asta Maskaliunaite (2015), "Exploring the Theories of Radicalization" . . ., pp. 11–12, op. cit.

91 Ibid., p. 12.

92 See Anthony Richards (2015), "From Terrorism to 'Radicalization' to 'Extremism' . . .", p. 377, op. cit.

93 Loc. Cit.

94 See Asta Maskaliunaite (2015), "Exploring the Theories of Radicalization" . . ., p. 12, op. cit.

95 See Alex P. Schmid (2016), "Research on Radicalization . . .", p. 27, op. cit.

The basic elements or ingredients in the dynamics of radicalization include ideological socialization away from the mainstream, political socialization, mobilization, and recruitment, and ultimately a conversion process to be inclined to conflict escalation.[96] The main portals or platforms for radicalization are the prisons, the mosques and madrassas, the internet and other social media outlets.[97] It is an acknowledged fact that the Iraqi authorities and the United States run prisons in Iraq that "acted as incubators for radicalization".[98] Of course, the most recognizably notorious among these Iraqi prisons that acted as "incubators for radicalization" was "in Camp Bucca, the infamous US-run prison near Umm Qasr in Southern Iraq" where the ISIS leader, Abu Bakr al-Baghdadi, also spent time.[99] The propensity or vulnerability to radicalization is usually conditioned by some internal or external (environmental) dynamics. In other words, radicalization is both a function of the "enabling environment" and the "vulnerable individual"; something that happens at the "intersection of an enabling environment and a personal trajectory".[100]

Whereas the internal dimension to radicalism and radicalization, especially for those embarking martyrdom through suicide missions, entails some personality modifications that are related to the expectation of rewards or the gratification "of the flesh in the afterlife [like the promise of the alleged dozens, about 70 virgins], seemingly unattainable in their societies";[101] the latter (the external influence in radicalization) consisting of such factors as the "foreign policy, historical legacies and cultural disagreements";[102] much of which is, for instance, adumbrated by the United States' foreign policy in the Middle East with respect to the Israeli-Palestinian conflict, the historical legacies of Anglo-French imperialism represented by the Sykes-Picot lines in the sand, and the clash of civilization narrative. In fact, U.S. vice admiral Lowell E. Jacoby, director of the Defense Intelligence Agency (DIA), had in 2005 unequivocally told the Senate Select Committee on Intelligence that "our policies in the Middle East fuel Islamic resentment".[103]

It is narratives of this nature that "serve as a springboard for resentment—most prominently, the notion of the unjust occupation of the Muslim nations of Iraq and Afghanistan".[104] As far as the explication of the substance of radicalization as a weapon is concerned, Fawaz Gerges offers an important view on why the ISIS

96 Loc. Cit.
97 Ibid., p. 28.
98 See Fawaz A. Gerges (2016), *ISIS: A History* . . ., p. 84, op. cit.
99 Ibid., p. 85.
100 See Alex P. Schmid (2016), "Research on Radicalization . . .", p. 27, op. cit.
101 See Sheila Macrine (2016), "The Psychology of Radicalization" . . ., p. 14, op. cit. Brackets mine.
102 See Asta Maskaliunaite (2015), "Exploring the Theories of Radicalization" . . ., p. 10, op. cit.
103 See Fawaz A. Gerges (2016), *ISIS: A History* . . ., p. 84, op. cit.
104 See Sheila Macrine (2016), "The Psychology of Radicalization" . . ., p. 14, op. cit.

makes a huge success of it. According to Fawaz, by the ISIS's use of the strategy of radicalization to present itself as "a powerful vanguard movement capable of delivering victory and salvation", it offers "alienated Muslim youths a utopian worldview and a political project"—the resurrection of the lost Caliphate.[105] It is, therefore, through the process of radicalization that the idea of the Caliphate, a political institution that was disposed of [by the Sykes-Picot lines in the sand] in the 1920s with the emergence of Turkey, [took] hold of the imagination of many Sunni Islamists who see it as redemptive, a means to salvation, and a worthy cause to do jihad for.[106]

And as Fawaz further reiterates, "at the heart of this utopian longing for the imagined Caliphate is the feeling of some Muslims that the modern nation-state has failed to build a just and inclusive order".[107] Hence, the extremists had to resort to this "sophisticated outreach campaign and strategy". This weapon of radicalization has remained a very potent weapon where the "ISIS's efficacy in attracting young recruits from around the world lies"; and through which "the group appeals to disaffected and disadvantaged Sunni youths around the world, who are often dealing with issues concerning their identities".[108] When taken together, the internal and external/environmental dynamics have made radicalization against Western societies a fad in the Middle East, a phenomenon that only grew more intense with the wave of conflicts in the region that came with the "Arab Spring", particularly the start of the Syrian civil war, the emergence of the ISIS, which witnessed "the influx of [radicalized] 'foreign fighters' with European passports".[109]

In the northeast of Nigeria—the hotbed of the Boko Haram insurgency—the insurgents' captives, especially women and children, are routinely gathered, addressed, and subjected "to series of lectures and preaching, all designed to indoctrinate them"—with the preaching tailored to incite and sometimes "accompanied by threats of decapitation should any of them attempt to escape".[110] In the indoctrination process, the terrorists urge their "supporters to take the law into their own hands" and particularly, as does the ISIS, call on "Muslims in the West to kill their countrymen", exhorting them that: "if you can kill a disbelieving American or European—especially the spiteful and filthy French—or an Australian, or a Canadian, then rely upon Allah and kill him in any manner or way, however it may be".[111] This hateful message is similar

105 See Fawaz A. Gerges (2016), *ISIS: A History* . . ., p. 46, op. cit.

106 Loc. Cit.

107 Loc. Cit.

108 Loc. Cit.

109 See Asta Maskaliunaite (2015), "Exploring the Theories of Radicalization" . . ., p. 10, op. cit. Parentheses mine.

110 See Abubakar Adam Ibrahim in "The Girl Who Defied Boko Haram", *Daily Trust* (Abuja), Saturday, October 29, 2016, p. 10.

111 See Fawaz A. Gerges (2016), *ISIS: A History* . . ., p. 230, op. cit.

to the al-Qaeda's religious doctrine of calling on every Muslim to "kill the Americans and their allies in every country", which is tantamount to "sanctioning lethal and mass casualty attacks against . . . virtually open-ended category of targets".[112]

It was in reaction to this sort of radical and hateful narrative that many countries began countering the terrorists with opposing narratives in the Countering Violent Extremism (CVE) strategy, which not only include such security tips like if you "see something; say something", but also "a sustained effort at the integration of marginalized Muslims" while weaning them away from vitriolic messages.[113] In 2010, the European Commission set up a Radicalization Awareness Network (RAN)—"an EU-wide umbrella network of practitioners engaged to prevent" and promote "counter-radicalization to violent extremism".[114] Since then RAN's Center of Excellence (RAN CoE) has become "a hub in connecting, developing and disseminating expertise" that "seeks to develop a state-of-the-art knowledge on de-radicalization.[115] However, despite the existence of RAN, there is still "no EU-wide programme to tackle the challenges of re-integrating" the numerous men and women that return from the Middle East after fighting with the ISIS.[116] But the dilemma that the EU faces with these brainwashed fighters returning from Syria is that in Belgium, for instance:

> [A]ll known returning fighters are questioned by the police, with the judicial authorities then deciding whom to prosecute. Some will serve prison sentences, but in cases where there is not enough evidence of a crime, the people will simply be returned to their home in Belgium, under varying degrees of surveillance. Then, it is up to the individual municipalities to decide how to reintegrate them. Right now, most are just leaving it to the security services.[117]

In all of this, Belgium starkly faces this dilemma, particularly in deciding whether "to treat the returning fighters as enemies of the state and potential attackers [as lone wolves], or the victims of brainwashing in need of treatment or help"[118] or de-radicalization. In other words, returning ISIS fighters are not given blanket amnesty and rehabilitated. Although the most dangerous ones are prosecuted, some still escape undetected into the society. The March 22, 2016 attacks at

112 See Anthony Richards (2015), "From Terrorism to 'Radicalization' to 'Extremism' . . .", p. 377, op. cit.
113 See Fawaz A. Gerges (2016), *ISIS: A History* . . ., pp. 230–231, op. cit.
114 See Alex P. Schmid (2016), "Research on Radicalization . . .", p. 26, op. cit.
115 Loc. Cit.
116 See Charlotte McDonald-Gibson in "The Former Neo-Nazi Helping Returning ISIS Fighters Let Go Hate" . . ., p. 36, op. cit.
117 Loc. Cit .Brackets mine.
118 Loc. Cit. Brackets mine.

Brussels Airport and the city's metro by a cell of Belgian Islamists[119] can be attributed, not only to the EU's failure in de-radicalization and re-integration owing to the non-existence of a EU-wide programme to that effect, but also to the dilemma of who to prosecute and who to de-radicalize—the dilemma in whether the so-called de-radicalization programme can actually successfully shift the hard line Islamists' allegiance away from violent jihad by challenging their belief about what it means to be a good Muslim.[120]

To appreciate what should be done in any de-radicalization programme, it must be equally appreciated that radicalization itself thrives more easily amongst the "isolated, marginalized and insecure", the frustrated and the alienated; which is why jihadists and even nationalists trawl the social media for this category of people, especially the "vulnerable youngsters".[121] In tackling the Boko Haram, the federal government of Nigeria was acutely aware of this inclination by terrorists to radicalize the most vulnerable through different portals of radicalization like the mosques and the social media. Consequently, it consistently warned the Nigerian populace to guard against this;[122] and, in fact, the regime of President Goodluck Jonathan also developed its own CVE programme in order to counteract the terrorist sect's toxic narratives.[123]

So, radicalism and radicalization essentially drive terror, particularly the lone-wolf terrorists.[124] It is in the radicalized lone wolf that terrorism has evidently witnessed a tremendous boost and transformation—"from so-called 'traditional' and relatively centralized forms (such as those of the IRA and the Basque separatist organization ETA) to the decentralized and horizontal forms where the threat is more amorphous"—manifesting in a "greater propensity for low-level 'small groups' and 'lone wolf terrorism'".[125] The danger of radicalized lone wolves is so great that President Obama—after rejoicing that it was "because of the extraordinary courage of our men and women in uniform, and the intelligence officers, law enforcement, and diplomats who support them" that no foreign terrorist organization has successfully planned and executed an attack on our homeland these past eight years"—still lamented that "Boston and Orlando remind us of how dangerous radicalization can be".[126]

In the lament aforementioned, President Obama implicitly recognized the danger of radicalism and radicalization as evasive and dangerous weapons

119 Loc. Cit.
120 See Emily Feldman in "And a Child Shall Lead Them" . . ., p. 26, op. cit.
121 See Charlotte McDonald-Gibson in "The Former Neo-Nazi Helping Returning ISIS Fighters Let Go Hate" . . ., p. 37, op. cit.
122 See Fred Aja Agwu (2016), *Nations among Nations* . . ., p. 563, op. cit.
123 Ibid., pp. 529, 564–565.
124 See Anthony Richards (2015), "From Terrorism to 'Radicalization' to 'Extremism' . . .", p. 373, op. cit.
125 Loc. Cit.
126 See "Full Text of President Obama's Farewell Speech" . . ., op. cit.

of terrorism, weapons that endlessly promote the resilience and spread of the scourge. In the same vein while expressing his vision for a revitalized United Nations, Secretary-General Antonio Guterres also lamented that in today's wars that no one wins, wars that everyone is a loser, "millions more children and young people are vulnerable to the cycle of . . . radicalization and conflict".[127] But in all of this, radicalism is an ambiguous concept that can be viewed positively or negatively, progressively or retrogressively; but either way, it is a mindset, the disposition of reformists or revolutionaries—be they construed as saints or villains—that fight for the expansion of the rights of social groups.[128]

Ideology, Radicalism, Violence, and Counter-Terrorism

It is in the foregoing context that it is recognizably self-evident that ideologies (like right-wing orientation or nationalism, left-wing orientation, and religion, etc.) have some relationships with radicalization that can be either compatible or even incompatible with terrorist acts.[129] However, although not all ideologies "have some intrinsic doctrinal connection to terrorism"—even if some religious ones are sometimes called "terrorist ideologies"—still, "there are belief-systems to which violence is integral, and there may also be ideologies that have been interpreted, adapted or distorted to explicitly justify the use of terrorism and in which terrorism may then become ideologically embedded".[130] So, the ideological dimension of radicalism can be paradoxical: although the basic character of radicalism is that "to be a radical is to reject the status quo", it is also clear that this rejection of the status quo might not necessarily be in a violent or even a problematic manner.[131]

However, "the idea of a non-violent ideology that is conducive to terrorism would seem to be something of a contradiction".[132] But the fact that there are non-violent ideologies that are conducive to terrorism makes it imperative that counter-terrorism does not increasingly or necessarily become counter-ideological;[133] otherwise, it will have huge "implications for the remit of counterterrorism".[134] By way of explication, in drawing a distinction between "extremism of thought and extremism of method or action", what often manifests is the existence of "extremist ideology that is [sometimes] non-violent but

127 See Antonio Guterres in "My Vision for a Revitalized U.N.: The New Secretary-General Calls for a Surge in Diplomacy for Peace in 2017", *Newsweek*, January 20, 2017, p. 32.
128 See Asta Maskaliunaite (2015), "Exploring the Theories of Radicalization" . . ., p. 12, note 2, op. cit.
129 See Anthony Richards (2015), "From Terrorism to 'Radicalization' to 'Extremism' . . .", p. 375, op. cit; see also Alex P. Schmid (2016), "Research on Radicalization . . .", p. 26, op. cit.
130 See Anthony Richards (2015), "From Terrorism to 'Radicalization' to 'Extremism' . . .", p. 375, op. cit.
131 Ibid., p. 378.
132 Ibid., p. 373.
133 Ibid., p. 372.
134 Ibid., pp. 373, 378.

is nevertheless deemed to be conducive to terrorism".[135] This trend is found in "those who deliberately [avoid] . . . open support for violence but knowingly [create] . . . an environment in which people can be drawn into terrorism itself".[136]

But it can also be argued that because radicalization takes place within the trajectories of this "non-violent but extremist ideology",[137] its practitioners "are surreptitiously or otherwise, culpable".[138] This is to recognize "ideology itself as a cause of terror, even where it is acknowledged that such doctrine is in and of itself non-violent".[139] The point here is that a counter-terrorism strategy that focuses on non-violent ideologies that are nevertheless conducive to terrorism (as implicit in U.S. President Trump's rhetoric and blanket travel ban) risks the alienation of "large sections of the population who might abhor the terrorist methods of Al-Qaeda and ISIS"; those who, although by implication, can be "seen as part of the terrorist problem", but could otherwise be potential, important, and effective allies in countering terrorism.[140]

As far as ideologies and terrorism go in the United States, nationalists or white supremacists share the same nuance with the al-Qaeda, but by President Trump focusing exclusively on Muslim groups like the al-Qaeda and the ISIS, "the white supremacists become emboldened" because, according to Christian Picciolini—a reformed Italian-American white supremacist—"our government just focus[es] on what they call radicalization in certain communities, and for the Muslim communities, that marginalizes them",[141] especially those of them that may be extremist in their thought, but not violent or terrorist in their actions. But beyond all of this, the notion of a non-violent ideology may be a myth after all; since the fact remains that "for a belief system itself to be conducive to terrorism, it must have at least some element of doctrinal endorsement or justification for violence, in which case one cannot legitimately refer to it as non-violent".[142]

But even if for hypothetical reasons the so-called non-violent ideologies are accepted as such, and although counter-terrorism strategies must not be too obsessed or exclusively focused on it so that it does not "impose a paradoxical situation on those who might adamantly urge peaceful methods but also simultaneously hold extremist views that are said to be conducive to terrorism",[143] the de-radicalization component of counter-terrorism must be involved in "countering non-violent ideologies"; it must "certainly be concerned with

135 Ibid., p. 371. Brackets mine.
136 Ibid., p. 372.
137 Ibid., p. 373.
138 Ibid., p. 372.
139 Ibid., p. 373.
140 Ibid., pp. 372–373.
141 See Charlotte McDonald-Gibson in "The Former Neo-Nazi Helping Returning ISIS Fighters Let Go Hate" . . ., pp. 36–37, op. cit.
142 See Anthony Richards (2015), "From Terrorism to 'Radicalization' to 'Extremism' . . .", p. 373, op. cit.
143 Ibid., p. 379.

doctrines and narratives of violence"; for "it would be foolhardy not to scrutinize the belief systems, whether themselves intrinsically violent or not, of those carrying out acts of terrorism".[144]

Particularly for the West that expound and irrevocably hold on to democratic values, those who propagate the so-called non-violent ideology that are paradoxically conducive to terror must have their extremist thought conceded to them, not just because it is "their democratic rights to hold such views—however unpalatable they may be—but also because to fail to concede this right to the "extremism of thought" to them would be tantamount to alienating and making them "part of the terrorism problem"; even when otherwise they can be "potential dissuaders against those who would resort to terrorism".[145] In fact, for the West, denying them this right will be tantamount to allowing terrorists orchestrate the desecration of Western values. Such people's right to the extremist thought must be conceded to them, more so when John Horgan has been quoted as saying that "the idea that the adoption of radical ideas causes terrorism is perhaps the greatest myth alive today in terrorism research".[146]

If a counter-terrorism measure does not skillfully deploy its de-radicalization aspect to meet the non-violent ideology that can induce violent or terrorist acts, it will risk the charge that "rather than focusing on the threat from terrorism", it "has itself become increasingly ideological—that it has gone beyond the remit of countering terrorism and has ventured into the broad realm of tackling ideological threats to the state".[147] Another implication for counter-terrorism of a blanket stigmatization of religious ideologies in the war on terror is the risk of promoting the so-called clash of civilization narrative that the terrorists are themselves bandying about. This was exactly what President Trump started in the United States with his anti-Muslim rhetoric, his travel ban, and his decision at a point in time "to change the government's Countering Violent Extremism programme . . . to focus purely on countering Islamic extremism".[148] Meanwhile, it is not all Muslim religious groups that endorse extremism and terrorism. So, the de-radicalization component of counter-terrorism is very critical, especially to countering those non-violent ideologies that can be conducive to terrorist acts.

The Sisyphean Task of De-Radicalization

As already adverted to earlier, from the perspective of Emily Feldman, de-radicalization essentially involves weaning the allegiance of the Islamist terrorists away from violent jihad by, amongst other strategies, challenging their belief

144 Ibid., pp. 379–380.
145 Ibid., p. 380.
146 Loc. Cit.
147 Loc. Cit.
148 See Charlotte McDonald-Gibson in "The Former Neo-Nazi Helping Returning ISIS Fighters Let Go Hate" . . ., p. 37, op. cit.

about what it means to be a good Muslim. But countering the radicalization weapon in the hands of the extremists, according to Alex Schmid, requires that a better understanding of "fanatical extremism and how to break or defuse it" is attained; and doing so also requires "the courage to enter the radical and extremist milieus and talk to the angry, the disillusioned and the forlorn who search for significance and recognition in their lives and hope to find it in fundamentalist religion".[149] The implication of this reality is that at the "vulnerable individual" level or "personal trajectory", the task of every CVE programme should be to figure out the ways to access this category of individuals and "bring them back into the midst of our society"—the mainstream.[150]

This is what the United States and some member nations of the EU try to accomplish in their CVE programmes.[151] In the United Kingdom for instance, a "Channel Project 2007" was established "following the London 7/7 attacks in 2005 with the aim of identifying people who are vulnerable to extremism", so as to "refer them to the appropriate agencies to address their extremist behaviour and keep them away from danger".[152] Since its launch in 2007, many UK residents of diverse ages were, as of 2014, referred to Channel Project; from where those that were determined to be at the risk of radicalization into "Islamic extremism" were in turn referred to the appropriate specialists for treatment in order to forestall that risk of radicalization into extremism.[153] However, the targeting of vulnerable individuals' personal trajectories to radicalization in order to de-radicalize them is clearly not cognizant of the environmental trajectory—the cultural, foreign policy, and historical circumstances.

But the fact that, by 2014, "a total of 3,934 UK residents of all ages" had been identified as "vulnerable to extremism" and prone to the risk of radicalization[154] is a stark indication of how the al-Qaeda and ISIS, amongst other terrorist groups, had effectively weaponized extremism and radicalization—and, indeed, counter-penetrated the West—being ever determined (in avenging the Caliphate) to operate even from a virtual Caliphate (the cyber-Caliphate) the moment it dawned on them that their physical Caliphate was a wild goose chase in a world militarily dominated and controlled by the West. The factors of age and degree of involvement in violent jihad are at the heart of the controversy over who to de-radicalize and who to prosecute for deterrence purposes.

Conceived in Nigeria as a blanket scheme that is indiscriminately "targeted at weaning 'penitent' Boko Haram members from their jihadist ideology"—that is,

149 See Alex P. Schmid (2016), "Research on Radicalization . . .", p. 31, op. cit.

150 Loc. Cit.

151 Ibid., pp. 26–31; see also Charlotte McDonald-Gibson in "The Former Neo-Nazi Helping Returning ISIS Fighters Let Go Hate" . . ., pp. 36–37, op. cit.

152 See Akimi Scarcella, Ruairi Page, and Vivek Furtado (2016), "Terrorism, Radicalization, Extremism, Authoritarianism and Fundamentalism . . .", p. 2, op. cit.

153 Loc. Cit.

154 Loc. Cit.

subduing the Salafists of all degrees without any form of prosecution for the diehards that had committed crimes from their murderous ideology—de-radicalization has been described as "a misplaced strategy" because, irrespective of the so-called penitence, the argument is that such a scheme "cannot persuade suicide bombers and mass murderers that have been brainwashed by a false heavenly utopia of martyrdom to retrace their steps".[155] The "heavenly utopia of martyrdom" under reference is the "darkling vision" of the hereafter by the Islamists yearning for martyrdom, their pining to be holy warriors in the fanatical belief that they are tied up in life, that the world means nothing to them, and that, in death, there is freedom since giving one's life in martyrdom is the "honourable life".[156] This belief that martyrdom is the "honourable life" is founded on the "darkling vision" of "heaven, near the Prophet Muhammed".[157]

It is in the attraction of this darkling vision of heaven that the hardened Salafist/Wahabbist terrorist is committed to either seeking martyrdom or installing an Islamic Caliphate where there would be pristine practices of the Islamic religion according to the radical tenets or interpretations of sharia law.[158] Even where attempts had been made to de-radicalize the hardcore Islamists, they have normally experienced very high recidivism—hence, in Australia, the de-radicalization programme has been restricted to those below 25 years of age—thereby disqualifying a Somali-born terrorist, Yacqub Khayre, who, in any case, relapsed after release from a 16-month jail term, taking a woman hostage and wounding three police officers in June 2017 in Brighton (Australia) before being shot dead by the police.[159] Given this proneness to recidivism, "the underlying principle in Europe, Australia and the United States [is now] to target de-radicalization programmes at young people holding extreme views, not those who had already participated in acts of terror".[160]

This is the reason why, "after the Charlie Hebdo massacre in 2015, France cracked down hard on returnees from ISIS and those suspected of terror at home", sending dozens to prison.[161] In fact, France had to close down its state-run prevention center against radicalization, particularly when Adel Kermichie demonstrated the difficulty in de-radicalizing hard-boiled terrorists by—despite confessing during his trial that "jihad is evil" and being granted leniency—invading a church in Normandy in October 2016 upon release from prison and slitting the throat of an 85-year-old priest, Jacques Hamel.[162] Even

155 See "Boko Haram: De-Radicalization, a Misplaced Strategy", *Editorial, The Punch* (Lagos), Wednesday, August 2, 2017, p. 20.
156 See Michael Weiss and Hassan Hassan (2015), *ISIS* . . ., pp. ix, 1, op. cit.
157 Ibid., p. xii.
158 Ibid., p. 1.
159 See "Boko Haram: De-Radicalization, a Misplaced Strategy" . . ., p. 20, op. cit.
160 Loc. Cit. Brackets mine.
161 Loc. Cit.
162 Loc. Cit.

in Saudi Arabia, some of the de-radicalized terrorists have been known to return to terrorist insurgency.[163]

In Nigeria, five commanders of the Boko Haram that were freed in the deal to swap the 82 Chibok girls returned to the terrorist organization and appeared with its leader, Abubakar Shekau, in a video.[164] It is for this reason that in most countries, "no attempt is made to de-radicalize the most committed extremists, particularly those who have been involved in serious plots, successful or otherwise".[165] And it was also for this reason that *The Punch* (Lagos) newspaper came down very hard on the Buhari government for—in advancement of President Jonathan's CVE with the creation in 2016 of the *Operation Safe Corridor* de-radicalization programme—purporting to be indiscriminately de-radicalizing the "over 90" hard-boiled Salafist Boko Haram insurgents who surrendered to Nigerian troops in the northeast without any major prosecution.[166]

While describing this approach to de-radicalization as an "appeasement" that would not work, *The Punch* expressed the view that "the incentive to join the [Boko Haram] group must be removed by first prosecuting offenders, particularly with building separated prisons so that they do not contaminate others"[167] as happened in Iraqi prisons where terrorist leaders, like the ISIS's Abu Bakr al-Baghdadi, were radicalized and graduated. It is because committed terrorist ideologues never give up their belief that in places like the United Kingdom—which initiated the de-radicalization programme in the wake of the 7/7 bombings in 2005—de-radicalization is designed to wean the vulnerable with low recidivism and prevent them from being drawn into terrorism, rather than seeking to reform the diehards ideologues with a high propensity for recidivism.[168]

163 Loc. Cit.
164 Loc. Cit.
165 Loc. Cit.
166 Loc. Cit.
167 Loc. Cit.
168 Loc. Cit.

5 The Jurisprudence of New and "Unregulated" Weapons

The Dilemma in "Unregulated" Weapons

As far as the escalation in the use of drones by the United States is concerned, it is, no doubt, a policy that was imposed by the ruthlessness and evasiveness of terrorism: the inclination of terrorists to avoid pitched battles. Although all is not fair in warfare,[1] meeting the contingency that is unavoidably imposed by terrorism necessarily demands adapting to the threats it poses as an adversary—an adaptation that may not necessarily "be integrated into a more conventional formula of confrontation", and which could involve "moving and expanding the field of conflict from a simple battlefield",[2] and even using dirty and unregulated weapons like armed drones. In the war on terror, this expansion of the battlefield is made possible by the use of modern technology-driven weapons, the hi-tech weapons that are amply exemplified by drones; weapons that can bypass the belligerents and strike at targets or objects behind the enemy line. Although these modern and hi-tech driven weapons are in use, some of them are inadmissible in armed conflicts.

This is because "Article 22 of the Hague Regulations [the First and Second Hague Regulations 1899 and 1907] stipulates expressly that the right of belligerents to adopt means of injuring the enemy is not unlimited".[3] As a matter of fact, some weapons are expressly prohibited by treaties, while others are prohibited or condemned by customary international law.[4] The assumption here is that, apart from the weapons expressly prohibited by treaties or by customary international law, all the means of killing and wounding the enemy that exists, or may be

1 See Ahmad Nazir Warraich (2013), "The Use of Drones . . .", p. 68, op. cit.
2 See Teodor Frunzeti (2013), "Asymmetric, Unconventional and Hybrid Actions . . .", pp. 8–9, op. cit. Brackets mine.
3 See L. Oppenheim (1952, edited by H. Lauterpacht), *International Law: A Treatise, Vol. 2: Disputes, War and Neutrality*, Seventh Edition, London, Longman, p. 340. Brackets mine; see also Fred Aja Agwu (2011), *The Law of Armed Conflict and African Wars* . . ., pp. 67–72, op. cit.
4 Ibid., p. 340.

invented in future, are lawful.[5] It is in this assumption that some ambiguity and dilemma exist with respect to those weapons that are not expressly prohibited by either treaties or customs (including the futuristic weapons). This ambiguity and dilemma cover weapons like the atomic bomb, the hydrogen bomb (and, indeed, all kinds of nuclear, chemical, and biological weapons). It is this same ambiguity and dilemma that are now faced in drones.

Ameliorating the Dilemma: The Martens Clause

But to ameliorate this ambiguity, the progenitors of the positivist law of armed conflict presciently recognized its inherent inability to prohibit unknown or futuristic weapons and therefore, prohibited, not the weapons themselves, but the effects or consequences of using the weapons not prohibited because their development had not been anticipated by the law. Hence, a customary rule of law was expressed in Article 23 of the Hague Regulations aforementioned, prohibiting, for instance:

> . . . the employment of poison and of such arms, projectiles and materials as [may] cause unnecessary injury. Accordingly, wells, pumps, rivers and the like from which the enemy draws drinking water must not be poisoned; poisoned weapons must not be made use of; rifles must not be loaded with bits of glass, irregularly shaped iron, nails and the like; cannons must not be loaded with chain shot, crossbar shot, red-hot balls and the like.[6]

The implication of the foregoing is that all the means of killing or wounding (be they swords and rifles, shrapnel, and machine guns for instance) that needlessly cause painful deaths or aggravate sufferings are unlawful.[7] The Hague Regulations under reference also prohibits the employment of explosive bullets, expanding (dum-dum) bullets and other arms or projectiles "the sole object of which is the diffusion of asphyxiating or deleterious gases".[8] It is worthy of note that Protocol 1 (1977) Additional to the Geneva Conventions has since weighed in to reinforce the Hague Regulations.[9] The Protocol specifically stated with respect to new weapons that:

> In the study, development, acquisition or adoption of a new weapon, means or method of warfare, a High Contracting Party is under an obligation to

5 Loc. Cit.
6 Ibid., pp. 340–341.
7 See Fred Aja Agwu (2011), *The Law of Armed Conflict and African Wars* . . ., pp. 67–68, op. cit.
8 See L. Oppenheim (1952, edited by H. Lauterpacht), *International Law: A Treatise, Vol. 2* . . ., pp. 341–342, op. cit.
9 See Part III, Articles 35 and 36; see also Fred Aja Agwu (2011), *The Law of Armed Conflict and African Wars* . . ., p. 71, op. cit.

> determine whether its employment would, in some or all circumstances, be prohibited by this Protocol or by any other rule of international law applicable to the High Contracting Party.[10]

Long before the 1977 Additional Protocol 1 to the Geneva Conventions addressed the issue of new weapons, it had been recognized in the Hague Regulations that because modern technological innovations move faster than the law, there was need to provide against the use of dangerous weapons that might not have been expressly banned in international law. Hence, the preamble of the Hague Convention (Regulation) IV (1907) provides (what is known as the Martens Clause) as follows:

> Until a more complete codes of the laws of war has been issued, the High Contracting Parties think it right to declare in cases not included in the Regulations adopted by them [that] populations and belligerents remain under the protection and empire of the principles of international law as they result from the usage established between civilized nations, from the laws of humanity and the requirements of public conscience.[11]

In addition to the Martens Clause, there is also the Cluster Munitions Coalition (CMC), a global network of countries campaigning for, and routing for a comprehensive ban on the use of these dangerous and unlawful weapons.[12]

Prohibited Weapons and Non-State Actors

But the question is this: does the law forbidding the use of prohibited weapons extend to non state actors, particularly in the light of the fact that they are the ones that have perfected the use of these objectionable weapons in the Improvised Explosive Devices (IEDs)? As lawless fighters, insurgents are adept at making and deploying the IEDs, which are basically the dirty weapons that are proscribed under Article 23 of the Hague Regulations under reference. On April 25, 2007, a convoy of American soldiers, including medics, was travelling at dusk in Afghanistan's Paktika Province when it was struck by an IED, setting one of their Humvees ablaze.[13] The IED attack was immediately followed by a burst of small-arms gunfire and mortar rounds from the insurgents, which seriously wounded some five soldiers in that convoy.[14]

10 See Article 36 of Additional Protocol I to the Geneva Conventions of 12 August 1949.

11 See Fred Aja Agwu (2011), *The Law of Armed Conflict and African Wars . . .*, p. 71, op. cit.

12 Ibid., p. 73.

13 See Dick Cheney (2011), *In My Time: A Personal and Political Memoir*, New York, Threshold Editions, p. 496.

14 Loc. Cit.

At a time when women's involvement in combat is a rarity[15]—with the Israeli Defence Force in the Supreme Court with a young woman requesting to be combat pilot[16]—and at a time when, in the words of Dick Cheney, U.S. "army regulations prohibit women from participating in combat missions", the IED attack on the U.S. convoy in the Afghan Province under reference by insurgents caught a 19-year-old female army medic, Specialist Monica Brown, in the crossfire; and even though she was caught under that heavy fire, she evinced a remarkable calmness, with no regard for her own safety, in stabilizing and preparing the wounded for evacuation.[17] But the instruction here is that the fact of a noncombatant medic like Brown inadvertently finding herself on the frontlines by dint of the application of dirty and prohibited weapons like IEDs informed the contemplative call by U.S. Vice-President Dick Cheney for an adjustment in law and public policy "to reflect the changing nature of twenty-first-century war, in which combat and non-combat, frontline and rear, are not always so easy to delineate".[18]

Thus, the development and use of new weapons, whether IEDs, nuclear weapons, biological weapons, chemical weapons (and now drones) constitute a nightmare to public policy and international law. And as will be seen later under the rubric of drones in international humanitarian law from the prisms of Robert Sloane (also invoking Hersch Lauterpacht), because non-state actors suffer a double incapacitation of being at the receiving end of both factual and legal asymmetry, they do not have any attraction in eschewing the deployment of prohibited weapons. As a matter of fact, these non-state actors use the prohibited or dirty weapons to compensate for the resource and numerical inferiority. And this is what they also use their peripatetic inclinations to accomplish. Thus, prohibited weapons are to non-state actors (in terms of value) what constantly shifting terrain is also to them; otherwise, they will be easily out-numbered, outgunned, and vanquished.

Other Controversies of Unregulated Weapons

Long before the invention and use of drones, the introduction of new weapons in armed conflicts had remained a source of controversy. This was aptly illustrated by the deployment or use of submarines in naval hostilities. In warfare on the high seas, it has been trite international law that the rule of engagement demands "visit and capture" as necessary safeguards for the safety of passengers and crew.[19]

15 See Yaakov Lappin in "More Women Soldiers Seeking to Serve in Combat Units, IDF Says", *The Jerusalem Post*, available at www.jpost.com/Defense/IDF-More-women-want-to-serve-in-combat-units-330641 (last visited on Sunday, May 28, 2017).

16 Available at www.youtube.com/watch?v=N8WjwkcWsgE (last visited on Sunday, May 28, 2017)

17 See Dick Cheney (2011), *In My Time . . .*, pp. 496–497, op. cit.

18 Ibid., p. 497.

19 See L. Oppenheim (1952, edited by H. Lauterpacht), *International Law: A Treatise, Vol. 2 . . .*, pp. 469–470, op. cit; see also Fred Aja Agwu (2011), *The Law of Armed Conflict and African Wars . . .*, pp. 43–49, op. cit.

Although there was the abolition of privateering by the Declaration of Paris of 1856,[20] there had nonetheless been this "distinction between converted armed merchant cruisers and defensibly armed merchantmen".[21] But in 1913, the British Admiralty, still insisting on the distinction between converted armed merchant cruisers and defensibly armed merchantmen, announced its intention in the event of war "to supply British merchant-vessels with guns and ammunition for the purpose of defending themselves".[22]

The consequence of that announcement was that when the Second World War broke out, "it became the practice of the Allied Powers in that war to arm their merchant-vessels defensively and so enable them more effectively to exercise their right . . . of resisting attack by force".[23] This was a huge problem for submarines that (being new weapons) had no surface capability. Meanwhile, an overwhelming weight of authority recognized that the defensive armament of these converted merchant vessels in no way altered their legal status, that is, the right to visit and capture rather that outright destruction with regard to the safety of the passengers and crew.[24] But the arming of merchant ships raised some substantial difficulties; the first of which was the difficulty of drawing a line of distinction between defensive and offensive acts; the second difficulty being the fact that it undermined the abolition of privateering; and the third difficulty being that "the fact that a merchantman is armed and that she is entitled to resist actual or anticipated attack makes it impossible for enemy submarines to exercise their right of visit and capture in accordance with international law"; that is, "without running the risk [because it lacks surface capability] of destruction by the superior armament of the merchant-vessel or being rammed by her".[25]

There was equally the difficulty in the armed merchantman being torpedoed by the submarine without regard to the safety of the passengers and crew. In fact, by early 1916, the United States "propounded suggestions for abandoning defensive armament in consideration of the clear obligation of the enemy not to sink merchantmen without warning [because] the use of submarine had effected a radical change in the situation";[26] for submarines cannot visit and capture. Unfortunately, it was "suggested that the obvious consequence of the inability of submarines to exercise the customary rights of visit and capture in relation to defensively armed merchantmen in accordance with international law is abstention from [or inability to enforce] activities prohibited by the law".[27] But on the

20 See L. Oppenheim (1952, edited by H. Lauterpacht), *International Law: A Treatise, Vol. 2* . . ., p. 469, op. cit.
21 Ibid., p. 468.
22 Loc. Cit.
23 Loc. Cit.
24 Loc. Cit.
25 Ibid., p. 469.
26 Loc. Cit, note 1.
27 Loc. Cit. Brackets mine.

other hand, it is also true; indeed, trite law that "the novelty of a weapon does not by itself carry with it a legitimate claim to a change in the existing rules of law".[28] In other words, the fact that the submarine (a new weapon) was unable to enforce the international law rule of visit and capture does not vitiate that rule of law or constitute a license for privateering.

Apropos drones and other new but precision-guided weapons: the fact that they fail in their "rigorous targeting procedures"[29] and incur prohibitive collateral damage (be it harm to the civilian populace or the destruction of protected non-military objects or objectives) does not mean that the rule of law protecting civilians and non-military objectives has been rendered a nullity. This is even as it may be argued that unlike the manned aircraft pilots, drone pilots have a greater opportunity to check and clearly discern their targets before firing their missiles. But the point at issue here is not that the avoidance of collateral damage can be absolutely avoided; it is the fact that such phenomena as "signature strikes" make nonsense of armed drones' technology of rigorous targeting because they inflict unacceptable collateral damage on the civilian population in a manner that contradicts the spirit and letters of the Additional Protocol I (1977) to the Geneva Conventions.[30]

A signature drone strike contradicts Article 51 (5) (b) of Additional Protocol I (1977); which advances the argument that, as a matter of fact, the fact that "international law must adapt itself to the changes necessitated by the advent of new weapons" does not mean that such adaptation would be inconsistent with the fundamental rules of warfare and, in particular, "the distinction between combatants and non-combatants".[31] In Oppenheim's unexpurgated rendition, "international law must adapt itself to the changes necessitated by the advent of new weapons so long as such adaptation is not inconsistent with the fundamental rules of warfare and, in particular, with the distinction between combatants and non-combatants".[32] This is the fundamental challenge that the United States faces today—that of reconciling its new armed drone technology with the demands of international law that excessive or intolerable collateral damage inherent in indiscriminate attacks as in signature strikes must be avoided. This is at the epicenter of the controversies surrounding the armed drones as part of the new and unregulated weapons of today.

28 Loc. Cit.

29 See Sam Roggeveen (2014) in "Proliferation of Unmanned Aerial Vehicles . . .", op. cit.

30 Article 52, paragraphs 5 (b) of the Additional Protocol considers an attack indiscriminate when it "may be expected to cause incidental loss of civilian life, injury to civilians, damage to civilian objects, or a combination thereof, which could be excessive in relation to the concrete and direct military advantage anticipated".

31 See L. Oppenheim (1952, edited by H. Lauterpacht), *International Law: A Treatise, Vol. 2 . . .*, p. 470, op. cit.

32 Loc. Cit.

Reconciling the Clash Between Technology and Law

But there is always a compromise in this clash between technology and the law, the dissonance between new weapons and the prevailing rule of law. With respect to submarines under reference, some degree of compromise was considered in the restriction of the activities of submarines (vis-à-vis converted merchantmen) "in exchange for the abandonment of the right to arm merchantmen for defence".[33] This restriction consisted

> either in the total abolition of the right to destroy merchant-vessels on the ground of carriage of contraband, or in its limitation to certain areas in close proximity to coasts, subject always to compliance with the rules ensuring the safety of crews and passengers.[34]

All in all, the noncombatant character of defensively armed merchant vessels was (and is always) preserved. They do not lose either their character as merchant vessels, or the concomitant right to be treated as such both by the enemy and by neutrals.[35] The rights of defensively armed merchant vessels, especially as they concern the enemy, includes immunity both from direct attack and from destruction without the necessary safeguards that include the safety of the crew and passengers.[36]

So, like the civilian population and civil aircraft that are not combatants or belligerents, there is prohibition of direct attack on enemy merchant vessels, whether or not they are defensively armed. But with respect to offensively armed or straight warships, "nothing forbids an attack on enemy vessels by the dropping of bombs from aircraft",[37] be it manned or unmanned, the unmanned being the drones. In that situation, if the bombed ship does not flee (or take flight) but remains to defend itself, all modes of attack (that is, with manned or unmanned aircraft, for instance) are also lawful against it, just as it is also justified to adopt any mode of counter-offensive.[38] In all theaters of armed conflict, be it on land, in maritime warfare, or in aerial combats, drones are new implements of warfare that are not only supremely suitable, they are also legitimate and even legal.

Being a form of aircraft, there may be a temptation to succumb to British Air Marshal Harris, who quipped that in the use of aircraft in warfare, there is no applicable international law at all; but this controversy has since been resolved in the *Shimoda* case where it was established that international law applies, and that in the use of aircraft, an indiscriminate bombardment is illegal.[39] Thus, the

33 Loc. Cit.
34 Loc. Cit.
35 Loc. Cit.
36 Ibid., p. 531.
37 Ibid., p. 471.
38 Loc. Cit.
39 See Fred Aja Agwu (2011), *The Law of Armed Conflict and African Wars* . . ., p. 63, op. cit.

legality of drones is incontestable. The only snag in the use of drones is that being in the family of unconventional weapons; that is, being a new and "unregulated" weapon, the "legality" of drones is dubious or analogous to the "legality" of nuclear weapons. In other words, like nuclear weapons, the use of drones is subject not only to the Hague rule that belligerents have not got unlimited right to the choice of means of injuring the enemy, but also to the Martens Clause, and the dictates of morality.[40]

Again, like nuclear, chemical and other weapons that are not expressly prohibited by any conventional (treaty) or customary international law but subject to Article 23 (a) and (e) of the Hague Regulations (1899 and 1907) and Article 35 of Protocol 1 (1977) Additional to the Geneva Conventions aforementioned as well as the 1925 Geneva Protocols, the impermissibility of drones as weapons of war will only be meaningful within the same context of the regulation or prohibition of the consequences; that is, if their use would provoke consequences such as enormous cruelty, needless painful deaths, and aggravated sufferings.[41] This is what Oppenheim meant when he said that the illegality of nuclear weapons (and here by extension, drones) can only be admitted based on the unacceptable consequences of their use.[42] And it was what propelled the Christof Heyns' report to the United Nations' General Assembly on extrajudicial, summary, or arbitrary executions to make the observation that "there is a broad agreement that drones themselves are not illegal weapons"; although "there is . . . a notable lack of consensus on how to apply the rules of international law that regulate the use of force to drones, the fact that drones are now an established technology notwithstanding".[43]

Attempting the Regulation of Drones

But it still beats the imagination how, despite the prolific deployment and use of drones during the Second World War and in Vietnam (the early or simple versions of the weapon used for reconnaissance in combat),[44] international jurists did not deem it fit to regulate these weapons within the framework of the 1977 Additional Protocol I to the Geneva Conventions. Could this oversight or lack of foresight be attributed to an inability to anticipate that in the future, drones were capable of modernization and weaponization, a clear illustration that human ingenuity is intractable, and that between technological development

40 Ibid., p. 77.

41 Ibid., pp. 77–78.

42 Ibid., p. 78.

43 See Christof Heyns' in "Report of the Special Rapportuer on Extrajudicial, Summary or Arbitrary Executions", sixty-eight session, item 69(b) of the provisional agenda, A/68/382, September 13, 2013, available at www.justsecurity.org/wp-content/uploads/2013/10/UN-Special-Rapporteur-Extrajudicial-Christof-Heyns-Report-Drones.pdf (last visited on September 17, 2015).

44 See Van Baldwin Carr (undated) in "Unmanned Aerial Vehicles . . .", pp. 4–11, op. cit.

and the development of international law, the latter is always helpless and confronted with a fait-accompli? Indeed, it was actually this inability to anticipate the future that informed the Martens Clause as the preamble of the 1907 Hague Convention Regulation IV aforementioned, and Article 36 (New Weapons) of Protocol I Additional to the Geneva Conventions, also aforementioned. The closest that countries have come in the regulation (not abolition) of the use of drones is in the 1987 Missile Technology Control Regime (MTCR);[45] but this is not a direct regulation. The MTCR only regulates the use of the drone technology by attribution.

This is because the MTCR is "an informal and voluntary multilateral arrangement comprising thirty-four states that attempt to constrain ballistic missile proliferation".[46] Thus, "under the MTCR, drones capable of delivering at least a five-hundred-kilogram payload [for] a minimum of three hundred kilometers are classified as Category I items, for which there will be a strong presumption to deny such transfers".[47] Thus, because the acquisition of drones (especially for use in reconnaissance) is allowed for countries that cannot develop it, it was under the MCTR framework that "the United States refrained from selling drones to states such as Pakistan, Turkey, Saudi Arabia, and the United Arab Emirate (UAE),[48] preferring rather, through the General Atomic, manufacturers of the Predator, to unveil the Predator XP surveillance drone that "lacks the hard points—or mounting brackets for aerial munitions—wing strength, and fire control system required for weaponization".[49] But outside the MCTR, any country that has the technological know-how can develop and weaponize drones without any restriction or inhibition.

The foregoing reality, therefore, leaves the tackling of the issue of drones (like nuclear weapons) only in the realm of consequences. And these unacceptable consequences of use can only flow from the inability of the weapon to meet up with the desired targeting procedure or precision, and to thereby indiscriminately hit the civilian population; that is, in drones not being able to thereby discriminate between combatants and noncombatants, and to, thus, cause untold collateral damage. But as long as drones can transcend such technological or technical foibles, there is certainly nothing illegal about their deployment as instruments of warfare. In other words, in the absence of unacceptable collateral damage, the use of drones is perfectly legit and, indeed, lawful in armed conflict. But also sometimes referred to as "America's drone warfare"[50] because it was the United States that pioneered the recent use of modern armed drones in support of its

45 See Micah Zenko (2013), "Reforming U.S. Drone Strike Policies" . . ., p. 19, op. cit.

46 Loc. Cit.

47 Ibid., pp. 19–20.

48 Ibid., p. 19.

49 Ibid., p. 20.

50 See Rudolph Herzog's report of Andrew Niccol's film in "Dealing Death by Remote Control", *Newsweek* (London), April 17, 2015, p. 66.

distant asymmetric wars in the Middle East to protect its national interests,[51] Washington's use of drones with its precision capability tries as much as possible to limit unacceptable consequences and the resultant association of drones with illegality.

Washington particularly does this in furtherance of the doctrine of "zero deaths"[52] in many of its conflicts. This practice of the doctrine of "zero deaths" also goes beyond the limiting of casualties amongst the local civilian populace to include the limiting of American deaths; and this is accomplished or leveraged, not only by the power of the drone technology, but also through proxy wars, including such approaches as the use of mercenaries and the domestication or indigenization of the combatants; known in Africa as the Africanization of the conflicts; or in Asia as the Vietnamization of the conflicts. It is perhaps because the United States assiduously tries to limit the casualties arising from drone strikes that it avoids hitting its targets unless they are in "lightly populated areas", as illustrated in its experience in the pursuit of Abu Musab al Zarqawi.[53] Through this way, the operators of the drones try to avoid the unfortunate incidences of "civilians suddenly walking into the crosshairs".[54]

51 This pioneering role in the deployment and use of drones is, however, shared between the United States and Israel; see Van Baldwin Carr (undated) in "Unmanned Aerial Vehicles . . .", pp. 7–8, op. cit.

52 See Teodor Frunzeti (2013), "Asymmetric, Unconventional and Hybrid Actions . . .", p. 8, op. cit.

53 See Stanley McChrystal (2015), *Team of Teams* . . ., p. 130, op. cit.

54 See Rudolph Herzog's report of Andrew Niccol's film in "Dealing Death by Remote Control" . . ., p. 66, op. cit.

6 The Armed Drone Weapon Platform

A Convenient Weapon for 9/11 Washington

> The combination of persistence and responsiveness, high-quality intelligence infrastructures, and tacit host-state support have made drones preeminent tool for U.S. lethal operations against suspected terrorists and militants where states are unable to singlehandedly deal with the threat they pose. As a result, drones are not just another weapons platform. Instead, they provide the United States with distinct capability that significantly reduces many of the inherent political, diplomatic, and military risks of targeted killings.
>
> (Micah Zenko)[1]

The epigraph is an aphoristic statement by Micah Zenko of the Council on Foreign Relations in the United States on the inherent benefits of armed drones to the United States. Since the September 11, 2001 (9/11) terrorist attacks, so much hoopla has surrounded the issue of drones as if the weapon directly resulted from the challenges posed by those attacks. On the contrary, and as Evan Baldwin Carr put it, "the notion of unmanned aerial flight has existed far longer than most Americans realize".[2] In other words, drones had long been in existence before 9/11. All that 9/11 did was to amplify its importance and popularize its existence in the consciousness of the general public, especially outside military circles. With 9/11, drones "received considerable news coverage . . . [because with] the start of the War on Terror, drone use [became] a common sight on the battlefield";[3] that is, on the apocryphal battlefield, apocryphal because (as seen below in the section of this book on *Drones and the Vanishing Frontline*) the battlefield properly so called in the "war on terror" is nonexistent.

War (although a human tragedy) has this paradoxical role of creating a boom in the military-industrial complex and the economy of mainly the industrialized nations. And so, as happen in many industrialized nations' war economies, 9/11

1 See Micah Zenko (2013), "Reforming U.S. Drone Strike Policies" . . ., pp. 7–8, op. cit.
2 See Van Baldwin Carr (undated) in "Unmanned Aerial Vehicles . . .", p. 4, op. cit.
3 Loc. Cit. Brackets mine.

actually provoked a boom in the United States' military-industrial complex. As reported by *Time* newsmagazine, "if one of bin Laden's goal[s] was to disrupt or destroy U.S. economy, he had the opposite effect" in the intelligence and surveillance sector of the economy as well as in drones manufacturing; for although controversial in its reputation as war, 9/11 and the attendant hunt for Osama bin Laden created not just a market for intelligence and surveillance, it also, as *Time* newsmagazine put it, "helped create a new market for unmanned aerial vehicles (UAVs), including Predator drones made by General Atomics"; while the stock for small drone-makers like AeroVironment skyrocketed.[4] Indeed, as the *Time* newsmagazine under reference testifies, in the wake of 9/11, "Predator drones have been particularly effective in hunting down al-Qaeda and Taliban leaders"; and with the eventual death of Osama bin Laden (though not from drone strikes but more from the effective intelligence and communication from drones), further recruitments by this terror organization (as distinct from ISIS) could be dampened.[5]

The interesting thing here is that this boom in the military-industrial complex and ipso facto the U.S. economy was happening at a time that these drones are facilitating some reductions in the country's usual military expenditure. How does this happen? With the onset of international terrorism, the nature and tactics of America's enemies have clearly changed. The emergent enemies (the terrorists and their tactics) have shifted to remote mountainous terrains where the expanded use of drones has become inevitable.[6] And so, the question is asked, do the U.S. military need a big budget or expenditure anymore for purposes of getting more, say, "50 attack submarines when America's main enemy hides in caves"; or even get the Air Force to expand its fleets of F-15s, F-16s and F-18s when it is cheaper to deploy such cutting-edge weapons as unmanned drones that easily seek out and destroy these enemies in their impossible hide-outs, saving, at the same time, the demand for troops?[7] In this way, the use of armed drones as a weapon against terror since 9/11 affects the United States' military budgeting positively by stemming the old large budget practice of the "era of sky's-the-limit defence budgets".[8]

The Early Development of Unmanned Aerial Vehicles (UAVs)

At the beginning, "the first drones were military" because "the use of pilotless flying machines as weapons dates back to the siege of Venice in 1849, when Austrian forces launched balloons laden with explosives against the city".[9] From

4 See Bill Saporito in "Terror Inc: How Bin Laden Made One Industry Boom", *Time* (New York), May 20, 2011, p. 10.
5 Loc. Cit.
6 Loc. Cit.
7 See Mark Thompson in "How to Save Trillion Dollars: You Can Start Right Here", *Time* (New York), April 25, 2011, pp. 20–22.
8 Ibid., p. 22.
9 See "Give and Take" in Taking Flight, *The Economist* Technology Quarterly pullout, June 10, 2017, p. 4.

the account rendered by Evan Baldwin Carr, "the concept of remote pilotless vehicles was born during the early days of electricity through a partnership between George Westinghouse and Nikola Tesla", thus, pioneering the invention of a simple remote boat called the "Teleautomaton" that could serve as a torpedo.[10] As a boat, the "Teleautomaton" was evidently a craft for maritime warfare. It was not until the period 1909–1920 that "scientific advancement of the aeronautical gyroscope by Elmer Sperry, and airframe construction by Glenn Curtiss allowed these early pioneers to begin testing aerial torpedoes".[11]

But these early version of drones—the remote-controlled flying machines—were rudimentary if not primitive, as they "were not designed to return", but only meant "to fly to a target remotely and through various mechanisms, terminate forward velocity, dropping themselves and presumably, bomb payloads, on the targets".[12] At the time under reference, these pilotless flying machines were actually "controlled through a series of on-board devices with pre-set operations".[13] However, "the origin of military drones is usually dated to the development of un-crewed, remote-controlled aircraft for use as targets by anti-aircraft gunners after the first World War".[14] Because it started after the first World War, the implication was that it was only during the First World War that the concept of aerial torpedo underwent rigorous testing and brief production under the supervision of Charles Franklin Kettering, resulting in the Kettering Bug that could fly 50 miles and deliver a 200-lb payload on target; even though it still fell short of this mark and was discontinued as the First World War came to a close.[15]

But it was, nevertheless, the first instance of an unmanned aircraft successfully performing a pre-designated flight pattern.[16] This had come to vindicate Evan Baldwin Carr's assertion that the early history of UAV development was sporadic, often taking place when armed conflicts required that the military looked for new technologies, and with the enthusiasm waning when the armed conflict ceased.[17] It was after the First World War that the unmanned aircraft was consistently steadied in its ability to take off and remain airborne, seriously turning attention to its remote control, with radio engineers working with Sperry to create the *Messenger*, "the world's first truly remote-controlled aircraft" that successfully achieved "two-hour flights and 90-miles accuracy", which was also "built as a relay vehicle and in an aerial torpedo configuration for the [U.S.] army".[18]

So, it was also after the First World War that the British, between 1934 and 1943, produced the de Havilland Queen Bee (the apiarian UAV from where the name drone was taken, and which inspired the Hollywood actor and model

10 See Van Baldwin Carr (undated) in "Unmanned Aerial Vehicles . . .", p. 5, op. cit.
11 Loc. Cit.
12 Loc. Cit.
13 Loc. Cit.
14 See "Give and Take" . . ., p. 4, op. cit.
15 See Van Baldwin Carr (undated) in "Unmanned Aerial Vehicles . . .", p. 5, op. cit.
16 Loc. Cit.
17 Ibid., p. 4.
18 Ibid., p. 5. Brackets mine.

plane enthusiast, Reginald Denny, to invent the Radioplane-I, RP-I for gunnery practice and anti-aircraft military defence), with the Germans only producing the V-I cruise missiles that were not necessarily regarded as drones during the Second World War, but which inflicted enormous casualties on the Allies.[19] So, talking about the antecedents of modern drones, "the first truly successful example" of "un-crewed, remote-controlled aircraft" was "the de Havilland DH82B Queen Bee, which entered service in Britain in 1935 and seems to have been the inspiration for calling such aircraft 'drones' (after stingless male bees); [while] Germany's V-1 flying bomb was another early drone".[20]

At that time, and as far as the development of the drone technology was concerned, attention was beginning to be turned to "producing an aircraft that would not fly to a target and self-terminate but deliver its payload and return to base for future deployment", unmanned aircraft with higher longevity and higher altitude; all of which were easily applied for reconnaissance for the needs of the Cold War that later ensued.[21] These early, crude forms of drones bore similar resemblance with modern-day surveillance drones with their possession of a 125-mm or a 70-mm film camera, flares for use with nighttime photography, an IR sensor, plumbing for dispensing chemical or biological agents from under wing tanks and a Side-Looking Airborne Radar (SLAR) that was capable of transmitting imagery back in real time via a ground sensor.[22]

Thus, the development of unmanned aerial technology has a long history, and its early version was principally tied to reconnaissance, "demonstrating that when used effectively, they [like today's drones] can help achieve combat objectives".[23] This long antecedent of unmanned aerial technology—dating, from its crudest forms, as far back as the siege of Venice in 1849 aforementioned and days of the Spanish-American War—meant that they had not only existed long before 9/11, they had equally been tied to wars (especially conventional wars), beginning with the primitive or early forms of drones, if unmanned aerial vehicles, used in the Spanish-American War under reference, to the more improved versions of these unmanned aerial vehicles used in the Second World War (like the Germans V-I cruise missiles).The more modern version (but not as modern as today's version) used during the Vietnam War, when unmanned aerial vehicles were not only ubiquitous—with 1,016 AQM-34 Lightning Bugs and Firebees flying 3,435 sorties with over 84% success rate—were also functionally prolific, that is, in terms of "their various missions, from air defense and communication intelligence to leaflet dropping", all of which solidified the functions of UAVs in modern military arsenals".[24]

19 Ibid., pp. 6–7.
20 See "Give and Take" . . ., p. 4, op. cit.
21 See Van Baldwin Carr (undated) in "Unmanned Aerial Vehicles . . .", p. 6, op. cit.
22 Loc. Cit.
23 Ibid., p. 7. Brackets mine.
24 Ibid., pp. 6–7.

The Technological Refinement of Drones

As far as the technological refinement of unmanned aerial vehicles—the precursor to the modern-day drones—goes, various schemes were tested, all ahead of their time, most prominently the perfection of the Inertial Navigation System of the 40s, the Star Tracker of the 50s, and the Transit system of the 60s, which was the first system to use satellite radio signals and which preceded [the Global Positioning System] GPS.[25]

In the '90s—when efforts were made to enable the unmanned vehicles to stay airborne for over 24 hours and above 50,000 feet, with new materials now used in the construction of the craft in order to make them lighter and stronger, harnessing solar power to propel them for indefinite periods of time—the NASA and AeroVironment Corporation developed the solar-powered Pathfinder and Helios, even though these craft were still "hindered by inefficient photovoltaic cells".[26]

But eventually, "fully autonomous flights that included take-off and landing were pioneered; and for the first time, the new Predator drone was outfitted with a laser-guided antitank missile, making it capable of patrolling, spotting, targeting and attacking at once".[27] It was at this juncture that it became clear that UAVs in combat could lessen the need for manpower and put fewer soldiers in the line of fire.[28] Today, there are, across the broad spectrum of drones that serve as a vital component of air power, two major types: (1) in one end of the spectrum is the "small, hand-launched fixed-wing surveillance drones such as the Raven, Wasp and Puma, all made by AeroVironment to either fly autonomously or under short-range remote; with the Raven—the world's most widely used military UAV with around 20,000 units deployed—capable of flying for up to 90 minutes.[29] (2) On the other end of the spectrum is the "larger drones like the Predator and Reaper", which "can typically stay aloft for 12 20 hours and carry weapons".[30]

There are also in this larger drone category, the biggest of them all—the "long-endurance, high-altitude reconnaissance drones such as the Northrop Grumman Global Hawk, which can loiter over an area for 32 hours, longer than any human pilot".[31] The U.S. armed forces alone "have a fleet of more than 11,000 drones, compared with just a handful in 2001[32]". Meanwhile, despite the

25 Ibid., p. 7.
26 Ibid., p. 8.
27 Loc. Cit.
28 Loc. Cit.
29 See "Give and Take" . . ., p. 4, op. cit.
30 Ibid., p. 5.
31 Loc. Cit.
32 Ibid., p. 4.

United States' dominance, about 80 countries are said to possess "military drones, including about 20 with armed forces, either already in use or in development; but the vast majority are unarmed surveillance aircraft of various shapes and sizes".[33]

Drones, Special Operations, and Targeted Killings

Unarguably the most poignant point made in the epigraph that introduces this chapter is the fact that, as modern instruments of warfare, drones are tailor-made, not just for conventional warfare, but also for the unconventional or asymmetric (insurgency) ones; more so because the latter (insurgency) is tinged with shifty and, thus, evasive terrorist campaigns. This is why "military drones are built to survive in demanding conditions, having special requirements (such as stealth capabilities or long-endurance) and tend to be expensive".[34] But it is only in the latter case (insurgencies thriving with terrorist campaigns) that targeted killings take place for preemptive purposes. Conceptually, "targeted killing is the intentional, premeditated and deliberate use of lethal force by states or their agents acting under colour of law, or by an organized armed group, against a specific individual who is not in the physical custody of the perpetrator".[35] In asymmetric warfare, targeted killings, as the name implies, can be done against people or terrorists behind enemy lines; that is, those that are not in an active participation in the hostilities, terrorists that are hiding amongst the civilian population.

But in a conventional or symmetric warfare, targeted killings are not permissible because deliberately or intentionally targeting those behind the battlefields or frontlines, or those in undefended cities (be they civilians or even members of the armed forces that are not in active hostilities) is unlawful. The objects of targeted killings are usually those individuals or groups that pose threats but cannot be dealt with in open or pitched conventional battles. Sometimes, these individuals or groups can be unarmed when they are targeted; and in conventional engagements, unarmed persons are almost the same as those rendered hors de combat. They are as vulnerable as pilots parachuting from distressed aircraft that must not be shot at until they are on the ground and refuse to surrender. Thus, to indulge in killings in conventional warfare that have the elements of targeted killing (deliberate, intentional, and premeditated killing or unarmed persons[36]) is clearly a war crime.

As an added weapon platform in asymmetric warfare, the proliferation and weaponization of drones have given the nation-state (and the United States in particular for now) an additional advantage at the level of what Micah Zenko referred to as "special operations raids".[37] These raids facilitate targeted killings in asymmetric warfare. Although "the decision to target specific individuals with lethal force" was not unprecedented (the United States had engaged in targeted

33 Loc. Cit.

34 Ibid., p. 5.

35 See Ahmad Nazir Warraich (2013), "The Use of Drones . . .", p. 67, op. cit.

36 Loc. Cit.

37 See Micah Zenko (2013), "Reforming U.S. Drone Strike Policies" . . ., p. 6, op. cit.

killings for a long time, "at least since a border war with Mexican bandits in 1916"), "the new elements of the targeted killing policy emerged in recent years in response to terrorism and its threats against the United States at home and abroad".[38] But the practice of "targeted killing quickly took a sharper focus soon after September 11" because "for the first time, pilotless drone aircraft were equipped both with sophisticated surveillance and targeting technology and with powerful Hellfire missiles capable of inflicting lethal force effectively from a safe distance".[39] The advanced and dramatic use of armed drones had promised enormous and effective gains in the war against terrorism, and with very little or no risk at all to U.S. service personnel.[40]

Other Advantages Offered by Drones

By 2013, the United States as the country that pioneered the use of drone strikes had in its arsenal of armed drones, "primarily the Predator and Reaper", two varieties of armed drones that offer immense advantages over other weapons platforms in special operations raids because in terms of "sustained persistence over potential targets", they "can remain aloft, fully loaded with munitions, for over fourteen hours, compared to four hours or less for F-16 fighter jets and A-10 ground attack aircraft".[41] Furthermore, as far as the advantages of drones are concerned, "unlike manned aircraft or raids, drones fly directly over hostile territory without placing pilots or ground troops at risk of injury, capture or death".[42]

The Christof Heyns' report to the United Nations' General Assembly wrote about drones as follows:

> Drones, assumed for the purpose of the present report to be armed drones, have moved from the horizon into the realm of the unknown. The appeal of drones is clear. Among other things, they provide the strategic advantage of greatly reducing the time between the identification of a potential target that could be a great distance away and the deployment of deadly force against that target. Drones, it can safely be said, are here to stay.[43]

Another report by a UN Special Rapporteur headed by Philip Alston was also of the view that although drones were originally developed to gather intelligence and conduct surveillance and reconnaissance, the appeal of armed drones (especially those that have the capacity to shoot laser-guided missiles, ranging from

38 See William C. Banks (2005), "The Predator", in Volker C. Franke (2005, ed.); *Terrorism and Peacekeeping* . . ., pp. 142–143, op. cit.
39 Ibid., p. 143.
40 Loc. Cit.
41 See Micah Zenko (2013), "Reforming U.S. Drone Strike Policies" . . ., p. 6, op. cit.
42 Loc. Cit.
43 See Christof Heyns' in "Report of the Special Rapportuer on Extrajudicial, Summary or Arbitrary Executions", op. cit.

35 pounds to more than 100 pounds) lies in their capacity to operate in hostile terrains, permitting targeted killings at little or no risk to the country's personnel that can remotely operate them from the home country.[44] But the foregoing examples are not all the advantages that drones can offer. They also "provide a near-instantaneous responsiveness—dramatically shrinking what U.S. military targeting experts call the 'find-fix-finish' loop—that most other platforms lack".[45] For instance, when in August 1998, the United States was targeting Osama bin Laden, the cruise missile "had to be programmed based on projections of where he would be in four to six hours, to allow time to analyze the intelligence, obtain presidential authorization, program the missiles, and fly them to the target".[46]

At that time in the Fall of 1998, a window of opportunity existed for taking out bin Laden; but then the reluctance of President Bill Clinton (the President being only desirous of "a guaranteed hit" and avoiding enormous civilian casualties), was not helped by the absence of armed drones when the only weapons of choice were Tomahawk missiles, a clandestine snatch by Special Operations Forces, and the "penetrating bombers or high-speed fighter aircraft" flown by U.S. Air Force and Naval forces;[47] but which might not guarantee the success of the mission or the avoidance of loss of American lives as well as civilian casualties as the armed drones could better guarantee. This lack of capacity for instantaneousness on the part of cruise missiles also applies to Inter-Continental Ballistic Missiles (ICBMs), which when "loaded with conventional munitions can reach distant targets much faster than cruise missiles, but they [the ICBMs] carry the dire risk of misattribution as a U.S. nuclear first strike against Russia or China".[48] But the near-instantaneous response of drones stands in stark contrast to the cruise missiles and ICBMs, and this inheres in the fact that "a drone-fired missile travels faster than the speed of sound, striking a target within seconds—often before it is heard by people on the ground".[49]

Drone-Targeted Killings and the Authority to Strike

President Barack Obama, while outlining his administration's counter-terrorism policy at the National Defence University in Fort McNair, acknowledged that (as new but unconventional, technologically driven weapons) armed drones raise this profound question of who is to be targeted and why, particularly in view of the

44 See Philip Alston in "Report of the Special Rapportuer on Extrajudicial, Summary or Arbitrary Executions", Human Rights Commission, Fourteenth session, Agenda item 3, promotion and protection of all rights, civil, political, economic, social and cultural rights, including the right to development, A/HRC/14/24/Add.6, May 28, 2010, available at www2.ohchr.org/english/bodies/hrcouncil/docs/14session/A.HRC.14.24.Add6.pdf (last visited on Thursday, September 17, 2015).

45 See Micah Zenko (2013), "Reforming U.S. Drone Strike Policies" . . ., p. 6, op. cit.

46 Loc. Cit.

47 See Robert "Buzz" Patterson (2003), *Dereliction of Duty* . . ., pp. 129–130, op. cit.

48 See Micah Zenko (2013), "Reforming U.S. Drone Strike Policies" . . ., p. 6, op. cit. Brackets mine.

49 Loc. Cit.

necessity to avoid civilian casualties, avoid the risks of "blowbacks" (that result in new enemies in countries whose territories are breached in pursuit of the terrorists), and make sure that the legality of the strikes are ensured alongside the requirement of accountability.[50] In fact, one of the problems that slow down the effectiveness or value of armed drones as weapons for instantaneous response is the authority to authorize strikes or targeting; that is, the authority to authorize the strikes after intelligence had identified and defined the targets to be struck as legitimate.

The controversy over the ultimate authority to authorize the firing of identified targets had allegedly "slowed the development of the new [drone] counterterrorism weapon".[51] But traditionally, it is an established principle in armed conflict and civil-military relations in general that civilian authorization is supreme.[52] And expectedly, the United States is the exemplar that leads the way in this tradition or ethos that "military commanders must be governed by the politics and directives issued to them" by the civilian authority.[53] Anything to the contrary is demurred and invites outright sanctions that include the relieving of command from the recalcitrant military officer. For instance, with a history of ignoring "the explicit instructions of [US President Herbert] Hoover", which dates back to 1932, when, "as a young Army Chief of Staff", General MacArthur orchestrated "a fiasco" when dispersing a crowd, he earned for himself a stigma and obviously became a marked man.[54]

General MacArthur was to be later excoriated as "self-glorifying", particularly in his running afoul of President Truman in his brushes with the President over Korea in the 1950s, when he ignored President "Truman's clearly stated war aims and [taking] it upon himself to campaign for a preemptive invasion of 'Red China' as the People's Republic of China was called in those days".[55] The consequence of his exuberant antecedence in overreaching the 1932 mission to disperse a crowd under President Herbert Hoover, including his overzealousness and refusal "to pipe down" in Korea, was that General MacArthur was relieved of his command, including the eternal opprobrium associated with his arrogance in thinking that "he was better equipped to decide such things than the civilians who then, as now, are elected to run the military".[56] What is the import of the foregoing in the question of who authorizes the drone strikes against identified and defined targets in the war on terror?

President Bill Clinton as far back as 1998 had authorized the CIA to use covert means to disrupt and preempt Osama bin Laden's terrorist operations,

50 See the "Full Transcript of President Obama's Speech on Counterterrorism Policy" . . ., op. cit.

51 See William C. Banks (2005), "The Predator", in Volker C. Franke (2005, ed.); *Terrorism and Peacekeeping* . . ., p. 145, op. cit.

52 See Fred Aja Agwu (2011), *The Law of Armed Conflict and African Wars* . . ., pp. 398–401, op. cit.

53 See Michael Duffy in "*Even Headstrong Generals Must Answer to Someone*", a book review in *Time* (New York), October 31, 2016, p. 47.

54 Loc. Cit.

55 Loc. Cit. Parentheses mine; see also Fred Aja Agwu (2011), *The Law of Armed Conflict and African Wars* . . ., pp. 398–400, op. cit.

56 See Michael Duffy in "Even Headstrong Generals Must Answer to Someone" . . ., p. 47, op. cit.

an authorization that was affirmed by President George W. Bush after 9/11, who also signed "an intelligence finding giving the CIA broad authority to pursue terrorism around the world".[57] In fact, although the intelligence finding aforementioned "contemplates a high and unprecedented degree of cooperation between the CIA and special forces", and although "the president delegated targeting and operational authority to senior civilian and military officials", the "precise approval mechanisms" remained classified.[58] But as it were, the factual and policy predicates of the document, the intelligence finding, indicated that the authorization to strike at pinpointed targets "must be personally approved by the President of the United States".[59]

Hence, "under the terms of an agreement, the CIA controllers did not have the authority to order a strike on the target", as in the case (on October 2001) of when its "officials . . . pinpointed the location of the supreme commander of the Taliban, Mullah Muhammad Omar" and had to delay to secure General Tommy R. Franks' approval, who also declined to approve that request and insisted on the personal approval of President Bush, within which time lag Mullah Omar changed his location, thus, disrupting the attack.[60] Had the CIA officials at that time been seized with the authority to authorize strikes on targets immediately as they are located or pinpointed, or had General Franks immediately authorized that strike without declining "on the basis of legal advice he received on the spot",[61] Mullah Omar would not have escaped. Thus, the disagreement lingered over who should have the ultimate authority for firing the hellfire missiles—the military or the CIA—even though this was apparently settled by the unfortunate incident of Mullah Omar's escape.[62]

That missed opportunity to take Mullah Omar out (caused by the traditional military chain-of-command reviews up to and apparently including the Commander-in Chief), "gave the CIA its first-ever authority to strike beyond a narrow range of preselected counterterrorism targets".[63] But the Obama administration congratulated itself for working "vigorously to establish a framework that governs" the United States' use of armed drones against terrorists—a framework that insists on "clear guidelines, oversight and accountability", and embodied in the codified "Presidential Policy Guidance" that President Obama signed in 2013, a day before his counter-terrorism speech at the nation's National Defense University.[64] These codes, as enunciated by President Obama, include

57 See William C. Banks (2005), "The Predator", in Volker C. Franke (2005, ed.); *Terrorism and Peacekeeping* . . ., p. 146, op. cit.

58 Loc. Cit.

59 Loc. Cit.

60 Ibid., p. 142.

61 Loc. Cit.

62 Ibid., pp. 145–146.

63 Ibid., p. 146.

64 See the "Full Transcript of President Obama's Speech on Counterterrorism Policy" . . ., op. cit.

(1) striking against high value al-Qaeda targets and "against forces that are massing to support attacks on coalition forces"; (2) not taking "strikes when we have the ability to capture individual terrorists—[as] our preference is always to detain, interrogate and prosecute them"; (3) not taking "strikes to punish individuals—[because] we act against terrorists who pose a continuing threat to the American people, and when there are no other governments capable of effectively addressing the threat"; and (4) to ensure that "before any strike is taken, there must be near-certainty that no civilians will be killed or injured—[being] the highest standard we can set".[65]

President Obama may have meant well in the enunciation of these codes, but there are still some inherent contradictions. For instance, the first inherent contradiction with the "Presidential Policy Guidance"—the codes aforementioned—is that the authorization of strikes against those massing to support attacks on coalition forces is an ideological justification for "signature strikes", those strikes that continually ruin the demand for the protection of civilians, more so when even large gatherings to bury victims of drone strikes are usually mistaken for terrorists massing to mount attacks. Second, the codes do not resolve the issue of who, apart from the President of the United States personally authorizing, should act on his behalf to avoid the kind of delay that led to Mullah Omar's escape—the CIA or the military? The involvement of the CIA is clearly antithetical to transparency and accountability because the CIA is a secret organization, the identity of whose members of which are never divulged, neither are they combatants in any war, thus, suffering the same rule of engagement incapacity as the terrorists themselves.

The result of the foregoing is that civilians still remain the ultimate victims despite the near-certainty in measures that the framework tends to suggest must be taken to avoid civilian casualties. But more significantly, the involvement of the CIA, which was not resolved by President Obama's codes, tends to relax the requisite rigorous oversight needed in maintaining safety for civilians, transparency, and accountability. Although personalities in the military like General MacArthur tend to suggest that the military itself is also vulnerable to over reach and overzealousness,[66] there is no doubt that the involvement of members of the CIA, who are more inclined to overreach and overzealousness than the professionalism-oriented members of the armed forces, is more ruinous to the noble philosophy embodied in the armed drones campaign.

However, on assumption of office, and especially in the wake of his new government's decision to drop the 21,000-pound-bomb (the Massive Air Ordnance Blast, MAOB) on Nangarhar (Afghanistan),[67] President Donald Trump gloated that "I authorized the generals to do the fighting", suggesting

65 Loc. Cit. Parentheses mine.

66 See Michael Duffy in "Even Headstrong Generals Must Answer to Someone" . . ., p. 47, op. cit.

67 See "Strategic Confusion: America Stokes Tensions on the Korean Peninsula, Then Tries to Lower Them Again", *The Economist*, April 22, 2017, pp. 45–46; see also Owei Lakemfa in "War without End", *Vanguard* (Lagos), Friday, May 5, 2017, p. 31.

that he had "shifted the authority for final approvals from the White House back to combatant commanders".[68] In a way that suggested that President Trump may have "revised the rules of engagement in the war on the Islamic State", he said about the combatant commanders' "requests for approval for drone strikes and Special Forces raids" that "they keep coming to me at weird times too".[69] The implication of abandoning the authority to authorize drone strikes to field or combatant commanders may have disastrous consequences, not only on humanitarian restraints, but also on the niceties of seeking authorization from the territorial state.

Drones as Dubious Weapons

Within the context of the normative framework that governs the means and methods of warfare, drones, even if not statutorily proscribed, are "dubious weapons", a terminology that was coined by the distinguished Dutch Professor, Bert Roling, and defined as such "because either the weapons themselves or the manner in which they are used are deemed not to be in accordance with principles of humanitarian law of armed conflict".[70] Drones characteristically fall into the bracket of prohibited or restricted weapons on account of being capable of actions that would lead to excessive injuries or indiscriminate consequences or effects, not only on the enemy "combatants" themselves but also on civilians and other protected persons and places.[71] This is because of their proclivity, like nuclear weapons, to produce indiscriminate or severe collateral damages or consequences, especially in "signature strikes" aforementioned that target large gatherings of people considered suspicious, even amongst a civilian population.

Other weapons that share the same dubious province with drones are nuclear weapons, chemical weapons, bacteriological weapons, incendiary weapons, non-detectable fragments, booby-traps, land and sea mines, and, of course, the IEDs, amongst other "dirty" weapons.[72] Like stealth bombers, Unmanned Aerial Vehicles (UAVs or drones) have not only come to establish themselves in this era of precision weapon revolution, they have also found their way into the inventories of the air forces of many of the advanced nations, transcending their hitherto futuristic nature and now tremendously adding to the air superiority of the possessing nations as well as the qualities and capabilities of the air forces of these nations.[73]

68 See "Trump after Hours: From Where the 45th President Works, Eats and Sleeps, Everything Is Going Just Great", *Time* (New York), May 22, 2017, p. 38.

69 Loc. Cit.

70 See Frits Kalshoven (1987), *Constraints on the Waging of War*, Geneva, International Committee of the Red Cross (ICRC), p. 147.

71 Loc. Cit.

72 Ibid., pp. 147–148.

73 See Richard P. Hallion (1997), "Air Power Past, Present and Future", in Richard P. Hallion (1997, ed.); *Air Power Confronts an Unstable World*, London, Washington, Brassey's, p. 9.

Value of Intelligence in Drone Strikes

The advent and profusion (or proliferation) of drones have offered a platform for the enhanced utilization of advanced sensor and intelligence, the two very key elements in aerial warfare.[74] Concerning intelligence in particular, as Micah Zenko has clearly shown, the use of drones cannot be possible without the aid of intelligence on the ground:[75] the same way that the prompt or instantaneous utilization of intelligence can also not be possible without the role of the drone platform in special operations raids.[76] As will be reiterated under the rubric of self-defence given later, it was for the sake of intelligence that the Central Intelligence Agency (CIA) maintained a paramilitary force of three thousand ethnic Pashtuns and even continued, alongside the U.S. military, to cooperate with their Pakistani counterparts.[77]

The release of the controversial U.S. Army Private First Class, Bowe Bergdahl, who, after being kidnapped in 2009, endured "five years as a hostage of the militant Haqqani network" (after being abducted in Afghanistan and spirited off to Pakistan),[78] provided a glimpse of the immense benefit of intelligence to drone strikes. Although put to trial after being accused of colluding with the Taliban enemy,[79] there was no doubt that his debriefers obtained vital information that enabled the CIA., after ten days of his recovery from the enemy, to open a sustained drone campaign in the place he was held in the tribal territory of Waziristan in northwestern Pakistan, a campaign that had been suspended "in the five months prior to Bergdahl's release".[80] Bowe Bergdahl was released on May 31, 2014,[81] but those drone strikes in North Waziristan led, on June 12, 2014, to the death of Haji Gul, a Haqqani commander and about six associated Haqqani militants; and "in the two months that followed, at least, six more strikes took out compounds, vehicles and dozens of suspected militants".[82]

By advancing the use of intelligence, and advanced sensor and targeting (hitherto very critical or key issues in aerial warfare), "the dividing line between what is now considered a precision-guided munition and an unmanned vehicle" is increasingly blurred.[83] Thus, conceptually, a drone (be it the Predator or Reaper) is that remotely piloted or "standard unmanned aerial vehicle . . . capable of

74 See Richard P. Hallion (1997), "Precision Air Attack in the Modern Era", in Richard P. Hallion (1997, ed.); *Air Power Confronts an Unstable World* . . ., pp. 125–126, op. cit.

75 See Micah Zenko (2013), "Reforming U.S. Drone Strike Policies" . . ., p. 7, op. cit.

76 Ibid., p. 6.

77 Ibid., p. 7.

78 See Michael Ames, "Traitor or Hero: What the U.S. Army Doesn't Want You to Know about Bowe Bergdahl", *Newsweek*, February 5, 2016, pp. 26, 33.

79 Ibid., pp. 26–33.

80 Ibid., p. 34.

81 Ibid., p. 29.

82 Ibid., p. 34.

83 See Richard P. Hallion (1997), "Precision Air Attack in the Modern Era", in Richard P. Hallion (1997, ed.); *Air Power Confronts an Unstable World* . . ., p. 125, op. cit.

providing real-time transmission of full motion video of objects on the ground",[84] permitting the remote pilot to discern a target from an "on-board" camera and decide when and how to fire. The significance of intelligence to drone strikes lies in the fact that, before its weaponization, the drone was used as a satellite and reconnaissance airplane. But the weaponization of the drone technology has led to the onset of its lethal dimension and controversies. Although this has been noted earlier, it is worth restating that 9/11 drew an unprecedented attention to unmanned aerial vehicles as these lethal weapons of war changed the nature of war because of their roles in the ensuing post-9/11 conflicts.[85] However, there is still a rough edge in the value of intelligence in the application of drones.

This rough edge is in the fact that the requirement of state consent often betrays the secrecy that is required for intelligence to be effective; this secrecy is usually given away by Trojan Horses within every system. But much as intelligence leverages drone strikes, the drone strikes themselves are paradoxically a nightmare to intelligence itself. Intelligence is of the essence, indeed, supreme in the war on terror; for it is only with the aid of intelligence that terrorist operations can be preempted or prevented at the point of origin from taking off.[86] But with targeted killings with or without drone strikes, and to the extent that these sorts of killings eliminate the possibility of capture and interrogation of the terrorists, they consequently destroy the possibility of getting the terrorists to speak and spill the beans. In other words, it is trite knowledge that "getting captured ISIS [and, indeed, any terrorist organization] fighters to talk is one of the crucial ways in which Western intelligence services have built up the picture of its . . . network and in particular, the role of its" principal commanders.[87]

It is for this reason that the terrorists themselves are always panicky and, in fact, on their toes whenever one of their own is arrested. This panic was amply illustrated by the speed with which the ISIS struck in Brussels the moment Salah Abdeslam, "one of the leading members of the cell behind the Paris attacks" of November 2015 was taken captive.[88] The group ostensibly struck the Brussels airport and metro station within one week of Abdeslam arrest apparently out of fear that the captive would divulge the plot. Although the ISIS commander in Europe, Abdelhamid Abaaoud, who took part in that Paris November 2015 attacks was not captured alive as he eventually blew himself up, part of the euphoria over the capture of Abdeslam was that he was going to provide more crucial intelligence on Abaaoud (even though posthumously), the way that Nicolas Moreau (arrested in 2015 after returning from the jihad fight in Syria) had provided valuable information on him as well as the department of ISIS he led, the ISIS's external operations department known as *Amni* (meaning security).[89]

84 See Stanley McChrystal (2015), *Team of Teams . . .*, p. 130, op. cit.
85 See Van Baldwin Carr (undated) in "Unmanned Aerial Vehicles . . .", p. 9, op. cit.
86 See Fred Aja Agwu (2013), *Themes and Perspectives . . .*, p. 373, op. cit.
87 See "Is in Europe . . .", p. 18, op. cit.
88 Loc. Cit.
89 Loc. Cit.

The *Amni* is a band consisting of 1,500 trained fighters that are hand-picked, paid 50,000 euros (about 40,000 British Pounds Sterling) and sent "back to Europe to inflict death and destruction on their homelands".[90] This network, its modus operandi, and leader were totally unknown to Western intelligence until the capture and interrogation of Moreau. It was Moreau that "revealed the *Kunya*, the nom de guerre of the person in charge of *Amni*—Abu Omar from Brussels"—who turned out to be Abdelhamid Abaaoud.[91] The point at issue here is that because the targeted killings inherent in drone strikes do not permit the capture of terrorists, it destroys the vital opportunity for the treasure troves of intelligence or information that would have otherwise been extracted from them. This is the reason President Obama emphasized in his speech on the United States' counter-terrorism policy that the likelihood of capture was Washington's preference.[92]

So the fact of not enabling capture is the contradictory role of armed drones in the war on terror vis-à-vis intelligence. The hell of missiles from drone strikes are not only equivalent to applying the sledge-hammer, it also entails the user shooting itself in the foot to the extent that it does not allow for capture and the extracting of valuable intelligence on the formations and operations of the dreaded terrorist networks. Although in the use of a team of Special Forces to raid his compound in Abbottabad (Pakistan), the United States deliberately did not want to capture Osama bin Laden in order not to iconize him (so much so that he was buried at sea rather than land from USS *Carl Vinson*[93]), many intelligence leads would have been obtained were the reverse the case. But in this relationship between armed drones and intelligence, the United States is clearly in a double bind. It must make use of the two, even though they can at times be mutually antagonistic as the foregoing indicates.

"Killer Robots": Nemesis of Abu Ali al-Hirithi and Mullah Mansour et al.

It was Richard Clarke that described the armed drones as "a bunch of flying killer robots".[94] But in order not to be deceived by the above sub-heading, it must be made clear here that compared to the autonomous weapons system that will be discussed later in this book, the armed drones are not entirely robotic because of the human input at the control points; but as it were,

90 Loc. Cit.
91 Loc. Cit.
92 See the "Full Transcript of President Obama's Speech on Counterterrorism Policy" . . ., op. cit.
93 See David Von Drehle in "Death Comes for the Terrorist: After More Than a Decade of Hunting, the U.S. Eliminates Its Most Hated Enemy", *Time* (New York), May 20, 2011, pp. 13–51; see also Mark Owen (2012), *No Easy Day: The Autobiography of a Navy SEAL (2012)*, England, Dutton (a member of Penguin group, USA), p. 272.
94 See Richard A. Clarke (2014), *Sting of the Drone*, New York, Thomas Dunne Books, St. Martin's Press, p. 85.

> the first notable event in the new era of drone warfare occurred when a remotely controlled Predator drone located, tracked and fired a hellfire missile on a car, killing Abu Ali al-Hirithi, al-Qaeda's top operative in Yemen and one of the planners of the 2000 *USS Cole* bombing.[95]

It was "the first use of an armed Predator outside Afghanistan, or indeed, the first military action in the war against terrorism outside Afghanistan", for "Al Harethi was described as the senior Al-Qaeda official in Yemen, one of the top ten to twelve Al-Qaeda operatives in the world".[96]

This was just one of the notable strikes that came to characterize the U.S. military operations in Afghanistan and Iraq, with the CIA also conducting a strike against the Afghani warlord, Gulbiddin Hetmatyar, "who, shortly after joining forces with the Taliban, was killed by a drone".[97] The CIA features very prominently in the United States' use of drones because being fundamentally intelligence-related from the outset, "the drones are CIA aircraft, part of the Special Activities division";[98] even though, as illustrated by the Mullah Muhammad Omar incident in Afghanistan in October 2001, the CIA, courtesy of an agreement, secures approval before hitting an identified target.[99] They may not be totally in control of the authority to strike identified targets; but with the CIA involvement, "the drones are controlled by civilian leaders outside the chain of command", civilian officials that "cooperate and share information and decision making with military commanders in a shared campaign against terrorism".[100]

It was a drone strike in South Waziristan, in what was curiously considered a "mysterious explosion" below Pakistani airspace that killed a Pakistani Taliban commander, Nek Muhammad, including other successful strikes that killed Haitham al-Yemeni, another high-ranking al-Qaeda weapon expert, and the Egyptian-born number three in al-Qaeda, Abu Abu Hamza Rabia.[101] Over a period of time, the persistent drones strike campaigns by the United States helped to successfully take out many of the Islamic fundamentalists that were sworn enemies of that country, its citizens and allies.[102] In fact, until he succumbed to the Hellfire of missiles from a U.S. drone strike, Islamic fundamentalists like the Afghan factional leader, Gulbuddin Hekmatyar, "had vowed to topple the government of Hamid Karzai and to attack U.S. forces".[103]

95 See Van Baldwin Carr (undated) in "Unmanned Aerial Vehicles . . .", p. 9, op. cit.
96 See William C. Banks (2005), "The Predator", in Volker C. Franke (2005, ed.); *Terrorism and Peacekeeping* . . ., pp. 144–145, op. cit.
97 See Van Baldwin Carr (undated) in "Unmanned Aerial Vehicles . . .", p. 9, op. cit.
98 See William C. Banks (2005), "The Predator", in Volker C. Franke (2005, ed.); *Terrorism and Peacekeeping* . . ., p. 143, op. cit.
99 Ibid., p. 142.
100 Ibid., p. 143.
101 See Van Baldwin Carr (undated) in "Unmanned Aerial Vehicles . . .", p. 9, op. cit.
102 See William C. Banks (2005), "The Predator", in Volker C. Franke (2005, ed.); *Terrorism and Peacekeeping* . . ., pp. 144–145, op. cit.
103 Ibid., p. 144.

Aside this catalogue of successful drone strikes, there were also some misses, like Abu Musab al-Zarqawi's first close shave with the drone. In combination with intelligence sources, a predator that was flying 10,000 feet above the ground had spotted Zarqawi travelling in a Sedan vehicle and moving across a lightly populated area west of Baghdad.[104] The drone operator had tracked the Sedan move into a cul-de-sac, stopped momentarily and drove out again, only missing al-Zarqawi through sheer bad luck as (to maintain surveillance) he had to adjust the drone's camera; thus, missing or failing to strike before Zarqawi jumped from the vehicle and moved away on foot.[105]

But a U.S. drone later successfully pinned down and killed al-Zarqawi on June 7, 2006, after dropping on him "a five-hundred-pound laser-guided bomb; . . . followed by a second, satellite-guided munition".[106] There was also another incident in which the drone missed al-Zawaheri, al-Qaeda's number two operative, destroying three buildings and killing 18 civilians, "including five women and five children", thereby, "enraging the Pakistani population".[107] However, others like Anwar Al-Awlaki and his passenger, Mr. Samir Kahn (both having U.S. citizenship) were both killed in Yemen in a hellfire missile strike by U.S. drones.[108]

As Richard Clarke put it, drones are "a bunch of flying killer robots"[109] that enables "guys . . . [to] go to war without leaving their desks".[110] Whereas "only ten years ago, the US Pentagon had an arsenal of approximately 50 drones at its disposal, nowadays over 7500 of these type of planes fly over the territories of Iraq, Afghanistan, Pakistan, Yemen and Somalia . . .".[111] Although the United States started the drone campaigns in 2004 under the President Bush Jr. administration in order to eliminate Osama bin Laden and other highly placed al-Qaeda members, the number of the attacks carried out by Washington since the advent of President Barack Obama rose sharply since 2009 and remained unabated till he left office.[112]

Whereas President George W. Bush reportedly authorized about 50 non-battlefield targeted killing strikes by drones, President Obama "more than septupled that number", having as at January 2013, authorized 350 strikes.[113] And even at the risk of scuppering a widely expected peace talk between the Taliban and the Afghan, President Obama also authorized the drone strike that,

104 See Stanley McChrystal (2015), *Team of Teams* . . ., p. 130, op. cit.
105 Ibid., p. 131.
106 See Michael Weiss and Hassan Hassan (2015), *ISIS* . . ., p. 61, op. cit.
107 See Van Baldwin Carr (undated) in "Unmanned Aerial Vehicles . . .", p. 9, op. cit.
108 See Geert-Jan Alexander Knoops (2012), "Legal, Political and Ethical Dimensions of Drone Warfare under International Law. . .", p. 699, op. cit.
109 See Richard A. Clarke (2014), *Sting of the Drone* . . ., p. 85, op. cit.
110 Ibid., p. 77.
111 See Geert-Jan Alexander Knoops (2012), "Legal, Political and Ethical Dimensions of Drone Warfare under International Law. . .", p. 698, op. cit.
112 Loc. Cit.
113 See Micah Zenko (2013), "Reforming U.S. Drone Strike Policies" . . ., p. 8, op. cit.

on Saturday, May 21, 2016, killed the Taliban leader, Mullah Akhtar Mansour, in South West Pakistan.[114] The Obama Presidency not only believed in the efficacy of the drone technology as a weapon against terror, it also believed in its pragmatism in dealing with the highly evasive terrorists; and remained with this conviction all through that Presidency, despite the controversies surrounding the weapon.

A Signal of American Arrogance

Drone strikes have, thus, come to be regarded as "just a signal of arrogance", a signal of American arrogance and an instrument of its foreign policy, which, paradoxically, was broadly becoming unpopular because they were contradicting the country's stated non-military foreign policy objectives, what with the drones overshadowing and diminishing the effectiveness of the country's civilian assistance programmes.[115] In the resource-rich but impoverished African nation of Niger Republic where viable public infrastructures are virtually nonexistent, "it is instructive that the single largest piece of US infrastructure [there] . . . was the $100m drone facility".[116]

In Niger, the United States financed "the construction of a new 3km runway and associated infrastructure for a drone base in Agadez", where Washington also had "drones, including MQ-9 Reaper drones, stationed at Niamey to support France's Operation Barkhane".[117] In fact, "Niger is the only country in the region accepting to host MQ-9 UD drones that can conduct airstrikes".[118] As it were, "Niger has positioned itself to become a crucial base for US operations in the region"; and "Agadez is a bridgehead for launching reconnaissance and surveillance [over Niger and Chad as well as Libya, Nigeria, and further afield] against a plethora of terrorist groups".[119] And Washington does not hesitate to deploy and apply these drones whenever occasions call for it, even if it had previously undertaken not to do so.

For instance, in 2012, the Secretary of State, Hillary Clinton, remarked at a press conference for the International Contact Group on Somalia as follows: "I know enough to say airstrikes would not be a good idea; and we have absolutely no reason to believe anyone—certainly not the United States—is considering that [for Somalia]".[120] But Secretary Clinton's outburst was not to deter subsequent attacks, as within hours of her statement, "a convoy was attacked in the

114 See "Afghan Confirms Death of Taliban Leaders", *Nigerian Tribune* (Ibadan), Monday, May 23, 2016, p. 37.

115 See Micah Zenko (2013), "Reforming U.S. Drone Strike Policies" . . ., p. 11, op. cit.

116 See Johannes Makar in "America's Good Cop", *New African*, February 2017, p. 47.

117 See Jeremy H. Keenan in "War Games in the Sahel", *New African*, January 2017, p. 37.

118 Loc. Cit.

119 Loc. Cit.

120 See Micah Zenko (2013), "Reforming U.S. Drone Strike Policies" . . ., p. 11, op. cit. Brackets mine.

Shabelle region of Somalia, killing between four and seven suspected Islamic militants".[121] Armed drones strikes have continued till date against the henchmen of the al-Qaeda, the ISIS, and other terrorist organizations in Iraq, Syria, Afghanistan, and Yemen.

In early February 2016, the United States' drone strike in Southern Yemen killed Jalal Baleedi, also known as Hamza al-Marqashi, along with two of his guards near the town of Azzan.[122] Apart from being identified since 2004 as the field commander of the al-Qaeda in the Arabian Peninsula (AQAP), Baleedi had also pledged allegiance and, indeed, joined the Islamic State of Iraq and the Levant (ISIL, also called ISIS),[123] which made him a veritable target with the Predator. There were also reports at that time that another U.S. drone attacks "killed six alleged al-Qaeda fighters in their car travelling in Yemen's southern Shabwa province".[124]

So, as a symbol of American power, if not arrogance, American drone attacks did not abate, even when Secretary Clinton said that "I know enough to say airstrikes would not be a good idea"—not just in Somalia, but elsewhere around the world in the "global" war on terror. But the Somalian strike that first contradicted Secretary Clinton was not the handiwork of the CIA; for "an anonymous U.S. official" confirmed that it was actually a Joint Special Operations Command, JSOC (which also conducts drone strikes like the CIA[125]) that was behind the drone attack that killed the militants.[126] This was the extent that the United States' use of drone strikes as an emblem of its national arrogance and foreign policy had been mired in confusion and marked by controversy and even ambiguity and secrecy too—secrecy in the sense that, unlike the Obama administration, the George W. Bush administration "never openly discussed any aspect of its targeted killing policies".[127]

The implication of this secrecy is that "both the American and International publics often misunderstand how drones are used"; with some countries even tending to blame the United States for their own attacks; that is, attacks by the host states' weapons systems.[128] In the United States, the tendency for some critics to single out the Obama administration for blames in the escalation of the drone strikes seems to miss the point that this symbol of American arrogance can also enjoy an escalated deployment by any President in the White House, irrespective of party or ideological affiliation. If President George W. Bush did not use drone strikes as massively as President Obama, it may well be that the situation did

121 Loc. Cit.

122 See "U.S Drones Strike Kills Senior al-Qaeda Leader in Yemen", *The Guardian* (Lagos), Friday, February 5, 2016, p. 50.

123 Loc. Cit.

124 Loc. Cit.

125 See Micah Zenko (2013), "Reforming U.S. Drone Strike Policies" . . ., pp. 7–8, op. cit.

126 Ibid., p. 11.

127 Ibid., p. 8.

128 Ibid., p. 15.

not so warrant. For the sake of America's security from terrorists, any American President must be inclined to deploy the drones as soon as possible, even in the President's first day in office.

For instance, although as a retaliatory measure against the al-Qaeda terrorist group, the U.S. drone strikes against suspected al-Qaeda targets had been commonplace in the years since the September 11, 2001 attacks; and although the use of this unmanned aircraft had dramatically spiked under President Obama, especially between 2012 and 2016, the first drone strike under President Donald John Trump (as he assumed office on Friday, January 20, 2017) took place the next day, Saturday, January 21, 2017, in Yemen's southwestern Bayda province, killing three alleged al-Qaeda operatives, Abu Anis al-Abi (an area field commander) and two others.[129] It cannot be logically said that it was the order President Obama left behind that legitimated that Yemen strike 24 hours after he exited office. The Yemen strike, a day after President Trump took office, must undoubtedly been under Trump's behest, not Obama; suggesting that President Trump was also keen on deploying the armed drones the way that President Obama did, if the situation in the war on terror called for such.

To consolidate its dominance in the armed drone technology, the United States has developed a Laser Weapon System (LaWS)—the U.S. Navy's drone-killing laser, which "is more precise than a bullet" and "begins with an advantage no other weapon ever invented comes even close to matching" because "it moves . . . at the speed of light"—comparable to about "50,000 times the speed of an incoming ICBM".[130] The "LaWS . . . is not science fiction; it is not experimental; it is deployed on board the USS Ponce amphibious transport ship, ready to be fired at targets"—[131] any U.S. adversary's drone targets. The U.S. Navy's drone-killing laser—as an invisible killer—operates at the silent and invisible speed of light; and immediately it is fired at any adversarial drone, "the drone's wing lit up, heated to a temperature of thousands of degrees, lethally damaging the aircraft and sending it hurtling down to the sea".[132] The drone-killing laser can enable the United States to confront and easily overwhelm any rival nation.

Weaponization/the Arming of Drones

Although the time that weaponized drones were deployed by the United States embodies some whiff of controversy, especially with the report crediting retired U.S. Air Force General John Jumper with first arming the predator seven months

129 See "Suspected US Drone Strike Kills 3 Alleged Al Qaeda Operatives in Yemen", available at www.bostonglobe.com/news/world/2017/01/22/suspected-drone-strike-kills-alleged-qaeda-operatives-yemen/8tlcAqfivlCiPQyCg5ZsUN/story.html (last visited on Tuesday, January 24, 2017).

130 See Jim Sciutto and Dominique van Heerden in "Exclusive: CNN Witnesses US Navy's Drone-Killing Laser", available at http://edition.cnn.com/2017/07/17/politics/us-navy-drone-laser-weapon/index.html (last visited on Tuesday, July 18, 2017).

131 Loc. Cit.

132 Loc. Cit.

before 9/11,[133] there is no doubt that before the September 11, 2001 terrorist attacks on the United States, Washington had restricted its use of drones to surveillance missions, and mostly employed "unmanned aircraft like the General Atomics Predator".[134] It was after the tragic event of 9/11 and the resultant U.S. invasion of Afghanistan and Iraq that weaponized drones became an essential tool of that nation's armed forces in counter-insurgency.[135]

And although "the combat debut of the Predator came in 1995 in the skies over Bosnia, (where it provided sharp "real time" [intelligence] images of the battlefield"[136]), the 9/11 attacks against the United States was actually the point in time that "the Pentagon armed the Predator and a larger hitherto unmanned surveillance plane—the Reaper—with missiles; so that their operators—sitting in offices in places like Nevada or New York—could destroy as well as spy on targets thousands of miles away".[137] From then on, up from fewer than 200 in 2002, the United States had, as at 2013, deployed more than 11,000 military drones to carry out a variety of missions; and all of this, primarily, has been allegedly to save "money and American lives".[138] In fact, William Banks invoked the authority of the United States' administration officials to support the assertion that "the decision to develop the Predator as a combat device was made specifically to attack [Osama] bin Laden".[139]

Washington's Drone Monopoly

Enjoying the latitude of unilaterally defining a generous scope of legitimate targets; and comfortable with all of its inherent benefits—despite the fact that, ethically, drone strikes lower the threshold for the use of force, making the latter easily attractive, irrespective of attendant cost to human life—the United States is reputed to also be capable to continue enjoying, for the foreseeable future, the unrivaled leadership in the development of Medium-Altitude Long Endurance (MALE) armed drone technology.[140] In fact, when he wrote in 2013, Micah Zenko was of the conviction that the United States was "projected to account for 62 percent of all drone research and development, and 55 percent of all procurement over the next decade", and that "with a projected $80 billion in global spending for the next ten years, drones constitute a potential growth industry for the aerospace and defense sectors".[141]

133 See Mark Thompson in "Can the drones be stopped? As the US' Edge in Unmanned Aircraft Fades, a Scramble for Defenses", *Time* (New York), February 23–March 2, 2015, p. 14.
134 See John Horgan in "The Drones Come Home", *National Geographic*, March 2013, p. 124.
135 Ibid., pp. 124–125.
136 See William C. Banks (2005), "The Predator", in Volker C. Franke (2005, ed.); *Terrorism and Peacekeeping* . . ., p. 145, op. cit. Br mine.
137 See John Horgan in "The Drones Come Home" . . ., p. 125, op. cit.
138 Loc. Cit.
139 See William C. Banks (2005), "The Predator", in Volker C. Franke (2005, ed.); *Terrorism and Peacekeeping* . . ., p. 145, op. cit.
140 See Micah Zenko (2013), "Reforming U.S. Drone Strike Policies" . . ., p. 18, op. cit.
141 Loc. Cit.

Since then, at least 50 other countries have acquired drones: the more notable of those are Russia, China, Israel, and Iran, which also have their own manufacturers.[142] "Nevertheless", as Micah Zenko was persuaded, "there is not yet public evidence of non-U.S. states—except Israel—developing an armed drone capability".[143] Actually, despite the present American leadership in the modern drone technology, Israel was actually more prolific in this regard and had begun research in the development of modern drones in 1970, remaining or continuing at the endeavour at a fervid pace till date.[144] Israel had also taken the lead in the deployment of drones (though not necessarily armed drones) in asymmetric warfare, having found itself in "a region mired in political turmoil and war"; and having, during Operation Peace in 1982 over the Syrian-occupied area of Lebanon, destroyed surface-to-air missile batteries by deploying unmanned decoys that the Syrians attacked, wasting resources and divulging the locations of the batteries for targeting by Israeli fighters.[145]

Indeed, it was in the late 80s and early 90s [that] the United States renewed its interest in unmanned aerial systems after observing that in both Lebanon and Syria, Israel was among the first nations to employ such vehicles regularly for combat, demonstrating that when used effectively, they can help achieve combat objectives.[146]

Expectedly, the two nations, as very close allies and joint pioneers, embarked, from then on, on a programme of joint development that ushered in the age of more modernized unmanned aviation.[147] They worked had in hand to develop the *Hunter* and *Pioneer* UAVs (all for reconnaissance missions), the latter of which was effectively used by the U.S. Navy during the second Persian Gulf War (that evicted Saddam from Kuwait) "to spot enemy fire for the delivery of munitions".[148] The *Pioneer* also successfully operated in a surveillance capacity for the Marines in the 1994 Balkan conflict, and in Kosovo in 1999, all successes that popularized the attraction of drones as well as an interest in exploring its use outside traditional military applications.[149]

In the apparent global competition for the ability to develop and be capable of deploying reconnaissance and armed drones, many countries embarked on either the development or the acquisition and addition of this new weapon into their arsenals. Drone development is different and, indeed, distinguishable from drone acquisition; but both are the function of the resources available to the nation, as

142 See John Horgan in "The Drones Come Home" . . ., p. 125, op. cit; see also Micah Zenko (2013), "Reforming U.S. Drone Strike Policies" . . ., p. 18, op. cit.

143 See Micah Zenko (2013), "Reforming U.S. Drone Strike Policies" . . ., p. 18, op. cit.

144 See Van Baldwin Carr (undated) in "Unmanned Aerial Vehicles . . .", p. 7, op. cit.

145 Loc. Cit.

146 Loc. Cit. Brackets mine.

147 Ibid., p. 8.

148 Loc. Cit.

149 Loc. Cit.

well as the soundness of its industrial base, enough to enable it to embark on the manufacturing of the weapon. Apparently because of the short supply of the two variables aforementioned (that is, financial resources and industrial manufacturing capability, the latter of which is tied to technological know-how), many countries, aside from the United States and Israel, became merely drone acquisition nations. Because of the fad that is the jostling for acquisition, "it is estimated that the number of states that have acquired a complete drone system has grown from forty-one in 2005 to seventy-six in 2012"; whereas, "over the same period of time, the number of total drone programs within those countries increased from one hundred [and] ninety-five to nine hundred".[150]

Although much of the acquired drones as well as those made from the various drone programmes were used by countries that developed or acquired them exclusively for government or civilian intelligence, surveillance and reconnaissance missions, some industrialized countries like Russia, Taiwan, and South Korea "have developed increasingly sophisticated and largely indigenous drone capabilities"; even though they have also largely missed the deadlines for the weaponization or the arming of the drones.[151] But the way the trend is going, and although Micah Zenko is optimistic that not many states would, within the near future, have "the complete system [or] architecture required to carry out distant strikes", either by dint of their financial resources or capacity to purchase/acquire, or their possession of the industrial base to manufacture drones, the scary truth is that many states are becoming increasingly interested in this lethal weapon.[152]

Below the Radar Development of Drones

One of the greatest dangers inherent in expressly unregulated weapons like armed drones is the tendency for some countries to develop it under the table; even when it may be publicly said that they missed the deadlines for the arming or weaponization of the lethal technology. It is this tendency towards the secret development that saw some countries like India, Pakistan, and even North Korea acquiring the nuclear weapon before the world could wake up to the reality that they had the capacity to do so. Although some underdeveloped nations like Nigeria may be underestimated in this regard because they putatively lack the industrial base, but this same prejudice cannot be held against human ingenuity for long. Nigeria, particularly since faced with the Niger Delta militancy and the terrorist campaigns of the Boko Haram, has been aspiring to cultivate the

150 See Micah Zenko (2013), "Reforming U.S. Drone Strike Policies" . . ., p. 18, op. cit. Brackets mine.

151 Loc. Cit.

152 Ibid., p. 20. Brackets mine.

drone technology, whether indigenously or through acquisition from countries like Israel.

In 2006, Nigeria struck a deal to purchase unarmed spy drones from the Israelis to be deployed in the oil-producing Niger Delta to checkmate the militants attacking oil pipelines and kidnapping oil workers.[153] But hopes were to rise that these hi-tech Aerostar unmanned surveillance drones, supplied by the Israeli Aeronautic Defence System, would also be deployed to hunt down the Boko Haram in the wake of the abduction of the Chibok girls.[154] Curiously, the country never commissioned the drones after they were purchased,[155] but the military authorities proceeded in December 2013 to unveil a locally made drone at an Air Force base in Kaduna.[156] Unarguably, the purchased but unused Israeli drones may have been cannibalized (stripped or diemembered) to aid the fabrication of the so-called locally made Nigerian drones which operational relevance remained in serious doubt because of Nigeria's weak technological base, and its equally weak support for research and development. But what remains clear is that the Nigerian so-called locally fabricated drone, clearly unarmed, would probably be restricted to surveillance or intelligence activities.

The unarming of the said Nigerian drone is surely the case because Nigeria does not have the wherewithal, the requisite industrial capacity to arm drones. And so, when on Wednesday, February 3, 2016, many Nigerian newspapers reported that Nigerian "air force drones hit" and destroyed "Boko Haram's base in Sambisa",[157] it was obvious that the reports never accurately or appropriately conveyed the message of the military authorities; or that if they did, the military spokesman that passed the message to the press was indulging in "the kinetic stuff"[158] or merely posturing because Nigeria never owned armed drones and could never have got the U.S. armed drones to strike the Boko Haram. Washington's priorities in the use of armed drones were only concentrated on strikes on the ISIS and al-Qaeda in Iraq, Syria, Afghanistan, and Yemen. But the larger point to be made here is that no research-based and inventive nation actually needs more than one specimen of any technology to develop its own; after all, it was only one U.S. drone that Iran reportedly captured that it used to fabricate

153 See Emma Emeozor in the report, "Drones Nigeria Bought from Israel Grounded, Reveals Manufacturer: Poor Maintenance Blamed", *Daily Sun* (Lagos), Wednesday, May 21, 2014, p. 16.

154 Loc. Cit.

155 Loc. Cit.

156 Loc. Cit.

157 See Our Reporters, "Air Force Drone Hit Boko Haram's Base in Sambisa: Troops Stop Two Suicide Bombers", *The Nation* (Lagos), Wednesday, February 3, 2016, pp. 1, 5; Timothy Olanrewaju and Molly Kilete in "NAF Drones Bombard Boko Haram Strongholds: Military Intercepts 2 Bombers in Maiduguri", *Daily Sun* (Lagos), Wednesday, February 3, 2016, p. 11; and Ronald Mutum in "Air Force Unmanned Aerial Vehicle Destroys B/ Haram Logistics Base", *Daily Trust* (Abuja), Wednesday, February 3, 2016, p. 4.

158 See Fred Aja Agwu (2011), *The Law of Armed Conflict and African Wars . . .*, pp. 419–420, op. cit.

and now claims to have manufactured its own drone surveillance machine. This is the extent to which the surreptitious development of this weapon in unlikely places, including even by individual gangs or brigands themselves, is real.

The UAE, for instance, is reported to have "spent five years building the armed United-40 drone with an associated Namrod missile"; and "a march 2011 analysis by [a] marketing research firm, Lucintel, projected that a fully developed [armed drone] product will take another decade".[159] Indeed, it is also true that "after the United States, Israel has the most developed and varied drone capabilities"; and that, although Tel Aviv "allows the United States to veto transfers of weapons with U.S-origin technology to select states,[160] including China", the same "Israel was responsible for 41 percent of drones exported between 2001 and 2011" (drones like Harop, a short-range attack variety, to France, Germany, Turkey, and India), while not a member of the MTCR, and having "used armed drones in the Palestinian territories".[161] This does not, in any case, prejudice the fact that Israel "has predominantly sold surveillance drones that lack hard points and electrical engineering".[162]

The Future of Drones and Implications for State and Non-State Actors

The very fact that, not being a member of the 1987 Missile Technology Control Regime (MTCR), Israel sold the Harop to some countries that would definitely improve on it or sell it to controversial countries is an indication that it is facilitating the spread of this weapon. In any case, the fact that some non-state actors like the Hezbollah has accessed drones, having "flown the Iranian-supplied Abibil that reportedly boasts an eighty-eight-pound explosive triggered by crashing the drone into a target",[163] is a cause for concern. This sort of drone may have been the primitive or "pristine" type, described by Evan Baldwin Carr as self-terminating, as opposed to the more technologically refined that is not self-terminating,[164] but it is all the same an apt instrument for terrorist operations because many terrorists do not intend to survive their operations by way of delivering their payloads and returning to base for future deployment.[165]

It is also not a boon either that individuals that are non-state actors, individuals like U.S. citizen Rezwan Ferdaus (who pleaded guilty to attempting to attack

159 See Emma Emeozor in the report, "Drones Nigeria Bought from Israel Grounded, Reveals Manufacturer . . .", p. 16, op. cit. Parentheses mine.

160 For instance, in the height of Nigeria's counter-insurgency operations against the Boko Haram, it sought to purchase certain advanced weapon grades from South Africa, but this was blocked by the United States; See Fred Aja Agwu (2016), *Nations among Nations*. . ., p. 906, op. cit.

161 See Micah Zenko (2013), "Reforming U.S. Drone Strike Policies" . . ., p. 20, op. cit.

162 Loc. Cit.

163 Ibid., p. 21.

164 See Van Baldwin Carr (undated) in "Unmanned Aerial Vehicles . . .", pp. 5–6, op. cit.

165 Ibid., p. 6.

the Pentagon and U.S. Capitol with three remotely piloted aircraft, laden with five pounds of homemade explosives that would have caused significant damage to the two federal buildings)[166] was in possession of these remotely piloted aircraft, a simpler variant of the armed drone technology. In fact, "primitive drones like those that Ferdaus sought to build could become more prevalent in domestic terror attacks".[167] But beyond the possibility of non-state actors possessing and deploying armed drones for terrorist activities, the awesome power (at times lacking in the principle of proportionality and discrimination) that these weapons put in the hand of the nation-state gives a terrifying dimension to warfare in the 21st century, be it conventional or unconventional.

In the future of drones also lies its added strategic advantage, which probably informed the decision of the United States to establish a drone base in the Republic of Niger, seen by critics as Washington's surreptitious way of establishing a "*de facto* Africom" in the West African sub-region.[168] The United States was faced with a stiff resistance in the region as it tried to set up the African Command (ARICOM), prompting it to move the Command's headquarters to Stuttgart in Germany.[169] But in addition to the efforts of other Western nations, the American Niger drone base was to seem very attractive when Nigeria found itself in a bind over the Chibok girls that were kidnapped from their school hostels by the Boko Haram insurgents, the kith and kin of the al-Qaeda.[170] The American drones provided a risk-free hope that the United States would be part of the rescue of the Chibok girls without the danger of imperiling its airmen.

But beside this risk-free opportunity that drones offer in aerial reconnaissance as well as combat, and with drones expected to be capable of replacing most manned military aircraft within a generation,[171] other traditional types of warfare like the use of infantry, cavalry (tanks), or even fighter jets and Apache helicopters would most probably be replaced too.[172] Thus, armed drones have become serious implements of warfare for the present, and will remain predictably so for the future. As the Christof Heyns' report of the United Nations' Special Rapportuer opined:

> Drones are expected to become more sophisticated and available in more compact form, and also to become less expensive and therefore more accessible. They are likely to form part of the arsenals of an increasing number of

166 See Micah Zenko (2013), "Reforming U.S. Drone Strike Policies" . . ., p. 21, op. cit.

167 Loc. Cit.

168 See, for instance, B. M. Sani in "A US Drone Base in Niger Would be de facto Africom", *Daily Trust* (Abuja), Tuesday, February 12, 2013, p. 51.

169 Loc. Cit; see also Fred Aja Agwu (2009), *National Interest, International Law* . . ., pp. 236–280, op. cit.

170 Even the British also mobilized their spy planes in search of the missing girls, see "RAF Spy Plane Breaks Down on Way to Find Chibok Girls", *Vanguard* (Lagos), Tuesday, May 20, 2014, p. 58.

171 See John Horgan in "The Drones Come Home" . . ., p. 125, op. cit.

172 See Geert-Jan Alexander Knoops (2012), "Legal, Political and Ethical Dimensions of Drone Warfare under International Law. . .", p. 697, op. cit.

> states that may be able to deploy such force across international borders in relatively non-intrusive and sometimes non-attributable ways, on the battlefield and to pursue targets far removed from what would traditionally be seen as zones of armed conflict. . . . Armed drones may fall into the hands of non-state actors and may also be hacked by enemies or other entities. In sum, the number of states with the capacity to use drones is likely to increase significantly in the near future, underscoring the need for greater consensus on the terms of their use.[173]

The drone technology may also probably "replace satellite reconnaissance-airplanes".[174] Meanwhile, all the nations that have acquired the drone technology, including those that aspire to acquire it, have very strong convictions about its necessity. For the United States' Air Force, the vision behind the weaponization of the drone technology is "to harness increasingly, automated, modular, and sustainable UAS [Unmanned Aircraft Systems]; resulting in leaner, more adaptable and tailorable forces that maximize the effectiveness of 21st century air power"; and this is particularly because "Unmanned Aircraft Systems have . . . some compelling advantages over humans because human physiological limits, such as speed of reaction and persistence, can prevent a proper mission execution".[175]

But although prided to be more effective in the execution of missions than humans, the compatibility of the weaponization of drones with the law of armed conflict (indeed, both international humanitarian law and international criminal law) is still very much as issue, especially "with the advent of the so-called 'seek and destroy' drones, drones capable of making autonomous decisions, life-or-death decisions that (though touted to be futuristic) have been tested by the United States' Navy".[176] Besides the problem of compatibility with international law, the authorization of drone strikes also raises some serious political problems verging on the tendency to arbitrariness by the political leadership, the executive arm of government, especially in the wielding of presidential powers as in the United States. In the United States, for instance, because drone strikes are easily inclined to be viewed as limited military operations, the President usually does not see himself as obligated to operate under the "War Powers Resolution" of the Congress,[177] the Authorization for the Use of Military Force (AUMF), a joint resolution that was passed by the U.S. Congress on September 18, 2001, in the wake of the 9/11 attacks.[178]

173 See Christof Heyns' in "Report of the Special Rapportuer on Extrajudicial, Summary or Arbitrary Executions" . . ., op. cit.

174 See Geert-Jan Alexander Knoops (2012), "Legal, Political and Ethical Dimensions of Drone Warfare under International Law. . .", p. 697, op. cit.

175 Ibid., p. 699.

176 Ibid., pp. 699–700.

177 Ibid., p. 701.

178 See Micah Zenko (2013), "Reforming U.S. Drone Strike Policies" . . ., p. 16, op. cit.

Thus maintaining that targeted killings with the instrumentality of drones are consistent with U.S. domestic law, the Obama administration was of the view that the White House would not seek congressional approval beyond the approval in the AUMF, made immediately the 9/11 attacks happened, and intended to strike al-Qaeda operatives elsewhere in the world, whether in Yemen, Somalia, or anywhere around the world.[179] This is the same way that the administration insisted that being consistent with international law, "targeted killings do not require a separated self-defence analysis"; and that once an imminent threat of violent attack against the United States was posed, Washington's response with drone drones attacks would "stem from the assertion that the United States is in a continuous state of international armed conflict with al-Qaeda and associated forces".[180] The Obama administration's argument can only be admissible because the war on terror is irregular and an extra-ordinary exigency.

In a conventional armed conflict, the argument of responding to an imminent threat without an armed attack would be inadmissible; but it is certainly admissible in the war on terror because terrorists do not attack in a conventional war. And unfortunately, they attack soft targets, civilians, and generally vulnerable groups. In both conventional and unconventional (the war on terror), the argument is that the "continuous state of international armed conflict can also be admissible". This is because, permanent aggression can necessitate permanent self-defence and even the occupation of territory, a scenario that Julius Stone invoked to justify the Israeli occupation of Arab lands in the absence of a peace treaty.[181] This is the only solid ground the Obama administration can stand in asserting a "continuous state of armed conflict" and its resultant continuous affirmation of the right of self-defence, putative or preemptive self-defence against the al-Qaeda with drone strikes. But it smacks of dictatorship or taking a unilateral measure for the U.S. President to evade congressional approval for any reason. Consequently, in not seeking the normal Congressional "war Powers Resolution" on the strength of the AUMF of September 18, 2001, or because of the assumed limited military operational nature of drone strikes, President Obama has been reported to have sometimes himself approved drone strikes and even personally selected the human targets through a "kill list".[182]

But the "kill list" is not fool-proof. Although it is claimed by John Brennan that due care is taken in drawing the "kill list", but "it seems that being put on such a list automatically legitimizes killing despite the many flaws and weaknesses in the process".[183] The "kill list" nonetheless more often than not contains valid targets. Abu Yahaya al-Libi, the second highest placed al-Qaeda member after the

179 Loc. Cit.

180 Loc. Cit.

181 See Fred Aja Agwu (2005), *United Nations System, State Practice and the Jurisprudence of the Use of Force . . .*, p. 79, op. cit.

182 See Geert-Jan Alexander Knoops (2012), "Legal, Political and Ethical Dimensions of Drone Warfare under International Law. . .", p. 701.

183 See Ahmad Nazir Warraich (2013), "The Use of Drones . . .", p. 76, op. cit.

death of Osama Bin Laden in May 2011, was one of those in the kill list; and he was, on June 4, 2012, eliminated by a U.S. drone in Pakistan.[184] Nevertheless, it is because of the United States' vague definition of the enemy as the "Al-Qaeda, Taliban and associated forces"[185] that the "kill list" is usually elastic and commodious, containing any conceivable suspect and making it possible for mistakes or the killing of innocent persons to occur. As it were, the U.S. Congress was made powerless here because President Obama, in authorizing the use of drones in the killing of the terrorists on the "kill list", wielded "his presidential powers to avoid judicial and congressional control".[186] The United States' age-old established principle that governs the authorization of the use of force is apparently being circumvented by the deployment of drone strikes: the laid-down institution of "War Powers Resolution" as "legal rights and guarantees" against presidential excesses.[187]

Thus, the authorization for drone attacks does not only create complications in international law (both international criminal justice and the humanitarian law aspect of the law of armed conflict), it also creates complications for the United States' political processes, the interface between the legislature and the executive arms of government vis-à-vis the authorization of the use of force and the "War Powers Resolution" of Congress. Beyond these legal and political niceties, there is the controversial issue of the targets of the drone strikes. These targets are distinguishable into two: the "personality strikes" and the "signature strikes".[188] Whereas the "personality strikes" are strikes "on high valued terrorists such as Al-Alibi"; the "signature strikes" are those "on training camps and suspicious grounds".[189]

But it is believed by Micah Zenko that there should be an end to the signature strikes; and that all strikes should, by implication, be limited to personality strikes, those "leaders of transnational terrorist organizations and individuals with direct involvement in past or ongoing plots against the United States and its allies".[190] Yet, even the personality strikes have their own peculiar controversy. This controversy is on who qualifies as a lawful target, and where and when should that person be target?[191] In addressing this question, Alexander Knoops is persuaded that "the mere fact that individuals engage in illegal action, for instance terrorist activities, does not by itself justify the conclusion that these persons fulfill the threshold or the criterion [of] direct participation in hostilities".[192]

184 See Geert-Jan Alexander Knoops (2012), "Legal, Political and Ethical Dimensions of Drone Warfare under International Law. . .", pp. 701–702, op. cit.
185 See Ahmad Nazir Warraich (2013), "The Use of Drones . . .", p. 75, op. cit.
186 See Geert-Jan Alexander Knoops (2012), "Legal, Political and Ethical Dimensions of Drone Warfare under International Law. . .", p. 702, op. cit.
187 Loc. Cit.
188 Loc. Cit.
189 Loc. Cit.
190 See Micah Zenko (2013), "Reforming U.S. Drone Strike Policies" . . ., p. 4, op. cit.
191 See Geert-Jan Alexander Knoops (2012), "Legal, Political and Ethical Dimensions of Drone Warfare under International Law. . .", p. 708, op. cit.
192 Loc. Cit. Brackets mine.

But the terrorist is not just engaging in an ordinary "illegal action", as Alexander Knoops is wont to frame the situation, he or she is engaging in the worst atrocity of its kind by targeting innocents and all other categories of people that are protected in armed conflicts. When Ahmad Nazir Warraich wrote that "targeted killing may be legal in certain circumstances", even though "international law imposes an obligation upon states to fulfill the requirement of transparency",[193] what readily comes to mind in this legality is the targeting of proven terrorists, be they low level or of a higher value. There is this prejudice that some of the people and places being targeted may not fit into the category of permissible targets, such as political and religious leaders or financial contributors, informants, collaborators and other service providers, targeted individuals in a number of civilian settings, including homes and urban centers.[194]

But this prejudice will find it difficult to stand in the precarious circumstances of asymmetric warfare where the collaborators may be taking part in the conflict "in isolated acts":[195] like, for instance, the religious leaders that embarks on the radicalization and recruitment of militants or jihadists. It is a known fact that even in symmetric or conventional warfare, civilian can lose their protection in circumstances in which they are known to aid and abet the enemy in advancing the cause of hostilities, or taking direct part in the hostilities.[196] Even the International Committee of the Red Cross (ICRC) was quoted to have held the view that "it is allowed to target a civilian while he is involved in a particular act of conflict, but not otherwise; whereas a continuous civilian combatant can be targeted anytime".[197] Whereas in conventional warfare it would be patently illegal to target anybody on account of his nationalist fervor cum rhetoric in terms of what he preaches, in the asymmetric war on terror, it is perfectly okay to target a toxic preacher like Al-Awlaki because his incendiary preachments clearly radicalize and, thus, attract recruits, the army of militants that themselves target civilians. Meanwhile, Micah Zenko noted that U.S. officials are persuaded that individuals targeted by drones are limited to high level al-Qaeda leaders who are planning attacks; individuals who are a threat to the United States; individuals involved in some sort of operational plot against the United States; and specific senior operational leaders of al-Qaeda and associated forces.[198]

This clarification on who the U.S. targets are was compelled by the fact that Washington sometimes targets terrorists that were not a direct threat to the United States and its allies, those that were predominantly fighting internal

193 See Ahmad Nazir Warraich (2013), "The Use of Drones . . .", p. 67, op. cit.
194 Ibid., p. 74.
195 Loc. Cit.
196 See Fred Aja Agwu (2011), *The Law of Armed Conflict and African Wars* . . ., pp. 114–116, op. cit.
197 See Ahmad Nazir Warraich (2013), "The Use of Drones . . .", pp. 74–75, op. cit.
198 See Micah Zenko (2013), "Reforming U.S. Drone Strike Policies" . . ., p. 10, op. cit.

insurgencies in their countries, thus risking dragging itself into other countries' civil wars.[199] But it is utterly restrictive, inappropriate, and inadmissible to limit U.S. drone strikes to only those posing direct threat to the United States because terrorists share the same infamy with pirates; that is, they are practically *hostis humani generis* (an enemy of mankind). If the United States refuses to target some terrorists because they do not pose direct threats to its homeland or interests abroad, these terrorists would ultimately turn to the United States whenever they are done with menacing other countries.

Meanwhile, whereas the President of the United States has the responsibility to authorize the drone attacks (with or without the Congressional "War Powers Resolution" as it now seems), the Central Intelligence Agency (CIA) is reputed for being the agency from where the drone operators are resident, thus triggering the severest criticism against itself, which is that "the criteria the CIA applies for carrying out signature strikes are too lenient while the CIA is not always certain before-hand, of the presence of terrorists at a targeted site".[200] According to the report to the United Nations General Assembly by the Special Rapporteur, the CIA controls its fleet of drones from its headquarters in Langley, Virginia, in coordination with pilots near hidden airfields in Afghanistan and Pakistan (not the cubicles in Las Vegas as portrayed in fiction[201]) who handle takeoffs and landings, a fleet reportedly flown by civilians, including both intelligence officers and private contractors (often retired military personnel).[202]

All in all, it is now obvious that the use of armed drones is now gaining traction for as many bad reasons as there are also the good ones. Even the United Nations has reportedly proposed the "use of [surveillance] drones to enhance the capabilities of peacekeepers monitoring the movement of armed groups [like M23 rebels] in the Democratic Republic of Congo (DRC)", a sensitive move that "could set a precedent that would worry some United Nations members" because the prospect exists that "the Security Council authorizing UN operations in the DRC could allow for the drones to be armed and would authorize the use of force if necessary to protect individuals from an imminent threat of violence".[203] How the legality of the deployment of armed drones by the United Nations Security Council will be acquired is certainly unknown because the United Nations does not have its own army or military-industrial complex.

199 Loc. Cit.

200 See Geert-Jan Alexander Knoops (2012), "Legal, Political and Ethical Dimensions of Drone Warfare under International Law. . .", p. 702, op. cit.

201 See Rudolph Herzog's report of Andrew Niccol's film in "Dealing Death by Remote Control" . . ., p. 66, op. cit.

202 See Philip Alston in "Report of the Special Rapportuer on Extrajudicial . . .", op. cit.

203 See Gregory S. McNeal in "United Nations Wants to Use Drones in Africa, Could be Legally be Armed", available at www.forbes.com/sites/gregorymcneal/2012/11/24/united-nations-wants-to-use-dron . . . (last visited on December 10, 2012). Parentheses mine.

This is made more complex because world government and world law are still elusive (for beyond the limit of statehood as conceived in political science, the international political society appears only a mere discernable "political chaos"[204]), while the armed drones–owning nations (the United States and Israel, perhaps being the only openly known ones at the moment) are still very conservative with the technology, so much so that the Security Council is viscerally incapacitated in terms of having access to the technology in the first place not to talk of the legality of its deployment. But about the most cheery aspect of the news or prospect of the United Nations deploying drones (surveillance or armed) is that the whole scheme will snugly fit into the pragmatic philosophy (rather than the talk about legality) of the doctrine of necessity or force majeure, which can even be extended to other crisis-ridden nations like Syria—the monitoring of the violations of human rights, international humanitarian law, and the protection of those threatened with harm; even if it meant violating international law and state sovereignty.[205]

204 See Fred Aja Agwu (2007), *World Peace through World Law . . .*, p. 279, op. cit.

205 See Gregory S. McNeal in "United Nations Wants to Use Drones in Africa, Could be Legally be Armed", . . . (last visited on December 10, 2012), op. cit.

7 Drones in Self-Defence Against Terrorists

Beyond the Pail of the Jurisprudence of Self-Defence

Today's drone strikes by the United States have so generated heated debates and so much hoopla that the inherent benefit of this lethal smart weapon as a critical component of air power (and instrument of self-defence in contemporary precarious environment of international security) is practically being obscured. As stated at the beginning of this book, contemporary international security environment has got the misfortune of habouring a surfeit of errant and very erratic non-state actors in the form of terrorist organizations like the Taliban, the al-Qaeda, the ISIS, and the Boko Haram, amongst many other assorted bands of brigands that do not fight in a conventional manner or play by the rules; yet, these terror organizations are ceaselessly threatening to overwhelm, override, or even nullify the nation-state as it exists and is recognized in law and in fact. The ISIS and its kindred spirit amongst the assortments of sub-state entities that are terrorist groups are part of the very extant dangers against which the nation-state must defend itself. The very existence of these terrorist organizations is not only a nightmare to the nation-state they are fighting to extinguish or dismember; these non-state actors also contaminate or introduce complications into contemporary international relations, the security, and the legal environment.

For instance, the jurisprudence of the use of force as established under the United Nations system did not anticipate the emergence of or the ferocity with which these terrorists hurtle down and constrain the sovereign state. So, because the law was totally oblivious of this now dangerous reality of terrorist organizations putting up robust appearance and having tremendous consequences in international relations, the provisions of the United Nations Charter are silent with regard to how to react to them in self-defence, having merely enjoined that "All members shall refrain in their international relations from the threat or use of force against the territorial integrity and political independence of any state, or in any other manner inconsistent with the purposes of the United Nations".[1] Not being an absolute interdiction or prohibition, this rule finds an exception in a counterpart provision that "Nothing in the present Charter shall impair the

1 See Article 2, paragraph 4 of the United Nations Charter.

inherent right of individual or collective self-defence if an armed attack occurs against a member of the United Nations, until the Security Council has taken measures necessary to maintain international peace and security", amongst other provisions in this exception from the rule of non-forcible measures.[2]

When these counterpart provisions of the United Nations Charter on non-forcible measure are taken together, they raise two fundamental questions as far as the proliferation and involvement of terrorists in the international security environment is concerned. The first question is this: are these non-state entities capable of the use of force or an armed attack within the context of the standard of this phenomenon, and as established by the Charter of the United Nations?[3] The second question is this: can an action in self-defence be taken by a state against a sub-state entity without impeding the territorial integrity and political independence of another state; whose territory is, perhaps, used by the insurgents without its consent, thus violating the principle of territorial inviolability as protected by the United Nations Charter? On the question of an armed attack, an insurgency may not be capable of inflicting one on the nation-state in a conventional manner, but it is nonetheless capable of using unconventional means to harm the state and its citizens.

Hence, "in April 1986, a terrorist bomb exploded in a West Berlin nightclub crowded with US servicemen", killing two soldiers and a Turkish woman and wounding 230 people, including 50U.S. military personnel.[4] When it was still wholly regarded as a terrorist organization, the Palestinian Liberation Organization (PLO) was also sponsoring attacks on Israel from its headquarters in Tunisia and other friendly countries; just as the al-Qaeda, operating from the Taliban-held Afghanistan, on August 7, 1998, simultaneously bombed two U.S. embassies in Nairobi (Kenya) and Dar es Salaaam (Tanzania).[5] Of course, with respect to the West Berlin nightclub bombing, the United States responded ten days later by bombing a number of targets in Tripoli (Libya); and with respect to the PLO menace, Israel in 1985 attacked the organization's headquarters in Tunisia, while President Clinton of the United States, two weeks after the East African nations' bombing of American embassies ordered the firing of "seventy-nine Tomahawk cruise missiles at six terrorist training camps around the town of Khowst, Afghanistan, and at a pharmaceutical plant on the outskirts of Khartoum".[6]

These countries justified their actions on the basis of self-defence, with the then U.S. Secretary of State, George P. Shultz, are that it is absurd to argue that international law prohibits us from capturing terrorists in international waters or airspace; from attacking them on the soil of other nations, even for the purpose

2 See Article 51 of the United Nations Charter.

3 See Fred Aja Agwu (2005), *United Nations System, State Practice and the Jurisprudence of the Use of Force* . . ., pp. 131–133, 167–173, op. cit.

4 See Michael Byers (2005), *War Law* . . ., p. 61, op. cit.

5 Ibid., p. 62.

6 Ibid., pp. 61–63.

of rescuing hostages; or from using force against states that support, train, and habour terrorists or guerillas.[7]

With respect to the throwing of Tomahawk cruise missiles in Afghanistan and Khartoum (Sudan), the latter of which the Central Intelligence Agency (CIA) erroneously thought that the pharmaceutical plant was producing precursors to chemical weapons, the then U.S. National Security Adviser, Sandy Berger, said: "I think it is appropriate, under Article 51 of the United Nations Charter, for protecting the self-defence of the United States . . . for us to try and disrupt and destroy those kinds of military terrorist targets".[8] A patient dissection of these two related rules of force and self-defence and how the nation-state can walk the minefield of defending itself against terrorist insurgents without contravening or circumventing them will offer a glimpse on the value, legitimacy, and legality of the deployment of drone attacks in the present-day international security environment.

The Code of Offences Against the Peace and Security of Mankind

It was to deal with this problem, to establish whether or not sub-state entities in the form of insurgents or insurgent terrorists can use force and ipso facto commit an armed attack (against which the state can invoke the right of self-defence), that the International Military Tribunal (IMT) sitting in Nuremberg, Germany, after the Second World War, established the liability of individuals (be they insurgents or insurgent terrorists) in this regard, arguing that crimes against international law are committed by men, not by abstract entities; and only by punishing individuals who commit such crimes can the provisions of international law be enforced.[9] The consequence of this ruling was that, in 1947, the General Assembly of the United Nations called upon the International Law Commission (ILC), which resultantly Drafted a Code of "Offences Against the Peace and Security of Mankind" that holds individuals as subjects of international law and as armed bands, responsible, amongst other offences, for any incursion into the territory of a state from the territory of another state.[10]

The validity of the Draft Code raised some dissension amongst some authorities in Jurisprudence. Derek Bowett cynically saw it as a mere expression of the views or desire of the ILC for the future of international law;[11] but Julius

7 Quoted in ibid., pp. 61–62.
8 Ibid., p. 63.
9 See Fred Aja Agwu (2005), *United Nations System, State Practice and the Jurisprudence of the Use of Force . . .*, p. 71, op. cit; see also Robert K. Woetzel (1962), *The Nuremberg Trials in International Law, with a Postlude on the Eichmann Case*, London, Stevens & Sons Ltd., p. 96.
10 See Fred Aja Agwu (2005), *United Nations System, State Practice and the Jurisprudence of the Use of Force . . .*, pp. 71–72, op. cit.
11 See Derek W. Bowett (1958), *Self-Defence in International Law*, Manchester, Manchester University Press, p. 57.

Stone was to more pragmatically call it the "programmschriften for an unborn world",[12] which was like a prescient glimpse into today's world that interlopers like the ISIS, the al-Qaeda, and the Boko Haram have become serious bugbears in the international security environment. But the legality or otherwise of the Drat Code cannot be stretched too far because it is "soft law"; and "soft laws" are ineluctably valid international law.[13] The legality of "soft law" derives not only from the fact that it is not a mere guideline—an instrument that does not in any way, even vaguely, pretend to express international law—but also because of its capacity as a basis for social action; since, like the recommendations of the General Assembly of the United Nations, the states or international organizations entering into them take their contents very seriously, thus, giving them some measure of respect.[14]

With respect to the Draft Code being a legitimate "soft law", it was actually the United Nations General Assembly Resolution 177 (1) of November 21, 1947 that authorized the ILC to draft it,[15] a Resolution that the United Nations itself as well as the states entering into it took very seriously and, thus, giving it some measure of respect aforementioned. The overall effect of the Draft Code is that, consistent with the recognition of individuals as both objects and subjects of international law, these individuals as insurgents are now held responsible when they commit acts that clearly and intentionally violate the law of nations, like the law on the inviolability of the territorial integrity and political independence of nations.[16] In fact, Quincy Wright made it clear that individuals as armed groups must be specifically held liable, not just because of the intentionality of their criminal act, and the fact their act is in breach of the principle of territorial inviolability recognized by the law, but also because the injury to the state is such that that victim state cannot adequately protect itself or punish the erring individuals through the normal exercise of its jurisdiction; and this is because these individuals are outside the territory of the victim state.[17]

Self-Defence Against Terrorists Vis-À-Vis Territorial Inviolability

The settlement of the first question that Article 2, paragraph 4 in conjunction with Article 51 (both of the United Nations Charter) raises with respect to the capacity of individuals (as armed bands/insurgents or terrorists) for the use of force

12 See Julius Stone (1954), *Legal Control of International Conflict* . . ., p. 23, op. cit.

13 See Fred Aja Agwu (2007), *World Peace through World Law* . . ., pp. 253–259, op. cit.

14 Ibid., pp. 255–256; see also Joseph Gold (1983), "Strengthening the Soft International Law of Exchange Arrangement", *AJIL*, Vol. 77, p. 443.

15 See Jorge Castaneda (1969), *Legal Effects of United Nations Resolutions*, New York, Columbian University Press, p. 191.

16 See Fred Aja Agwu (2005), *United Nations System, State Practice and the Jurisprudence of the Use of Force* . . ., p. 72, op. cit.

17 See Quincy Wright (1952), "Proposal for an International Criminal Court", *AJIL*, Vol. 46, pp. 71–72.

and armed attack as well as their responsibility therein, now brings the second question into focus. This question is this: can there be an action in self-defence against insurgents or terrorists without impeding the territorial integrity and political independence of any state whose territory is inhabited and employed by the terrorists in staging their operations, thus violating that hallowed principle of territorial integrity and inviolability as established by the United Nations system? The inviolability of the territorial integrity and political independence of the sovereign nation-state is an issue that is taken very seriously in positivist international law as well as the writings of the law's renowned publicists. As a positivist formation or formulation, Article 2, paragraph 4 of the United Nations Charter is clear on this matter.

Learned publicists also hold that this principle of inviolability of territory and political independence are very dear to the heart of contemporary international law, that is, the jurisprudence of the use of force under the United Nations. Since the emergence of the United Nations, this has, for instance, been the meat of the controversy at some point between Michael Reisman and Oscar Schachter, and between Robert Tucker and Oppenheim. Whereas Michael Reisman believed that the inviolability of territorial integrity and political independence of a nation can be subordinated to the policy or principle (of democratic values) that animated it,[18] Oscar Schachter firmly opposed this subordination, arguing that the inviolability of territorial integrity and political independence is a "higher" value to which no other value can be subordinated, particularly when a state is arbitrarily invading another state to restore the value of democracy, no matter how brief that arbitrary invasion might be.[19]

Similarly, Robert Tucker had argued that because belligerent reprisals are based on the conditions of necessity and proportionality, it cannot be said to be directed against the territorial integrity and political independence of the state, unless, perhaps, there is the dainty or fastidious standard of territorial integrity or political independence being equated with territorial inviolability.[20] It is this strict or fastidious standard that Oppenheim favours in his affirmation that "territorial integrity, especially when coupled with political independence, is synonymous with territorial inviolability".[21] This affirmation apparently inheres in the fact that the United Nations system has a very strict regime or restriction on the use of

18 See Fred Aja Agwu (2005), *United Nations System, State Practice and the Jurisprudence of the Use of Force . . .*, p. 23, op. cit; see also W. Michael Reisman (1984), "Coercion and Self-Determination: Construing Charter Article 2(4)", *AJIL*, Vol. 78, pp. 643–645.

19 See Oscar Schachter (1984), "The Legality of Pro-Democracy Invasion", *AJIL*, Vol. 78, pp. 648–649.

20 See Fred Aja Agwu (2005), *United Nations System, State Practice and the Jurisprudence of the Use of Force . . .*, p. 143, op. cit; see also Robert W. Tucker (1972), "Reprisals and Self-Defence: The Customary Law", *AJIL*, Vol. 66, pp. 589, 594, fn. 5.

21 See Fred Aja Agwu (2005), *United Nations System, State Practice and the Jurisprudence of the Use of Force . . .*, p. 143, op. cit; see also L. Oppenheim (1952, edited by H. Lauterpacht), *International Law: A Treatise, Vol. 2 . . .*, p. 154.

force; and this is consistent with its determination, as seen in the preambles of the Charter, "to save succeeding generations from the scourge of war, which twice in our life-time has brought untold sorrow to mankind . . .".[22]

This strict interpretation, the conception that a confluence of territorial integrity and political independence amounts to territorial inviolability, does not give room for any inordinate or cavalier application of force in international relations, not matter the aim or objective, the limited nature, brevity or transience.[23] As, thus, conceived, every bullet that whizzes through the airspace of a sovereign state without its consent constitutes a violation of its territorial integrity and political independence. This strict if positivist interpretation, therefore, probably accounted for the decision of the United States to back down in its standoff with the defunct Soviet Union over the Cuban Missile row; for Washington's policymakers reckoned that "a bombing attack, even one strictly restricted in purpose and effect, would probably be deemed as use of force against the territorial integrity (and perhaps the political independence) of Cuba".[24]

There is, however, no absolutism to this strict preservation of the territorial inviolability and political independence of the nation-state, the so-called territorial inviolability. Perhaps, the only absolutism to it is with respect to the arbitrary or unilateral use of force by a state outside the context of self-defence in Article 51 of the United Nations Charter. The first exception to this seeming absolutism is in a collective use of force that is authorized by the United Nations Security Council acting under Chapter VII of the Charter. The second exception is in when the nation-state is reacting to the armed attack by individuals as insurgents. This phenomenon is inherent in the existing exigency that the entrant of modern insurgents in the international security environment has created. As Bowett insisted, the territorial integrity and political independence (that is, territorial inviolability) of a state must be contingent upon the condition of the non-existence of any threat to the security of another state within its borders (that is, a state not allowing its territory to be a safe haven for insurgents).[25]

Lauterpacht also affirmed this position that a state is entitled to expect the exclusiveness of other states' jurisdiction over its territory only if that will not result to its territory being used directly or indirectly to menace the safety of those other states.[26] In every situation that things went contrary to this expectation, a

22 See the Preamble of the United Nations Charter.

23 See Fred Aja Agwu (2005), *United Nations System, State Practice and the Jurisprudence of the Use of Force . . .*, p. 146, op. cit.

24 Ibid., p. 143, fn 71, op. cit; See also Louis Henkin (1968), *How Nations Behave: Law and Foreign Policy*, Washington, Praeger Publishers, p. 226.

25 See Fred Aja Agwu (2005), *United Nations System, State Practice and the Jurisprudence of the Use of Force . . .*, p. 138, op. cit; see also D. W. Bowett (1958), *Self-Defence in International Law . . .*, p. 152, op. cit.

26 See Fred Aja Agwu (2005), *United Nations System, State Practice and the Jurisprudence of the Use of Force . . .*, p. 73, op. cit; see also H. Lauterpacht (1928), "Revolutionary Activities by Private Persons against Foreign States", *AJIL*, Vol. 22, p. 106.

victim state must defend itself; and every sovereign state that found its territory being used without its consent, or which was impotent, indifferent, or was incapable of reining in the insurgents, must oblige its victim counterpart.[27] Before the coming into being of the United Nations, when a British force commanded by Colonel McNab entered the U.S. territory of fort Schlosser in the State of New York to dislodge a band of insurgents that were crossing the border into Canada and acting in cahoots with Canadian rebels during a rebellion in Canada, this principle, resulting from the *Caroline case*, was the *locus classicus* of self-defence under customary international law.[28]

And in the wake of 9/11, while broadening support for the U.S. invasion of Afghanistan, John Negroponte, the U.S. ambassador to the United Nations, wrote to the President of the Security Council on October 7, 2001, stating that:

> The attack on 11 September 2001 and the ongoing threat to the United States and its nationals posed by the al-Qaeda organization have been made possible by the decision of the Taliban regime to allow the parts of Afghanistan that it controls to be used by this organization as a base of operation. Despite every effort by the United States and the international community, the Taliban regime has refused to change its policy. From the territory of Afghanistan, the al-Qaeda organization continues to train and support agents of terror who attack innocent people throughout the world and target United States nationals and interests in the United States and abroad.[29]

The recalcitrance of the Taliban, as John Negroponte indicates, carries some consequences. One of these consequences is the imposition of a sense of righteous indignation on the United States as well as the feeling of being obliged to act in response to a force majeure whenever it takes an arbitrary action in the face of the Taliban's refusal to flush out the al-Qaeda. The situation of the United States acting arbitrarily could only have been saved if the Taliban were either not complicit in the activities of the al-Qaeda, or the extremist regime were honestly unable to flush the terrorist group out of its territory. To remain adamant or insensitive to the security concerns of the United States was to invite trouble to itself, the trouble that Washington gave the Taliban regime when it invaded Afghanistan on March 20, 2001 to dismantle its governmental authority over the state of Afghanistan and get rid of the al-Qaeda.

Even after the dismantling of the Taliban in Afghanistan, the United States continued to pursue its leadership and the group's other identifiable ranks and

27 See Fred Aja Agwu (2005), *United Nations System, State Practice and the Jurisprudence of the Use of Force* . . ., p. 73, op. cit.
28 Ibid., pp. 66–69; see also R. Y. Jennings (1938), "The Caroline and Mcleod Cases", *AJIL*, Vol. 32, p. 82.
29 Quoted in Michael Byers (2005), *War Law* . . ., p. 66, op. cit.

file beyond Afghanistan and into Pakistan, claiming the very controversial right to putative or anticipatory self-defence. For instance, when on Saturday, May 21, 2016, a U.S. drone strike that was reportedly authorized by President Obama killed the Taliban leader, Mullah Akhtar Mansour, near the city of Quetta in South West Pakistan (Waziristan), the U.S. Secretary of State, John Kerry, explained that Mansour (who assumed the leadership of the Taliban, circa 2013, replacing the group's founder and spiritual leader, Mullah Mohammed Omar) had posed "a continuing imminent threat to US personnel".[30]

Between Consent and Obligation to Waive the Right of Inviolability

Thus, Fred Nielsen posits that self-defence against insurgents belongs to the class of cases in which every sovereign nation is understood to expressly, tacitly, or implicitly waive the exercise of a part of that complete or exclusive territorial jurisdiction and inviolability to enable other states, victims of armed bands' armed attack to repel such attacks.[31] This is particularly so (as stated earlier earlier) wherever, being not actively supportive of the insurgents, the state in which the insurgent found a haven was indifferent or incapable of stopping them. It is at this point that the issue of consent is invited and could be offered expressly or implicitly. However, there is still some whiff of controversy over whether or not consent must be obtained, irrespective of whether or not, like the Taliban in relation to the al-Qaeda, a regime was in support of the terrorists. Ahmad Nazir Warraich contributed to a perspective in the assertion that the use of force in this context "is only permitted with the consent of the host state or when the host state is either unwilling or unable to take action against the non-state actor".[32] But consent may not be sought when the victim state (like the United States) is inclined to act arbitrarily where, as in the Taliban in Afghanistan, the local regime is supportive of the terrorists.

However, an express consent is not too necessary in other cases where the host-state is striving to stave off some domestic political backlash; that is, if for some reasons of domestic exigencies, the brigands have some measure of local support.[33] In the case of Qaed Salim Sinan al-Harethi, a notorious and top-notch al-Qaeda member in Yemen, the Yemeni authorities had failed to nab him and had to subsequently give up trying because, apart from their "insufficient training in counter terror operations", Yemen became reluctant to act on account "of a perceived debt that President Ali Saleh owes to Usama bin Laden's forces, which

30 See "Afghan Confirms Death of Taliban Leaders" . . ., p. 37, op. cit; see also "Afghans Confirm Taliban Leader's Death", *The Nation* (Lagos), Monday, May 23, 2016, p. 44.

31 See Fred Aja Agwu (2005), *United Nations System, State Practice and the Jurisprudence of the Use of Force* . . ., pp. 72–73, op. cit; see also Fred K. Nielsen (1919), "The Lack of Uniformity in the Law and Practice of States with Regard to Merchant Vessels", *AJIL*, Vol. 13, p. 13.

32 See Ahmad Nazir Warraich (2013), "The Use of Drones . . .", p. 69, op. cit.

33 See Fred Aja Agwu (2005), *United Nations System, State Practice and the Jurisprudence of the Use of Force* . . ., p. 70, op. cit.

assisted in putting down a separatist movement in 1994".[34] Even the United States' drone strikes in Yemen that were publicly acknowledged by the authorities in Washington met with the ire of the Yemeni authorities that argued that such public acknowledgement on the part of Washington was insensitive to the domestic situation in Yemen, the fear of "domestic unrest in Yemen, and reprisals by al-Qaeda sympathizers still active in Yemen".[35]

So, on the part of a haven state like Yemen, this sort of domestic tension would demand an ad hoc, rather than a loud or express waiver of the right of territorial inviolability, which is, thus, a right that is not negotiable, and which inures to the victim state of the attack; provided that in exploring that waived right to defend itself, it takes all proper or reasonable care to ensure that it is only the terrorist or insurgents' camp that is hit, not the state infrastructures or institutions.[36] Although there is this ad hoc waiver of the right of territorial inviolability, the consent of the state waiving this right must nonetheless be sought and secured. It is important to know that the United States, unarguably the greatest user of drone strikes, does not just proceed on the drone attacks without the consent of the territorial authorities. As far as state consent or authorization goes, Micah Zenko outlined the critical infrastructures of support that the United States requires to advance its drones campaigns in Afghanistan and Pakistan as follows:

> U.S. drones have benefited from host-state support, which the United States has helped to secure with extensive side payments in foreign aid and security assistance. The few hundred Predators and Reaper drones that currently conduct distant airstrikes leverage a system-wide infrastructure that includes host-state permission to base drones and associated launch and recovery personnel, over flight rights in transit countries, nearby search-and-rescue forces to recover downed drones, satellite or assured access to commercial satellite bandwidth to transmit command-and-control data, and human intelligence assets on the ground to help identify targets.[37]

This host-state permission or support creates the "relatively permissive environment, largely unthreatened by antiaircraft guns or surface-to-air missiles"; otherwise, "some of the [drones] that we have today, you put in a high-threat environment, and they'll start falling from the sky like rain".[38] It is also for this reason of using the host-state's permission to support intelligence, according to Micah Zenko, that "the Central Intelligence Agency (CIA) reportedly maintains a paramilitary force of three thousand ethnic Pashtuns to capture, kill, and collect

34 See William C. Banks (2005), "The Predator", in Volker C. Franke (2005, ed.); *Terrorism and Peacekeeping* . . ., p. 147, op. cit.

35 Ibid., p. 152.

36 See Fred Aja Agwu (2005), *United Nations System, State Practice and the Jurisprudence of the Use of Force* . . ., p. 74, op. cit.

37 See Micah Zenko (2013), "Reforming U.S. Drone Strike Policies" . . ., p. 7, op. cit.

38 Loc. Cit.

intelligence".[39] In addition, "the CIA and U.S. military also cooperate with their Pakistani counterparts to collect human and signals intelligence" in order to identify and track suspected militants.[40] Implicitly, therefore, the Pakistani authorities give consent to the United States' drone strikes. This fact, however, is not without some controversies. According to Ahmad Nazir Warraich:

> Some confusion persists regarding the Pakistani government's consent to the drone programme conducted before 2011. Though no clear statements are available in its favour, since 2011, the Pakistani government, the Foreign Office as well as the Parliament have been unequivocal in their assertion that drone strikes in FATA are illegal and a violation of Pakistan's sovereignty.[41]

Although this assertion did not go down well with many observers in the Western world (as it is emblematic of the fact that Pakistan was not taking the requite action needed to rein in the terrorists, thus, warranting arbitrary U.S. intervention); the NYU-Stanford study, "*Living Under Drones*",[42] actually reported that Pakistan had at times shown both the willingness and the ability to take action, a clarification that evidences the fact that it was not at all times that Pakistan evidenced that willingness to cooperate; meaning that at such times, Washington took arbitrary measures, putting the so-called Pakistan's consent in doubt.[43] Another typical example of when the United States' drone strike was carried out without Pakistan's consent was the strike of Saturday, May 21, 2016 that killed the Taliban leader, Mullah Akhtar Mansour, because the Pakistani authorities complained that it was a violation of the country's sovereignty.[44] But these controversies notwithstanding, it is the support of the host-state of Pakistan that makes it possible for the Pakistani army to always clear the airspace for U.S. drones, and for the Pakistani troops to fight with the Taliban for the recovery of the drones whenever they inadvertently crash.[45]

In Yemen too, according to the United Nations Special Rapporteur, the United States routinely sought prior consent on a case-by-case basis for drones operations on its territory through recognized channels; and where consent was withheld, a strike would not go ahead.[46] Regarding the legal implication of the

39 Loc. Cit.
40 Loc. Cit.
41 See Ahmad Nazir Warraich (2013), "The Use of Drones . . .", p. 78, op. cit.
42 Ibid., p. 75.
43 Ibid., p. 78.
44 See "Afghan Confirms Death of Taliban Leaders" . . ., p. 37, op. cit.
45 See Micah Zenko (2013), "Reforming U.S. Drone Strike Policies" . . ., p. 7, op. cit.
46 See Ben Emmerson in "Report of the Special Rapporteur on the Promotion and Protection of Human Rights and Fundamental Freedoms While Countering Terrorism", UNHuman Rights Council Twenty-fifth session, Agenda item 3, Promotion and protection of all human rights, civil, political, economic, social and cultural rights, including the right to development, A/HRC/25/59, 10 March 2014, available at www.justsecurity.org/wp-content/uploads/2014/02/Special-Rapporteur-Rapporteur-Emmerson-Drones-2014.pdf (last visited on Thursday, September 17, 2015).

United States conducting drone strikes in the territory of a state with its permission or consent vis-à-vis carrying out the same strikes in the territory of a state without permission; whereas the former (with state consent) would not constitute an act of aggression in the sense of being a breach of Article 2, paragraph 4 of the United Nations Charter, the latter (without state consent) is clearly an act of aggression or breach of Article 2, paragraph 4 of the United Nations Charter.

It is in this sense that the use of armed drones is antagonistic to *jus ad bellum* (the law before the outbreak of war). Drone strikes in the territory of a state without its consent raises the same issues that were demurred at by the International Court of Justice (ICJ) in the case, *Military and Paramilitary Activities in and against Nicaragua (Nicaragua v. United States of America)*, in which the court said that the right to sovereignty and political independence possessed by Nicaragua was violated; and that the United States violated its obligation in international law not to intervene and infringe the sovereignty of another state.[47] But at the same time, there were also arbitrary strikes by the United States; for it was the same Yemeni President Hadi that also informed Human Rights Watch during a meeting on 28 January 2014 that some specific drone strikes were not pre-approved; even though such strikes were "generally permitted" pursuant to an agreement concluded between the United States and former President Abdullah Saleh, which remained binding.

It is also worthy of note that "on the day the AU convened a Heads of State meeting in Nairobi in September 2014 to discuss terrorism, a US drone attack killed several people at a meeting [ostensibly a signature strike] in the port town of Barawe in Southern Somalia"; and that "it speaks volumes about Africa's role in Western counter-terrorism that the Barawe attack was conducted without the knowledge of any of the Heads of State gathered in Nairobi".[48] Although the Somali state had failed since 1992 and the south of the country taken over by the al-Shabaaab terrorists, the knowledge of the drone strike by any of the surrounding countries in the region ought to have been apposite; more so when it was such a consequential operation in the sense that the al-Shabaab leader, Ahmed Abdi Godane, was among those targeted and successfully killed in the drone strike.[49]

While laying pretentions to state consent, that southern Somali operation was typical of the veil of secrecy that shrouds the United States' drone strikes. Aside from drone strikes, state consent used to be particularly necessary where there would be a direct invasion of the state's territory; but for the sake of creating a permissive or safe airspace as well as an environment for intelligence to thrive, it has also become imperative in the use of drones. In 1995 while the Serbian war raged, it was apparently because of lack of state consent, as well as the fact

47 See ICJ Report (1984), 169, 392, and ICJ Report (1986), 14; see also "The International Court of Justice, ICJ (1986), The Hague", Third Edition, p. 104.

48 See Kalundi Serumaga in "Terrorism in Africa . . .", p. 36, op. cit.

49 Loc. Cit.

that the U.S. drones at that time lacked speed, stealth, and *resilience*, that the "relatively unsophisticated Serbian antiaircraft guns shot two of the first three Predator drones deployed outside the United States"; the same way that in 2002, "Iraqi jet fighters shot down a Predator".[50]

Drones: Balancing Consent, Secrecy, Intelligence, Transparency, and Reasonableness

However, in this era of hi-tech cruise missiles and drones that make ground invasion totally unnecessary, consent can still be dispensed with, especially for the sake of the preservation of the integrity of intelligence and the drone operation in a country whose alliance is doubtful, a country like Pakistan that the United States would describe as a "frenemy"; that is, a friendly enemy,[51] more so because despite being a friend/ally of the United States, Pakistan is still the life-blood of the Taliban; with the Afghan President Ashraf Ghani confessing as a matter of fact that the Taliban insurgency would not survive a month if it loses its sanctuary in neighbouring Pakistan;[52] and with some groups in that country still re-arming the insurgents for their comeback in Afghanistan.[53]

As a "frenemy", *Time* wrote that "Pakistan is both arsonist and fireman in the war on terror".[54] An arsonist sets the fire and the fireman quenches it; so when one doubles as both, then the individual, nation, or organization becomes a bundle of contradiction that will be very difficult to deal with because of this embodiment at once of both the negative and the positive. In a relationship like this, there is usually no love lost. The Pakistani fearsome Inter-Services Intelligence (ISI) directorate is emblematic of this "double mirror" or "strange duality" in the country's relationship with the United States, thus, playing a "double game".[55]

The ISI tends to put up a friendly facade that it wants the United States (or, indeed, any other countries it has a love-hate relationship with) to understand, but its "private face" or hidden disposition towards Washington is duplicitous or imbued with so many nuances (Janus-like, "at once very secretive and very open"), usually "coldly ruthless, to the point of silently condoning attacks on US soldiers by their allies".[56] The foregoing situation explains why the United States sneaked into Afghanistan "without so much as a warning" and conducted

50 See Micah Zenko (2013), "Reforming U.S. Drone Strike Policies" . . ., p. 7, op. cit.

51 See Condoleezza Rice (2011), *No Higher Honor* . . ., pp. 74–75, 90–91, op. cit.

52 See "Afghan President Says Taliban Wouldn't Last a Month without Pakistani Support", *Vanguard* (Lagos), Monday, December 5, 2016, p. 40.

53 A view expressed by an interlocutor in the CNN Programme, *Amanpour*, monitored in Lagos (Nigeria) on Wednesday, November 16, 2016, 8pm to 9pm local time.

54 See Aryn Baker in "How Can We Trust Them?", *Time* (New York), May 20, 2011, pp. 54–57.

55 See David Ignatius in "The Double Mirror: How Pakistani's Intelligence Service Plays Both Sides", *Time* (New York), May 23, 2011, p. 22.

56 Loc. Cit.

a military operation that killed Osama bin Laden just 75 miles (120 km) from Pakistan's capital, betraying the incompetence of the Pakistani military which prestigious defence academy lay just "a mere mile from" the ground zero (Osama bin Laden's house) in Abottabad (Pakistan).[57] But as opposed to "frenemies" like Pakistan, or totally hostile territories like the Taliban-controlled Afghanistan, dispensing with the consent of friendly countries by the United States has the implication of promoting secrecy, with all its concomitant negative effects.

Writing on the need to reform U.S. drone strike policies with increased transparency (so that state sovereignty would not be attacked by dint of lack of consent or authorization), Micah Zenko made the point that consent can sometimes be dispensed with while deploying drones because of the "need to protect sensitive intelligence sources and methods" and serve the national interest.[58] But despite this assertion that consent can be dispensed with, Zenko also acknowledged the ineluctable fact that the fog of secrecy promotes "myths and misconceptions", and that these are serious threats to the legitimacy of drones' use over the years; insisting that these problems needed to be addressed by the United States in order to secure other nations' cooperation at the level of "intelligence support and host-state basing rights".[59]

The need for the United States to reform its use of drones with sustained transparency through ensuring things like state consent or authorization is to play the dual role of not only ensuring the legitimacy of Washington's continued use of drones, but also exerting "a normative influence on the policies and actions of other states" that have acquired and may, with time, be compelled to use the armed drones to counter terrorism-imbued insurgency.[60] As Micah Zenko quoted the U.S. President Obama to have said, "if we want other nations to use these technologies responsibly, we must use them responsibly".[61] In fact, President Obama confessed that "from our use of drones to the detention of terrorist suspects, the decisions we are making will define the type of nation—and world—that we leave to our children. . . .".[62] This may be an honest declaration by President Obama; but ensuring the so-called responsible use of drones is actually a tall order because the exigencies in the war on terror can hardly permit this reform.

In other words, as far as President Obama's avowal of a responsible use of drones is concerned, the United States may not keep faith and bequeath a positive legacy because the conduct of the terrorists (like hiding within civilian populations) is clearly antithetical to the so-called responsible application of the lethal weapon. The President's next remark after the avowal of commitment to a

57 See Aryn Baker in "Frenemies: The U.S.-Pakistan Relationship Is No Love Match", *Time* (New York), May 23, 2011, pp. 16–18.
58 See Micah Zenko (2013), "Reforming U.S. Drone Strike Policies" . . ., p. 4, op. cit.
59 Ibid., pp. 4–5.
60 Ibid., p. 5.
61 Loc. Cit.
62 See the "Full Transcript of President Obama's Speech on Counterterrorism Policy" . . ., op. cit.

responsible use of the weapon does not even help matters as its focuses more on the imperative of rooting out the terror instead of any pretentions to the niceties of any form of responsible application of the weapon. According to President Obama:

> . . . America is at the crossroads. We must define the nature and scope of this struggle, or else it will define us, mindful of James Madison's warning that "no nation could preserve its freedom in the midst of continual warfare". Neither I, nor any President, can promise the total defeat of terror. We will never erase the evil that lies in the hearts of some human beings, nor stamp out every danger to our open society. What we can do—what we must do—is dismantle networks that pose a direct danger, and make it less likely for new groups to gain a foothold, all while maintaining the freedoms and ideals that we defend.[63]

If as President Obama said (invoking the authority of James Madison), "no nation could preserve its freedoms in the midst of continual warfare", it then means that America may not be able to be the lodestar that Micah Zenko would want it to be in the use of armed drones. From President Obama's foregoing statement, it is clear that his escalated use of drones puts more premium on the eradication of terror than on "maintaining the freedoms and ideals" the United States defends. President Obama noted that the United States "will never erase the evil that lies in the hearts of some human beings"; and there is no evil much more than the targeting of civilians by terrorists, or sheltering in the midst of civilians, knowing full well that in doing so, they put these civilians in harm's way. And in being compelled to hit the terrorists amidst the civilian population, there is hardly any magic, level of caution, or responsibility that would make the United States to achieve zero collateral damage in such drone strikes.

Whether or not the use of armed drones can be reformed by the United States to attain the requisite responsibility, the fact remains that the deployment of the weapon is the future of the war on terror, more so because a ground invasion against terrorists in self-defence is pretty difficult if not impossible now that the terrorists straddle both contiguous and far-flung borders. In the words of President Barack Obama, the terrorists "try to gain foothold in some of the most distant and unforgiving places on Earth".[64] Many of them (like the 9/11 attackers) have transcended beyond contiguous territories, having morphed from the typical terrorism-insurgency of Canadian rebel leaders, Mckenzie and Rolfe (who operated and organized partisans across a contiguous U.S. territory

63 Loc. Cit.

64 See the "Full Text of Pope Francis' Speech to US Congress: Pope Takes His Case for Action on the Death Penalty, Climate Change and Immigration to US Congress in Historic Speech", available at www.aljazeera.com/news/2015/09/full-text-pope-francis-speech-congress-150924152204132.htmlSee (last visited on March 4, 2016).

of Buffalo[65]), to the 9/11 attackers under reference that organized from the far-flung Taliban-controlled territory of Afghanistan.

In this circumstance, ground invasions cannot be viable options, not with the availability of these armed drones that make confronting the terrorists very convenient. And President Obama himself also confessed in his counter-terrorism policy speech, mentioned earlier in this book, that "it is not possible for America to simply deploy a team of Special Forces to capture every terrorist"; more so when there are places where it would pose profound risks to our troops and local civilians—where a terrorist compound cannot be breached without triggering a firefight with surrounding tribal communities that pose no threat to us, or when putting U.S. boots on the ground may trigger a major international crisis.[66]

Barring the humanitarian law, ethics, and the concern about the loss of the pride of chivalry, this convenience inheres primarily in the elimination of the danger of losing personnel and incurring body bags and all the associated political complications and liabilities.

So, with the invasion of territories pursuant to the right of self-defence against terrorists not a viable military and political option, it is now perfectly alright in international law (as the law is helplessly indifferent to these unregulated weapons) to employ cruise missiles or armed drones from the territory of the victim state (even the high seas or anywhere else that the victim state has a military base[67]) in pursuit of the realization of this right of self-defence, provided the principle of reasonableness or due care not to hit state infrastructures or institutions is observed. Hence, when on August 20, 1998 (in response to the simultaneous bombing of U.S. embassies in Kenya and Tanzania on August 7, 1998), the U.S. President Clinton ordered the synchronized airstrikes in Afghanistan and Sudan in pursuit of the destruction of the Osama bin laden al-Qaeda terrorist camps in those countries, the attendant controversy was not necessarily about the legality of the attacks; rather, it was about the intelligence failure that led to the hitting of a wrong target, a pharmaceutical plant on the outskirts of Khartoum that was erroneously thought to be a chemical weapons factory.[68]

Use of Drones: A Matter of Pragmatism, Not Law

Like cruise missiles, drones come in handy when the exigency of self-defence against predatory individuals from far-flung territories becomes imperative or totally unavoidable. The State Department in the United States makes no bone

65 See Fred Aja Agwu (2005), *United Nations System, State Practice and the Jurisprudence of the Use of Force . . .*, p. 66, op. cit.
66 See the "Full Text of Pope Francis' Speech to US Congress . . .", op. cit.
67 See Fred Aja Agwu (2005), *United Nations System, State Practice and the Jurisprudence of the Use of Force . . .*, p. 74, op. cit.
68 See Robert "Buzz" Patterson (2003), *Dereliction of Duty . . .*, pp. 180–181, op. cit.

about the country's use of drones in self-defence, as contained in the report of the United Nations Special Rapporteur.[69] In a memorandum by the Office of Legal Counsel (OLC) of the State Department, the following parameters were canvassed as the threshold of the permissibility of the use of drones in self-defence by the United States:

> (1) Suspects, such as Mr. Al-Awlaki, can only be killed through drone attacks in the event that an incarceration of such person is illusory; (2) The person in question has to be involved in perpetrating 'acts of war' against the U.S; (3) Consequently, that individual should pose an immediate and significant threat to the U.S.; (4) The State "hosting" such an individual must not be able or willing to apprehend him or her.[70]

This threshold that the United States has defined is very much like a *periculum in mora* (impending threat[71]) scenario rather than an actual armed attack situation; and with respect to the drone strike that killed Al-Awlaki in Yemen, the United States maintained its claim to the right of self-defence (with the use of drone attacks) because it (the United States) was taking part in a war with the al-Qaeda while the Yemeni authorities were not able to apprehend Al-Awlaki, and, indeed, were unwilling to apprehend him.[72] Thus, Washington is clearly unapologetic about what seems like its disobedience of the rules governing the use of force under the United Nations system. It makes no bone about the fact that it can do anything to defend itself from the devastating impacts of terror attacks when all other options (including the failure of other nations to stop the terror attacks) are closed; and including the option of preemptive strikes. Listen to President Obama's righteous indignation on this controversial issue of self-defence against terrorists:

> . . . America's actions are legal. We were attacked on 9/11. Within a week, Congress overwhelmingly authorized the use of force. Under domestic law, and international law, the United States is at war with the al-Qaeda, the Taliban, and their associated forces. We are at war with an organization that right now will kill as many Americans as they could if we do not stop them first. So, this is a just war—a war waged proportionally, in last resort, and in self-defense.[73]

69 See Philip Alston in "Report of the Special Rapporteur on Extrajudicial . . .", op. cit.

70 See Geert-Jan Alexander Knoops (2012), "Legal, Political and Ethical Dimensions of Drone Warfare under International Law. . .", p. 700, op. cit.

71 *Periculum in mora* is a customary international law rule of self-defence that means that a state is faced with a threat that is "instant, overwhelming, and leaving no choice of means and no moment for deliberation"; see Fred Aja Agwu (2005), *United Nations System, State Practice and the Jurisprudence of the Use of Force* . . ., pp. 177, op. cit. This is contrary to the positivist law condition in Article 51 of the United Nations Charter that the right of self-defence can only be raised or enforced if an armed attack occurs.

72 See Geert-Jan Alexander Knoops (2012), "Legal, Political and Ethical Dimensions of Drone Warfare under International Law. . .", pp. 702–703, op. cit.

73 See the "Full Transcript of President Obama's Speech on Counterterrorism Policy" . . ., op. cit.

The death of Al-Awlaki in Washington's action against terror in self-defence also raised some dust because the authority of the government to kill a U.S. citizen outside the judicial process is very contentious.[74] But, it is obvious that the practical necessity for defence against terrorism trumps all considerations. However, although not explicitly defined, the right or authority of the U.S. government to target U.S. citizens like Al-Awlaki and other Yemeni-Americans like Kamal Derwish (struck with Hellfire drone missiles while in the same car with Qaed Salim Sinan al Harethi[75]) is believed to be implicitly condoned in "situations where the American is threatening, directly, the lives of other Americans or their allies".[76] As a matter of fact, Americans that collaborate with the country's adversaries are therein viewed as enemy combatants whose constitutional rights as an Americans were nullified by their terrorist actions.[77] As President Obama put it:

> . . . when a U.S. citizen goes abroad to wage war against America—and is actively plotting to kill U.S. citizens; and when neither the United States, nor our partners are in a position to capture him before he carries out a plot—his citizenship should no more serve as a shield than a sniper shooting down on an innocent crowd should be protected from a swat team. That's who Anwar Awlaki was—he was continuously trying to kill people . . . I would have detained and prosecuted Awlaki if we captured him before he carried out a plot. But we couldn't. And as President, I would have been derelict in my duty had I not authorized the strike that took out Awlaki.[78]

In fact, and as seen earlier from the position of President Obama, the drone operation that killed Al-Awlaki was to be analogized to the right of force by a state within the anticipatory self-defence customary international law framework,[79] which is not allowable under the United Nations system, and which goes a long way to underline the United States' unrepentant attitude about apparently taking an action that (were it not in pursuit of terrorists) could have been in violation of international law. As has been alluded to earlier, the same inflexible and righteous appropriation of a legitimate right of anticipatory self-defence was also made by the U.S. Secretary of State, John Kerry in the wake of the drone strike that killed the Taliban leader, Mullah Akhtar Mansour, in Pakistan when he insisted that Mansour had posed "a continuing imminent threat to US personnel".[80] In

74 See William C. Banks (2005), "The Predator", in Volker C. Franke (2005, ed.); *Terrorism and Peacekeeping* . . ., p. 151, op. cit.
75 Ibid., pp. 144–145, 147–148, 151.
76 Ibid., p. 51.
77 Loc. Cit.
78 See the "Full Transcript of President Obama's Speech on Counterterrorism Policy" . . ., op. cit.
79 See Geert-Jan Alexander Knoops (2012), "Legal, Political and Ethical Dimensions of Drone Warfare under International Law. . .", p. 709, op. cit.
80 See "Afghan Confirms Death of Taliban Leaders" . . ., p. 37, op. cit.

condemnation of the United States' anticipatory use of force in the war on terror, Ahmad Nazir Warraich invoked the Daniel Webster principle and wrote as follows:

> For "anticipatory" self-defence to be operative, the qualifying attack must be "instant, overwhelming, and leaving no choice in response to an armed attack—either as a response to the attacks of choice of means, and no moment of deliberation". This standard seems to be absent with regard to drone attacks in FATA. The U.S. practice of preparing 'kill lists' which are maintained for long periods of time and serve as the premise for carrying out 'signature strikes' show that the threat does not meet these requirements. In anticipatory self-defence, the state is not supposed to have time to decide on alternative methods or means.[81]

It must be stated here right away that Ahmad Nazir Warriach presented anticipatory self-defence as if it is still lawful under the United Nations framework. But the truth is that anticipatory self-defence is not lawful today. What is presently lawful, that is, what obtains now is the right of self-defence "if an armed attack occurs".[82] But in the "war on terror", being not just a response to an unconventional war, but also a response to an aggravated unconventional war (in the sense of terrorist campaigns being an unconventional tactic used by an equally unconventional group, the al-Qaeda and ISIS insurgents), anticipatory self-defence can be defensible, even if not statutorily legal. But one of the observed contradictions in the United States' application of anticipatory self-defence in the war on terror is the fact that some of those targeted by armed drones never actually attacked the United States; persons like Al-Awlaki were mere collaborators with their intoxicating, toxic, or incendiary extremist messages. There is also the contradiction of some of the terrorist attacks not being attacks on the United States, like the bombing of the *USS Cole* off the coast of Yemen, for which there cannot be response in self-defence.

So, the whole Daniel Webster idea pursued by Ahmad Nazir Warraich earlier, the idea that the practice of maintaining "kill lists" for a long period of time (which forms the basis of carrying out "signature strikes") does not meet the requirement of instant, overwhelming, and leaving no choice of means, and cannot be argued in self-defence against terrorist campaigns or attacks. In an attempt to effectuate its "inherent" right of self-defence in the war on terror, the United States has found itself in the position of the African proverbial *eneke-nti-oba* (a kind of bird). In the words of Chinua Achebe:

> Eneke the bird was asked why he was always on the wing and he replied: "Men have learnt to shoot without missing their mark and I have learnt to fly without perching on a twig".[83]

81 See Ahmad Nazir Warraich (2013), "The Use of Drones . . .", p. 78, op. cit.

82 See Fred Aja Agwu (2005), *United Nations System, State Practice and the Jurisprudence of the Use of Force* . . ., pp. 94–436, op. cit.

83 See Chinua Achebe (1958), *Things Fall Apart*, London, Ibadan, Nairobi, Heinemann Educational Books, p. 183.

This proverb was told in the context of the dilemma of how to deal with the "shameful sacrilege" and the "abomination" orchestrated in "Umuofia", Achebe's fictional Igbo clan in *Things Fall Apart* where, owing to the encroachment and absorption of the natives into Christianity and the attendant missionary crusades that had desecrated the land so much that the "gods" were angry: "Idemili is weeping; Ogwugwu is weeping; Agbala is weeping, and all the others".[84] What to do? The dilemma was chillingly unacceptable: "If we fight the stranger we shall hit our brothers and perhaps shed the blood of a kinsman. But we must do it. Our fathers never dreamt of such a thing, they never killed their brothers. But a white man never came to them".[85] Apropos the United States: if the United States played by the rule of Article 2, paragraph 4, and Article 51, it will continue to be ruthlessly savaged by terror. It is only logical that Washington, putatively or in a preemptive manner, defend itself.

Those that built the United Nations' architecture that prescribes self-defence only when there was an armed attack never anticipated that there would be war on terror; and they never thought that countries should behave otherwise. But terrorist campaigns never came the way of states that foreswear anticipatory self-defence. This *eneke-nti-oba* analogy is clearly a pragmatic explanation for the United States' resort to anticipatory self-defence against terrorists. Terrorists—being so unconventional and elusive, being amorphous non-state entities that are not capable of frontal or open battlefield engagements, being not recognizable because they do not wear uniforms, and having made virtue of the knack for dissolving into the civilian population after an attack—leave the United States with no option but to act in anticipation of the attacks. Hence, Washington draws "kill lists" and takes the terrorists out with drones whenever the opportunities present themselves. Ashley Deeks put it in a very stark manner when he said with respect to the "war on terror" that: ". . . states that are currently fighting a particular kind of conflict, which I'm going to refer to as a transnational armed conflict, are in a situation in which the governing international law is nonexistent, unclear, or potentially a somewhat awkward fit for the facts on the ground".[86]

These are the circumstances, ironically also recognized by Ahmad Nazir Warraich,[87] which made for Washington's seeming apotheosis of deliberate, targeted, or premeditated killings in its prosecution of the war on terror, using the armed drones. The "kill lists" join with intelligence to make the preemption terrorist attacks feasible. In the war on terror, intelligence (even if it is not everything) is very important because the moment intelligence fails and the terrorist is not stopped, he or she will have his or her way. And the moment some terrorist

84 Ibid., p. 182.
85 Ibid., p. 183.
86 See Ashley Deeks (2011), "New Battlefield/Old Laws: Shaping a Legal Environment for Counterinsurgency", Proceedings of the Annual Meeting (American Society of International Law), Vol. 105, March 23–26, p. 373.
87 See Ahmad Nazir Warraich (2013), "The Use of Drones . . .", pp. 67, 72, op. cit.

attacks are accomplished, especially in suicide missions, the attacker leaves no objective trails behind; except, perhaps, complications that leaves the victim with a paroxysm of attributions that ultimately culminates in searching and killing suspects many years later. An aspect of this complication is in the query that a UN Special Rapporteur, Christof Heyns, posed as to whether some killings carried out in 2012 (ostensibly in self-defence against terror) can constitute a justifiable response to an event that took place earlier in 2001?[88] These are some of the complications in the war on terror as far as the right of self-defence within it is concerned. It is for this reason that the requirement of an armed attack for self-defence in WoT is not practicable because the terrorist, if he or she survived the attack, can elude capture for years; and his or her elusiveness can even lead many years later to hitting a wrong target in response.

Thus, because of the obvious force majeure that the emergence of terrorists like the al-Qaeda in the arena of insurgency has imposed on the United States, the killing of al-Al-Awlaki in putative or anticipatory drone attack in self-defence can be admitted into legality; but this was not supposed to be the case if it were not in an asymmetric warfare in which the al-Qaeda, a non-state and terrorist strategy-inclined entity were involved; and if the elements of the al-Qaeda were capable of conventional means and could be responded to through conventional means. When Micah Zenko argued that "reforming U.S. drone strike policies can do much to allay concerns internationally by ensuring that targeted killings are defensible under international legal regimes",[89] stressing also that the way and manner the United States uses drones, especially in the signature strikes or "drone strikes in non-battlefield settings" should be reformed,[90] this argument was clearly without cognizance of the fact that battlefields are elusive in the war on terror.

And wherever these so-called battlefields exist, say in Afghanistan and north-western Pakistan as will be seen later, the dynamics of drones' use in the pursuit of terrorists in personality strikes in particular do not admit of battlefield operations; not only because the targets (the terrorist leaders or operatives) lurk behind the battlefields amongst the civilian population, drones are also in the family of modern-day precision weapons that can bypass and hit targets behind the enemy. Thus, though not an illegal weapon (because not yet, like the nuclear weapon, regulated by any treaty or customary law) the armed drone technology, as Micah Zenko put it, is still "without the requisite normative framework".[91] And the development or shaping of this normative framework is not what the United States can unilaterally bring into being through good behaviour or the enthronement of transparency in the way it uses its own armed drones as Micah Zenko argues;[92] it is something that will happen through the concerted efforts of

88 Ibid., p. 79.
89 See Micah Zenko (2013), "Reforming U.S. Drone Strike Policies" . . ., p. 3, op. cit.
90 Ibid., p. 4.
91 Ibid., p. 3.
92 Ibid., pp. 3–4.

nations, and through the instrumentality of treaty arrangements like the Hague Regulations and the Geneva Conventions.

Much as playing by the rules of engagement is desirable, drones in asymmetric armed conflicts typically illustrate the saying that it is difficult to make omelets without breaking an egg. It is very difficult to engage terrorists or insurgents in armed conflict the same way that the nation-state would be engaged because insurgents do not engage in conventional warfare, being not capable of any pitched battle or frontal engagement. They erratically hit, run, and dissolve in the civilian population, thus making self-defence in the expectation of Article 51 of the United Nations Charter very difficult if not absolutely impossible. In this case, the victim state would not have any option than to engage them from an anticipatory or preemptive manner; that is, if from intelligence revelations, the state is faced with Daniel Webster's (in the *Caroline case*) *periculum in mora* in the sense of a threat that is "instant, overwhelming, and leaving no choice of means and no moment for deliberation".[93]

Daniel Webster's formulation was entirely of customary law orientation, not positivist law within the context of the United Nations' demand of an armed attack as a condition precedent. But the United States does not pretend to act within the context of the United Nations' jurisprudence on self-defence. It operates from the customary law anticipatory or preemptive self-defence and makes no bone about it. This U.S. practice of preemptive self-defence is generously expressed in the "Clinton Doctrine" and the "Bush Doctrine".[94] In fact, President Bush Jr. is said to have argued that "if the United States deferred action, hesitated at striking those who were threats, the consequences might not be immediate; but the prospect of losing half the population of an American city was so horrible to contemplate that it created an urgent duty".[95]

President Bush aforementioned was also quoted to have told nearly 1,000 graduating cadets and their families in West Point's Michie Stadium that "the war on terror will not be won on the defensive. . . . We must take the battle to the enemy, disrupt his plans, and confront the worst threats before they emerge".[96] The Defence Secretary, Donald Rumsfeld, also opined that "it is certainly within the President's power to direct that, in our self-defence, we take this battle to the terrorists, and that means to the leadership and command and control capabilities of terrorist networks".[97] This preemptive self-defence argument is also stretched further to justify the policy of using armed drones in targeted killings, citing President Ronald Reagan's 1981 Executive Order 12,333 that reiterated President Ford's ban on political assassination, but "does not restrict the lawful

93 See Fred Aja Agwu (2005), *United Nations System, State Practice and the Jurisprudence of the Use of Force* . . ., p. 177, op. cit.

94 Ibid., pp. 433–434.

95 See Bob Woodward (2004), *Plan of Attack*, London and New York, Pocket Books, p. 132.

96 Loc. Cit.

97 See William C. Banks (2005), "The Predator", in Volker C. Franke (2005, ed.); *Terrorism and Peacekeeping* . . ., p. 150, op. cit.

use of force against legitimate enemy targets".[98] Hence, the argument goes, the Executive Order as a U.S. operational policy or instrument of defensive use of force in targeted killings (with the Predator) while in pursuit of "Al Qaeda combatants", has a firm root, not only in U.S. law, but also in customary international law and the United Nations Charter.[99]

And even in this inclination of Washington to preemptive measures, there was report that at the 70th New York meeting of the United Nations General Assembly (UNGA), President Obama himself also unequivocally stated that the United States will not hesitate to use force unilaterally in protection of itself and allies.[100] But even in their deployment in preemptive self-defence, the status of the drones as new and unregulated weapons has certainly not proved its illegality or illegitimacy in asymmetric armed conflicts; but this is not to justify the questionable way or circumstance of its preemptive application in ways that are inconsistent with Article 51 of the United Nations Charter. But it must be accepted that this preemptive application of armed drones in self-defence is foisted on the United States by the very character of the war on terror as one without any geographic or territorial content in the sense of identifiable frontlines. The terrorists diffuse and get lost in the anonymity of the civilian population.

But for conventional or non-terror-related armed conflict, the U.S. practice of anticipatory self-defence in the war on terror does not change the fact that the United Nations system no longer admits of the use of force in any customary international law manner. The provision of Article 51 of the United Nations Charter is that a state is only entitled to the right of self-defence if an armed attack occurs. And if the positivist reasoning that the United Nations Charter demands is strictly followed, it would not matter whether or not the enemy is a regular force or an insurgent force, an armed attack must be a physical and strategic phenomenon that must involve an active firing of weapons,[101] to which the attacked state must immediately respond in defence of itself. In other words, this self-defence must not be embarked upon just because the victim state was in a situation of *periculum in mora*; it should be because there was an actual armed attack.

But a change in this rule of the game has clearly been foisted on the United States by circumstances; that is, the advent of the al-Qaeda brand of terrorism-related insurgency. In the killing of Al-Awalaki in Yemen, Washington showed no pretention about using force in a preemptive manner[102] that is contrary to the expectations of Article 51 of the United Nations Charter. Thus, the exigency of terrorist campaigns has changed (for the war on terror) what ordinarily should be

98 Ibid., p. 149.

99 Loc. Cit.

100 This was not just a report, the U.S. President was shown making this declaration on Channel Television (Lagos, Nigeria), monitored in Lagos on September 28, 2015, at 10 pm.

101 See Fred Aja Agwu (2005), *United Nations System, State Practice and the Jurisprudence of the Use of Force*. . ., pp. 167–173, 186–194, op. cit.

102 See Geert-Jan Alexander Knoops (2012), "Legal, Political and Ethical Dimensions of Drone Warfare under International Law. . .", pp. 702–703, 709, op. cit.

incontestable legal cannon: that "law cannot be changed to accommodate state necessity"; and that "laws can only be changed through acceptable methods of law development, which in the domain of international law are treaty and custom".[103] But at the same time, it must be made clear here that what the United States has changed in its pragmatic approach (the resort, apparently informed by the *eneke-nti-oba* analogy) to the war on terror is not the law.

In its response with anticipatory self-defence and the "kill lists" in the war on terror, the United States was not trying to change the law to accommodate its interests; it was merely into a pragmatic policy that was imposed on it by the necessity of self-preservation against the evil of terrorism, just like Okika in Chinua Achebe's character in *Things Fall Apart* urged his people, the people of Umuofia, to be guided by the wisdom of *eneke-nti-oba* the bird to root out the "evil" that the white man's religion was planting in their land. For President Obama, the essence of the drone strikes in self-defence is that "by narrowly targeting our action against those who want to kill us, and not the people they hide among, we are choosing the course of action least likely to result in the loss of innocent life".[104] However, irrespective of this expressed caution in the application of armed drones, the use of the weapon is still heavily criticized; and the United States is still living with the consequences of the drone strikes, some of which are high collateral damage among the civilian population and the attendant "blowbacks" that are tantamount to building an "industrial terrorist complex".

But for President Obama, the alternative to the drone strikes is to use Special Forces or conventional air power.[105] This, however, has its own peculiar limitations, some of which are unthinkable. According to President Obama:

> . . . small Special Operations carry enormous risks. Conventional airpower or missiles are far less precise than drones, and likely to cause more civilian casualties and local outrage. And invasions of these territories lead us to be viewed as occupying armies; unleash a torrent of unintended consequences; are difficult to contain; and ultimately empower those who thrive on violent conflicts. So, it is false to assert that putting boots on the ground is less likely to result in civilian deaths, or to create enemies in the Muslim world. The result [of boots on the ground] would be more U.S. deaths, more Blackhawks down, more confrontations with local populations, and an inevitable mission creep in support of such raids that could easily escalate into new wars.[106]

President Obama stood by his preference for the drone strikes and continued to authorize it until his last day in office. His successor, President Donald Trump,

103 See Ahmad Nazir Warraich (2013), "The Use of Drones . . .", p. 78, op. cit.
104 See the "Full Transcript of President Obama's Speech on Counterterrorism Policy" . . ., op. cit.
105 Loc. Cit.
106 Loc. Cit. Brackets mine

has not shown any inclination to abandon the path of drone strikes, being himself even very critical of Obama (while campaigning for the White House in the November 8, 2018 presidential election) for a glove-in-hand approach to the ISIS. Donald Trump vowed to use his bare-knuckles to defeat the ISIS in his umpteenth avowal during his campaigns to make America great again.

8 Drones, Vanishing Frontlines, and the Emergence of "Battlespace"

Shifting Theaters in the War on Terror

The enlistment of terrorist campaigns by insurgents and the attendant use of armed drones in targeted killings to repel them are some of the dimensions of modern asymmetric warfare that have made the comprehension or location of the theaters of the warfare a very arduous if not an absolutely elusive task. In the war on terror, the frontline or battlefield is nomadic, ubiquitous and almost incomprehensibly omnipresent in nature. As theaters of engagement in this genre of asymmetric conflict, they are inherently complex because they are borderless. Interchangeably used in this book, although the frontline or battlefield constitutes the geographic confine within which every armed conflict takes place, the borderless nature of the war on terror is one of its major and inherent controversies.

Although in the form of whole countries, there are multiple frontlines in terror and counter-terror operations, these frontlines are also not only shifty in nature, they are increasingly vanishing because the nomadic and evasiveness of terrorists characteristically eviscerates the idea of any distinctive battlefield in the conventional sense of it. This is probably why the U.S. President George W. Bush administration characterized its anti-terror and counter-terror campaigns as a global war on terror, implicitly signifying that entire countries and, indeed, "that the entire world is a battlefield in this regard".[1] In other words, although having few fixed frontlines in Africa (Algeria, Nigeria, Libya, etc.), the Middle East—(Iraq, Syria, Afghanistan, and Pakistan) and the Southeast Asian countries of Indonesia, Malaysia, Philippines, Thailand, and even Singapore and Brunei where the al-Qaeda-linked pan-Asian terrorist group (the Jemaah Islamiya, JI) wants to establish a pan-Islamic realm[2]—the war on terror is also literally omnipresent.

In its virtually omnipresent character, it extends beyond its primary theaters in Africa, the Middle East, Southeast Asia, and even cyber sphere, to also being waged in the West by lone wolves; so much so that the war affects practically every aspect of international relations, from things as basic or rudimentary as

1 See Robert D. Sloane (2011), "New Battlefields/Old Laws . . .", p. 372, op. cit.

2 See Rosemary Foot (2005), "Collateral Damage . . .", p. 414, op. cit.

international travels to even how foreign aid is prioritized and delivered by donors.[3] From Afghanistan, Pakistan, Iraq, and Syria, to New York, Washington, and Pennsylvania (on 9/11), Bali (Indonesia), London, Madrid, Paris, San Bernardino (United States), Tunisia, Libya, Nigeria, and Belgium (Brussels' Zaventem Airport and Maelbeek Metro), the frontlines in the war on terror intractably exist, not in a territorially definitive or conventional manner, but in a whole country, including civilian neighbourhoods, being parts of the frontlines. So, it is certainly not a contradiction in terms for the former U.S. President Bush to have characterized the war on terror as global in nature. This is because the war on terror truly thrives globally, both literally and figuratively.

Thus, the war clearly does not possess definite frontlines as the terrorists are permanently shifting their "theaters" of operations and striking soft targets amongst the civilian population while not engaging the military in frontal combats. The al-Qaeda in the Islamic Maghreb (AQIM) does not recognize any definitive frontline, explaining why in November 2015, the "terrorists struck a tourist hotel in the Malian capital of Bamako, killing 20 people"; in January 2016, they also carried out an "attack on a hotel in the Burkina Faso capital of Ouagadougou [that] left 30 dead"; and on March 13, 2016, the "militants besieged a beach resort in Grand Bassam, Cote d'Ivoire's former capital, leaving at least 13 dead".[4] This is the manifestation of the vanishing frontlines on the part of the terrorists. And as Robert Sloane put it, the terrorists do this "in order to offset the stronger party's advantages".[5]

So, President George W. Bush's description of this conflict as a global war on terror can be apprehended in both the literal and figurative sense, not just on account of the fact that the conflict actually has a global manifestation, but also because there have been regional coalitions that emerged to tackle it. For instance, and as will be alluded to later in this book, apart from the NATO coalition in Afghanistan, the U.S.-led coalition against the ISIS in Iraq and Syria, and the Saudi-Arabia-led Muslim countries coalition tackling terrorism in Yemen, there is also the regional coalition of Asian governments that has not only moved to enact new anti-terrorism laws in addition to the strengthening of the existing ones, they have also formed organizations that are designed to fight this menace.[6] On the other hand, having adverted to the notion of the vanishing frontlines on the part of the terrorists, this notion on the part of the nation-state also derives from the fact that, because the terrorist "combatants" are irregular, shifty, and chronically unwilling to enter into frontal or pitched battles, the result or culmination is that the counter-terrorism operations embarked upon by countries also happen beyond the literal or physical frontlines.

3 See Ngaire Woods (2005), "The Shifting Politics of Foreign Aid . . .", p. 393, op. cit.
4 See "Mali, B'Faso, Senegal, Cote d'Ivoire Raise Efforts to Fight Terror", *The Guardian* (Lagos), Friday, March 25, 2016, p. 18.
5 See Robert D. Sloane (2011), "New Battlefields/Old Laws . . .", p. 372, op. cit.
6 See Rosemary Foot (2005), "Collateral Damage . . .", p. 414, op. cit.

Meanwhile, because of the shifty nature of the war on terror, the physical frontlines consist of the points or moments at which the terrorists execute their plots; as, for instance, in the moment they struck the United States on 9/11, or when, on March 22, 2016, they struck the ticketing area at Brussels' Zaventem Airport and Brussels Maelbeek metro station as well.[7] Counter-attacks against them are accomplished with the intelligence that leads to their detection outside that frontline. It is in this behind the frontlines attacks by terrorists (and the equally behind the frontlines intelligence-led counter-attacks by countries) that frontlines vanish or diminish in specific terms, paving the way for whole countries to become frontlines in the war on terror. In these countries that have become massive frontlines of terror—the United States (New York et al.), Russia (Chechnya), Nigeria (the northeast region in particular), France (Paris), or Belgium (Brussels)—the civilian population is characteristically targeted; and no discrimination is shown between combatants and noncombatants.

By extrapolation, the global war on terror in a literal sense of it came from President George W. Bush's address of September 20, 2001 to the joint session of the Congress, in which the President declared that the war on terror that was beginning with the al-Qaeda "will not end until every terrorist group of global reach has been found, stopped, and defeated".[8] The U.S. President also warned that "we will make no distinction between the terrorists who committed these acts and those who habour them".[9] Thus, the attribution of a global dimension to the war on terror practically arose from these Presidential statements because that is what, at first blush, the statements are liable to be interpreted as, among other possible varied interpretations. And apart from President Bush, many officials of his government also made statements that could be subject to the war on terror being construed in a global sense. In July 2002, Secretary (of Defence) Rumsfeld made a similar statement when he "ordered Special Forces commander and Air Force General Charles Holland to develop a plan to capture or kill members of terrorist organizations on a global scale".[10]

Even the Vice-President, Dick Cheney, declared, with respect to the al-Qaeda, that:

> There's no piece of real estate. It's not like a state or a country. The notion of deterrence doesn't really apply here. There's no treaty to be negotiated, there's no arms control agreement that's going to guarantee our safety and security. The only way you can deal with them is to destroy them. The reach

7 See Brief in *Time* (New York), April 4, 2016, p. 8; and "Europe Has Suffered Another Series of Murderous Attacks by Jihadists: They Will Not Be the Last", *The Economist*, March 26, 2016, p. 11; see also Abdullateef Aliyu in "Security Alert at Lagos over Brussels Attacks", *Daily Trust* (Lagos), Thursday, March 24, 2016, p. 7.

8 See William C. Banks (2005), "The Predator", in Volker C. Franke (2005, ed.); *Terrorism and Peacekeeping* . . ., p. 144, op. cit.

9 Ibid., pp. 144, 153.

10 Ibid., p. 148.

> of our efforts must be as broad and deep as the tentacles of the terrorist networks.[11]

The emphasis on Vice-President Dick Cheney's statement is on the fact that "the reach of our efforts must be as broad and deep as the tentacles of the terrorist networks": networks that are, of course, practically global in some relative sense. In addition, the United States' Congress also granted a sweeping authority to the President in a Resolution that "is not time-limited; nor does it have a geographic constraint"; nor is the President's "discretion on choice narrowed in any way, so long as the target is connected to September 11".[12] And because al-Qaeda members do not wear uniforms or serve in any nation's army, or even fight on conventional battlefields, according to William Banks, the battlefield against them "was declared to be the entire world after September 11".[13] The totality and global spread of the war on terror also appear to be captured in the remark of an intelligence official who said that "you have to go after the Gucci guys, the guys who write the checks",[14] explicitly meaning that you do not only go after the bad guys, you also go after the people that fund them.

And in going after the sources of terrorist funding, you must be invariably scouring the entire nooks and crannies of the globe because the sources of terrorist funding are far-flung and global in nature; either directly or indirectly. It is "broad and deep", with widespread tentacles or network, to deploy some of the vocabularies of the U.S. Vice-President Dick Cheney earlier. So, this literal interpretation is certainly one of the credible perspectives to President Bush's, his government officials', the Congress', and others that weighed into the public debate in the aftermath of 9/11 because they all implicitly suggest that the terror attacks and the United States' responses thereafter are akin to a World War, one in which, at least, by virtue of the North Atlantic Treaty Organization's (NATO) participation, many nations were involved; and in which the battlefields were well neigh globally spread in the literal and figurative sense of it; that is, wherever the terrorists were found and armed drone deployed to take them out.

However, the Obama administration that came immediately after Bush "strived to distance itself from the Bush Administration's literal [or global] characterization of the conflict".[15] This reluctance to characterize it in global terms arises from the inability to precisely define the borders of this "war on terror" due to the serious evasiveness of the terrorists. It is for the reason of the terrorists' evasiveness that Philip Alston is attributed with the position that the war on terror is not amenable to being "stated within a category or geographic scope"; and that "the contours of the right to self-defence were not defined" within it;

11 Ibid., p. 152.
12 Ibid., p. 150.
13 Ibid., p. 151.
14 Ibid., p. 153.
15 See Ahmad Nazir Warraich (2013), "The Use of Drones . . .", p. 74, op. cit. Brackets mine.

that is, that the right of self-defence is not capable of being realized in terms of the expectations of Article 51 of the United Nations Charter.[16]

It is certainly because of the absence of a geographic or territorial frontline content to the war on terror that it is difficult to talk in terms of realizing the right of self-defence against terrorist campaigns within the ambience of Article 51 of the United Nations Charter. This is why laying claims to exercising the right of self-defence, which the United States often does, is better apprehended as an exercise in expediency or pragmatism that does not meet the textbook conception of the right of self-defence in this positivism and even post-positivism era of the United Nations.

It Is "Battlespace", Not Battlefield or Frontline

Conceptually, and as distinct from a battlefield or frontline, a "battlespace" is an arena of warfare that is contaminated by civilians.[17] This contamination is peculiar to the shifty war on terror and creates operational difficulties for the Air Force, not just in its use of drones. In northeast Nigeria in the battle against the Boko Haram, the Nigerian Air Force had reported that "there are times when the pilots would return to base with their bombs because they sighted women and children".[18]

But the hitting of civilians could not be avoided by the Nigerian Air Force on Tuesday, January 17, 2017, when a fighter jet misfired, killing not civilians in an Internally Displaced Persons (IDP) camp in Rann (Kala Balge, Borno State), but also humanitarian workers.[19] Although the federal government had announced the defeat of the Boko Haram by dint of the domination of the terror group's "camp Zero" in Sambisa Forest by *Operation Lafiya Dole*, the military in the morning of the unfortunate incident had "received a report about the gathering of Boko Haram terrorists around Kala Balge area of Maiduguri" and authorized an airstrike; but it "turned out that other civilians were somewhere around the area and they were affected".[20] Scores of people were killed; but as it were, not many people accepted that the action of the jetfighter was in error and called for a probe.[21]

16 Ibid., p. 73.
17 See Markus Wagner (2012), "Beyond the Drone Debate: Autonomy in Tomorrow's Battlespace", Proceedings of the Annual Meeting (American Society of International Law), Vol. 106, March 28, pp. 81–82.
18 See Seun Akioye in "Air Force Flies Ezekwesili, Others to Sambisa Forest: Troops Discover Bodies of Boko Haram Fighters", *The Nation* (Lagos), Tuesday, January 17, 2017, p. 9.
19 See Muyiwa Adeyemi, Terhemba Daka, Karls Tsokar and Njadvara Musa in "Fighter Jet Kills Civilians in Borno Anti-Terror Raid", *The Guardian* (Lagos), Wednesday, January 18, 2017, p. 1.
20 Ibid., pp. 1, 6.
21 See John Alechenu, John Ame, Olusola Fabiyi et al in "NAF Jet Bombed Borno Camp Thrice, Survivor Recounts", *The Punch* (Lagos), Thursday, January 19, 2017, pp. 7, 34; see also Ademola Oni, Olusola Fabiyi, Friday Olokor, Olaleye Aluko and Kayode Idowu in "IDP Camp Bombing: NAF Panel Summons War Commander, Pilots", *The Punch* (Lagos), Friday, January 20, 2017, pp. 1, 7.

Even in the so-called Federally Administered Tribal Areas (FATA), an area of Pakistan that is putatively or recognizably the epicenter of the war on terror,[22] it is still very difficult to talk in terms of the existence concrete battlefields or frontlines in the pristine sense of the words. This is because, over there in FATA, "the U.S. is fighting against a diffused group that cannot easily be identified from the civilian population".[23] In an armed conflict, a battlefield properly so-called does not contain civilians. Even when the war moves into the cities, the civilian population is advisedly evacuated. Between the belligerents, the attacking enemy commander can warn that civilians be evacuated from a besieged city before bombardment, while the authorities of the defended city have the responsibility to put civilians to safety.[24]

This imperative is also amplified by Articles 57 and 58 of Protocol I (1977), additional to the four Geneva Conventions. This cautionary measure is to avoid the contamination of the battlefield or frontlines and the attendant high level of civilian casualties. But in FATA and other places where the war on terror is waged, "civilian and military targets become increasingly intertwined"; and it is because of this contamination that Markus Wagner used the word, "battlespace", "as opposed to the conventional battlefield",[25] to designate the combat zone of drone strikes in the war on terror. The challenge that armed drones face in the "modern battlespace" as opposed to the conventional battlefield that is not contaminated with civilians will be further discussed later in the rubric on automated or autonomous drones.

It is, therefore, because of this borderless nature (which also arises from the fact that insurgents are ambidextrous by way of combining conventional approaches with terrorist or unconventional ones) that terrorist campaigns (as part and parcel of insurgency) are disqualified from being characterized as armed conflicts from the standpoint of IHL. To this extent, it will be apposite to reiterate here that, unlike in conventional armed conflicts, terrorist campaigns and the counter-campaigns waged by the victim states do not have strict frontlines. They are shifty in nature and often take place behind the so-called enemy lines in places with heavy civilian presence or contamination. Thus, the observance of IHL is hard to be meaningfully attained. And this is essentially because, to compensate for their weaknesses, the terrorists are inherently averse to IHL.

Their aversion to IHL leaves the nation-state with the option to only concede the protection of the law to them, partly from a philosophical inspiration and partly from their consciousness of the Martens Clause and Article 3 common to the four Geneva Convention that has not only obliged them to observe IHL whenever the armed forces are deployed, but has also abolished the notion that only the High Contracting Parties to the IHL instruments would observe them,

22 See Ahmad Nazir Warraich (2013), "The Use of Drones . . .", p. 74, op. cit.
23 Ibid., p. 75.
24 See Fred Aja Agwu (2011), *The Law of Armed Conflict and African Wars* . . ., p. 37, op. cit.
25 See Markus Wagner (2012), "Beyond the Drone Debate . . .", pp. 81–82, op. cit.

including the extension of the law to irregular forces and the Levees en Masse in occupied territories.[26] The terrorist components of modern insurgencies make the armed engagements with them to be conflicts without borders. In fact, as already stated earlier, it was for this reason, particularly with the insurgents' use of IEDs, that the former Vice-President of the United States, Dick Cheney, wrote that the policy towards insurgency "ought to be adjusted; that it [the policy] needs to reflect the changing nature of twenty-first century war, [one] in which combat and noncombat, frontline and rear, are not always so easy to delineate".[27]

Cyberspace as an Epicenter-Frontline

The frontline or battlefield of the war on terror may be in treat or facing increased contamination, resulting to what is now called "battlespace"; but this definitive or concrete may after all be in existence in cyberspace. Here, the literal and the figurative frontline converge to provide a concrete arena of hostilities from which none of the parties or "combatants" can practice any form of evasiveness. In other words, with the deployment of IEDs by the terrorists, and armed drones (an example of precision-guided munitions that can bypass enemy forces and strike at targets beyond the combat zones[28]) by the nation-state (the United States in particular), the unfortunate reality of a very murky frontline may have come into existence in the war on terror; but it is also safe to say that, in cyberspace, there is no vanishing frontline, neither is there any "battlespace" in the sense of a contaminated frontline or battlefield. Cyberspace is a concrete and undiluted arena of confrontation between terrorists and the nation-state.

Cyberspace is one of the most literal, un-receding, un-changing, and un-vanishing combat zones in the "war on terror". In fact, as an arena, cyberspace most effectively captures President George W. Bush's promulgation or framing (consistent with the conception that the conflict in borderless terms) of the war on terror in global terms.[29] Whereas the U.S. President's promulgation may have as well asserted the global dimension of the war on terror in literal and figurative terms, digital space, the cyberspace as an internet platform, is about the most apt representation of that global dimension in literal terms. This aptness also derives from the fact that cyberspace is where the ugliest face of the war on terror can be found because, as a weapon at the disposal of the terrorists, it, like "battlespace" on land, is highly contaminated. In the use of cyberspace to radicalize and recruit followers, sympathizers and lone

26 See Article 3 common to the four Geneva Convention; see also Fred Aja Agwu (2011), *The Law of Armed Conflict and African Wars. . .*, pp. 354–355; see also L. Oppenheim (1952), *International Law:A Treatise, Vol. 2. . .*, p. 258, op. cit.

27 See Dick Cheney (2011), *In My Time . . .*, p. 497, op. cit. Parentheses mine.

28 See Fred Aja Agwu (2005), *United Nations System, State Practice and the Jurisprudence of the Use of Force . . .*, pp. 338, 364, op. cit.

29 See Geert-Jan Alexander Knoops (2012), "Legal, Political and Ethical Dimensions of Drone Warfare under International Law. . .", p. 706, op. cit.

wolves, the terrorists do not discriminate between adults and children, and even women. In terms of recruitment and radicalization, all is fair game on the internet.

As discussed earlier in this book, the cyberspace as a frontline for both the insurgents and those countering them cannot be underestimated or even overestimated. As a frontline, insurgents use cyberspace to try to close up the asymmetric gap in the engagement vis-à-vis the nation-state; since victory in that domain, as alluded to earlier, is a function, not of the quantum of resources available (or even the numerical strength of the adversary); it is rather a function of the available skill. And cyberspace is also a frontline in the sense that it provides the insurgents with the avenue for the radicalization and recruitment of its members.[30] It is also an arena for propaganda, used to appeal to and win the hearts and minds of the local population whenever the nation-state displaces the insurgents the way the United States sacked the al-Qaeda and the Taliban from Afghanistan in the wake of 9/11 attacks. In the war on terror, the United States and other Western nations are morbidly apprehensive about ungoverned spaces around the world because these spaces are characteristically easily taken over and converted to safe havens by insurgents. This makes all ungoverned spaces perfect frontlines in the war on terror.

Paradoxically, the internet (the worldwide web) where cyberspace is domiciled is also an ungoverned space in the sense that it is so open and free that about anything under the sun can be posted there by about any person or group of persons that have the ability to do so. Like every other ungoverned territory, cyberspace is, therefore, the "virtual sanctuary [that] enables global insurgency" to thrive;[31] and there is absolutely nothing that the West or any nation-state for that matter can do about it. But there is no doubting the fact that the so-called ungoverned spaces, defined here in terms of those places that are playing host to insurgents, are actually the incubating centers and, thus, the epicenter of the battlefields in the war on terror.

Other Epicenters of the Frontlines

In conservative terms, and talking especially about the drone strikes, other epicenters of the battlefields or frontlines of this war on terror are Afghanistan and northwestern Pakistan (Waziristan).[32] The drone strikes, however, are more pronounced in the FATA region of Pakistan.[33] It was on account of the centrality or prominence of FATA as one of the frontlines on the war on terror that for the first time in 2010, it was the first place the United States officially acknowledged using the CIA to embark on targeted killings, using armed drones.[34]

30 See "How to Fight Back . . .", p. 13, op. cit.

31 See Richard Shultz (2009), "Virtual Sanctuary Enables Global Insurgency", in Jeffrey H. Norwitz (2009, ed.); *Pirates, Terrorists, and Warlords* . . ., p. 425, op. cit. Brackets mine.

32 See Geert-Jan Alexander Knoops (2012), "Legal, Political and Ethical Dimensions of Drone Warfare under International Law. . .", p. 710, op. cit.

33 See Ahmad Nazir Warraich (2013), "The Use of Drones . . .", p. 64, op. cit.

34 Ibid., p. 65.

With the emergence of the ISIS in Syria and Iraq, the frontline in the war on terror has also moved there—including the West African nation of Nigeria (on account of the Boko Haram), and the Horn of African nation of Somalia (on account of the Al-Shabab)—even though American drone strikes are not prominent in Nigeria and Somalia. The frontlines in the war on terror are, therefore, scattered across the Middle East and Africa, even though some frontlines also exist in the West, especially wherever the lone wolves strike and are confronted. But it is doubtful whether President George Bush's characterization of the war on terror as global arises from this fact that the frontlines are strewn across several regions, having made that definition only after 9/11; that is, before the emergence of the Boko Haram, or the escalation of the Al-Shabab insurgency and terror campaigns.

There is a strong imprint (or fingerprint) of an "ungoverned" or inadequately governed territory in the FATA region because "general Pakistani law does not apply in FATA, [the] tribal areas in the north west of Pakistan that border Afghanistan, due to the special status of the area since pre-partition days".[35] It is pretty difficult to see the basis of the assertion that "the U.S use of drones in FATA is illegal under international law [because] it does not fall in any of the situations allowed where such use of force is permissible".[36] This statement is highly contentious because, as at this moment, there is no extant international law that governs the use of armed drones; and as far as international law is concerned (as explored earlier under the rubric of drones in self-defence), it is perfectly permissible in the use of force for a state to leverage its right of self-defence against individual brigands in another state's territory, provided that it does not violate that state's territorial integrity by hitting the state itself (its institutions or infrastructure) rather than the insurgents or terrorists.

The successful assertion of this form of the right of self-defence has been made possible with modern technological innovations like the armed drones. But this is not to say that there is no concern about international law in these drone strikes. The most visible or credible concern about the law here is in relation to IHL, the perversion of the principle of distinction by signature strikes, which easily leads to unacceptable civilian casualties. The suspicion that the United States may deny the proneness of signature strikes to orchestrate unacceptable collateral damage was what led Philip Alston (former UN Special Rapporteur) to recommend the invoking of U.S. former President Ronald Reagan's wisdom of "trust but verify";[37] that is, that the international community should accept such denials, but that it should nonetheless not fail to verify them.

But as far as the use of armed drones is concerned, it is in the character of the war on terror that "both the enemy and the war theatre are vaguely defined"; and that the frontline is sometimes "increasingly remote from the aggressor".[38]

35 Ibid., p. 66.
36 Loc. Cit. Brackets mine.
37 Ibid., p. 76.
38 Ibid., p. 64.

This is not only on account of the fact that drones bypass the battlefield and hit targets behind enemy lines, it is also on account of the fact that these drones sometimes go after the collaborators with the real enemy or "aggressor" in an entirely different location, away from the real aggressor, here defined in terms of characters like Osama bin Laden (the sponsor of the al-Qaeda) or Abu Bakr al-Baghdadi (the leader of ISIS). Although in the light of the fact that terrorist campaigns by insurgents are truly worldwide (including African countries of Nigeria, Libya, and Egypt, other parts of the Middle East like Syria and Iraq, and the homegrown ones in the West), some controversy may attend the designation of Afghanistan and Waziristan as the major frontlines in the war on terror.

But this controversy can be attenuated by the fact that until the emergence of the ISIS in Syria, Iraq, Libya, and the Boko Haram in Nigeria, it was only in Afghanistan that an insurgent group like the Taliban conducted combat operations that later spilled over into northwest Pakistan (Waziristan).[39] It was also in Afghanistan that the al-Qaeda was born; and it was from there that the terrorist organization began planning and executing its terrorist campaigns elsewhere around the world, under the leadership of Osama Bin Laden that was later killed in Abbottabad, Pakistan, even though not through a drone strike.[40] In fact, the Afghan President Ashraf Ghani once said of his country: "this is the frontline" of the war on terror.[41]

Apparently supporting the Afghan President's assertion that his country is the frontline in the war on terror is the fact that (1) a record number of the people have died from terrorism; (2) the Afghan government only controls about 60% of the country's territory while "almost 10% of the population now lives in areas under insurgent control or influence; (3) "of the 98 U.S.-designated terrorist organizations worldwide, 20 operate in the borderlands between Afghanistan and Pakistan"; (4) there is "the presence of 8,400 American troops (along with some 4,600 NATO soldiers") and "the possibility of more to come" to Afghanistan; (5) "more than 2,200 U.S. troops have been killed in Afghanistan since 2001, and some 20,000 have been wounded", yet the insurgents (especially the Taliban) are resurgent; (6) the U.S. cannot afford to walk away from Afghanistan, lest the Taliban roll back and reconstitute the threat it posed, and which culminated in9/11; and (7) "in addition to the foreign soldiers in the country, Afghanistan now has more than 300,000 of its own troops in the field fighting the Taliban and other groups".[42]

In fact, it was on account of all of this and more that on April 13, 2017, the United States "dropped a 21,000-Ib. bomb—daubed the 'mother of all

39 See Geert-Jan Alexander Knoops (2012), "Legal, Political and Ethical Dimensions of Drone Warfare under International Law. . .", p. 710, op. cit.

40 Loc. Cit.

41 See Nikhil Kumar in "Afghanistan Is the Front Line", *Time* (New York), June 12, 2017, p. 20.

42 Loc. Cit.

bombs'—on an ISIS cave complex in eastern Afghanistan", destroying "a very significant group of ISIS leaders", even though "the terrorist group still has hundreds of lethal fighters in the country".[43] Apparently in response to the United States dropping of the MAOB, the undeterred terrorists, on May 31, 2017, dropped their own powerful bomb in the Kabul ARG area that houses the Afghan President's office and residence, around the corridor from the German embassy, killing at least 90 people and wounding "more than 400 in what was one of the worst terrorist atrocities to shake Afghanistan".[44]

However, the better view in the conception of the battlefield or frontline in the war on terror may be to say that there are multiple battlefields or frontlines spread across the whole world. Every state or territory that habours terrorists is a battlefield or frontline, both in terms of drone strikes or in other confrontations with terrorists. Although a drone strike might not have killed Osama bin Laden in Abbottabad, and although this city may not have been situated in northwestern Pakistan,[45] it was a battlefield. The mere fact that bin Laden was confronted and killed in Abbottabad made the place a frontline or battlefield in the war on terror, even if ad hoc. This appears to be in accordance with Washington's "view that virtually every state which harbours potential terrorists posing a threat to the U.S. could constitute a battlefield, i.e. is part of a global armed conflict which the U.S. have declared between Al Qaeda (and its affiliates) and itself".[46]

It is, however, noteworthy that although the United States may have declared this war, the threat posed by insurgents and their terror campaigns are not limited only to the United States and its citizens; it is now a threat against every nation in the world (and its citizens) because any terrorist bomb that brings down an airplane does not discriminate between U.S. citizens and those of other nations by way of sparing the latter. The same applies when a terrorist bomb pulverizes a place of worship, be it in Nigeria or Beirut (Lebanon); it does not discriminate or spare anybody. It was also this theory that there is a battlefield in the war on terror anywhere in the world that terrorists take refuge and pose threats that animated the decision of the United States to go after Al-Awlaki in Yemen. So, although he fled to Yemen, "the U.S. contemplated that Al-Awlaki . . . was taking part in a war between the U.S. and Al Qaeda and therefore posed a threat to . . . Americans, while the Yemeni authorities were not able or unwilling to apprehend him".[47]

This action was, thus, in consonance with the view that across the whole wide world, there are different battlefields on the war on terror, which was why irrespective of the fact that Al-Awlaki was thousands of miles away from the actual battlefield of Afghanistan and northwestern Pakistan, the United States

43 Loc. Cit.
44 Loc. Cit.
45 See Geert-Jan Alexander Knoops (2012), "Legal, Political and Ethical Dimensions of Drone Warfare under International Law. . .", p. 710, op. cit.
46 Ibid., pp. 706–707.
47 Ibid., pp. 702–703.

struck and killed him with a drone strike.[48] Indeed, in Yemen, the U.S. predator drones were launched some 10,000 miles away from some of the battlefields in Afghanistan and Waziristan, killing Al-Awlaki and his passenger, Mr. Samir Kahn, in a hellfire of the missile strike from drones.[49] Because of the safe haven that the al-Qaeda in the Arabian Peninsula (AQAP) had converted Yemen into, that country can effectively, from the American promulgation aforementioned, be regarded as one of the battlefields in the war on terror; but then, the place that Al-Awlaki was killed in Yemen by the drone strikes could hardly be regarded as a battlefield or frontline. In other words, even if the so-called battlefields were to be easily discernable, the drone operators would still not restrict their strikes to these battlefields. And this is for the obvious fact that because the drone operators work with intelligence reports that seek to unravel the hiding places of insurgent terrorists in the civilian population, they have the penchant to strike in cities behind the enemy or frontlines.

In this conception of frontlines on the war on terror, there is also the Garissa county, the "sun-baked frontier town located 230 miles northeast of Nairobi" and dominated by Somali-speaking Kenyans that are suspected of colluding with the al-Shabaab in the terror group's constant raids in the area.[50] The hallmark of this Kenyan northern frontier district being a frontline is in the constant al-Shabaab attacks, one of the most horrendous being the April 2, 2015 attack on Garissa University College in which 142 students were massacred.[51] This has long paralyzed tourism and economic activities in the area, forcing the Kenyan government (especially following the withdrawal of Uganda from the project) to halt the oil pipeline project—that "would have linked Uganda's, South Sudan, and Kenyan oil fields to a refinery at a new deep-water port that Kenya is building in Lamu, not far from the border with Somalia"—because the area had been listed as "a security operation zone".[52]

Controversies in Drone Strikes Behind the So-Called Frontlines

In the law of armed conflict, the criterion for being targeted is being a combatant; that is, being in direct participation in hostilities.[53] Aside from direct participation in hostilities, any member of the armed forces of the belligerent that falls into enemy hands in conventional warfare can only be held as a Prisoner of War (POW).[54] So, the question is this: behind the enemy line, that is, away

48 Ibid., p. 703.
49 Ibid., p. 699.
50 See Bevertone Kipchumba Some in "Kenya's al-Shabaab Paradox", *New African*, June 2017, pp. 48–49, op. cit.
51 Loc. Cit.
52 Ibid., p. 51.
53 See Fred Aja Agwu (2011), *The Law of Armed Conflict and African Wars*. . ., p. 33, op. cit.
54 Ibid., pp. 117–122.

from the battlefield or frontline, can any individual be validly considered to be taking an active part in hostilities, enough to warrant being validly targeted the way drone operators do? It was in this context that Philip Alston, the United Nations Special Rapporteur, made the point that "the greatest source of the lack of clarity with respect to targeted killings [by drones] is in the question of who qualifies as a lawful target, where and when can the person be target?"[55] But, against the background of this unresolved question, Alston is of the opinion that the mere fact that individuals engage in illegal actions like terrorist activities does not by itself justify the conclusion that these persons fulfill the threshold of the criterion of direct participation in hostilities and, thus, should be targeted.[56]

However, with these insurgents like the ISIS, the al-Qaeda, or even the Boko Haram in Nigeria that combine their insurgency with terrorist campaigns, parsing over issues of legality in the application of armed drones against them appears totally sterile because these brands of insurgents themselves are a bunch of illegality simplicita; that is, plain and simple. These terrorists are not only incapable of playing by the rules of the game, they are unwilling and unrepentantly committed to the violation of the rules of armed conflict; such that, whatever modicum of humanity that nation-states like the United States extend to them in places like Guantanamo Bay[57] only comes from the spark of divinity in all humans, that spark that enable fellow-feelings in all circumstances, and which had animated the humanitarian considerations in armed conflicts. Because the terrorist does not play by the rules, there is hardly any meaningful way he or she can be engaged within a legal framework.

As already noted in the early pages of this book, it was out of sheer frustration at the inability of the terrorist insurgents to fight a conventional war that a military officer agonized, quipping that: "if only the little bastards would just come out . . . and fight like men, we'd cream them".[58] Since the terrorists don't come out to fight like men, the drones are inexorably employed to hit them behind the frontlines, then that is the only way to preempt or disrupt the plans and execution of their terrorist activities that neither lead to honourable deaths amongst humans nor discriminate between combatants and the civilian population. Thus, the fact that the frontlines in specific terms have vanished is the inevitable corollary of their unconventional or terrorist approaches; and the determination of the nation-state to eliminate their nuisance, even if it means enlisting ruthless approaches like the employment of drones that do not respect

55 See Geert-Jan Alexander Knoops (2012), "Legal, Political and Ethical Dimensions of Drone Warfare under International Law. . .", p. 708, op. cit. Brackets mine.

56 Loc. Cit.

57 See George W. Bush (2010), *Decision Points*, New York, Crown Publishers, pp. 166–167.

58 See P. H. Liotta (2009), "Takin' It to the Streets: Hydra Networks, Chaos Strategies, and the 'New' Asymmetry", in Jeffrey H. Norwitz (2009, ed.); *Pirates, Terrorists, and Warlords . . .*, pp. 414, op. cit.

the rule of engaging the enemy on the frontlines where it is in active participation in hostilities.[59]

It is in this context that (as pragmatic instruments in asymmetric warfare) "drones are critical counterterrorism tools that advance U.S. interests around the globe", and the suggestion that the secrecy surrounding its use, that its "lack of transparency threatens to limit U.S. freedom of action and risks proliferation of armed drone technology without the requisite normative framework"[60] is highly contestable. It is also in this context that it cannot be valid to cavil the practice of "drone strikes in non-battlefield settings"[61] because the war on terror has no definitive battlefield or frontline properly so called, having converted entire nations into frontlines.

Neither is it appropriate to submit that "targeted killings [of terrorists with drone strikes] are indefensible under international legal regimes"[62] because, as will be seen immediately in the implication in international humanitarian law of the use of drones, there is no extant international humanitarian legal regime that is governing the "war on terror", being not entirely an armed conflict in the real sense of the phenomenon. The war on terror is part law enforcement and part armed conflict. That is why it is a grey area or penumbra in the law of armed conflict, a status mixtus. Because terrorists are a peripatetic punch that is constantly in motion, striking any soft target within their reach, it is as well allowable to have them struck wherever they are encountered, be it within or without the frontline.

59 See Fred Aja Agwu (2011), *The Law of Armed Conflict and African Wars* . . ., p. 33, op. cit.
60 See Micah Zenko (2013), "Reforming U.S. Drone Strike Policies" . . ., p. 3, op. cit.
61 Loc. Cit.
62 Loc. Cit. Brackets mine.

9 Drones in International Humanitarian Law, IHL

Drones: The Pitilessness and Ghoulish Impact

> When a drone looks at a thing, that thing has a way of looking like a target. People become silhouettes at a shooting range. Buildings look vulnerable, their roofs helplessly exposed and defenseless. Most colors disappear, and the remaining blacks, whites and grays evacuate the scene of all human meaning. What we see becomes data: body counts, damage reports, strategic value.[1]

This epigram illustrates the complication that drone strikes bring to International Humanitarian Law (IHL)—the pitilessness inherent in the utter lack of the weapon's capacity for distinction and discrimination. And, indeed, the controversial lack of the ability to attribute responsibility for IHL violations to some of those (like the CIA as intelligent agents) involved in the drone strikes, all of them being not combatants in the expectations of the law of armed conflict. It is in this same manner that drones bring complications to IHL that the incidence of terrorism itself also does. When CIA agents that are traditionally involved in espionage and law enforcement become involved in drone strikes that ordinarily should be a full combatant activity, they simply get lost in the anonymity of their profession, which is espionage, and hence cannot be easily revealed and brought to account for their infractions.

In the case of terrorists, the question becomes this: who is to be held accountable for the consequences of terrorist attacks when the actual perpetrators had obliterated themselves in their suicide missions? It will be recalled that in the wake of the U.S. Congress voting (97–1) "to overturn President Obama's veto of a bill that would allow survivors and families of the victims of 9/11 to sue Saudi Arabia's government over the attacks",[2] critics began to raise the fear that the action by the U.S. Congress might have breached the age-old principle of

1 See Lev Grossman in "Middle Vision: Easily Accessible, Affordable Drones Are Giving Us a New—Perhaps Temporary—Vantage on the World", *Time* (New York), December 29, 2014–January 5, 2015, p. 70.

2 See "Senate Overturns Obama Veto", *Ticker, Time* (New York), October 10, 2016, p. 10.

sovereign immunity known to international law; for the result would be that the court processes would lead to the victim families attaching the Saudi government's property in order to realize the judgment awards by the courts.[3]

Without necessarily digressing here, it must be pointed out that this is a real complication because what is at issue here is not sovereign immunity that only applies in a diplomatic context of general international law when the sovereign is not in the marketplace, illustrated by the age-old distinction between *jure gestionis* and *jure imperii*.[4] What is at issue when dealing with the breaches of the law of armed conflict is not diplomatic or general international law; it is rather those International Criminal Court (ICC) crimes that international criminal justice is focused on. Unfortunately, although terrorism is sometimes considered a non-ICC crime,[5] acts of terrorism could admittedly form the basis of a charge under Articles 6, 7, and 8 of the Rome Statute that established the ICC—charges relating to "killing members of the group", murder and extermination of a group as well as torture and inhuman treatment, amongst other crimes.

It is by virtue of these Articles of the Rome Statute under reference that the ICC can assume jurisdiction over matters within the domain of terrorism, even though by dint of their modus operandi, terrorists see victory in death. Thus, many of them are hardly liable to capture as they blow themselves up in suicide missions and may never get arraigned before the ICC. Otherwise, trial at the ICC could be the most credible platform to remove them from the jurisdiction of municipal courts. This is more so because the ICC is now a new dispensation in which (like the decisions of the United Nations Security Council that bind all nations willy-nilly) there is a vertical (without state consent) rather than a horizontal (with state consent that is one of the fundamental principles of international law[6]) binding nature of international law.[7] The implication is that all terrorists will be subject to the jurisdiction of the court, irrespective of whether or not their countries are members of the Rome Statute.

The United States, not being a member of the Rome Statute, was acutely aware of this reality; hence, it proceeded to sign bilateral non-surrender treaties with some member states of the Rome Statute like Cambodia and Nigeria in order to vitiate the possibility of handing over U.S. personnel to the court, which

3 This was the position of the interlocutors in Fareed Zakazia's GPS programme on CNN, monitored in Lagos (Nigeria) on Sunday, October 2, 2016, between 8pm and 9pm local time.

4 See Fred Aja Agwu (2013), *Themes and Perspectives . . .*, pp. 486–488, op. cit.

5 See Leila Nadya Sadat (2012), "The Legacy of the International Criminal Tribunal for Rwanda", Occasional Paper, Whitney R. Harris World Law Institute, Washington University in St. Louis, July 3, p. 15.

6 See George Schwarzenberger (1965), *The Inductive Approach to International Law*, London, Stevens & Sons, pp. 53, 85, 97, 175.

7 Article 39 of the United Nations Charter; see also Fred Aja Agwu (2009), *National Interest, International Law . . .*, p. 106, op. cit; and Christian Reus-Smit (2004, ed.), *The Politics of International Law*, Cambridge, University Press, pp. 182, 187.

will have jurisdiction over such personnel whether or not the United States is a member of the Rome Statute that created the ICC.[8] But the argument can still be pursued that terrorism is largely a non-ICC crime; for it is certainly its consideration as a non-ICC crime that might have, perhaps, accounted for the decision of the United Nations Security Council, in prosecuting the "perpetrators, organizers and sponsors of the terrorist bombing that assassinated [the] Lebanese Prime Minister Rafiq Hariri on February 14, 2005, to establish a tribunal, which though of an international character, is devoid of international law" as it is exclusively meant to apply domestic law.[9]

Furthermore, terrorism can be considered a non-ICC crime because both terrorism itself and the war against it are not armed conflicts in the expectations of international law. But this is not to suggest that the ICC is only seized with jurisdiction over crimes committed in armed conflicts as the court also has jurisdiction over crimes (like genocide) that could be committed in peace time; and some of which can be perpetrated through terrorist activities. But at best, the atrocities by terrorists on 9/11 can only be appraised within the context of the penumbra (grey area) of IHL, being not an armed conflict properly so called. It is a grey area of the law of armed conflict because the armed response by the victim state straddles between armed conflict and law enforcement.

Since terrorism is a penumbra in the law of armed conflict, being neither ICC nor non-ICC crimes, if the municipal court in the United States (or indeed any other state whose national was a victim) decide to arbitrarily take jurisdiction, there is still a high onus of prove that officials of the Saudi government were complicit in the planning and execution of the attacks. Thus, the war on terror truly raises complications for IHL at the level of state responsibility. For instance, in Nigeria, fears could be expressed that the human rights community would hold the government responsible for the recruitment of child-soldiers by the Boko Haram, or even by the civilian Joint Task Force (JTF). For the latter, the attribution of responsibility to Nigeria is very difficult because the civilian JTF is not an arm of the Nigerian military. And for the former, it is equally difficult in the principle of state responsibility to attribute the sins of the terrorist Boko Haram to the Nigerian State; just as Saudi Arabia cannot be held responsible for the terrorism of Salafism or Wahabbism.

But in all breaches of extant IHL in mainstream armed conflict properly so called, the attendant international criminal court processes and their execution can only involve individuals and as such cannot concern the state in such a manner as to involve the infraction of sovereign immunity; for as long as war crimes and their associated infractions are concerned, it is individuals and not

8 See Fred Aja Agwu (2009), *National Interest, International Law* . . ., pp. 29, 107, note 47, op. cit; see also *The Guardian* (Lagos), May 19, 2005, p. 11.

9 See Janice Yun (2010), "Special Tribunal for Lebanon: A Tribunal of International Character Devoid of International Law", *Santa Clara Journal of International Law*, Vol. 7, p. 181, op. cit.

states that are held accountable. This is consistent with the affirmation of the Nuremberg Tribunal that crimes against international law are committed by men, not by abstract entities that states represent; for it is only by punishing individuals who commit those crimes can the rules or provisions of international law be enforced.[10] But because terrorism is still a grey area in the law of armed conflict (including the fact that elements of the Saudi government have not been established to be in cahoots with the Osama bin Laden network in the 9/11 attacks), the 9/11 attacks and the attendant consequences, just like the armed drones that rain hails of missiles on terrorists (thereby advertently or inadvertently killing civilians), produce complications at the level of accountability in IHL.

Although some optimistic views exist that suggest that in the deployment of the drone technology in armed conflicts, there is "a combination of persistent surveillance and precision-guided weaponry [that] allows for more deliberative targeting, and which reduces civilian death",[11] the epigram above conveys a contrastively different impression. One of these optimistic views was expressed by Jessica Stern who maintained that "unarmed aerial vehicles . . . are significantly more discriminating than any other weapon when fired from afar"; and that the "accuracy is one reason Obama has come to rely so heavily on them".[12] But Jessica admitted nonetheless that drones are still imperfect as "their targeting is entirely dependent on the quality of the intelligence available to the pilots", and that "it is not possible to completely avoid civilian casualties".[13]

So, it is as if to vindicate Jessica Stern's assertion about the imperfection of drones that the epigram at the beginning of the chapter portrays the weapon as one with a devastating and ghoulish impact. Apparently bearing this gory scenario in mind, that is, the scenario of "the pitilessness in the drone's stare", Lev Grossman[14] stated that there is an undiscriminating tendency and, hence, some destructiveness in the application of drones in warfare, especially at the level of collateral damage among the civilian population. Meanwhile, it is trite knowledge that the quality of the precision of a drone strike (in terms of avoiding unnecessary civilian casualties) is a function of the vast intelligence network on the ground, the effectiveness and accuracy of intelligence, both human and signal.[15]

10 See Fred Aja Agwu (2005), *United Nations System, State Practice and the Jurisprudence of the Use of Force* . . ., p. 71, op. cit.

11 See Sam Roggeveen (2014) in "Proliferation of Unmanned Aerial Vehicles . . .", op. cit.

12 See Jessica Stern (2015), "Obama and Terrorism . . .", p. 64, op. cit.

13 Loc. Cit.

14 See Lev Grossman in "Middle Vision: Easily Accessible, Affordable Drones Are Giving us a New—Perhaps Temporary—Vantage on the World", p. 70, op. cit.

15 See Micah Zenko (2013), "Reforming U.S. Drone Strike Policies" . . ., p. 7, op. cit, see also Geert-Jan Alexander Knoops (2012), "Legal, Political and Ethical Dimensions of Drone Warfare . . .", p. 715, op. cit.

UN Special Rapporteurs Assessment of Washington's Drones in IHL

In fact, in the very important issue of assessing drone strikes in the context of International Humanitarian Law (IHL), the United States was, within the space of a three-year time period (2010, 2013, and 2014), practically indicted in three separate reports of the United Nations Special Rapporteurs, on the way and manner it uses armed drones in the asymmetric engagement with the terrorist insurgents; and this is despite the very scrupulous steps that the United States[16] tries to take in order to avoid excessive collateral damage.

In the third annual report on the promotion and protection of human rights and fundamental freedoms while countering terrorism, submitted to the Human Rights Council of the United Nations General Assembly, the United Nations Special Rapporteur (dated March 10, 2010) examined the use of these remotely piloted aircraft (the drones) in extraterritorial lethal counter-terrorism operations, especially in the context of asymmetrical armed conflict, the allegations that the increasing use of drones had caused a disproportionate number of civilian casualties.[17] In Yemen, the Rapporteur, using estimates provided by Human Rights Watch, reported that, since 2009, the United States conducted at least 86 lethal drone counter-terrorism operations, killing up to 500 people, and that although the majority of those killed were believed to have been individuals with a "continuous combat function" in the Yemeni internal armed conflicts and therefore legitimate military targets, media monitoring organizations, however, alleged that between 24 and 71 civilians were confirmed killed in those drone strikes between 2009 and 2013.[18]

According to the Rapporteur Reports, civilian casualties owing to drone attacks are also prevalent in Afghanistan and Pakistan.[19] In fact, the Rapporteur Report alluded to the United Nations Mission in Afghanistan's (UNAMA) confirmation that up to the end of 2012, drone strikes inflicted more civilian casualties than aerial attacks carried out by other air platforms, a report that also implicated the International Security Assistance Force (ISAF) in the use of drone and casualties.[20] There was also the report of the Christof Heyns Special Rapportuer (dated

16 From all indications, the United States does not embark on drone strikes without being cognizant of the implication of such attacks on the civilian population. When, for instance, in February 2005, it was confirmed that Abu Musab al-Zarqawi, one of the al-Qaeda top leaders, was inside Iraq, the United States (even though through sheer bad luck the drone missed him) only moved in on him when "a combination of intelligence sources confirmed" this fact, and a drone "spotted his "vehicle moving across a lightly populated area west of Baghdad"; apparently to avoid incurring serious collateral damage or casualties within the civilian population; see Stanley McChrystal (2015), *Team of Teams*. . ., pp. 130–131, op. cit.

17 See Ben Emmerson in Report of the Special Rapporteur on the promotion and protection of human rights and fundamental freedoms while countering terrorism, op. cit.

18 Loc. Cit.

19 Loc. Cit.

20 Loc. Cit.

September 13, 2013) that observed that "the claim that drones are more precise in targeting cannot be accepted uncritically"; and that "drones enable a state to perform targeted killing without exercising effective control over territory and without having the individual in custody".[21]

But characteristically (as only a superpower would), Washington dismissed these and other Special Rapporteurs' Reports, arguing that it was exercising its inherent right of self-defence under Article 51 of the United Nations Charter, and that "inquiries related to allegations stemming from military operations conducted during the course of an armed conflict with Al-Qaeda do not fall within the mandate of the Special Rapporteur".[22] Perhaps, Washington is bolstered in its ways by the intellectual justification of its action that is provided by likes of writers like William Banks. Even though acknowledging that the war on terror is not a traditional war, William Banks offered this untenable suggestion that "during war . . . , targeted killing of individuals is lawful"; and that "in peacetime, any extra-judicial killing by a government agent is lawful only if taken in self-defence or in defence of others".[23]

But Banks' assertions do not serve the juridical interests of the United States because in traditional or conventional war, targeted killing is not permissible or lawful, whereas the war on terror is neither traditional nor nontraditional war; it is, as will be seen later, a *status mixtus* that is not within the coverage of any law of armed conflict and as such, any action taken within that state of *status mixtus* cannot be justified in terms of lawfulness but rather a pragmatic action in response to *force majeure* or compelled by the principle of necessity. In this response, the United States by dint of its deployment of drones in targeted killings, especially through its signature strikes, inevitably runs afoul of the demands of international humanitarian law (IHL).

The Tragedy of Signature Strikes in IHL

The problem of precision, associated with drone strikes, is more acute with respect to signature strikes because the CIA operators in particular usually do not get to "know beforehand if terrorist suspects are present when carrying out a signature strike (i.e. a strike on training camps and suspicious compounds)".[24] Because there can be "strikes on mosques, funerals, schools and meetings of elders (jirgas)" with "a large civilian presence",[25] signature strikes (also known as "crowd killing" or terrorist attack disruption strikes") enable CIA officials to target anonymous suspected militants that bear the characteristics of al-Qaeda or

21 See Christof Heyns in "Report of the Special Rapportuer on Extrajudicial . . ., op. cit.

22 See Micah Zenko (2013), "Reforming U.S. Drone Strike Policies" . . ., p. 17, op. cit.

23 See William C. Banks (2005), "The Predator", in Volker C. Franke (2005, ed.); *Terrorism and Peacekeeping* . . ., p. 149, op. cit.

24 See Geert-Jan Alexander Knoops (2012), "Legal, Political and Ethical Dimensions of Drone Warfare . . .", p. 716, op. cit.

25 See Ahmad Nazir Warraich (2013), "The Use of Drones . . .", p. 75, op. cit.

Taliban leaders on the run; thus, counting and killing without discrimination, "all military-age males in the arena of the drone strike".[26]

This is why signature strikes are also said to be "based on behavior patterns"; and reports indicate "a strong correlation between political events and drone strikes" within this context.[27] The worst aspect of signature strikes is the second strike that is principally aimed at the first responders or rescue workers that gather to assist the victims, those that evidently cannot be identified as rightful or lawful targets.[28] Thus, there is hardly any consciousness in signature strikes about the obligation to observe the principle of distinction; added to which is the "concerns regarding the military necessity and whether sufficient precautions were taken";[29] at least, to prevent unacceptable casualties among the innocent as well as ensure absolution from legal indictments.

It all goes a long way to show that signature strikes embody some "extraneous considerations"[30] that might not have any factual relationship with, or even be complicit in terrorist activities, both the planning and execution. Thus, in signature strikes, civilians or the innocent are normally caught in the "crossfire", or inadvertently killed in the process of targeting senior terrorist (al-Qaeda) members in what becomes an unintentional but "vast majority of collateral deaths".[31] Later, (perhaps, through an explicit intelligence), the innocent amongst the dead are posthumously justified, a post hoc methodological justification that has been roundly condemned because the targeted killing itself did not meet a priori, "the principle of distinction for the use of lethal force".[32]

The signature strikes have increasingly failed to answer such questions as to whether or not legitimate targets should include children, ordinary folk attempting to rescue drone strike victims, and people in the funeral processions of killed or deceased militants or terrorists; all three occasions (and more) of which U.S. drones have allegedly targeted.[33] One estimate in 2013 by the New American Foundation had it that "since 2004, 420 drone attacks have killed between 2,000 to 3,200 militants, including 275 to 360 civilians".[34] But it is important to stress the point that the targeting of evasive terrorists is certainly one of the circumstances in which the use of armed drones are permissible and justified, even if the legality is controversial.[35] It appears to be the only way that these lawless elements can be brought to heel, being extremely destructive and evasive because the nature of the war they wage forecloses any frontal combat. In them, the

26 See Micah Zenko (2013), "Reforming U.S. Drone Strike Policies" . . ., p. 12, op. cit.
27 See Ahmad Nazir Warraich (2013), "The Use of Drones . . .", p. 75, op. cit.
28 Loc. Cit.
29 Loc. Cit.
30 Loc. Cit.
31 See Micah Zenko (2013), "Reforming U.S. Drone Strike Policies" . . ., p. 12, op. cit.
32 Loc. Cit.
33 Ibid., p. 14.
34 See Van Baldwin Carr (undated) in "Unmanned Aerial Vehicles . . ., pp. 9–10, op. cit.
35 See Ahmad Nazir Warraich (2013), "The Use of Drones . . .", p. 67, op. cit.

nation-state is waging "a struggle against an amorphous non-state enemy", enemies that do not wear uniforms; and so, the asymmetrical nature of the warfare legitimizes the use of armed drones to engage and eliminate them.[36]

However, problems arise in the inability of the signature drone strikes in particular to discriminate between the terrorists and innocents, and this is despicable and condemnable. Signature strikes are particularly destructive and in utter negation of IHL because they are "conducted on the basis of surveillance of suspected [not actual] terrorists", they incur huge "collateral damage, a euphemism for civilian deaths" or high civilian casualties; and this is particularly so in the second strike that immediately follows.[37] The second strikes have "the potential to kill first responders who are helping the wounded".[38]

CIA Drone Strikes as a Violation of Combatancy and IHL

Another realm in which the U.S. drone strikes are antagonistic to IHL is in the use of the CIA to effect or carry out such strikes. It is here that the contradiction in using spies (the CIA) in drone strikes clearly manifests itself. By using the CIA (that as a spy agency is not an organization of combatants that can engage in warfare), the United States is deliberately obfuscating. Washington is obfuscating because "a spy agency is by definition working either beyond or below the legal radar whereas the military functions within the legal paradigm".[39] This "raises serious issues of transparency and accountability", being a practice of "double-hatting" that, "coupled with the lack of publicly available information, makes it difficult to provide justification in legal terms, of such action"; that is, the employment of the CIA in drone strikes and the ability to take responsibility for their actions.[40]

In fact, the former UN Special Rapporteur, Philip Alston, said categorically that by deliberately indulging in "double hatting", the United States is "purposefully confusing the lines between military and intelligence work and domain".[41] This is more so because, as discussed later in the section about the incompatibility of WoT/drones in IHL, members of the CIA (just as the terrorists themselves) are not combatants. Double hatting is clearly a strategy for the evasion of responsibility and accountability in IHL; and as Ahmad Nazir Warraich wrote with respect to the participation of spy agencies (rather than regular or military combatants) in hostilities through drone strikes:

> . . . the issue is not covered by the Laws of War. While traditional information gathering by spy agencies is considered a factual reality, states do not

36 Ibid., p. 72.
37 Ibid., p. 71. Brackets mine.
38 Loc. Cit.
39 See Ahmad Nazir Warraich (2013), "The Use of Drones . . .", p. 65, op. cit.
40 Loc. Cit.
41 Ibid., p. 76.

consider it a legal reality. Any protection or acceptance spy agencies enjoy is in that regard; though the issue remains to be addressed by [U.S.] officials.[42]

The use of the CIA in drone strikes leaves Washington with the aperture to create the alibi that (since, in the argument of Oppenheim, the belligerent that employs spies and traitors acts lawfully even though the opposing belligerent also has the right to punish them[43]) spies in armed conflict are its de facto entitlement; in which case, it cannot surrender them to be prosecuted for some serious infractions like the huge civilian casualties that sometimes attend signature strikes. And by the nature of asymmetric warfare as well as the confidentiality surrounding the operations of the CIA, the identity of the CIA agents behind the infraction can hardly be known; neither would the United States ever voluntarily reveal their identities to enable the possibility of their capture/arraignment by either the adverse party or the International Criminal Court (ICC). Thus, it would be difficult for the CIA agents to fall into the hands of the ICC or the insurgents who themselves cannot even prosecute them because they too cannot be brave enough to come before the law.

This is a quintessential case of the collision of two earthen pots. It is a collision in which the two items must break because none has the integrity to withstand the test, the severity of the collision. This matter will be revisited later in ethical considerations in drone strikes. Like in Syria where it is not implausible that the arraignment of President Bashar al-Assad (in either the ICC that exclusively apply international law, an ad hoc tribunal that also applies international law, a hybrid tribunal that apply both international and municipal law, or even a tribunal like the special tribunal of Lebanon that is unique in being "the first international tribunal to apply domestic law exclusively"[44]) might be contemplated, the Prosecutors at the ICC have hinted that "the U.S. and the CIA may have committed war crimes by torturing detainees in Afghanistan",[45] but it is yet to be seen how they will launch a full probe because of the United States' inclination (just as Russia is wont to veto any attempt to prosecute al-Assad) to veto it at the United Nations Security Council. Referrals to the ICC are either initiated by the Security Council, or by the state, or by the Prosecutors himself. As a state, the United States cannot initiate it because it is not even a party to the Rome Statute that created the ICC.

On its part, the post-Taliban state of Afghanistan cannot initiate any proceeding in the ICC because being an ally of the United States; such a move would be tantamount to a hostile act. Of course, it is inconceivable that any Prosecutor

42 Ibid., p. 73, op. cit. Brackets mine.

43 See Fred Aja Agwu (2011), *The Law of Armed Conflict and African Wars . . .*, p. 85, op. cit.

44 See Janice Yun (2010), "Special Tribunal for Lebanon: A Tribunal of International Character Devoid of International Law", *Santa Clara Journal of International Law*, Vol. 7, No. 2, p. 181.

45 See "U.S. Forces Face War-Crime Probe", in *Ticker, Time* (New York), November 28–December 5, 2016, p. 12.

would have the nerve to initiate the prosecution of American military personnel or even a CIA personnel, given the hegemonic presence of Washington, which was demonstrated when Washington allegedly masterminded the pressure on Meron, the President of the International Criminal Tribunal for former Yugoslavia (ICTY), which ensured the acquittal of General Perisic[46] as well as the acquittal of Ante Gotovina and Mladen Markac, the two Croatian nationals charged with crimes against humanity and the violation of the laws and customs war, the latter (Gotovina and Markac) because the United States and Israel "feared that the ICTY law was getting too tough on military leaders and might potentially rebound on their own forces".[47] Given this antecedent, it is clearly unlikely that the United States will ever permit from any corner, the launch of any full-scale investigation or of its military and the CIA in Afghanistan or anywhere else, be it for violations related to the treatment of detainees or even for violations relating to drone strikes under reference. Such a move will stand vetoed in the UN Security Council, or killed with a monstrous political pressure somewhere else.

The Incompatibility of WoT/Drones in IHL

There are critics that believe that in the contexts in which drone strikes have taken place, the United States was merely throwing missiles where international armed conflicts did not and does not exist; and that by so doing, Washington is destabilizing the international legal order.[48] But the point that must be pointedly and unambiguously made here is that the justification for the use of Predators/drones in targeted killings in the war on terror cannot be dressed in the garb of lawfulness; instead, it should be that of necessity, compelled (as seen in the allegory of *eneke-nti-oba* the bird) by a pragmatic policy of self-preservation. Thus, a dispensation of lawfulness cannot be honestly attributed to drone strikes. In fact, as experience has shown "in the tribal areas along the border of Afghanistan and Pakistan", there is no doubt that "the precision and discrimination of drones are only as good as the supporting intelligence", both human and signal intelligence that are derived from multiple sources like the paramilitary force composed of ethnic Pashtuns, and the Pakistan's intelligence, a counterpart of the CIA.[49]

Because drones (especially where not supported with effective or accurate intelligence) lack the fabled precision attributed to them and, thus, kill indiscriminately, the consequence is that drones' deployment and use, invariably, do

46 See John R.W.D. Jones, Kevin Jon Heller, Elies Van Sliedgret, and Elizabeth Wilmshurst (2013), "Milestones in International Criminal Justice: Recent Legal Controversies at the UN Yugoslav Tribunal", *International Law Summary*, Chatham House, October 16, 3, 5, note 12.

47 Ibid., pp. 2–3.

48 This is an argument some interlocutors espoused in an *Aljazeera* documentary entitled *Drone*, monitored in Lagos (Nigeria) on Monday, August 22, 2016, between 9pm and 10pm local time, op. cit.

49 See Micah Zenko (2013), "Reforming U.S. Drone Strike Policies" . . ., pp. 6–7, op. cit.

not even allow for the possibility of sparing civilians that come into harm's way, or (even though terrorists are not entitled to be taken prisoners) the taking of "Prisoners of War" (POWs), were terrorists amenable to capture. Thus, drones are in this sense also intrinsically antagonistic to international humanitarian law. Being not combatants, a captured terrorist is not entitled to the POW status but may even be liable to the death sentence after the due process of a lawful trial (in a manner consistent with the demands of the principles of fair trial procedures set out in the various human rights instruments) that also guarantees human dignity.

The point is that the use of drones in targeted killings does not allow terrorists to be captured. This is because the use of drones to target or counter these terrorists themselves is a special operation, since the terrorists do not engage in pitched combats, and do not allow themselves to be captured, even though they are not entitled to be taken as POWs, preferring instead to blow themselves up in a determined act of suicide. And because terrorists do not allow themselves to be captured, they themselves, in the instances they capture U.S. troops or kidnap civilians, do not take anybody prisoner. Rather, terrorists prefer to execute their captors or kidnap victims in cold blood, like the case of the al-Qaeda's abduction in Pakistan, in late January 2002, of the *Wall Street Journal*'s reporter, Daniel Pearl.[50] In fact, it is an established fact that terrorist insurgents do not comply with IHL, that they "in most cases try to counterbalance their asymmetric position against a state's regular army, which necessarily leads to the violation of the law on warfare and the criminal law".[51]

In his broadcast to the people of Borno State (in the Boko Haram-besieged northeast Nigeria) on Friday, February 10, 2017, the Governor of the state, Kashim Shettima, said that the Boko Haram terrorists, especially after being disrupted in Sambisa forest with the capture of their camp zero, had "resorted in their cowardly fashion, to stepping up attacks on soft targets", comprising "schools, places of worship, markets and other soft targets".[52] In carrying out these "cowardly and vile attacks", according to Governor Shettima, the terrorists "even strap babies on the back of their recruits in order to slip through our security dragnets", thus, underlining the heinousness of terrorist acts, sequel to which the Governor unequivocally declared that even mere "support for insurgents is a crime against humanity".[53] It is more so essentially because the modus operandi of terrorists is a clear indication that they do not set stock by humanitarian values or restraints.

For these reasons, terrorists are pure criminals from the perspectives of IHL. And because of the status mixtus nature (mixture of law enforcement and limited armed or military operations) of the war on terror, the status of terrorists in it is

50 See George W. Bush (2010), *Decision Points* . . ., p. 167, op. cit.

51 See Bordas Maria (2014), "Current Issues of International Law in Regulating Counter-Insurgency and Counter-Terrorism" . . ., p. 574, op. cit.

52 See Kashim Shettima in "Boko Haram . . .", back page, op. cit.

53 Loc. Cit.

analogous to what spies (in conventional wars or armed conflicts) are in relation to the members of the armed forces of parties in conventional armed conflicts. The import of this is that terrorist insurgents are entirely or completely outside the cover of IHL; and that countries conducting the "war on terror" have the discretion to extend or remove them from the cover of IHL. It was because the war on terror is a mishmash sort of thing, consisting of both law enforcement and military operations, that in the Nigerian anti-terrorist battles against the Boko Haram, the Nigerian anti-terror forces were not restricted to the armed forces.

The Nigerian anti-terrorism forces against the Boko Haram were rather a seamless combination (in the words of Governor Kashim Shettima of Borno State) of "our gallant security agencies, our civilian JTF [Joint Task Force], vigilance groups and hunters".[54] But civilians and hunters do not fight in armed conflicts. However, in the fight against terrorists, even when civilians and hunters were not involved in the fight, terrorists show no mercy to such categories of people or indeed to anyone else. For this and other considerations, the IHL as a protective embrace can only be extended to terrorists out of sheer consideration of the principle of humanity. But this extension does not mean that they would be treated as POWs; it only means that they, like spies, would not be summarily executed upon capture. Rather, such terrorists upon capture must be given a fair trial before the appropriate punishment is meted out.

However, the regular insurgent (who does not wage terrorist campaigns) that engages in conventional or pitched battle confrontation with enemy forces is under the protection of IHL by dint of Article 3 common to the Geneva Conventions, but the moment that insurgent embarks on terrorist tactics or campaigns, he or she falls out of the carapace of IHL; the same way that a member of the armed forces of a belligerent (both as an ordinary member, and as a combatant) is protected by IHL, but the moment he or she embarks on espionage, he or she falls out of the pail of IHL, except he or she was caught in uniform while acting as a spy.[55] Of course, one of the greatest dilemmas that the Western world faces in the fight against terrorism is (in the absence of a legal regulatory framework that regulates the war at the moment) in the task of balancing their values with the actions they take. As *The Economist* put it:

> . . . the West has two things to defend: the lives of its citizens, and the liberal values of tolerance and the rule of law that underpins its society. Where these are in conflict, it should choose policies that minimize the damage to values in order to make large gains in protection.[56]

It was apparently for the reason of this lack of an extant legal framework that some commentators equally reasoned that there are some gains in extending

54 Loc. Cit. Brackets mine.

55 See Fred Aja Agwu (2011), *The Law of Armed Conflict and African Wars . . .*, pp. 83–86, op. cit.

56 See "How to Fight Back . . .", p. 13, op. cit.

protection to terrorists, even if they neither set stock by it nor deserve it; that is, as *The Economist* couched it, there is the "need to make gains in protection".[57] Although these gains are hardly made (because the terrorists hardly reciprocate), there is also another imperative factor to be preserved; and this is the need to act for the sake of protecting Western values, with respect of which the U.S. President George W. Bush said that the United States' treatment of the al-Qaeda with dignity at Guantanamo-Bay was just a function of Washington's philosophical inspiration and disposition to concede to them the basic demands of sheer humanity, not that they deserve such treatment. In President Bush's words:

> While our humane treatment of Guantanamo detainees was consistent with the Geneva Conventions, al-Qaeda did not meet the qualification for Geneva protection as a legal matter. The purpose of Geneva was to provide incentives for nation-states to fight wars by an agreed set of rules that protect human dignity and innocent life—and to punish warriors who do not. But the terrorists do not represent a nation-state. They had not signed the Geneva Conventions. Their entire mode of operation—intentionally killing the innocent—defied the principles of Geneva. And if al-Qaeda captured an American, there was little chance they would treat him humanely.[58]

This sentiment by President George W. Bush (the sentiment that the treatment of terrorists with dignity is only discretionary and at best based on Western philosophical inspiration) is also reinforced by the belief, for instance, that the torture of terrorists has remained justified for centuries in all parts of the world.[59] And the simple explanation for this belief or consideration is in "the fact of the terrorists' seeming rejection of the inviolability of innocent human life and their contravention of basic principles of humanity and, in more recent times, international humanitarian law".[60] This is the basis of the thinking that "the terrorists' indifference to a victim's suffering increases the danger that the counterterrorist will respond in kind".[61]

In fact, it is based on the foregoing that the problem of the al-Qaeda, and indeed all terrorist organizations, is neither not being a nation-state nor not signing the Geneva Conventions. However, the point is that the moment a conventional or even war of insurgency devoid of terrorist campaigns breaks out, the consequence is usually the application by the armed forces of Article 3 common to the four Geneva Conventions, whether or not the parties to the conflict are signatories (as nation-states or High Contracting Parties) to the Geneva Conventions. All of this has been made possible with the incident of the Martens

57 Loc. Cit.
58 See George W. Bush (2010), *Decision Points* . . ., pp. 166–167, op. cit.
59 See Rosemary Foot (2005), "Collateral Damage . . .", p. 421, op. cit.
60 Loc. Cit.
61 Loc. Cit.

Clause as well as the nullification of the "general participation clause" by the same Article 3 common to the four 1949 Geneva Conventions.[62] In this context, the Afghan Taliban fighters are beneficiaries of the Geneva Conventions, but not the al-Qaeda. Thus, the problem with the al-Qaeda is in being ordinary terrorists; that is, in not being belligerents or combatants known to the Geneva Conventions.

Meanwhile, the Philip Alston-led United Nations' Special Rapporteur also reported that, by November 3, 2002 ("when a predator drone fired a missile at a car in Yemen, killing Qaed Senyan al-Harithi, an al-Qaeda leader allegedly responsible for the *USS Cole* bombing" and the time of its report), there had been over 120 drone strikes, with casualties in Pakistan alone ranging between approximately 20 to many hundreds.[63] Ironically this same report cited the U.S. legal adviser to the State Department as opining that America uses drones in self-defence and in a manner cognizant of the codes of IHL because it is in an armed conflict with the al-Qaeda, the Taliban, and the associated forces.[64] But the contentious issue here remains that this sort of armed conflict with the al-Qaeda, the Taliban, and the associated forces is not only asymmetric in nature, the deployment of a weapon as new and utterly unregulated as drones raises significant questions of compatibility with the IHL under reference.

But the incompatibility of drones with international humanitarian law would, however, be probably more regrettably manifest any time it falls into the hands of terrorists or insurgents with their prodigal ways. Although one of the UN Special Rapporteur groups was of the view that it is inconceivable that non-state armed groups can obtain the drone technology,[65] there is, however, a well-informed fear that this lethal drone technology may not long be within "the sole province of wise and responsible nations" as "certain categories of state and sub-state terrorists will possess increasingly sophisticated weapons [including drones] . . . , enhancing the threat posed by nuclear, biological, and chemical weapons and thus holding at risk populations far distant from their own".[66] And there is no doubt that drones would be very attractive to terrorists and insurgents because "looking at the air warfare case, the overall reliability and costs associated with piloted systems have traditionally been less than the costs associated with operating purely unmanned weapon systems".[67]

This relationship between drones attacks and IHL is problematic because the law of armed conflict as it concerns terrorist campaigns as tools in insurgencies

62 See Fred Aja Agwu (2011), *The Law of Armed Conflict and African Wars . . .*, p. 156, op. cit; see also. Fred Aja Agwu (2011), *From Rebellion, Insurgency to Belligerency . . .*, pp. 9–11, 73–79, op. cit.

63 See Philip Alston in "Report of the Special Rapportuer on Extrajudicial . . .", op. cit.

64 Loc. Cit.

65 See Philip Alston in "Report of the Special Rapportuer on Extrajudicial . . .", op. cit.

66 See Richard P. Hallion (1997), "Air Power Past, Present and Future", in Richard P. Hallion (1997, ed.); *Air Power Confronts an Unstable World . . .*, p. 10, op. cit.

67 See Richard P. Hallion (1997), "Precision Air Attack in the Modern Era", in Richard P. Hallion (1997, ed.); *Air Power Confronts an Unstable World . . .*, p. 128, op. cit.

(that is, the handling of terrorists) is still a "status mixtus" (mixed or ambivalent status); meaning that it still exists in a state of intermediacy that contradicts Hugo Grotius' ***inter bellum et pacem nihil est medium*** (that literally implies that between war and peace, there is no medium).[68] In other words, the law of armed conflict as it concerns terrorist campaigns in insurgencies is still a grey and indeterminate area, characterized by a de facto or quasi-belligerency[69] that makes it unclear whether or not the "war on terror" exists in the sense of being denominated into an armed conflict, and whether it could trigger the law of war.[70] Robert Sloane holds the view that asymmetric warfare, in addition to its "factual asymmetry", also adds a "legal asymmetry" to its nature, an asymmetry in which one of the belligerents enjoys less or even no status in international law.[71]

The belligerent Sloane has in mind here is the insurgent who, because the law of armed conflict sometimes "deliberately" tries to be exclusive, does not adhere to that law, "except maybe in circumstances where it's politically or strategically advantageous".[72] In reinforcing the point that legal asymmetry discourages compliance to IHL as well as brings about the absence of geographic borders in the war on terror (as a variant of asymmetric warfare), Robert Sloane, referring to what Hersch Lauterpacht said circa 1950, wrote as follows:

> . . . it's impossible to visualize the conduct of hostilities in which one side would be bound by the rules of warfare without benefiting from them, while the other would be benefiting from the rules without being bound by them. That's roughly the situation that obtains in asymmetric conflicts. The legal asymmetry discourages IHL compliance by the weaker party, and it also eventually discourages compliance by the stronger party. That should be a source of concern for us, and the basic idea is that if the weaker party appreciates that it's going to be outgunned on the traditional battlefield, there is no question that it will try to shift the terrain, literally and figuratively, in order to offset the stronger party's advantage.[73]

But if, to use Ashley Deeks' expression, "the law is thin"[74] on the ground for insurgency; in the case of terrorism, there is practically no law because there is no armed conflict. And the terrorist has no pretentions about playing by any rule of engagement in the execution of its operations, no matter the perceived political or strategic expediency. For this reason of a visceral inability to give or accept the protections of the law, the terrorist is out rightly under no protection by the

68 See Fred Aja Agwu (2011), *The Law of Armed Conflict and African Wars . . .*, p. 11, op. cit.
69 Loc. Cit.
70 See Geert-Jan Alexander Knoops (2012), "Legal, Political and Ethical Dimensions of Drone Warfare . . .", p. 701, op. cit.
71 See Robert D. Sloane (2011), "New Battlefields/Old Laws . . .", p. 371, op. cit.
72 Ibid., pp. 371–372.
73 Ibid., p. 372.
74 Ibid., pp. 371–372.

law of armed conflict, except the right to a fair trial before punishment; unlike the privileged belligerent who cannot be tried or punished but held as a Prisoner of War to be unconditionally released to go home at the end of hostilities. As a phenomenon that is highly disruptive of the human society, the existence of an armed conflict (or declaration of war) is reckoned with by the law right from the beginning;[75] that is, from the *casus belli* or *jus ad bellum* (the reason war is fought), even though the *jus ad bellum* is indifferent to the *jus in bello* (the methods used to fight it), all these are very critical in determining whether or not a war has been legitimately declared in the eyes of the law, and whether an armed conflict exists as well.[76]

Within the framework of the United Nations Charter (Article 2 paragraph 4, and Article 51), it will certainly not be out of place to have issues with the United States' declaration of the "war on terror"; that is, in the obvious light of the fact that it may not have met the United Nations' laid down conditions for the existence of *casus belli.* Apart from 9/11 and the Paris attacks (amongst some others) there are many terror attacks that can definitely not be denominated as armed attacks. Attacks like the al-Qaeda's 2000 bombing of *USS Cole* in Yemen, or the ISIS's downing of the Russian metro jet over Egypt's Sinai region, all happened outside the territories of the United States and Russia and, therefore, cannot be rightly taken as armed attacks that would create a *casus belli.* Again, to reinstate Ashley Deeks' view stated earlier, states are currently fighting a particular kind of conflict in which they have found themselves in "a situation in which the governing international law is nonexistent, unclear, or potentially a somewhat awkward fit for the facts on the ground".[77]

However, although the United States only declared the "war on terror" after the event of 9/11 that was truly an armed attack, these issues can also be taken up with some Arab and Western nations that joined the war without a legitimate framework for collective self-defence.[78] But beyond the foregoing, and in both conceptual and practical terms (particularly as opposed to a state of war or war as a condition[79]), "an armed conflict requires that the violence be of a certain minimum threshold and obtain a certain intensity that lasts for certain time period, in addition to being taken against an entity that is both organized as a group and can be identified".[80] Considered in the light of the foregoing definition, the "war on terror" is certainly beset with contradictions because first, it does not have the quality of a sustained intensity over a long period of time; second, it essentially utilizes a hit-and-run strategy; and third, terrorist organizations are

75 See Fred Aja Agwu (2005), *United Nations System, State Practice and the Jurisprudence of the Use of Force . . .*, pp. 25–41, op. cit.

76 See Ahmad Nazir Warraich (2013), "The Use of Drones . . .", p. 78, op. cit.

77 See Ashley Deeks (2011), "New Battlefields/Old Laws . . .", p. 373, op. cit.

78 See Fred Aja Agwu (2005), *United Nations System, State Practice and the Jurisprudence of the Use of Force . . .*, pp. 159–167, op. cit.

79 Ibid., pp. 32–33.

80 See Ahmad Nazir Warraich (2013), "The Use of Drones . . .", p. 75, op. cit.

organized groups, but they are hardly ever easy to be identified because, being not uniformed, they are faceless.

It is in the context of the war on terror not possessing the features of an armed conflict that it has actually been considered that this war is after all a "law enforcement issue" rather than a military operation properly so called.[81] This impression of the war on terror as a "law enforcement" rather than "military engagement" persists because terrorism is actually an attack on soft targets like the civilian population and government authorities[82] rather than an attack on the government's military strength,[83] the way an insurgency would do. In other words, insurgent terrorists are considered as criminals because "they commit terrorist and organized crimes, or crimes only against public safety, public order or the state power"; in which case they are under the authority of law enforcement, that is, "come up for trial based on the rules of criminal procedure".[84]

Although this is not entirely true with the cases of guerilla war in Afghanistan and the civil war in Syria she mentioned, in distinguishing law enforcement activity from military engagement, Bordas Maria made the point that, with respect to law enforcement (with exception to peaceful demonstrations permitted by public authorities), people offend or try to remove existing governments other than by democratic elections; hence: the conspiracy (Bolshevik Party in Russia), revolution (fundamentalist Islamists in Iran), freedom fight (Che Guevara in South America), guerilla war (Taliban in Afghanistan), civil war (Syria), and military putsch (Chile), are all riotous or violent actions that (as law enforcement) domestic laws normally regulate as crimes against state power.[85] However, it is not totally true that the war on terror is a "law enforcement issue". Although because of the nature of the modus operandi of terrorists (the lethal weapons and force they deploy against ordinary folk), their activities are taken to be something short of war (inviting a limited response that would be categorized as law enforcement); but at the same time, even when this limited military response cannot be categorized as a full-fledged military operation, it is at the same time not full-fledged law enforcement.

This is where the characterization that is called status mixtus weighs in. In other words, the implication of this status mixtus is that the "war on terror" is still not within the full-fledged regulation of the law of armed conflict. The use of the qualifier, "full-fledged", is deliberate and very critical because the Israeli Supreme Court (ISC), in its ruling of December 13, 2006, had expressed the

81 Ibid., p. 77.

82 See Bordas Maria (2014), "Current Issues of International Law in Regulating Counter-Insurgency and Counter-Terrorism" . . ., p. 571, op. cit.

83 See David L. Bongard and William R. Schilling (2002), "Terrorist Operations in Nontraditional Warfare", in William R. Schilling (2002, ed.); *Nontraditional Warfare: Twenty-First Century*, p. 54, op. cit.

84 See Bordas Maria (2014), "Current Issues of International Law in Regulating Counter-Insurgency and Counter-Terrorism" . . ., p. 575, op. cit.

85 Loc. Cit.

view that "the laws of war are applicable to the (international) armed conflict between Israel and the terrorist organizations operating in the region".[86] This ruling (which is a clear case of a municipal court affirming a basic principle of the law of armed conflict in the sense that it is trite law that wherever the armed forces are used, IHL must apply[87]) may be true with the Israeli military's conventional engagements with the Hezbollah or the Hamas in Lebanon and West Bank respectively, but it cannot be true with the downright terrorist operations of these two groups of insurgents. In the latter case, the "war on terror" is, thus, not an armed conflict from the point of view of IHL.

And this is evidently so because the insurgent terrorists themselves and many of those like the CIA operatives engaged in countering them with armed drones are unlawful combatants in the purview of IHL, implying that they are not fit to take part in hostilities.[88] This is why in dealing with terrorists in the war on terror, and apart from taking care (with the principles of distinction) that the territorial integrity of other nations are not violated if the terrorists are taking refuge there, not many aspects of the law of armed conflict are applied, apart from, perhaps, IHL—making sure that unacceptable civilian casualties do not occur in addition to other unacceptable collateral damage.

So many bizarre strategies are adopted by both the insurgents and the counter-insurgents in the so-called war on terror (using unconventional tools like IEDs and drones), thus leaving international jurists in a dilemma as to whether or not to classify their deeds or acts as legitimate armed conflicts that transcend the stigma of pure brigandage or outright criminality, since these strategies and the weapons employed are in violation of IHL, both from the standpoint of the Hague laws that regulate the means and methods of warfare and the standpoint of the Geneva Conventions that seek to protect the victims of warfare.[89] Thus, most of the actors, including the nation-state actors in this "war on terror", are no "combatants" in the expectation of this law. It is incontestable and, indeed, self-evident that insurgents are no combatants; but it is also true that unlike their military counterparts, the counter-insurgents in the CIA in the United States that operate the drones are also themselves not combatants because the CIA (as civilians) is not a recognizable party in IHL with rights to take part in hostilities.[90]

Given the above scenario, and as far as IHL is concerned, what is clearly undeniable is that the "war on terror", especially with the use of armed drones

86 See Geert-Jan Alexander Knoops (2012), "Legal, Political and Ethical Dimensions of Drone Warfare . . .", pp. 707–708, op. cit.

87 See Fred Aja Agwu (2011), *From Rebellion, Insurgency to Belligerency* . . ., pp. 9–11, 73–79, op. cit; see also Fred Aja Agwu (2011), *The Law of Armed Conflict and African Wars* . . ., p. 1156, op. cit.

88 See Geert-Jan Alexander Knoops (2012), "Legal, Political and Ethical Dimensions of Drone Warfare . . .", p. 710, op. cit.

89 See Fred Aja Agwu (2011), *The Law of Armed Conflict and African Wars* . . ., p. 13, op. cit.

90 See Geert-Jan Alexander Knoops (2012), "Legal, Political and Ethical Dimensions of Drone Warfare . . .", p. 710, op. cit.

in targeted killings, is undoubtedly confronted or being dealt with, not in the context of the principles governing the prosecution of armed conflicts; rather, the prosecution of this asymmetric "war" is ostensibly governed by "state security" imperatives, which is why it has this troubled relationship, not only with international human rights requirements (peace time requirement of killing after a fair trial according to the rule of law), but also with the laws of warfare, especially the demand for compliance with IHL.[91] The attempt by the United Nations Special Rapporteur to provide a nuance that could exculpate the CIA does nothing but only to highlight the unresolved debate about whether or not the "war on terror" is truly an armed conflict properly so called. In trying to define the contexts that could exonerate the CIA from criminal prosecutions in the use of drone strikes, the Special Rapporteur differentiated between two situations as follows:

> a) if the targeted killings by the CIA are committed in the context of armed conflict, civilians (and thus also CIA agents) can participate in hostilities. However, the consequence thereof is that they lose their protection as civilians and therefore may be targeted and killed, or prosecuted; (b) if targeted killings by the CIA through drone attacks are not committed in the context of armed conflict, they may constitute extrajudicial killings. In the event these killings do not comply with human rights law, CIA agents can be prosecuted for murder, either domestically or internationally.[92]

Although civilians (the CIA) can take part in hostilities in an armed conflict and ipso facto lose their protection,[93] the United Nations Special Rapporteur's submission in (a) above is practically and undoubtedly over the top (or is not tenable) because the "war on terror" is not an armed conflict, and this is because it does not have all the essential ingredients of an armed conflict, especially on the part of the insurgents; or within the context of having a fixed or conventional theaters of engagement (on land, sea, or air), the armed forces of the "belligerents" (be it regular, irregular, or as levees en masse, and volunteers), and the possession of combatant status.[94] It is on the strength of these contradictions that it becomes impossible for the United States to apply the drone strikes in ways that are fully compliant with IHL. Expectedly, the United States has been unsparingly criticized for this failing.[95]

91 See Ahmad Nazir Warraich (2013), "The Use of Drones . . .", pp. 76–77, op. cit.
92 See Geert-Jan Alexander Knoops (2012), "Legal, Political and Ethical Dimensions of Drone Warfare . . .", pp. 710–711, op. cit.
93 See Fred Aja Agwu (2011), *The Law of Armed Conflict and African Wars* . . ., pp. 114–116, op. cit.
94 Ibid., pp. 22–33.
95 See, for instance, Ahmad Nazir Warraich (2013), "The Use of Drones . . .", p. 80, op. cit.

The Minimum Obligation of WoT/Drones in IHL

However, every military engagement has an obligation to observe IHL. An insurgency, including when it is on terrorist campaigns, may wrongly not feel obliged to obey the laws of war, especially IHL, but a counter-insurgency, including the "war on terror", is obliged, at least, by virtue of Article 3 common to the Geneva Conventions under reference. The parameters of engagement may differ,[96] for insurgents (inclusive of their terrorist campaigns) habitually disavow conventional parameters as contradictory of their own deviant ways, but state authorities, whether in counter-insurgency or in the "war on terror", are obliged, especially with respect to IHL since "avoiding civilian casualties and collateral damage as much as possible is a delicate balance", to be aligned with the rules of engagement.[97]

Thus, it is completely immaterial that the United States is not conducting its self-defence against terror in manners consistent with the United Nations' requirement of armed attack. This is another layer of legality upon which Washington cannot be judged harshly because, as stated earlier under the rubric of drones in self-defence, the framers of the Charter themselves never envisioned the resort to terrorist campaigns by insurgents. But a nation must defend itself even in a state of *status mixtus*. To affirm the unconventional nature of *status mixtus* and reiterate the inevitability of self-preservation, William Banks posits that the recognition that the United States was right in asserting that the September 11 attacks "were acts of war" directed against it and giving it "the legal right to repel the horrific attacks" is validly in juxtaposition with the acknowledgement that "whether waged against us by a state or a non-state terrorist organization, war is defined by what it does, not by the identity of the perpetrator".[98] What this means is that even in *status mixtus* kind of "war", a nation cannot stand akimbo and refuse to defend itself just because the "aggressor" is a non-state terrorist organization against which war cannot be waged. It is within this context of *status mixtus* that Banks stated the obvious that has also been stated earlier, which is that:

> . . . the law of armed conflict has not yet evolved to account adequately for the twilight zone between conventional war and conventional peace, when nations are subject to the continuing threat of terrorist attacks. . . . [W]ithin this twilight zone of threat from terrorist attacks, it is not clear exactly what distinguishes a combatant and, thus, a proper target, from a civilian who may not be targeted. Nor is it known what evidence will suffice that someone who does not wear a uniform and who does not fight for a sovereign state is sufficiently implicated in terrorist activities so as to warrant targeting with

96 See Giuseppe Caforio (2013), "Officer and Commander in Asymmetric Warfare Operations" . . ., pp. 13, 17, op. cit.

97 Ibid., p. 17.

98 See William C. Banks (2005), "The Predator", in Volker C. Franke (2005, ed.); *Terrorism and Peacekeeping* . . ., p. 150, op. cit.

> lethal force. Clearly, someone who is positively identified as an Al Qaeda operative is an enemy combatant, one who may be targeted with lethal force. But . . . what factual showing will demonstrate that [the target] had warlike intentions against us and who sees that evidence before an action is taken.[99]

The issues raised by William Banks, partly in conjunction with Professor Harold Hongju Koh of Yale, are intrinsic questions in *status mixtus*. They also pose a dilemma in targeted killings, particularly the issue of how to correctly identify who may be implicated in terrorist activities prior to targeting and strikes. This will be addressed later in this book when dealing with Autonomous Weapons Systems (AWS) and their inherent or congenital inability to observe the principles of distinction and proportionality in the war on terrorism, being able to make the requisite quantitative and qualitative distinctions necessary to observe the principle of proportionality, the avoidance of unacceptable collateral damage, especially in the sparing of civilians. But in all circumstances of putative or anticipatory self-defence by Washington, the minimum demand from the principle of humanity is that civilian casualties or unacceptable collateral damage must be astutely avoided in line with IHL.

The protection of civilians and prevention of wanton collateral damage are about the only aspects of the law of armed conflict that no nation can escape from, whether or not it is fighting an aggravated unconventional or asymmetric warfare (as in the "war on terror"), or it is using an equally unconventional weapon (as in armed drones) to prosecute the "war". Nevertheless, although it is difficult to treat terrorists in ways consistent with IHL because they hardly make themselves available to be so treated, especially with their inclination to suicide missions, there are still sentiments that "even terrorists must be treated according to international law" in order not to open a floodgate of intractable violations; more so with the United States that (with the incidence of armed drones) is "basically opening up and crafting a new tool and tactic", which, if misused, can put its leadership in this regard at risk or create unwholesome precedence of violations of IHL.[100]

In an unrestrained orgy of violations, any "nation can start executing those whom they consider terrorists".[101] Although it is difficult to see how the extension of IHL to terrorists who basically evade capture and prefer suicide can be realized, it is, however, also important to prevent the frightful scenario of nations embarking on the wanton execution of terrorists, perceived or real; for to do so would engender an orgy of abuses that would not serve but rather diminish humanity. It will bring back afresh "the contempt shown for human rights during the Second World War" that "resulted in acts of barbarism so outrageous as to call fundamentally into question the assumption that non-interference in

99 Loc. Cit.
100 Ibid., p. 152.
101 Loc. Cit.

the domestic affairs of states should hold as an immutable building block of world order"; and which, thankfully, resulted in "the creation after 1945 of several human rights treaties and declarations, promoted either through the United Nations or through regional Charters".[102]

Unfortunately, although the Cold War may have ended, taking along with it the ideological confrontations that had militated against the guaranteeing of humanitarian rights necessary for a life of dignity for all peoples, there are still geopolitical confrontations,[103] like the one between the United States and Russia in Ukraine, Crimea, and beyond, geopolitical confrontations that have inhibited a common resolution to tackle the scourge of terrorism in the contemporary world, be it the al-Qaeda, ISIS, or in Syria. It is this geopolitical confrontation (now dangerously spiraling into cyber conflict) that the new American President Donald Trump sees as pointless[104] as he seems prepared to get along with Russia's President Vladimir Putin.[105] It is when this geopolitical confrontation is transcended that the two countries may, perhaps, join hands with the rest of the world to find a common ground for dealing with terrorism and its consequences within the ambit of IHL.

102 See Rosemary Foot (2005), "Collateral Damage . . .", p. 411, op. cit.
103 Ibid., pp. 411, 412.
104 See Ian Bremmer in "Trump Will Thaw Chilly U.S.-Russia Relationship", *Time* (New York), November 28–December 5, 2016, p. 12.
105 See Owen Matthews in "With Friends Like This", *Newsweek*, November 25, 2016, pp. 28–37.

10 Drones and Ethics in WoT

President Obama Disavows Unethical Conducts in WoT

> Where force is necessary, we have a moral and strategic interest in binding ourselves to certain rules of conflict. And even as we confront a vicious adversary that abides by no rules, I believe the United States of America must remain a standard-bearer in the conduct of war. That is what makes us different from those whom we fight.
>
> (President Barack Obama)[1]

The discourse on drones in international humanitarian law inevitably leads to the related issue of moral or ethical questions in WoT, including as these questions concern the use of unregulated weapons like drones. It is obvious that as the United States discretionally binds itself to IHL in relation to terrorists, so is it also expected that it would behave with respect to moral or ethical questions in relation to terrorists, as President Barack Obama implies in the epigraph. The relationship between law and ethics is obvious: the law, even for those it is not binding on, influences "the highest moral standards".[2] The United States, for instance, may not be bound by the decisions of the European Court of Human rights (ECtHR), but the status of this court as human rights protection legal norm setting platform must certainly influence it as a nation that claims to be upholding "the highest moral standards".[3]

In the epigraph, the U.S. President Barack Obama spoke in his Noble Prize acceptance speech about the moral imperative of playing by the rules of warfare with those (the terrorists) so vicious that they do not have the capacity to abide by rules. Implicit in the foregoing is the fact that President Obama demands that officials of the United States hold themselves to the highest possible standards in every step they take in the conduct of the country's asymmetric war with the al-Qaeda, the ISIS, and other terrorist organizations; a fact that the White House

1 U.S. President Barack Obama in his Nobel Peace Prize Acceptance Speech, quoted in Ahmad Nazir Warraich (2013), "The Use of Drones . . .", p. 72, op. cit.

2 Ibid., p. 79.

3 Loc. Cit.

counter-terrorism adviser, John Brennan, reiterated while speaking on May 1, 2012, at the Woodrow Wilson Center.[4] Ironically, although the escalation in the use of this unregulated drone weapon was experienced more under the Obama administration, Brennan particularly exhorted the virtues of drone strikes in the achievement of moral ends when he "argued that the drones' ability to precisely target the enemy helps it to distinguish between terrorists and innocent civilians".[5] The irony here is that drones may be fabled to be imbued with precision; but, nevertheless, shorn of the liability of body bags, they make resort to arms and the shedding of blood easy to be embarked upon. This assertion will be amplified in due course here.

But for the United States, the pretension to, at least, rhetorically, moral or ethical obligations in the "war on terror" is inescapable in the light of what *The Economist* terms the West's imperative need to balance the protection of citizens' lives with its liberal values of tolerance and the rule of law.[6] Since the fact that (like nuclear weapons) the use of drones as a weapon of war has not been legislated upon by way of abolition, and since, perforce, a state possessing drones and seeking to protect itself (its citizens) from acts of terrorism may be forced to use the weapon, attaining the ethical threshold of resisting a facile or easy resort to violence with the weapon, minimizing the orchestration of undue human carnage, and generally attaining the noble goal of using the weapon constructively to attain good if ethical ends is a major and ever present challenge.

But try as the countries that now possess and use armed drones may to avoid intense humanitarian carnage, this unfortunate incident still occurs. It raises the moral or ethical question of why use the weapons when it unavoidably puts innocents in harm's way. But like in the anti-nuclear weapon movement that has elicited a cavalcade of ethical supporters for nuclear disarmament, the use of armed drones has equally amassed its own antagonists. Those against the use of unconventional weapons like the nuclear weapons argue that because nuclear weapons, rather than win military objectives, have the capacity to blow up everything, they cannot be integrated into usable and effective fighting plans; and that as such, they are not usable weapons; and that reliance upon them is a sign of national weakness, not military strength.[7]

The Unethical and Inadmissibility of Unregulated Weapons

Today, the deployment of drones too has equally begun to elicit similar ethical opposition. Unfortunately, the moral or ethical assessment of unregulated/unconventional arsenals like nuclear weapons and newer weapons like armed

4 Ibid., p. 72.
5 Loc. Cit.
6 See "How to Fight Back . . .", p. 13, op. cit.
7 See Douglas P. Lackey (1989), *The Ethics of War and Peace*, Englewood Cliffs, NJ, Prentice Hall, p. 129.

drones is sometimes met with the antagonism of political realism, those political realists who think that all is fair in love and war;[8] and that such moral assessments are useless if not pernicious[9] in international affairs where moral discussions amount to waste because there is no world government.[10] The political realists insist that whereas conflicts within a society can be morally assessed and regulated, those conflicts between societies cannot because, while one society has a common moral standard, there is no mutually acceptable procedure for reaching moral conclusions between two societies with disparate judicial ways of enforcing moral judgments.[11]

But this antagonism against ethical consideration in the use of unconventional weapons like the nuclear weapons and drones rests on over-stretched and, thus, weak premises. As opposed to political realism, there is the traditional philosophical realism that asserts the objective existence of abstract properties (including moral properties) that transcend the so-called differences in societies' moral standards.[12] This traditional philosophical realism denounces the "bogus" realism of political science as a sub variety of the subjectivist interpretation of moral judgments that might be excusable in the past (among middle age college freshmen), but rejected in contemporary ethics.[13] Evidently, contemporary ethics derives its conviction about ethical or moral principles that transcend societal differences from the fact, as Grant put it, "that each and every human being possesses a spark of divinity . . . , that force that pervades and animates the whole of nature".[14]

This is a critical aspect of the sanctity of human lives, which obligates every society to preserve life, and is a strong pillar in International Humanitarian Law[15] that unconventional weapons like drones are supposed to preserve. Even if it can be granted that there is also an element of subjectivism in ethics, but this subjectivism cannot be as justifiable as the realism of political science; for:

> . . . the very fact that we engage in debates about the morality of our policies indicates that we are not simply applying the conventional beliefs of our own society to the solution of these problems. When we judge the actions of our highest political authorities, we are judging our society as a whole, and thereby show our own deep belief in standards that are "outside" our present social system.[16]

In any case, the casting of ethical questions as things that are relative to different societies (allegedly because there is no world government, or because

8 Ibid., p. 1.
9 Ibid., p. 2.
10 Ibid., p. 1.
11 Loc. Cit.
12 Ibid., p. 2.
13 Loc. Cit.
14 See Michael Grant (1971, trans.), *Cicero: On the Good Life*, London, Penguin Books, p. 7.
15 See Fred Aja Agwu (2011), *The Law of Armed Conflict and African Wars . . .*, p. 354, op. cit.
16 See Douglas P. Lackey (1989), *The Ethics of War and Peace*, p. 2, op. cit.

ethical issues are subjective) is no longer absolutely applicable in today's world of international organizations and treaties; a world in which the United Nations Security Council can now legislate for every nation.[17] We now live in a world where (because of the decisions of the UN Security Council, and the existence of institutions like the International Criminal Court, ICC, that bind vertically rather than horizontally) nation-states can now be obligated to international norms without their consent.[18] Hence, treaties like the Hague Regulations and the Geneva Conventions (and their Additional Protocols) that limit the freedom of the nation-state to use any means or method of warfare, or any form of weapons at their disposal to prosecute their wars, national or international, can be imposed upon non-signatories by virtue of the United Nations Security Council decision under Article 39 of the Charter.

Nation-states, under Article 25 of the same Charter, "agree to accept and carry out" the decisions of the Security Council. Even non-members of the United Nations are obliged to carry out the decisions of the Security Council because Article 2(6) of the Charter provides that "the organization shall ensure that states which are not members of the United Nations act in accordance with these principle . . ." As noted earlier, the obvious relationship between law and ethics is that the law, even for those it is not binding upon, influences the emergence of the highest moral standards. It is because of the existence of those international institutions that create laws capable of influencing the development of ethical principles that ethics may not be said to be absolutely relative. As a matter of facts, huge ethical questions attended the United States invasion of Iraq in search of Weapons of Mass Destruction (WMD); with world leaders like President Chirac of France sharing the opposing view at that time that "war is not inevitable", not only because diplomacy could be given a chance, but also because "it's a question of morality".[19]

And it is also because of the transcendence of some moral questions in and between societies that ethical considerations in the use of unconventional weapons not only pose the question, is war ever morally justified? it also asks the question, is there a morally correct way of fighting a war?[20] The latter question is very relevant within the context of the means and methods of warfare, like the use of nuclear weapons and armed drones. Ethics as "the philosophical analysis of human morality and conduct", the "system of conduct or behavior", the "moral principles" in the human society,[21] is, according to Aristotle, that pursuit that aims at something good; which is why "the Good has been rightly defined as that at which all things aim".[22] Although (as Grant persuaded earlier) each and every

17 See Article 25 of the United Nations Charter.
18 See Fred Aja Agwu (2009), *National Interest, International Law* . . ., p. 106, op. cit.
19 See Bob Woodward (2004), *Plan of Attack* . . ., p. 313, op. cit.
20 See Douglas P. Lackey (1989), *The Ethics of War and Peace* . . ., p. 1, op. cit.
21 See Geddes & Grosset New English Dictionary and Thesaurus (1994), new edition, p. 217.
22 See Aristotle (1955, trans. J. A. K. Thomson), Ethics, London, Penguin Books, p. 63.

human being possesses a spark of divinity (that force that pervades and animates the whole of nature), this, in itself, is not the ethical conviction but only a source of conviction to want to acquire ethical values.

Ethics is, therefore, beyond theory. As an ultimate virtue or goodness, it "consists not in gaining theoretical knowledge of the several points at issue, but rather in putting our knowledge into practice".[23] Thus, ethics or moral goodness is not something that comes by divine dispensation or inspiration; it is something that is "acquired by habituation",[24] including in the ways and manner, the methods and means that societies or nation-states prosecute their warfare. There has always been an inclination towards ensuring that war and the methods and means of prosecuting it meet ethical or moral standards. For instance, the ancient Romans tended to meet this moral obligation by satisfying or ensuring formal procedures for the declaration of war; while the occidental Christians tried to ensure an intrinsic justice or merit in the cause of war.[25]

As recent as the United States' war in Iraq, questions about the morality of the war were rife;[26] and these questions were provoked by the fact that there were some other possibilities or alternative solutions that could have obviated the recourse to war, like the possibility of diplomatic means, or in the event of the failure of diplomacy, the need to satisfy the expectations of the United Nations system on the use of force. And although they are legal documents, there is also something immoral or unethical in applying armed drones in willful violation of Article 22 of the Hague Regulation that prohibits belligerents from using unlimited means and methods of injuring or killing the enemy in armed conflicts; or indeed, the violation of the Martens Clause that obligates them, in all cases of inadequate codes of law, to observe the dictates of public conscience and the principles of humanity as inherent in customary international law. In other words, it is not only illegal to employ armed drones to violate these positivist and customary law regulations, such violations are downright immoral or unethical.

Drones and the Moral Threshold to Kill

The most considered ethical impact of the deployment or use of armed drones is in its propensity to make the resort to the use of force very attractive, and to lower "the moral threshold to kill human beings because of the distance between the drone operator and its target".[27] Although at the beginning of this chapter, President Obama was seen disavowing unethical conduct against even the

23 Ibid., p. 335.
24 Ibid., p. 80.
25 See Fred Aja Agwu (2005), *United Nations System, State Practice and the Jurisprudence of the Use of Force . . .*, pp. 36–37, op. cit.
26 See Bob Woodward (2004), *Plan of Attack . . .*, pp. 272–273, 313–314, op. cit.
27 See Geert-Jan Alexander Knoops (2012), "Legal, Political and Ethical Dimensions of Drone Warfare . . .", p. 718, op. cit.

terrorist; he is however in an ethical bind, indeed, a double bind when it comes to dealing with this brand of insurgents, using armed drones. As he puts it, the very precision of drone strikes, and the necessary secrecy involved in such action, can end up shielding our government from the public scrutiny that a troop deployment invites; [but] it can also lead a President and his team to view drone strikes as a cure-all for terrorism.[28]

With the advent of drones, "decision-makers are now much more likely to use lethal force against a range of perceived threats than in the past".[29] There is also the issue of this ethical looseness or laxity on the part of the drone operators, which is that "a drone pilot does not fully comprehend the implications of a drone attack, being simply positioned behind a control screen instead of on the battlefield itself".[30] Yet, the suggestion that drone pilots do not fully comprehend the implications of their actions may be overstretching credulity because they actually fully understand the consequences in distant places like Waziristan (Afghanistan) of the missiles they launch by merely wielding the joysticks in their hands that control the unmanned flying machines while secured seated, for example, "in a cubicle at an air force base near Las Vegas".[31]

The full knowledge of the ethical consequences of the drone strikes often leads the pilots to the feeling of personal guilt and a sense of schizophrenia, as poignantly illustrated by Andrew Niccol[32] in a fictional work he adapted from *Predator: A Pilot's Story*, an account of America's "war on terror", written by a "former drone top gun", Matt J. Martin. As narrated by Rudolph Herzog, fighter pilot Tom Egan (Ethan Hawke) walked into a store after the day's work and the man behind the counter pointed at his uniform in amazement and asked him if he ever got to fly in war. Egan replied in the affirmative and told the inquisitive store keeper that, from his desk in a cubicle at the air force base in Las Vegas, he had as a matter of fact killed six Taliban that morning in far away Pakistan.[33]

Although some of Egan's colleagues would have no qualm of unease about remotely blasting the Taliban warriors to bits, Tom was increasingly troubled, not just by the inherent contradiction in the juxtaposition of the horror of his job with his private life, but also by the uncomfortable fact that sometimes, civilians suddenly walk into the crosshairs while he watched helplessly, unable (even though

28 See the "Full Transcript of President Obama's Speech on Counterterrorism Policy" at the National Defense University, Fort McNair, available at http://news.yahoo.com/full-transcript-president-obama-speech-counter-terrorism-policy-18 . . . (last visited on May 24, 2013), op. cit. Brackets mine.

29 See Micah Zenko (2013), "Reforming U.S. Drone Strike Policies" . . ., p. 8, op. cit.

30 See Geert-Jan Alexander Knoops (2012), "Legal, Political and Ethical Dimensions of Drone Warfare . . .", p. 718, op. cit.

31 See Rudolph Herzog's report of Andrew Niccol's film in "Dealing Death by Remote Control" . . ., p. 66, op. cit.

32 Loc. Cit.

33 Loc. Cit.

Micah Zenko is of the view that drones offer an advantage in which "drone-fired missiles can be—and have been—diverted at the last moment if noncombatants enter the likely blast radius"[34]) to stop the missile he had launched just a second earlier.[35] Given the capacity of drones for near-instantaneous responses, and the speed at which a drone-fired missile moves, indeed, faster than the speed of sound,[36] it is doubtful that the diversion that Micah Zenko talks about whenever a noncombatant enters the blast radius is ever possible. The consequence of the impossibility of diverting an already drone-fired missile when a noncombatant strays into the blast radius is that civilians are inexorably amongst the dead, women, old people, and children; and Egan himself, though out of danger, would feel guilty about it, coupled with the apparent sense of cowardice.[37]

But all in all, the fact that with drones, the body bags do not come home because "no pilots need be put at risk", is evidently a source of lowering the ethical restraints that otherwise would exist and made the conflict and the concomitant shedding of blood less attractive.[38] Jessica Stern certainly captured the ethical debate when she wrote as follows:

> Drones are a terrifying instrument of war. They sometimes cause the deaths of innocents. [But] there is something that feels not quite right about a weapon whose use entails no direct physical risk to the user, And although most Americans approve of the use of drones in counter-terrorism operations, if drones were to someday target U.S. government officials or American citizens themselves, such opinions would quickly shift.[39]

The approval by most Americans at the moment of the use of drones in counter-terrorism operations is indicative of the fact that this lethal instrument of modern asymmetric warfare is actually lowering the political cost of going to war, which makes the resort to war a very cheap or easy option that has its own enormous ethical implications.

Drones and the Ethical Implications of Autonomous Weapons Systems (AWS)

The ethical dilemma in the use of armed drones remains heightened or is prone to be made more acute whenever the introduction of the Autonomous Weapon System (AWS) becomes a reality. This is because the emergence of these

34 See Micah Zenko (2013), "Reforming U.S. Drone Strike Policies" . . ., p. 6, op. cit.

35 See Rudolph Herzog's report of Andrew Niccol's film in "Dealing Death by Remote Control" . . ., p. 66, op. cit.

36 See Micah Zenko (2013), "Reforming U.S. Drone Strike Policies" . . ., p. 6, op. cit.

37 See Rudolph Herzog's report of Andrew Niccol's film in "Dealing Death by Remote Control" . . ., p. 66, op. cit.

38 Loc. Cit.

39 See Jessica Stern (2015), "Obama and Terrorism . . .", pp. 65–66, op. cit.

automated drones and their capacity for autonomous decision making capability will lead to mindless killings as machines cannot ensure any rational decision making or be able to observe restraints. Markus Wagner is very explicit on this in his declaration that:

> . . . the decision to deploy AWS—at least in democratic countries—may carry a lower political cost. While the idea of military forces consisting entirely of AWS is futuristic at best, the idea of incurring fewer casualties is attractive for decision-makers. When putting greater emphasis on AWS, there is a danger that entering into combat operations or prolonging them will no longer inflict the number of casualties that would otherwise be encountered. The attendant political cost of a public averse to such casualties would thereby decrease. The idea of lowering such political costs when going to war—as opposed to making it more difficult—is troubling.[40]

But with the AWS, the ethical problem in the facile resort to war because of the decrease in the political cost of going to war will be compounded by the fact that this automated and autonomous weapon system will easily negate the "individual responsibility for one's own action and those of subordinates".[41] Markus Wagner is of the view that "when analyzing AWS through the lens of morality", particularly in a situation where "one of the fundamental characteristics of the current *jus in bello* is the element of personal responsibility; one problem that the use of AWS presents is that it allows for the dilution of personal responsibility to the point that deterrent effects for those who decide to deploy an AWS may vanish".[42]

In fact, it has even been argued that the tremendous build-up of collateral damage that escalates the ethical dilemma arises from the fact that "drone operators suffer from 'emotional exhaustion' because of their long working hours and monotonous work", which "carries the risk of job burnouts and accidents".[43]

The question, again, is this; can it be assumed that the incident of high collateral damage in drone strikes can be obviated with the deployment of the AWS? The answer here is that this is most unlikely because of the total absence of emotions on the part of the automated machines (emotions that can sometimes restrain the individual operators). When Abu Musab al-Zarqawi had his first close shave with the drone, he was encountered by the drone operator while travelling in a Sedan vehicle and moving across a lightly populated area west of Baghdad.[44] The drone operator only missed him the moment it became necessary to pause and adjust the drone's camera, during which he hopped out of the

40 See Markus Wagner (2012), "Beyond the Drone Debate . . .", p. 83, op. cit.
41 Ibid., pp. 83–84.
42 Ibid., pp. 82–83.
43 See Geert-Jan Alexander Knoops (2012), "Legal, Political and Ethical Dimensions of Drone Warfare . . .", p. 718, op. cit.
44 See Stanley McChrystal (2015), *Team of Teams* . . ., p. 130, op. cit.

car and escaped on foot.[45] The same thing applied to the Taliban leader, Mullah Muhammad Omar. Besides being restricted by an agreement that needed that the CIA obtained authorization from higher authorities (either from the military High Command or the White House), it was speculated that the unmanned armed drone's attack on Mullah Omar when he took cover in a house near Kabul with his retinue of about one hundred guards "was aborted because of the possibility that others in a crowded house might be killed".[46]

An AWS would not possess the emotions to make that rational judgment or show restraint. It would have struck Abu Musab al-Zarqawi and Mullah Muhammad Omar wherever those terrorist leaders were found, even if their locations were in heavily populated areas of Baghdad (Iraq) and Kabul (Afghanistan). Herein lies the thick ethical question that will be found in a machine that would indiscriminately take human lives and not even show any sense of proportion as will be seen later in this book. But there is also this already highlighted overarching question of "individual criminal responsibility" vis-à-vis "state responsibility for drone attacks".[47] In the case of responsibility and accountability in the automated drone attacks (although this will be further explored in the analysis on the automation of drones and the principle of accountability), it is important to state here that the principle of transparency and accountability, ensuring compliance by the drone operators with (if no existing laws), at least, the ethical demands in ensuring that the operators are careful and guided by a sense of responsibility,[48] is seriously impeded by the practice of secrecy that goes with the drone strikes.[49]

Ethical Implications of the CIA Involvement in Drone Strikes

However, arguments are sometimes advanced in favour of the secrecy, the argument that operational "opaqueness and vagueness is necessary due to the clandestine nature of the operations";[50] and that there is need to use the confidentiality "to keep information secret to protect the lives of informants".[51] But plausible as this argument in favour of secrecy may seem, the inadequate transparency in the conduct of drone strikes by the United States undermines the country's liberal culture, which is a blot on the face of its ethical standing. In fact, within the

45 Ibid., p. 131.

46 See William C. Banks (2005), "The Predator", in Volker C. Franke (2005, ed.); *Terrorism and Peacekeeping* . . ., p. 142, op. cit.

47 See Geert-Jan Alexander Knoops (2012), "Legal, Political and Ethical Dimensions of Drone Warfare . . .", p. 718, op. cit.

48 See Ahmad Nazir Warraich (2013), "The Use of Drones . . .", pp. 69, 70, op. cit.

49 Ibid., p. 65.

50 Ibid., p. 69.

51 Ibid., p. 73.

context of ethics as well as domestic and international law, Ahmad Nasir Warraaich had observed that "any action aimed at killing requires transparency";[52] yet, this transparency is lacking in the United States' practice of obscuring the role of the CIA, which is among "the two main departments [the other is the Defence department] believed to be conducting this global [drones] operation".[53]

This lack of transparency in the conduct of drone strikes is unbecoming of a country that prides itself with the moral element or content of its foreign policy,[54] especially a country that is deemed a "globocop", a "global policeman".[55] As Ahmad Nasir Warraich wrote, it is trite knowledge that subject to international law as well as moral norms, war is a sovereign right of every nation; that it is "an honour to die for one's country and permissible to kill for one's country", but it is also trite knowledge that these cannot be carried out outside the context of the laws that define and regulate the means and method of war as well as the combatants and targets.[56] The asymmetric nature of the war on terror may have justified the enlistment of armed drones, but in the involvement of a spy agency (the CIA) in the deployment and execution of attacks with these drones, the United States (like the insurgents themselves that deploy terrorists and IEDs), are thereby using noncombatants in the war; and this invites the attendant ethical question, the dilemma over whether to regard these CIA agents (and, indeed, other regular members of the U.S. armed forces involved in the drone strikes) as warriors or to regard them as murderers.[57]

The fact is that "spy agencies may gather intelligence information but never get involved in the killing itself" because "even in the most violent of human experience, all is not fair"; and the so-called Machiavelli principle of the end justifying the means does not apply.[58] Otherwise, the situation in which a spy agency like the CIA is involved in drone strikes, as obtains in the United States, carries with it some huge legal and ethical burdens. The insurgents that apply terrorist tactics do not see themselves as obligated by any rule of engagement; but because as a state authority that is under obligation to apply international as well as domestic laws—and since all military manuals, including that of the Air Force, have clear rules that obligate the state to act in accordance with IHL in the conduct of warfare or armed action—the United States is bound not to renege from these obligations and shift the goal post.[59] There is definitely an ethical burden in willfully violating the law when there is the relevant knowledge or awareness

52 Ibid., p. 65.
53 Loc. Cit. Parentheses mine.
54 Loc. Cit.
55 See Thomas P. M. Barnett (2004), *The Pentagon's New Map . . .*, p. 350, op. cit.
56 See Ahmad Nazir Warraich (2013), "The Use of Drones . . .", p. 68, op. cit.
57 This dilemma was highlighted by the presenter of an *Aljazeera* documentary entitled *Drone*, monitored in Lagos (Nigeria) on Monday, August 22, 2016, between 9pm and 10pm local time.
58 See Ahmad Nazir Warraich (2013), "The Use of Drones . . .", p. 68, op. cit.
59 Loc. Cit.

about the existence of that law, and the capacity to implement the law too. The statement that "the goal posts cannot be shifted to accommodate individual situations of conflict but rather individual situations of conflict must conform to the relevant *lex speicialis*"[60] may not be entirely correct because the war on terror is clearly an exigency that was never anticipated and thus not covered in any *lex speicialis.*

It was this extraordinary situation (or the exigency) of the war on terror not being on the radar of any extant domestic or international law governing armed conflicts that compelled the shifting of the goal post with the deployment of drones; but where this goal post must not be shifted is in the area of those that wield the "joystick" that controls the drones. In other words, having involved the armed forces in the war on terror, the United States was obliged to play by the rules, meaning that those that prosecute the war in the area of drone strikes must be members of the armed forces as combatants, not the CIA, who are not members of the armed forces or even irregular forces for that matter and, as such, cannot be combatants. The United States cannot be seen to be joining insurgents in the deployment of noncombatants. This is because the status of anonymity or persona non grata before the law of the individual that is deployed by the insurgent group to embark on terrorist campaigns is the same status that the spy agent (the CIA) that embarks on drone strikes finds himself or herself.

The irreducible requirement for the involvement of IHL and other laws of armed conflict in general is the application of the armed forces in any armed conflict, be it symmetric or asymmetric. For this reason, the employment of noncombatants like terrorists (by insurgents) or spies as drones operators (by the United States), apart from not being covered by IHL and other laws of armed conflict, also have serious ethical consequences. At the best of circumstances in armed conflict, spying is only a de facto reality that is not deserving of any legal cover.[61] This reality is behind the ambiguous status of the spy[62] that led to the paradox (enunciated by Oppenheim) that "although a belligerent acts lawfully in employing spies and traitors, the other belligerent who punishes them, likewise acts lawfully".[63] In the employment of spies (the CIA as drone strikers), the United States has successfully created this ambiguity with a "deliberate vagueness" that seems to blur the "lines between the roles of the military and the CIA".[64] This is believed to be a patent abuse of the civilian nature of the CIA as an intelligence agency.[65]

60 Loc. Cit.
61 Ibid., p. 66.
62 See Fred Aja Agwu (2011), *The Law of Armed Conflict and African Wars . . .*, pp. 83–85, op. cit.
63 Ibid., p. 85.
64 See Ahmad Nazir Warraich (2013), "The Use of Drones . . .", p. 66, op. cit.
65 See the *Aljazeera* documentary entitled *Drone*, monitored in Lagos (Nigeria) on Monday, August 22, 2016, between 9pm and 10pm local time, op. cit.

And in doing this, the United States apparently damns all the strong whiff of ethical contradictions: that using the CIA instead of the U.S. military or Air Force is in contradistinction and contradicts the traditional role of the CIA as a spy agency.[66] The contradiction here (and this is paradoxical as well) is that having employed the CIA in drone strikes, the United States is expanding the role of the spy agency "from intelligence gathering to killing, while at the same time enjoying the same de facto protection accorded to all clandestine operations".[67] The implication, and this is where the protection comes in, is that in highly calamitous cases like signature strikes where huge collateral damage is incurred, the United States may argue along the line of Oppenheim's submission that the belligerent that employs spies have the legitimate right to do so and, thus (in the veil of secrecy that spies operate), not submit the erring CIA drone strikers responsible for high civilian casualties to the long arms of international law, say, for prosecution at the International Criminal Court (ICC). Of course, the United States is not a party to the Rome Status and, as such, will not be obliged to handover the CIA agent to the ICC. This is where Ahmad Nazir Warraich is concerned that:

> The United States of America prides itself on having a moral dimension to its foreign policy, and distinguishing its international actions from those of European nations. [Consequently], the U.S. has therefore partially condemned the use of targeted killings by other states; and as the self proclaimed "Leader of the Free World" has taken upon itself to push the agenda for international law compliance by other states.[68]

But the ethical bind here is not in the United States' condemnation of targeted killings, since the exigencies of the war on terror have rightly imposed it on Washington. The moral or ethical bind here is in the use of the CIA rather than the Defence Department (the members of the armed forces). The paradox captured earlier that the U.S. (as the leader of the free world) pushes the agenda for other states to comply with the international law it now itself violates by blurring the line between the CIA and its military in the application of drone strikes, is a reinforcement of the power of hegemony and the tyrannical burden that a global hegemon like the United States imposes on international law, the positivist dimension (international institutions like the United Nations) of which is "meant to order international relations".[69] The United States' actions clearly exemplify the negation of the post-Second World War wave of international legal positivism

66 See Ahmad Nazir Warraich (2013), "The Use of Drones . . .", p. 66, op. cit.
67 Loc. Cit.
68 Loc. Cit. Brackets mine.
69 Ibid., p. 65.

that saw "the establishment of the United Nations" with all its noble aims, objectives and ideals.[70]

Again, in underlining the implicit moral or ethical burden in all of this, Ahmad Nazir Warriach expressed the view that the perceived compromise of some of these ideals has been viewed as a retrogressive step, prompting some commentators and analysts to criticize the way in which the U.S. perhaps acts as an empire of yesteryears, making laws for the other states to follow while considering itself to be above those same laws.[71]

70 Ibid., p. 67.
71 Loc. Cit.

11 Drones, WoT, and the Principle of Chivalry

Importance of Chivalry in Armed Conflicts

Without prejudice to the discussion in the preceding chapter on ethics in the war on terror, this chapter must commence with an exploration of the importance or relationship between chivalry and ethics in armed conflicts in general; but also with a special reference to the war on terror under reference. In conventional armed conflicts, ethics and chivalry are very critical components of the philosophy of the cultivation of restraints. They are particularly so in the sense that whereas ethics serves as a moral restraint to wanton killings, chivalry appeals to the ego and thus, prevents the really courageous or gallant soldier from exhibiting an effeminacy in killing noncombatants, especially children, women, and aged persons. Thus, a chivalrous conduct is much more than the legal restraints offered by IHL. A chivalrous conduct, in addition to inducing the feeling of pride or self-satisfaction in the observance of IHL (a statutory legal restraint), also entails that restraint that is congenitally induced from the ego, the sense of honour and the innate satisfaction in doing the right thing.

Hence, apart from killings, a chivalrous soldier would not indulge in pillaging and kidnapping for ransom that would aid the war effort, the kind of practice that is habitually indulged in by terrorist organizations like the Taliban, the ISIS, the Boko Haram, or the al-Shabaab, amongst other terrorist organizations.[1] But its focus on other misbehavior beyond killings does not vitiate the fact that when considered within the ambits of the Geneva Conventions of 1949 and other legal instruments that embody the IHL, ethics and chivalry also enable the protection of human dignity and innocent lives. Ostensibly, terrorists do not set stock by ethics and chivalry. Nation-states are expected to do so. But the question here is this: for states that possess, deploy and apply armed drones for targeted killings, would these weapons be permissive of the observance of the demands of ethics and chivalry in the war on terror?

1 See Fred Aja Agwu (2011), *The Law of Armed Conflict and African Wars* . . ., pp. 172–174, op. cit; see also *Time* (New York), September 7, 2009, pp. 18–21.

Ethics and chivalry constitute the philosophical background that enables states to, as U.S. President George W. Bush would put it, "punish warriors who do not" comply with this necessity of human dignity and innocent lives protection.[2] Nevertheless, ethics, as a moral concern, must be differentiated from chivalry. This differentiation was aptly done by Douglas Lackey when he opined that:

> Since good moral character is something that is possible for each and is required of all, the moral quality of chivalrous virtues can be established only by demonstrating that everyone is morally obliged to be a knight—and that demonstration cannot be supplied. . . . Certainly, chivalrousness is a virtue, but it is not obviously a moral virtue. [This is because] it is a mark of genuine moral virtues that people of good character act not only in accordance with moral virtues, but also for the sake of them: the just man does just things, and does them because they are just.[3]

Thus, much as ethics and chivalry are both institutions of restraint, they are still different from each other. Although paradoxical, it is nonetheless true that chivalry in armed conflicts can hardly attain high moral virtues because in war, it must destroy. But in its destructiveness, chivalry must be cognizant of the utilitarian principle of necessity and proportionality in its destruction of the enemy. Ethics or morality, on the other hand, differs from chivalry in the sense that it abjures destructiveness in all its dimensions, for it holds that "it is wrong to destroy the good things of the world, even good things belonging to enemies that are waging unjust wars".[4]

Chivalry is, therefore, principally more about courage than about morality;[5] for in medieval times, it "presented the ideal of the virtuous knight: courageous in battle, fair with enemies, [and] compassionate toward the weak".[6] Yet, like ethical principles, chivalry also has the additional import of being concerned with the principles of humanity in armed conflicts, particularly because "the idea of noncombatant immunity developed in the High Middle Ages as part of the medieval traditions of chivalry".[7] In other words, like ethics, chivalry is concerned, not just about justice, but also about the prevention of cruelties and the preservation of the principles of humanity through putting an end to needless and indiscriminate killings, especially of civilians, noncombatants and those active fighters that willingly surrendered or had already been rendered hors de combat.

2 See George W. Bush (2010), *Decision Points* . . ., pp. 166–167, op. cit.
3 See Douglas P. Lackey (1989), *The Ethics of War and Peace* . . ., p. 65, op. cit.
4 Ibid., p. 64.
5 Ibid., p. 65.
6 Ibid., p. 66. Brackets mine.
7 Ibid., p. 65; see also Fred Aja Agwu (2011), *The Law of Armed Conflict and African Wars* . . ., p. 148, op. cit.

In fact, "to act in violation of the principle of discrimination was to use force contrary to chivalrous virtues", especially when "it takes no courage to kill women and children, and little more to kill an enemy who has laid down his arms".[8] As a matter of fact, "the moral content of the principle of discrimination . . . consists in the fact that respect for noncombatant immunity is a mark of virtuous character".[9] Although the logic of civilized warfare is that "a belligerent is entitled to apply such force as is necessary to produce the submission of the enemy as early and as cheaply (in men and substance) as possible", the principle of humanity prohibits "any kind or degree of violence beyond what is necessary to produce such submission".[10] It is in this context that the "old principles of chivalry . . . demand a certain fairness in offence and defence, and a certain mutual respect between opposing forces, independently of the needs of victory".[11]

Weapons in the Negation of Chivalry

The "sonorous and largely harmonious notes of humanity" that are inherent in the ideal of chivalry is principally ascribed to the decayed medieval or feudal society; but this ideal has largely exploded today with "the rise of explosive weapons [like drones] for killing and maiming at a distance".[12] Even though deliberate human intentions are sometimes involved, but weapons are very critical in the capacity to enforce chivalrous and ethical principles, the ability to prevent cruelties or indiscriminate deaths, especially amongst protected populations. In this regard, both the sub-national entities like the ISIS, the al-Qaeda or even the Boko Haram in Nigeria that use IEDs; or the nation-state that uses drones in asymmetric warfare, all hold the short end of the stick in ethical and chivalrous considerations.

In other words, ethical and chivalrous considerations get a short-shrift from the parties in asymmetric conflicts because they deploy controversial weapons, be they the IEDs or the drones. Yet, chivalrous considerations may have been very significant in the medieval times, but as Douglas Lackey said, "it would be perverse in analyzing twentieth-century [and indeed twenty-first century] wars to say that soldiers are placed on the battlefield for the purpose of exhibiting chivalry".[13] This statement is truer with respect to the use of weapons such as IEDs and drones because, with them, chivalry is out of the consideration. In the medieval times, "medieval knights, at least in legend, fought each other on

8 See Douglas P. Lackey (1989), *The Ethics of War and Peace* . . ., p. 65, op. cit.
9 Loc. Cit.
10 See Julius Stone (1954), *Legal Control of International Conflict* . . ., p. 337, op. cit.
11 Loc. Cit.
12 Loc. Cit. Brackets mine.
13 See Douglas P. Lackey (1989), *The Ethics of War and Peace* . . ., p. 65, op. cit. Brackets mine.

roughly equal terms, one on one, with similar equipment",[14] but this is no longer the case today with the emergence and use of all manner of sophisticated weapons that remove "combatants" from level playing grounds. During medieval times when weapons were similar and "combatants" were on level playing grounds, victory was usually obtained by a side with the unequal advantage, the side with the larger phalanx, the side with more men engaged in the "push of the pike", the larger cavalry, and the bigger guns.[15]

Law, Technology, and the Negation of Chivalry in WoT

There is a contradiction in the application of chivalrous codes in asymmetric warfare, especially the war on terror; and this owes largely to the contradictory relationship between law and technology in modern times. As a product of the dynamism or intractability of human ingenuity, technology out-paces the law. This is particularly because whereas ingenuity is a product of human imagination that can thrive and easily manifest at an individual level within a very short time, the law is a socio-cultural thing that entails social mobilization and consensus attainment. This is a procedure that takes quite a while to crystallize, especially internationally. And as seen earlier in the dynamics of self-defence, it is clear that it was the backwardness of the law (international law) vis-à-vis technological advancements that made it possible for the use of armed drones in self-defence (deep in the territories of other states) to thrive, even though these weapons remain largely unregulated as it were.

Self-defence under the United Nations normative legal order can only take place if an armed attack occurred and must be limited to the restoration of the status quo ante, meaning that it cannot take place beyond the threshold of national frontiers, except in cases of permanent aggression that requires territorial occupation before such aggressions can be halted.[16] But the use of armed drones in targeted and defensive killings against terrorists right inside the territories of terror-hosting nations is now akin to the rule of capture in the law of the sea that makes it lawful for one state to explore and tap mineral resources (like hydro-carbon) from the territory of another state with advanced technology[17] (provided it did not physically enter that territory[18]). Thus, because technology

14 Loc. Cit.

15 Ibid., p. 66.

16 See Fred Aja Agwu (2005), *United Nations System, State Practice and the Jurisprudence of the Use of Force* . . ., pp. 79, 167–177, op. cit.

17 The rule or law of capture is of common law origin from England; see "The Rule of Capture", available in Wikipedia at https://en.wikipedia.org/wiki/Rule_of_capture (last visited on Friday, November 6, 2015).

18 In the most influential decision on the "rule of capture", which was in *Westmoreland & Cambria Natural Gas Co. v. De Witt*, the Pennsylvania Supreme Court embraced the application of the proprietary analysis to hydrocarbons migrating across wells, holding as

here leverages the inadequacy of this aspect of the law of armed conflict that still exists as a penumbra (grey area), there is an explicit tolerance of one state using drones to strike at the safe haven or training centers of insurgents in another state's territory, provided that the drone-striking state was guided by the principles of proportionality and discrimination—an ability to distinguish or discriminate between the state institutions and the terrorist insurgents and, thus, not striking at the facilities of the state.

As far as the use of drones (or even IEDs on the part of insurgents) is concerned, it is this same contradiction in the relationship between the law and technology that buoys the infraction of chivalrous codes in the war on terror. In the matter of chivalry and the principles of humanity, as Julius Stone put it, the advent of "technological developments with which . . . the law of weapons has not caught up, have dwarfed in importance, the well-settled rules of the law of war built upon the medieval ideals of chivalry and the post-Renaissance and nineteenth century principles of humanity".[19] In air warfare, the technological development that now facilitates the deployment of long-range missiles from drones ostensibly makes bombardments quite gratuitous and a platform for wanton destructions.[20] Although drones are for precision targeting that could forestall the bombardment of an entire city from the air, but there is no doubt that such precision targeting (if even not called by its proper name, bombardment) would implicitly involve moving against an undefended city.

The act of bombarding an undefended city in whatever guise (even if to target a solitary insurgent) could implicate a state in illegality because bombardment is basically a preliminary measure to capture a defended city by softening or dislodging the defences in order to enable troops to move in and effect occupation.[21] In any case, the precision targeting that is ascribed to drones is not absolutely assured, for the weapon eventually becomes indiscriminate, causing the collateral damage that results in the "blowback" earlier referred to earlier. Thus, the civilian deaths that result from the failure in achieving precision targeting and the implicit indiscriminate nature of these attacks make the deployment of drones to be not only in violation of the Hague Regulations (Articles 22 and 23 in particular) but also the lives of innocents.[22]

---

follows: "If an adjoining, or even a distant owner, drills his own land, and taps your gas, so that it comes into his well and under his control, it is no longer yours, but his". And this happens when hydrocarbons are straddling either side of disputed boundary lines, the traditional answer usually being to drill first and answer questions later, what in technical terms is known as the "rule of capture"; see Dominic Roughton in "The Right (and Wrongs) of Capture: International Law and the Implications of the Guyana/Suriname Arbitration", available at http://hsfnotes.com/arbitration/wp-content/uploads/sites/4/2012/11/document.ashx_.pdf (last visited on Monday, November 9, 2015).

19 See Julius Stone (1954), *Legal Control of International Conflict* . . ., p. 557, op. cit.

20 Ibid., p. 560.

21 Loc. Cit.

22 Ibid., pp. 557–558.

Drones, the Death of Chivalry, and Courage in Combat

The inappropriateness of drones is emphasized by the fact that, "the more terrible the weapons, the less protection is offered to human life" by the principle of chivalry.[23] In fact, chivalry is hardly given thought today with weapons like drones, as "in contemporary war, men in tanks and amoured vehicles and bombers kill men not in tanks or amoured vehicles or bombers".[24] Thus, "the idea of courage in equal combat is largely absent in these situations".[25] As it were, "the bomber pilot and tank commander take risks on occasion, but on many other occasions, they kill in battle with little risks to themselves".[26] Before the advent of drones, aircrews (as opposed to soldiers and sailors, including civilians), especially during the Second World War, were victims of extreme callousness, devoid of any form of chivalrous feeling, as despite chivalrous impulses, there were divergences in state practice, some of which even verged on the "licence to shoot an airman who bailed out of a disabled machine".[27]

Admittedly, as Julius Stone argued, there was "no doubt, it is difficult for the attacker to be sure that the dangling human being is in distress, rather than a spy or saboteur; yet, the effect is to cancel the chivalrous analogy of land and sea rules".[28] But the Additional Protocol I to the Geneva Conventions of 12 August 1949, has unified and transcended the divergences; and, indeed, ipso fact abolished those Second World War state practice that lacked in chivalrous impulse.[29] When on November 24, 2015, a Russian warplane (a Sukhoi Su-24) was shot down for allegedly violating the Turkish airspace a multiple times while on a mission to Syria, the attendant outrage was not so much about the shooting down of the warplane (especially when Turkey had reportedly warned the Russian crew five times) as it was about the fact that the Russian pilots were shot at as they were descending in a parachute from the disabled machine, killing one of them.[30] According to the report, "one pilot was shot as he drifted to the ground in

23 Ibid., p. 558.
24 See Douglas P. Lackey (1989), *The Ethics of War and Peace . . .*, p. 66, op. cit.
25 Loc. Cit.
26 Loc. Cit.
27 See Julius Stone (1954), *Legal Control of International Conflict . . .*, p. 615, op. cit.
28 Ibid., pp. 615–616.
29 Article 42 (1) of the Protocol under reference states that "No person parachuting from an aircraft in distress shall be made the object of attack during his descent"; while 42 (2) provides that "upon reaching the ground in the territory controlled by an adverse Party, a person who has parachuted from an aircraft in distress shall be given an opportunity to surrender before being made the object of attack, unless it is apparent that he is engaging in a hostile act".
30 See Afeez Hanafi with agency reports in "Tension as Turkey Downs Russian Fighter Jet", *The Punch* (Lagos), Wednesday, November 25, 2015, p. 7.

his parachute, while the other was captured by the local militia called the 10th Brigade".[31]

The shooting was clearly in violation of Article 42 (occupants of aircraft) of Additional Protocol I (August–September 1977). It was, indeed, a war crime. Lamentably, old habits die hard. Or was it that the soldiers responsible for the shooting were not adequately informed about the dictates of IHL, of which the military high command has a responsibility? Today, however, with the advent of drones, the table has turned and the odds are no longer against "airmen" (if drones' operators can be validly referred to as such). It is now the "airmen", the drones' operators, that are caught in the contradictory web of not possessing or lacking "chivalrous impulses", as Julius Stone put it.[32] This total lack of chivalrous test "is true of men in the artillery and those engaged in laying mines"[33] as it is true of drones' operators. Like the insurgent or guerilla leader that overwhelmed an isolated outpost, or the field commander who sent a battalion against a company,[34] there is nothing chivalrous in a predator or drone pilot killing six Taliban in Pakistan while sitting in a cubicle at an air force base in Las Vegas wielding the joystick.[35]

As a matter of fact, a drone pilot, Tom Egan (Ethan Hawke), who had risked his life in Iraq flying manned missions, could not help but be increasingly troubled and seized with a sense of guilt and cowardice in now using the predator to kill the Taliban in far away Waziristan from Las Vegas.[36] Even in the realm of honour for gallantry, the ceremony and nomenclature of the ritual in "the real Air Force", according to Richard Clarke in his fictional rendition or account of the flying of drones, are distinct from those that take place amongst pilots of the UAVs.[37] Whereas the ceremonies are secret amongst UAV pilots (ostensibly because their activities are secret, not because they are not recognized), a special honour is also created for them—"the Distinguished Warfare Award", pejoratively referred to in the real Air Force as the "Desk Warfare Award", given only to "guys who go to war without ever leaving their desks, Cyber geeks and Xbox gamers"; and these are medals that "cannot ever be given for valor in combat".[38]

This has been known to trigger nostalgia in many a drone pilot that had flown manned missions; making them "want to fly again [the F-16s] . . . [as they] used

31 Loc. Cit.
32 See Julius Stone (1954), *Legal Control of International Conflict* . . ., p. 615, op. cit.
33 See Douglas P. Lackey (1989), *The Ethics of War and Peace* . . ., p. 66, op. cit.
34 Loc. Cit.
35 See Rudolph Herzog's report of Andrew Niccol's film in "Dealing Death by Remote Control" . . ., p. 66, op. cit.
36 Loc. Cit.
37 See Richard A. Clarke (2014), *Sting of the Drone* . . ., p. 77, op. cit.
38 Loc. Cit.

to do [because what they] really like is a crack at an F-22".[39] With the armed drones, American forces are prone to be disparaged and even taunted for cowardice in taking to the skies and not coming down to gallantly face the enemy on the ground of combat.[40] In Waziristan (the epicenter of the war on terror in Afghanistan), the al-Qaeda henchmen lament the failure of the Americans "to meet us face-to-face", taunting them as follows: "they send drones without pilots; they are cowards".[41] This charge of cowardice against the United States is part of al-Qaeda's "war" propaganda. Listen to Osama bin Laden in one of his propaganda pieces under the theme "The Afghan-Soviet Paradigm: The Myth of the Superpower and U.S. Cowardice":

> After our victory in Afghanistan and the defeat of the oppressors who had killed millions of Muslims, the legend about the invincibility of the superpowers vanished. Our boys no longer viewed America as a superpower. So, when they left Afghanistan, they went to Somalia and prepared themselves carefully for a long war. They had thought that the Americans were like the Russians, so they trained and prepared. They were stunned when they discovered how low (sic) was the morale of the American soldier. America had entered with thirty thousand soldiers in addition to thousands of soldiers from different countries in the world . . . . As I said, our boys were shocked by the low morale of the American soldier, and they realized that the American soldier was just a paper tiger. He was unable to endure the strikes that were dealt to his army, so he fled, and America had to stop all its bragging and all that noise it was making in the press after the Gulf War . . .[42]

Although this was a cheap propaganda campaign, Osama bin Laden was ostensibly taunting the United States on account of the Somali syndrome, the downing (as the United States operated in the skies as it hunted for General Mohammed Farah Aidid) of the Blackhawk, an American combat helicopter, leading, not only to casualties and the body bags that the American public dread the most, but also to the body of one of the dead soldiers being dragged in the streets of Mogadishu amid the Somalis' kicks and jeers.[43] In conventional battles, few countries can

39 Loc. Cit. Parentheses mine.

40 This reality is very much prevalent in Afghanistan and northwestern Pakistan where the war on terror has its most recognizable epicenters,

41 Again, this assertion is as gleaned from the *Aljazeera* documentary, *Drone*, aforementioned and as monitored in Lagos (Nigeria) on Monday, August 22, 2016, between 9pm and 10pm local time.

42 See Raymond Ibrahim (2007, ed.), *The Al-Qaeda Reader*, New York, Broadway Books, p. 260.

43 See Fred Aja Agwu (2009), *National Interest, International Law* . . ., pp. 450–451, op. cit.

rival the United States, how much less the al-Qaeda, the Taliban, or other rag-tag terrorist forces. But Osama bin Laden's bluster, for whatever it is worth, is ironical for a nation that the Pope described in his September 24, 2015, address to the joint session of the U.S. Congress as "the land of the free and the home of the brave".[44] This taunting and the concomitant attitude of condescension towards the Americans (a mighty superpower) is quite troubling because it portrays an otherwise gallant people as less chivalrous if not displaying outright cowardice.

44 See the "Full Text of Pope Francis' Speech to US Congress: Pope Takes His Case for Action on the Death Penalty, Climate Change and Immigration to US Congress in Historic Speech", available at www.aljazeera.com/news/2015/09/full-text-pope-francis-speech-congress-150924152204132.htmlSee (last visited on March 4, 2016).

12 Drones

Miniaturization, Automation, and Accountability in WoT

The Importance of Transparency

If in the current development of the drone technology, the coming up of a generation of armed drones that is resilient, that possesses speed, stealth, and decoy capabilities (enough to enable them protect themselves against air defence systems[1]) sounds ominous and threatening, then the development of an Autonomous Weapons System (AWS) that will witness the miniaturization and development of robotic and mindless drones that would not have anything to do with human interventions should even pose a greater concern to humanity. Miniaturization and automation of armed drones in the AWS are very critical dilemmas in the now intractable sophistication of this new technology in the military arsenal of some developed nations. But in the confluence of the miniaturization and automation of armed drones (particularly with respect to the latter, even though futuristic), there lies this hard nut, the problem of accountability, that is yet to be cracked.

Ordinarily, in a conventional warfare that involves human beings that are locked in the exchange of firearms, the condition that must be obtained before the vital issue of accountability can be attained is transparency, the absence of opaqueness in the means and methods of the warfare; it is only this transparency that can lead to the apportionment of guilt in the event of the infraction of the rules of engagement. Transparency is the key to the ultimate unraveling of liability, responsibility, and the determination of guilt. The focus of accountability is on the individual and the state itself; but in international criminal justice, the state is an abstract entity. As the International Criminal Tribunal in Nuremberg asserted, it is only by punishing the individual that the state can be vicariously punished and justice upheld. In other words, accountability demands that "if state agents are found guilty, the state is expected to publicly prosecute them and consequently impose punishments".[2] But in the absence of the willingness or ability of the state to prosecute and impose this punishment, the responsibility to do so will now devolve on the international community, through either an international tribunal or, now, the International Criminal Court (ICC).

1 See Micah Zenko (2013), "Reforming U.S. Drone Strike Policies" . . ., p. 7, op. cit.
2 See Ahmad Nazir Warraich (2013), "The Use of Drones . . .", p. 70, op. cit.

But one question that cries for attention in the domain of the automation of drones (the expected invention of the robotic species of this machine), is that of what will happen when the machines rather than the human beings make the decision to kill, and to do so in excess of the required principle of proportionality and discrimination between "combatants" and "noncombatants". Although the idea of "combatancy" is foreclosed for terrorists, accountability in asymmetric warfare, particularly in its variant of the "war on terror", is still very critical with respect to the nation-state that has military manual as well as being bound by the law of armed conflict, especially the IHL dimension. By dint of Article 3 common to the four Geneva Conventions (1949), the law of armed conflict is activated as soon as a state applies its armed forces. But before discussing this automation in full here, it is important to say something about miniaturization, no matter how tangentially.

Miniaturization

As a modern phenomenon, miniaturization has taken such sudden turn that as at 1998, starting with the RQ-4A Global Hawk drones with a length of 13.4 meters and a wingspan of 35.3 meters, "the refinement of the drone technology [had] developed drastically towards drones with the size of a big insect".[3] Advancing further in this project of miniaturization in 2011, the AeroVironment Nano Hummingbird drone announced that it had a wingspan of only 16 centimeters; while it is currently anticipated that future drone technology would "culminate into devices no larger than a fruit fly (micro air vehicles)".[4] As a matter of fact, it has already been said that miniature drones now inundate the field so extensively "that now, there are thousands of small, unarmed aerial surveillance drones being used by troops on the ground—so many, in fact, that it is difficult to obtain an accurate estimate of their number".[5]

And these small or miniaturized drones "can be deployed by hand and operated with an Xbox controller through a visual headset that allows troops on the ground to gain actionable intelligence at their command".[6] A miniaturized drone, even if of a primitive category, like the explosive-laden variety that U.S. citizen Rezwan Ferdaus wanted to use to attack the Pentagon and the Capitol,[7] is certainly an easy or convenient implement that terrorist organizations can potentially use to ply his or her trade. The implication of miniaturization is that an armed drone will be difficult to discern and track down. In other words, it will be very evasive, deadly, and capable of being misapplied to unimaginable ends,

3 See Geert-Jan Alexander Knoops (2012), "Legal, Political and Ethical Dimensions of Drone Warfare . . .", p. 698, op. cit.
4 Loc. Cit.
5 See Van Baldwin Carr (undated) in "Unmanned Aerial Vehicles . . .", p. 10, op. cit.
6 Loc. Cit.
7 See Micah Zenko (2013), "Reforming U.S. Drone Strike Policies" . . ., p. 21, op. cit.

ends that would contradict the rules of engagement in warfare as established since antiquity, from customary practices to their more recent conventional or treaty formulations.

But more ominously, miniaturization can easily lead to the militarization of domestic law enforcement. At the moment, and as far as critics of the deployment of armed drones across borders for targeted killings is concerned, these weapons are merely used in a "law enforcement issue"; that is the enforcement of international human rights law (even though it contradicts due process) rather than the law of armed conflict.[8] But this increased miniaturization has the potential of leading the full engagement of these weapons in domestic law enforcement; for their portability would then mean that they would be "used in the areas of policing and violent situations that fall short of armed conflict", thus, further complicating the already dubious status or legality of armed drones.[9]

Autonomous Weapon System (AWS)

Incidentally, the miniaturization feat is increasingly achieved at a time that this armed drone technology is also facing the prospect of automation. Presently, all the Unmanned Aerial Vehicles (UAVs) or drones are all generically referred to as Unmanned Systems (UMS).[10] They all operate "with direct human input",[11] with their operators "connecting to the aircraft via satellite link from thousands of miles away"[12] and often striking by dint of authorization from superior authorities. But with the increasing move toward a greater autonomy for the UAVs or drones, "the next generations of UMS are designed to operate wholly independently from human input" as automated machines.[13] As Markus Wagner put it, "from target selection, to the decision whether to employ weapon systems in the particular moment in time (and if so, which weapons), Autonomous Weapon Systems (AWS) will be in a position to carry out their missions without direct human input".[14] Many questions remain unresolved and beg for answers here. For instance, how can these machines identify the terrorists? Would the DNA of the terrorist be programmed or fed into the machine to enable it make the decisive distinction between the terrorist and an innocent person? How many of such terrorists' DNA would be readily available to be captured and fed into the automated or robotic drones?

The dramatic difference between unmanned weapons systems (UMS) and the autonomous weapons systems (AWS) can be illustrated with the case that involved a Taliban leader, Mullah Muhammad Omar in October 2001. As told by

8 See Ahmad Nazir Warraich (2013), "The Use of Drones . . .", pp. 76–77, op. cit.
9 Ibid., p. 77.
10 See Markus Wagner (2012), "Beyond the Drone Debate . . .", p. 81, op. cit.
11 Loc. Cit.
12 Ibid., pp. 80–81.
13 Ibid., p. 81.
14 Loc. Cit.

William Banks,[15] the narrative goes that, on that date, an unmanned but armed CIA drone patrolling the roads near Kabul (Afghanistan) pinpointed the location of that supreme commander of the Taliban at the time and "trained its crosshairs on Omar in a convoy of cars fleeing the capital".[16] Because, under an agreement, the CIA had to obtain an authorization to strike on its targets from a higher authority, the CIA operator of the unmanned but armed drone "sought approval from the United States Central Command (CENTCOM) in Tampa to launch the Hellfire missile from the Predator drone positioned above Omar".[17]

The process of seeking authorization caused some delay, prompting the Predator to "follow the convoy to a building where Omar and about one hundred guards sought cover".[18] However, the authorization or approval to strike that was sought from General Tommy R. Franks was refused by the General, who cited as an alibi, a legal advice on the matter he received on the spot.[19] The General, because of the magnitude of the target, rather preferred that the White House approved the strike, which, although granted by President Bush, had prompted a delay that enabled Mullah Omar to change his location, thus, aborting or disrupting the attack.[20] Unlike the UMS, the AWS is an autonomous weapon system that is programmed to take the decision to strike without any human input or approval, either from a military High Command, or from the White House. Were it to be an AWS that was involved in the Mullah Muhammad Omar's incident, it would have taken out the target right away without the need for authorization or approval from any quarters.

But the achievement of the AWS is futuristic and, thus, may not take place immediately; its introduction as a full-fledged weapon system may be a gradual process with the current generation of UAVs (or UMS) being the starting point. But, as Markus Wagner was confident of, "there is no doubt that future combat will see AWS as new players in battlespace",[21] the new name that battlefields or frontlines have come to assume as contaminated combat zones, contaminated with the presence of civilians. As at 2011, the U.S. Navy had experimentally begun testing the X-47B drone that is capable of making autonomous decisions.[22] When perfected, the X-47B can take off and land on its own, and be able to accomplish this even from an aircraft carrier.[23] The implication is that, although nowadays armed drones are controlled by humans, the future drones like the X-47B would no longer have any form of human intervention as it is

15 See William C. Banks (2005), "The Predator", in Volker C. Franke (2005, ed.); Terrorism and Peacekeeping . . ., p. 142, op. cit.
16 Loc. Cit.
17 Loc. Cit.
18 Loc. Cit.
19 Loc. Cit.
20 Loc. Cit.
21 See Markus Wagner (2012), "Beyond the Drone Debate . . .", p. 84, op. cit.
22 See Geert-Jan Alexander Knoops (2012), "Legal, Political and Ethical Dimensions of Drone Warfare . . .", p. 698, op. cit.
23 Loc. Cit.

"intended to make life-or-death decisions" on its own "without a human operator deciding how and when to hit a target".[24]

But what is the attraction in the AWS? Markus Wagner tried to explain that there are arguments that "because humans are prone to commit *jus in bello* violations on account of the high stress level of combat operations, and because AWS are better in any event at carrying out combat operations, there is a moral duty to employ AWS"; and that this argument was "buttressed by a U.S. government report that found that roughly 10 percent of soldiers and marines reported mistreating noncombatants".[25] The assumption here is that the AWS will not only solve the high stress that humans experience in combat operations, it will also resolve the problem of highly stressed soldiers and marines mistreating noncombatants or civilians. It is expected that "these automated (so-called 'seek-and-destroy' drones) will most likely dominate the battlefields in the future".[26] Nevertheless, it is not all automated weapon systems that are a part of the AWS. According to Markus Wagner:

> It is important to distinguish AWS from already existing technologies such as remotely operated systems or automated systems. Remotely operated systems have been in place for some time (with early examples going back to the end of the 19th century) and have received increased attention in recent years with the increase of attacks carried out by UAVs, including so-called targeted killings. Automated weapons have been employed regularly over the last half century, one example being the use of cruise missiles. AWS differ from these weapons. Unlike remotely operated systems and automated systems, AWS do not require a human operator to be in the loop. Rather, by design, they operate without direct human input.[27]

AWS and Proportionality

The ordinary meaning of proportionality is symmetry, balance or evenness.[28] In the law of armed conflict, it follows, therefore (and this is pursuant to the principle of humanity), that proportionality means the achievement of balance or evenness through limiting the "application of power to the necessary extent".[29] Francis Lieber, who on account of his drawing up the Lieber Code is widely recognized as the most renowned jurist in the codification of the law of armed

24 Loc. Cit.
25 See Markus Wagner (2012), "Beyond the Drone Debate . . .", p. 83, op. cit.
26 See Geert-Jan Alexander Knoops (2012), "Legal, Political and Ethical Dimensions of Drone Warfare . . .", p. 698, op. cit.
27 See Markus Wagner (2012), "Beyond the Drone Debate . . .", p. 81, op. cit.
28 See *Roget's International Thesaurus*, Third Edition (1962), New York, Thomas Y. Crowell Company, 247 (1), p. 132.
29 See Frits Kalshoven (1971), *Belligerent Reprisals*, Leyden, A. W. Sijthoff, p. 223.

conflict,[30] underlined this element of balance or evenness in the making of proportionality. In his letter to General Halleck some time after the issue of the 1863 Lieber Code (which was the United States' Army General Order No. 100),[31] Lieber wrote as follows:

> Is the threat of General Burnside true, that he would hang ten Confederates officers for every Union officer hung by the Confederates? Whether true or not, you are aware that this is the spirit which generally shows itself when a barbarous outrage is committed, but which it is very necessary promptly to stop. The wanton insolence of our enemy has been growing so fast, and is so provoking, that I am plainly and simply for quick retaliation; but in retaliation, it is necessary strictly to adhere to sections twenty-seven and twenty-eight of General Order 100 [the Lieber Code], to the elementary principle which prevails all the world over—*tit for tat*, or eye for eye—and not to adopt ten eyes for one eye. If one belligerent hangs ten men for one, the other will hang ten times ten for the ten; and what a dreadful geometrical progression of skulls and crossbones we should have.[32]

What Francis Lieber emphasized is the cathartic and humanitarian significance of adhering to the principle of proportionality, the fact that proportionality, as Frits Kalshoven put it, is not only a logical requirement for elementary justice for reprisals as for sanctions generally, but that it also represents a positive element contributing to their effectiveness: the measured reprisal stands a far better chance of achieving the desired effect than the disproportionate policy of terror.[33]

Also inherent in the principle of proportionality is the fact that "the number of persons executed must have been proportionate to the gravity of the act retaliated against".[34] But contrary to the Lieber Code, Robert Sloane believes that "proportionality is not an old, venerable principle of international law", and that it "probably was not part of customary international law until at least 1977; which, according to him, is why "to this day, you won't find the word "proportionality" in any international humanitarian law treaty".[35]

Yet, Sloane admits that the Additional Protocol I (1977) defines it indirectly by speaking of, among other indiscriminate attacks, those which may be expected to cause incidental loss of civilian life, injury to civilians, damage to civilian objects, or a combination thereof, which we can shorten to the euphemism "collateral damage", which would be excessive in relation to the concrete and direct military advantage anticipated.[36]

30 See Fred Aja Agwu (2011), *The Law of Armed Conflict and African Wars*. . ., p. 119, op. cit.
31 Loc. Cit; see also Frits Kalshoven (1971), *Belligerent Reprisals*. . ., p. 46, not 5, op. cit.
32 See Frits Kalshoven (1971), *Belligerent Reprisals*. . ., loc. Cit. Brackets mine.
33 Ibid., pp. 213–214.
34 Ibid., p. 210.
35 See Robert D. Sloane (2011), "New Battlefields/Old Laws . . .", p. 370, op. cit.
36 Loc. Cit.

This introduction of the element of excessiveness brings in the questions of weighing/weighting, assessing or the valuation of proportionality. What is the value of proportionality in qualitative terms? How can proportionality be quantified, particularly when what is involved is difficult to be measured? How can a number that is tangible be measured with the gravity of the act that is intangible and, thus, immeasurable?

This is the crux of the matter in the qualitative dimension of the principle of proportionality, which is equally as critical as the quantitative aspect. Unlike the quantitative dimension to proportionality in which "it is not open to doubt that the ratio of 50 or 100 to 1 was shocking disproportionate in any circumstance",[37] the qualitative dimension of proportionality is controversial. This qualitative dimension of proportionality will be reverted to again later. But for now, this question must be posed: how can AWS deal with the critical issue of distinction that is very decisive in the principle of proportionality? The issue is that "in the context of *jus in bello*, two cornerstones of international humanitarian law are of particular relevance: the principle of distinction and the principle of proportionality".[38] Although "both principles are designed to protect civilians", they "also allow for attacks, provided that the military advantage gained by the attacks (as anticipated at the time of the attack) does not disproportionately harm the civilian population"[39] or produce unacceptable collateral damage.

So, to be capable of attaining the principle of proportionality, whether quantitative or qualitative, the AWS must first be capable of also attaining the principle of distinction in this regard; for proportionality itself, according to Markus, Wagner, is also imbued with quantitative and qualitative dimensions.[40] Meanwhile, the principle of distinction as spelt out in Article 48 of Additional Protocol 1 (1977) to the four Geneva Conventions (1949) "mandates that when carrying out an attack, combatants must distinguish between combatants (as well as military objects) and civilians (as well as civilian objects)", and this extends to the ban on weapons that are by nature indiscriminate.[41] However, it is strongly believed that at the moment, the AWS only possesses the quantitative capacity for analyzing or recognizing "a tank which has specific characteristics that make it distinguishable from a car or a bus"; but that in the changing or unclear circumstances that are less amenable to mechanistic or quantitative analysis, like qualitatively recognizing "a person carrying a tool over his shoulder that looks very similar to a gun", the AWS is not capable of the qualitative distinction involved.[42]

37 See Frits Kalshoven (1971), *Belligerent Reprisals* . . ., p. 210, op. cit.
38 See Markus Wagner (2012), "Beyond the Drone Debate . . .", p. 81, op. cit.
39 Loc. Cit.
40 Ibid., p. 82.
41 Ibid., p. 81.
42 Ibid., p. 82.

In other words, it is a fact that, at least, at this point in time, this qualitative analysis is beyond the ken or what softwares like the AWS are capable of doing.[43] Meanwhile, this capacity for making quantitative and qualitative distinctions is very critical to the capacity to observe the principle of proportionality. But matters are not helped by the fact that, as Robert Sloane is cited to have said the reference to proportionality is indirect or does not seem to be very explicitly articulated by the Additional Protocol 1 (1977) to the four Geneva Conventions, a very vital aspect of IHL.[44] Neither does the opaque way and manner that the Additional Protocol articulated proportionality in relation to excessiveness help in dealing with the issue of determining its value or qualitative dimension.

Consequently, Sloane groups proportionality and collateral damage together, referring to them as a euphemism that seems to be "saying that for any given attack, here is the number of civilians—this is in a very rough sense, of course—and the type and amount of civilian infrastructure that can be destroyed".[45] The vagueness of proportionality makes it liable to exploitation by the weaker party in asymmetric warfare (especially the war on terror), causing Robert Sloane to query as follows:

> if you think about a good-faith commander trying to implement proportionality, can he be expected to systematically expose his forces to risks of the sort that are created by an enemy who is exploiting the rules of warfare, including proportionality?[46]

And without intending "anything pejorative", Sloane argued that the indeterminate nature of proportionality makes "moral philosophers have a field day" in raising or posing such questions as these: "what are the relative values that you assign to military advantage gained, injury to noncombatants, damage to civilian objects? What do you include or exclude in totaling various sums? What is the standard of measurement in time and in space? And to what extent is a military commander obliged to expose his own forces to risk in order to minimize damage to civilians?"[47]

And to drive home his critique of the imprecise character of the contents of proportionality, Sloane submits (invoking W. Hays Park's position on the matter) that "under U.S. law, the concept of proportionality would be void for vagueness".[48] In proportionality, Sloane continues, "each of its key terms is highly subjective, highly open-textured"; so much so that "it requires a weighing of

43 Loc. Cit.
44 Loc. Cit.
45 See Robert D. Sloane (2011), "New Battlefields/Old Laws . . .", p. 370, op. cit.
46 Ibid., p. 372.
47 Ibid., p. 371.
48 Ibid., p. 370.

incommensurables at the highest level of abstraction—military necessity against humanitarian aspirations and human life".[49] The possibility of achieving "a very determinant calculus" in this pursuit, according to Sloane, is a discouraging exercise in futility, even though this is not to imply that "cynicism and nihilism" should be the correct response to this dilemma.[50] The evident impracticability of the realization of distinction and proportionality in the deployment of AWS cannot engender a fatalistic resignation to nihilism; neither would it discourage the full exploration of this impossibility, given the vagueness of the substantive dimension of, especially the principle of proportionality.

In armed conflict, the duty to observe the principles of distinction and proportionality with respect to the civilian population is divided among two parties viz: between the belligerents as a whole on the one hand, and the individual commander on the other. Hence in this division, whereas Article 51 (5) (b) of the Additional Protocol under reference prohibits (an imposition on the belligerents as a whole) "an attack which may be expected to cause incidental loss of civilian life, injury to civilians, damage to civilian objects, or a combination thereof, which would be excessive in relation to the concrete and direct military advantage anticipated"; Article 57 (2) (a) (i–iii) (b–c) of the Protocol outlines the precautionary measures a commander must observe to "avoid or minimize damage, injury, or loss of life", etc. (amongst the civilian population) that is "excessive in relation to the concrete and direct military advantage anticipated".[51] The recurrent issue in the two Articles is excessiveness of action in relation to the concrete and direct military advantage sought or anticipated. So, this raises here again, the issue of the qualitative dimension of proportionality, the assigning of value, as Markus Wagner put it, to what is destroyed pursuant to the attainment of military objectives.[52]

This issue of valuation came to the fore during the Second World War, when, for instance, doubts were expressed "as to whether a ratio of one person executed for every German killed was the absolute maximum tolerable".[53] The issue was attended to very much later down the line in the history of armed conflicts. Concerned with applying or assigning values to the principle of proportionality to concrete situations, a 2000 report to the Prosecutor of the International Criminal Tribunal for the former Yugoslavia (ICTY) observed that "[o]ne cannot easily assess the value of innocent lives as opposed to capturing a particular military objective".[54] The import of this observation in the report is that "proportionality is a concept that is difficult to define in the abstract"; and that "each situation must be evaluated on its own merits at the time of an attack".[55]

49 Loc. Cit.
50 Loc. Cit.
51 See Markus Wagner (2012), "Beyond the Drone Debate . . .", p. 82, op. cit.
52 Loc. Cit.
53 See Frits Kalshoven (1971), *Belligerent Reprisals* . . ., p. 210, op. cit.
54 See Markus Wagner (2012), "Beyond the Drone Debate . . .", p. 82, op. cit.
55 Loc. Cit.

It is "because of the differing variables, which often change over time [that] proportionality determinations are by their very nature subjective".[56] And it is for this very reason of subjectivity that the employment of the AWS will be riddled with contradictions, since they have no capacity for emotions in order to determine proportionality, quantitatively, or qualitatively.[57] Although the proponents of AWS often posit the argument that in replacing humans, there can be a reduction in the high stress levels that lead to *jus in bello* infractions seen in the mistreatment of noncombatants; but the AWS also have their own problems in embodying a lack of compliance with the principles of distinction and proportionality, which themselves can even lead to a higher level of *jus in bello* violations. In the proportionality violations, the opposing argument on the suitability of AWS insists that "emotions, while they can be detrimental [as in stressed up soldiers and marines mistreating noncombatants], play an essential role in human decision-making".[58] This argument insists that:

> [T]he ability to empathize and fully appreciate a situation depends to a large degree on the involvement of human emotions and may play a constructive or even decisive role in determining which of the options available at any moment in time an individual will actually take. Moreover, there is a difference between the admission of having committed what could amount to a war crime *ex post facto*, and the programming of non-human AWS software for which the acceptable *a priori* failure rate is 10 percent. Furthermore, the approach does not resolve the problem of whether AWS software is actually capable of making proportionality assessments.[59]

Thus, the importance of human emotions as opposed to the "decisions" of robotic machines cannot be over-emphasized. In this very issue of seeking to deploy the AWS and at the same time, aspiring to attain proportionality in counter-insurgency, there is a problem; and this problem is principally that "the confluence of geostrategic objectives" and "humanitarian aspirations" creates an undue tension; that is, tension in an effort to "mediate between diametrically opposed impulses—one, military necessity, and the other, humanitarian considerations".[60] As Robert Sloane said, balancing military necessity with humanitarian considerations (even in conventional warfare) within the "highly subjective" and "highly open-textured" demand of proportionality is like trying to weigh the "incommensurables", which is a complicated and complex calculus to attain, especially in the asymmetric warfare on terrorism,[61] and particularly when the AWS is involved.

56 Loc. Cit.
57 Loc. Cit.
58 Ibid., p. 83. Brackets mine.
59 Loc. Cit.
60 See Robert D. Sloane (2011), "New Battlefields/Old Laws . . .", p. 370, op. cit.
61 Ibid., pp. 370–371.

The attainment of proportionality (achieving a determinant calculus or balancing military necessity with humanitarian considerations) with the application of AWS cannot be possible because, lacking in a precisely determined substance (both quantitatively and qualitatively), proportionality, as Sloane insisted, can only be attained by approximation, an approximation that is obtained through "the reasonable person standard . . . the extent that the reasonable military commander—and this was reinforced by Carla del Ponte's report on the Kosovo operation and so on—is supposed to take into account the various factors and decide what would be proportional".[62] As something that can only be achieved through the mediation of human emotions (not something mechanically achievable by robotic machines, the AWS), Robert Sloane, borrowing what Eyal Benvenisti called "dyadic reciprocity",[63] summed up that "proportionality worked, to the extent that it did work, because of the dynamic" of what I would rather prefer to ascribe to the fear of belligerent reprisals[64] instead of the so-called dyadic reciprocity.

It is true, as Slone affirmed, that "the claim and response nature of warfare essentially resolves most of these subjectivities of the proportionality formulation on the battlefield".[65] Apart from the use of conventional weapons in the pursuit of proportionality, belligerent reprisals can also guarantee the belligerents the deployment and counter-deployment of AWS if this highly probable robotic weapon is in the possession of the parties to the conflict. But by and by, two possible scenarios exist in the attainment or enforcement of proportionality in the age of AWS, and this is implicit in Robert Sloane's submission: (1) if one force is overwhelmingly superior to the other, where the "conventional [or even unconventional] determinants of military force are very much in favour of one side—things like technology, manpower, training, and so forth—the stronger party can afford, so to speak, to adhere very strictly to proportionality"; and (2) when there are belligerents of roughly equal strength, and in that case, over the course of time, there's a battlefield dynamic of reciprocity and retaliation, claim and response, that eventually creates a baseline that both parties will abide by because they know, at least traditionally, that reprisals could follow violations.[66]

62 Ibid., p. 371.

63 Instead of reciprocity, this should rather be called reprisals because unlike reciprocity that takes place in an atmosphere of amity and friendliness, reprisals take place in an environment of hostilities that proportionality is expected of the parties; see Fred Aja Agwu (2010), "Reciprocity and its Implications in International Relations", in Osita C. Eze (2010, ed.); *Reciprocity in International Relations: Nigeria's Foreign Policy in Retrospect*, Lagos, Nigerian Institute of International Affairs, pp. 27–35.

64 See Fred Aja Agwu (2005), *United Nations System, State Practice and the Jurisprudence of the Use of Force* . . ., pp. 11–16, op. cit.

65 See Robert D. Sloane (2011), "New Battlefields/Old Laws . . .", p. 371, op. cit.

66 Loc. Cit.

This is belligerent reprisals simplicita as the ultimate guarantor of the obligation to proportionality. This fear of belligerent reprisals can only be entertained by humans with emotional impulses, not the AWS.

Accountability

But this revolutionary development of armed robotic drones will certainly do nothing but usher in an era in which the deployment of this weapon would witness some rampant incidences of mass murder. This is owing to the fact that faced with a "battlespace" as opposed to a conventional battlefield or frontline), an automated or robotic machine, devoid as it were, of an emotional capacity to effectuate discriminatory attacks; that is, the capacity to show discrimination between lawful targets and innocent civilians, especially in the so-called signature strikes, will simply orchestrate an unbridled orgy of mass murder. In the light of this impending advent of the "seek-and-destroy" drones that are capable of making autonomous life-or-death decisions, and being the imminent future of the armed drones technology that will take control of the "battlespaces" rather than the battlefields, queries have been raised as to who will be accountable for the mass murder or intolerable collateral damage when crucial decisions are left to the computer?[67]

Another query concerns the question of how the chain of accountability can be assessed in relation to individuals' criminal responsibility vis-à-vis state responsibility. Who, between the army commander, the political leader, the manufacturer of the drone, the developer that programmed the drone, and the CIA drone operator, for instance, would be liable for the intolerable casualties or collateral damage?[68] As it were, accountability can only be possible in an atmosphere of transparency; that is, if the facts are made available, for in the absence of the sacred facts, neither the public nor the press, nor even the international community can "conclusively judge the legality and necessity of such actions".[69] Although in the practical term of judicial accountability, the resolution of the question of who should be held accountable for violations is ultimately determined by the law courts wherever the unfortunate incident arises; but in juridical terms, and since "the programming of the drone can be perceived as human involvement" or input,[70] little doubt exists that accountability will be all-embracing or inclusive of different parties, depending on the circumstances.

Thus, as far as accountability is concerned, a wide range of issues must be involved, ranging from command responsibility, to superior orders; and

67 See Geert-Jan Alexander Knoops (2012), "Legal, Political and Ethical Dimensions of Drone Warfare . . .", p. 699, op. cit.

68 Ibid., p. 719.

69 See Ahmad Nazir Warraich (2013), "The Use of Drones . . .", p. 77, op. cit.

70 See Geert-Jan Alexander Knoops (2012), "Legal, Political and Ethical Dimensions of Drone Warfare . . .", p. 719, op. cit.

logically, all those that programmed the machine to automatically operate, make autonomous decisions or behave in certain ways without any form of human intervention must be involved. This is the point that Markus Wagner made in the declaration that a number of individuals may be considered to incur responsibility for AWS, beginning with the programmer, the officer responsible for ascertaining whether a new weapon fulfills the requirements of Article 36 of Additional Protocol I, and the commanding officer at various levels of the decision-making process.[71]

The Article 36 (on new weapons) of the Additional Protocol under reference has been quoted earlier in this book under the rubric of the jurisprudence of new and unregulated weapons.

71 See Markus Wagner (2012), "Beyond the Drone Debate . . .", p. 83, op. cit.

13 Globalization, Postmodernism, and the WoT

Prefatory Remarks

Primarily anchored on globalization, this chapter is an application of the international political economy approach to the understanding of international terrorism. Globalization exerts a two-pronged impact on the war on terror. The first, which has been alluded to earlier, is in the creation of cyberspace as a platform that terrorists utilize to transcend their constraint in the loss of physical territory. The second, which this chapter explores, is the socio-economic contradictions inherent in the mismanagement of globalization, contradictions that can lead to conflict or mass poverty, the former leading to the refugee scourge while the latter leads to migration.

Although there is a socio-psychological dimension to terrorism—the so-called millenarian terrorism that arises more from radicalism, radicalization and its violent manifestation in Islamist jihad[1]—globalization provides a broad spectrum for the appreciation of the economic nexus (dialectical materialism) in people's propensity for terrorism,[2] both millenarian and secular; for much of the predisposing factors for terrorism are inherent in failed socio-economic and political expectations (be it legitimate or prebendal) as was the case in the failed prebendal expectation that partly led to the rise of the Boko Haram in Nigeria.[3] Globalization may have been a massive success in terms of its creation of global interconnectivity, the conquest of distance and the dominance of capitalism; but it has failed the low income and middle class in the developed nations, the same way it has in the developing and the underdeveloped, as well as caused the destruction of the viability of the state in the latter.

In the developing and the underdeveloped nations, globalization has torpedoed the prospect of socio-economic and political development because it brought about a "wave of economic dislocation"; particularly because these nations were

1 See Fred Aja Agwu (2009), *National Interest, International Law* . . ., p. 126, note 146, op. cit; see also Fred Aja Agwu (2013), *Themes and Perspectives* . . ., pp. 262–263, op. cit.

2 See Fred Aja Agwu (2013), *Themes and Perspectives* . . ., pp. 263–281.

3 See Animasawun Gbemisola Abdul-Jelil (2016), "Agential and Structural Explanations of Radical Islamism in Northern Nigeria in the Fourth Republic . . ., op. cit.

prematurely integrated into the global capitalist system. Thus, globalization has virtually reduced them to failed states by destroying in them the Almond and Powell's "political structure and political culture", the capacity to function effectively as political systems, especially in terms of their capacity for "capabilities, conversion processes, and system maintenance and adaptation functions".[4] In fact, this is more pronounced wherever these nations lose the Almond and Powell "six categories of the conversion processes: interest articulation, interest aggregation, rule making, rule application, rule adjudication, and communication".[5]

It is for reasons of failed expectations from globalization that, in the United States, most people tend to frame "every economic issue as a struggle between a deserving hardworking white middle class and undeserving minorities", be they minorities in the United States itself or immigrants and refugees across the globe.[6] It is also for this same reason of failed expectations from globalization that the struggle of these minorities tends to be against "the middle-aged white man who from the outside may seem like he's got all the advantages, but who's seen his world upended by economic, cultural, and technological change" that globalization has intensified.[7] Hence, in the United States, the economy evidently does not work for all; as the working/middle class is "convinced that the game is fixed against them", thus, constituting "a recipe for more cynicism and polarization in our politics".[8]

Globalization is perceived as nothing but the "ruthless demands of capitalism that they've foisted on the rest of the world".[9] This has made resentment against it a global one, with the 2016 backlash against it expressed in Brexit, the election of Trump, and the rise of ultra-nationalist political parties in many European countries—all of which had been foretold by the late 2011 and early 2012 "occupy" movement that flared in Europe, the United States, Asia, and the Middle East.[10] In fact, owing to its massive debts, Greece had put up with street protests;[11] with Germany unable to help Greece and the entire Europe because Angela Merkel was "being squeezed on all sides".[12] In the United States,

4 See Claude Ake (1979), *Social Science as Imperialism: The Theory of Political Development*, Second Edition, Ibadan, Ibadan University Press, pp. 2, 3.
5 Ibid., p. 3.
6 See "Full Text of President Obama's Farewell Speech" in Chicago on January 10, 2017, available at www.wsj.com/amp/articles/BL-WB-67205?responsive=y (last visited on January 11, 2017), op. cit.
7 Loc. Cit.
8 Loc. Cit.
9 See Rana Foroohar in "Firing Bankers for Fun and Profit: Wall Street Escaped the Past Three Years of Layoffs; the Pink Slips Are Arriving at Last", *Time* (New York), August 29, 2011, p. 14.
10 Loc. Cit.
11 See Roya Wolverson in "Smoke and Mirrors: As Greece Copes with Street Protests, the Day of Reckoning for Its Massive Debts Is Drawing Near", *Time* (New York), July 4, 2011, pp. 20–23.
12 See Michael Schuman in "Why Germany Can't Save Europe, Much Less the World", *Time* (New York), October 3, 2011, pp. 28–31.

the Occupy Wall Street protests began in "lower Manhattan in September, with Occupiers adopting the slogan: we are the 99%"; this was in addition to the allied movements that cropped up nationwide in the same United States.[13] In the United Kingdom, an outbreak of arson, looting, and lawlessness had caught its leaders by surprise.[14]

In Rome, there were also protests against painful austerity measures.[15] And, of course, there were the "occupy" protests in the Arab world where a 26-year-old Tunisian street vendor, Mohammed Bouazizi, became the final straw that ignited the Arab Spring.[16] These "occupy" protests against extreme capitalism was also witnessed in Nigeria when the government tried to deregulate the downstream sector of the petroleum industry by attempting to remove the so-called fuel subsidy.[17] Thus, all over the world, from New York, through Toronto (Canada) to South America (Chile), Europe, Eurasia (Russia), Middle East (Israel, the Arab Spring), and Asia (China, Burma, India), etc., "the protest network" against extreme capitalism or the manifestation in globalization of what Rana Foroohar[18] described as "supercapitalism" spread like wild fire.[19]

Cynicism gives way to grievances; and grievances are amongst the oldest factors in people's propensity for radicalization, revolt, terrorism, and even political violence.[20] Owing to the marginalization created by globalization, "deviance" has held sway in poor and marginalized nations, regions, ethnic groups, and religions, with these discontented mocking and rejecting with "deviance"—terrorism—against those perceived as oppressors, mobilizing to reject the values and culture of the perceived oppressors.[21] The cynicism and polarization that globalization engendered were seismic enough to contribute to the election of President Donald Trump for whom anti-globalization and protectionism were at the heart of public policy; causing an undoubtedly flummoxed out-going President Obama to enjoin

13 See Kurt Anderson in "2011 Person of the Year: The Protester", *Time* (New York), December 26, 2011–January 2, 2012, p. 65, 68.

14 See Nathan Thornburgh in "London's Long Burn", *Time* (New York), August 22, 2011, pp. 16–19; see also Rana Foroohar in "The End of Europe: Its Economic Union Is Unraveling, London Is Ablaze, and the Continent's Once Dependable Trading Partner, the US, Is too Feeble to Save the Day or the Euro; Say Goodbye to the Old Order", *Time* (New York), August 22, 2011, pp. 21–25.

15 See Stephan Faris in "Irked by Perks: Italians Are Growing Tired of Picking up the Check for Their Pampered Politicians", *Time* (New York), September 26, 2011, p. 40.

16 See Kurt Anderson in "2011 Person of the Year: The Protester", p. 22, op. cit.

17 See Ochereome Nnanna in "Hungry Youths Have Turned Angry", *Vanguard* (Lagos), Monday, January 6, 2017, p. 34.

18 See Rana Foroohar in "Firing Bankers for Fun and Profit: Wall Street Escaped the Past Three Years of Layoffs; the Pink Slips Are Arriving at Last", p. 14, op. cit.

19 See Kurt Anderson in "2011 Person of the Year: The Protester", pp. 68–69, op. cit.

20 See Asta Maskaliunaite (2015), "Exploring the Theories of Radicalization" . . ., p. 19, op. cit.

21 See The thought of Professor Badie, Director of the International Relations Programme at Political Sciences School of Paris as analyzed by Tobia Princewill in "Humiliation in African Context", p. 40, op. cit.

the reiteration of faith in democracy because "democracy does not require uniformity", only "a basic sense of solidarity"—more so because "for all our outward differences, we are all in this together; that we rise or fall as one".[22]

In the institutions of globalization, the poor in both the center and the periphery get a short-shrift owing to insensitivity to the imperative of post-modernism—an attitudinal framework that tolerates differences, an era in which nations cohere and tolerate one another because they recognize that frames of reference are relative and, thus, determine "individual and societal perceptions of reality".[23] It is because of this insensitivity to the poor and the demands of the postmodernist culture that many in the developed nations of North America and Western Europe retreated from globalization into protectionism and nationalism, thereby sounding a *Nunc Dimitties* on the kind of global coalescence that the world needs to defeat international terrorism.

The relationship between terrorism and globalization inheres in the fact that being an extreme manifestation of capitalism—a global super capitalist formation (or "supercapitalism") that has been foisted on the rest of the world, not just by financial services but also by the "real economy"; a phenomenon that is itself a testament to the fact that capital is superior to labour[24]—globalization has been grossly mismanaged, thus, triggering mass pauperization, global economic misery, ultra-nationalism and conflicts around the world. The cumulative result has been migration and refugee flows (including the environmental or climate change refugees). The migration and refugee flows have been more pronounced from the Middle East; and have been largely blamed for the dispersal of terrorists.[25]

Mass pauperization, migration, and the flow of refugees arising from climate change and conflicts all cumulatively provide the context in which the extremely poor from various parts of the world compete for survival against one another at the level of the global economy.[26] This is one of the primary triggers of xenophobia. It is worse when the manipulations by ultra-right ideologues add the scare of terrorism, both real and imagined. Meanwhile, populism and xenophobia weaken

22 See "Full Text of President Obama's Farewell Speech" in Chicago on January 10, 2017, available at www.wsj.com/amp/articles/BL-WB-67205?responsive=y (last visited on January 11, 2017), op. cit.

23 See George Washington (2002), "Staffing the Post Modern Army", *Military Review*, No. 6, November–December, p. 28.

24 Whereas capital is waxing strong and making waves across borders, either as "casino capitalism" (see Fred Aja Agwu (2009), *National Interest, International Law* . . ., pp. 515–519, op. cit.) or in the real economy, labour is increasingly impoverished everywhere with improved technology and automation, leading to loss of jobs, especially by workers with skills that cannot be retooled because they are not compliant with extant demands in the labour markets; see also Rana Foroohar in "Firing Bankers for Fun and Profit: Wall Street Escaped the Past Three Years of Layoffs; the Pink Slips Are Arriving at Last", p. 14, op. cit.

25 See Joe Klein in "The Ideological Challenge at the Core of Donald Trump's Radical Presidency", *Time* (New York), February 6, 2017, p. 12.

26 See Margaret C. Lee (2014), *Africa's World Trade: Informal Economies and Globalization from Below*, London, Zed Books, p. 141.

support for the very multilateral frameworks that would otherwise enable a successful confrontation of the terrorism monster.

Globalization: A Double-Edge Sword

One of the paradoxes in the reality of globalization is that it is a highly contested terrain that functions, according to Christine Lagarde of the IMF, as a double-edge sword; thus, engendering a groundswell of distrust, nationally and internationally.[27] Globalization is intrinsically dictatorial and tyrannical.[28] Emblematic of the dictatorship of globalization is the insistence by its neo-liberal protagonists (those that A. H. Snow would characterize as forces of "stand pat-ism and vested interests"[29]) "that markets are always efficient";[30] thus, implicitly pushing the worrisome unilineal/teleological understanding of globalization that intrinsically advances the improbable suggestion that the forces of implacable ethnocentrism and neo-liberalism, including the homogenization and subjection of all cultures by the West, be accepted as catechism.

But despite "all its accomplishments", globalization, according to Michael Hayden, has "jammed together the good and the bad and the weak and the strong in ways that had never been experienced before".[31] Defined in historical context, and as a matter of objective or scientific reality, globalization reflects the situation in which the world is progressively "molded into a shared social space by economic and technological forces".[32] In addition to being a phenomenon that reduces the world into a "shared social space", globalization is also practically the closer integration of the countries and peoples of the world which has been brought about by the enormous reduction of costs of transportation and communication, and the breaking down of artificial boundaries to the flow of goods, services, capital, knowledge, and (to a lesser extent) people across borders.[33]

The paradox in the entire world being molded into "a shared social space" by globalization is that "developments in one region of the world could have profound consequences for the life chances of individuals and communities on the other side of the globe"; while at the same time globalization is also

27 See Chijoke Nelson in "Globalization Is Double-Edge Sword—IMF Admits", *The Guardian* (Lagos), Wednesday, September 21, 2016, p. 26.
28 See Fred Aja Agwu (2016), *Nations among Nations*. . ., pp. 337–437, op. cit.
29 See A. H. Snow in Fred Aja Agwu (2005), *United Nations System, State Practice and the Jurisprudence of the Use of Force* . . ., p. 34, op. cit.
30 See Joseph Stiglitz in "Questions", *Time* (New York), August 29, 2016, p. 48.
31 See Michael V. Hayden (2016), *Playing to the Edge* . . ., p. 132, op. cit.
32 See Henry J. Steiner and Philip Alston (2000), *International Human Rights in Context, Law, Politics, Moral: Text and Materials*, Second Edition, Oxford, Oxford University Press, p. 1307.
33 See Joseph E. Stiglitz (2003, 2002), *Globalization and Its Discontents*, New York and London, W. W. Norton & Company, p. 9.

"associated with a sense of political fatalism and chronic insecurity because the sheer scale of contemporary social and economic change appears to outstrip the capacity of national governments or citizens to control, contest or resist that change".[34] To the extent that globalization is about the shrinking of the world into a shared social space by dint of the human ingenuity that has enabled faster means of transportation and communication, it is a fait-accompli; but as an economic and security force, globalization can be a nightmare for the vulnerable. Insecurity and economic and financial liberalization that arise from globalization can bring misery, especially to the underdeveloped and developing nations, making globalization an avoidable human policy of imposition that has aroused a world of terrorists.

Even where globalization is not tyrannical and negative and is, thus, admissive of some wholesome aspects,[35] the fact remains that, being Janus-faced, in the same way that it can make people take advantage of medicine or cures available for diseases elsewhere in the world that it can also enable the spread of epidemics, diseases, and terrorism.[36] This is why globalization is not just a historical, objective, or scientific phenomenon, but also an ironical and paradoxical phenomenon that is deeply capable of fostering "convergence and fragmentation".[37] Today, in the face of globalization, Syria and most of the Middle East region have become a haven or hotbed of terrorist attacks because the "Responsibility to Protect" has failed or succumbed to the national interest; in which "a few powerful nations" thwart "well-meaning efforts and chose to look the other way while . . . pogrom"[38] takes place or nations fail in many other ways and give haven to terrorists.

Despite the conception of globalization by the globalist as something that is capable of delivering an implicit change in economic growth and cultural formations,[39] an opposing radical assessment denounces it as viscerally capitalist, a capitalist imperialism, an epitome of "capitalist's chaos" (characterized by core capitalist values like deregulation, structural adjustment, denationalization, global interdependence, integration into the global market, neo-liberal, etc.), the "deification of liberal ideology", and a "new mercantilism based on relentless pursuit of strategic advantage, conquest, domination, exploitation, inequity, disorder and crisis".[40] Thus, globalization cannot but be ideological and double-faced; and as Jeffrey Norwitz pointed out, "globalization and interconnectedness . . . fuel

34 See Henry J. Steiner and Philip Alston (2000), *International Human Rights in Context* . . ., p. 1307. Brackets mine.
35 See Joseph E. Stiglitz (2006), *Making Globalization Work*, London, Penguin Books, p. 10.
36 Ibid., p. 280.
37 See Dele Seteolu (2004), "Globalization: Challenges for the State in Africa", *Nigerian Forum*, Vol. 25, Nos. 1–2, January–February, p. 5; see also Fred Aja Agwu (2016), *Nations among Nations* . . .; pp. 337–372, op. cit.
38 See Richard Bagudu (2007), *Judging Annan*, Bloomington, IN, AuthorHouse, pp. 7, 8.
39 See Dele Seteolu (2004), "Globalization . . .", p. 6, op. cit.
40 Loc. Cit.

discontent in some regions while dissuading disputes in others".[41] The discontented is part of those that that engage in the extremism that sometimes culminate in terrorist activities.

Globalization and Terrorism: Between Connectedness and Disconnectedness

> Whether we realize it or not, we are all—right now—standing present at the creation of a new international security order. You might think that the global war on terrorism is nothing more than the twisted creation of a warmongering Bush Administration, but you would be wrong. The global conflict between the forces of connectedness and disconnectedness is here and it is not going away anytime soon. Either America steps up to the challenge of defining this new global security rule set, or we will see those rules established by people who dream of a very different tomorrow.
>
> (Thomas P.M. Barnett)[42]

The epigram speaks to the contribution of the contrasting forces of globalization—"the forces of connectedness and disconnectedness"—to the creation of terrorism and some of the impediments in the fight against it. It is an affirmation of the fact that terrorism is caused by a combination of factors while the response to it transcends any conception of the war against it as "the twisted creation of a warmongering Bush Administration". Here, Thomas Barnett places a heavy responsibility on the United States to step up its efforts in the war on terror, face the challenge, not just as the leading military power of the moment, but also a leading neo-liberal actor that can make the difference by redefining the dynamics of globalization in a way that the phenomenon will be more inclusive. At a horizontal level, globalization will work for all nations and individuals in the developed, the developing, and the underdeveloped nations; but vertically, it will only work for the privileged in all spheres.

It is for this reason that, causatively, terrorism is not so much about the "clash of civilization" and the millenarian conviction as it is about the fact that some people have developed a sense of victimhood and hurt owing to marginalization, oppression, and dispossession by the forces of globalization. It is in the light of this (and apart from the practitioners of "sacred terror") that it is admissible that terrorists have "specific grievances";[43] here, grievances against the "polluting forces of globalization". It is also for this reason that not many people can be flummoxed by the groundswell of opposition against globalization, which has

41 See Jeffrey H. Norwitz (2009), "Introduction", in Jeffrey H. Norwitz (2009, ed.); *Pirates, Terrorists, and Warlords . . .*, p. 12, op. cit.

42 See Thomas P. M. Barnett (2004), *The Pentagon's New Map . . .*, pp. 45–46, op. cit.

43 Ibid., p. 84.

surged in the Western world in particular.[44] In the West, the down-trodden in particular reject the interconnectedness of globalization and implicitly angle for disconnectedness because globalization affects their lives in some negative ways, including loss of jobs and the invasion of their countries by immigrants.

When liberty is taken in the classification of terrorists, they would include all the extreme nationalists that distaste immigrants and harbour reservations against the state for allowing immigrants; the rank of terrorists can also expand and probably be inclusive of the xenophobes and other right-wing or secular terrorists that, goaded by their "righteous indignation", do not brook any challenge to their "self-righteous" and "homicidal resolutions" in challenging the status quo; and this is obtained from their ideological perception of reality, a perception that is often tainted by zealotry and irredentism.[45] These extreme nationalists (be it in the Middle East or the United States) may be right or wrong, but it is probably within this context of their angst that the former U.S. President Bill Clinton was credited with saying that "most terrorists were misunderstood, had legitimate grievances, and could be appeased".[46] These rabid nationalists employ terrorist tactics in reaction to the "pollution" of globalization and perpetrate heinous terrorists acts comparable to the conducts of the so-called sacred terrorists—the organized groups like the al-Qaeda that reject foreign forces on Arab soil.

In the United States and Europe, many rabid nationalists have latched on to the widening objection to migration to terrorize the general populace, ranging from Anders Brevik of Norway, Tim McVeigh of the infamous Oklahoma bombing in the United States, to some proponents of Brexit.[47] Illustrative of this terrorism was the right-wing white extremist, the 52-year-old Thomas Mair, a white supremacist who assassinated the young British Parliamentarian, Jo Cox, on Thursday, June 16, 2016 in her constituency in broad day light.[48] But unlike the ultra-nationalists, the millenarian terrorists are not amenable to rational political negotiations and appeasement as they see suicide as victory and go for complete destruction of lives and property. In the Middle East, the genre of terrorists that is amenable to appeasement is long gone in the pre-al-Qaeda and ISIS era. Since the al-Qaeda (and later the ISIS) emerged, negotiations (except for ransom payment in isolated cases for freeing hostages) are no longer an option in solving the terrorism plague.

44 In her programme on CNN, *Amanpour*, Christiane Amanpour was of the view that people were beginning to be flummoxed by the groundswell of opposition against globalization. This programme was aired live at the United Nations headquarters in New York and was monitored in Lagos (Nigeria) on September 21, 2016, at 7pm local time.

45 Wole Soyinka, cited in Fred Aja Agwu (2013), *Themes and Perspectives* . . ., pp. 240–241, op. cit.

46 See Robert "Buzz" Patterson (2003), *Dereliction of Duty* . . ., p. 131, op. cit.

47 See Charlotte McDonald- Gibson in "EU Might Not Be So Bad: After Britain's Vote to Leave the European Union, the Continent's Leaders Are Debating Whether It's Wise to Beat up on Their Departing Partners", *Newsweek*, August 5, 2016, p. 14.

48 See Phil Noble in Big Shots, "England: Brexit Murder", *Newsweek*, July 1, 2016, p. 6; see also Justin Forsyth in "Jo Cox: British Lawmaker", *Time* (New York), July 4, 2016, p. 11.

Is Globalization Globalizing Terrorism Threats and Xenophobia?

It is an objective fact that since the then existing European powers agreed to end the 30-year war by recognizing the sovereignty of one another in the Westphalia treaty of 1648,[49] several factors had been inundating the phenomenon of state sovereignty, some of which include the emergent vertical binding nature of some rules of international law.[50] But none had challenged the Westphalian sovereign state so hard in recent times more than globalization and the evolution of the "European state"—the state in Europe as known by Westphalia standards being threatened by the European Union through the process of sustained economic, monetary and, eventually, political integration. However, not many ordinary Europeans were as enthusiastic as the "Eurocrats" (that set of bureaucrats committed to carrying the integration project to its logical end"[51]) in the consummation of the European Union integration project.

The reason for the decision of some people to reject the European Union project as put forward by the "Eurocrats" is the fear of globalization. As the IMF boss, Christine Lagarde, reportedly said in a lecture at the International Bar Association Conference in Washington D.C. entitled "Mending the Trust Divide", although globalization was premised on mutual benefit, it has now unfortunately eventually solidified the foundation of global inequality, implicitly leading to a groundswell of distrust.[52] It was because of the factor of capitalist manipulations that the ordinary people in many industrialized (not just the European nations) have grown very fearful of globalization, culminating in what the IMF boss, Christine Lagarde, referred to as the "growing backlash against globalization",[53] a growing backlash that was orchestrated by the fact that globalization had made them scapegoats, afflicting them with poverty, privation, and misery, all of which had heightened their sense of xenophobia.[54]

Of course, the xenophobia was partly as a result of the economic and security concerns that had manifested as real objective issues in the EU countries and the United States (fueling distrust and misplaced aggression against immigrants): including the Euro crisis, the reasons of which have been partly described by Joseph Stiglitz to be a lack of the requisite political institutions to support a single currency.[55]

49 See the argument by Jibrin Ibrahim in "Brexit, Eurocrats, Europeans and others", *Daily Trust* (Abuja), Monday, June 27, 2016, p. 68; see also Fred Aja Agwu (2016), *Nations among Nations*. . ., pp. 481–486, op. cit.

50 See Fred Aja Agwu (2009), *National Interest, International Law* . . ., p. 106, op. cit.

51 See Jibrin Ibrahim in "Brexit, Eurocrats, Europeans and others", p. 68, op. cit.

52 Report on the conference by Chijoke Nelson in "Globalization Is Double-Edge Sword—IMF Admits", p. 26.

53 Loc. Cit.

54 See Jibrin Ibrahim in "Brexit, Eurocrats, Europeans and others", p. 68, op. cit.

55 See Joseph Stiglitz talking about his new book, *The Euro*, in "Questions", *Time* (New York), August 29, 2016, p. 48.

The pressure on globalization has invariably confirmed the Marxists' thinking that international organizations are a mere "superstructural froth on bourgeois society",[56] in which the nation-state and bureaucrats (like the Eurocrats) place more emphasis on vertical relations in international relations, rather than on the horizontal or "transnational relations"—relations between the proletarians or ordinary people of all countries.[57] Meanwhile, an emphasis on transnational rather than international relations will mean that class instead of state relations will be accentuated with a view to lifting the oppressed from poverty and misery.[58] But, as some have argued, international relations (as opposed to just mere transnational relations) must thrive because of a number of supernational, supranational, or transnational agendas like "climate change, pandemics, terrorism, organized crime, and cyber crime".[59]

But globalization has not help matters because, as Christine Lagarde noted, for example, the syndrome of "the shift in global production which it brought meant job losses or environmental damage for millions of people".[60] In addition to conflicts, the economic pressure is part of the explosion that causes the dispersal of people; either as migrants in search of greener pastures, or as refugees fleeing from conflicts. One of the greatest backlashes against globalization in this regard is not just the fear by the impoverished citizens of many industrialized nations that immigrants are coming to take their jobs, but also that these immigrants are harbingers of terrorism. Hence, in many of these countries in North America and Western Europe, migration has become extremely polarizing.[61] In the United States, the Republican Presidential candidate, Donald Trump, and his campaigners whipped up a groundswell of nationalist sentiment in opposition against immigrants and the Syrian refugees in particular, so much so that his eldest son likened the Syrian refugees to poisoned Skittles.[62] As a matter of fact, "Donald Trump Jr. set out to illustrate what he saw as the danger of letting Syrian refugees into the United States" when he queried in his twitter handle that if he had a bowl of Skittles and says that just three pieces would harm, would anybody

56 See Clive Archer (1983), *International Organizations*, London, George Allen & Unwin, p. 104.

57 Ibid., p. 106.

58 Loc. Cit.

59 See Joseph S. Nye, Jr. (2015), *Is American Century Over?*, Malden, MA, USA, Polity Press, p. 68.

60 See Chijoke Nelson in "Globalization Is Double-Edge Sword—IMF Admits", p. 26, op. cit.

61 Queen Rania of Jordan and Christiane Amanpour also made this point in the CNN programme, *Amanpour*, monitored in Lagos (Nigeria) on Wednesday, September 21, 2016, at 8pm local time.

62 See Sean Sullivan in "Donald Trump Jr. Sparks Outrage after Likening Syrian Refugees to Poisoned Skittles", available at www.chicagotribune.com/news/nationworld/politics/ct-donald-trump-jr-skittles-refugees-20160920-story.html (last visited on Wednesday, September 21, 2016); see also Karl Vick in "What Terrorists Acting Alone Says about the Loyalty of U.S. Muslims", p. 8, op. cit.

take a handful?[63] This anxiety is heightened because increased immigration into the United States had, for instance, "resulted in the influx of terrorists who mixed with genuine refugees".[64]

In Germany, the German Chancellor, Angela Merkel, paid dearly in the polls for her open-minded embrace of migrants and refugees in particular as her Christian Democratic Party was bitterly trounced in Berlin state elections.[65] Apparently because of the fear of migration and refugees, in addition to terrorist and other security threats, there was an epidemic of border walls/barriers around many countries of the world in 2016 alone; while some of these walls were at the proposal stage, the building of others had already commenced by that year. Like Donald Trump who, in reaction to globalization and the inherent angst against human migration, proposed building a wall (when elected President) on the United States' southern border with Mexico and have the latter pay for it,[66] the United Kingdom also "said Sept. 6 [2016] that it would fund a wall in the French port of Calais to keep out migrants".[67]

Other border walls/barriers "in the works around the world" against migrants in obvious negation of the spirit and letter of globalization are illustrated by the meeting on September 9, 2016 between the Prime Minister of Malaysia (Najib Razak) and his Thai counterpart where the duo discussed "building a wall along the border dividing their countries in an attempt to control trans-national crime"; the announcement by Israeli officials on September 7, 2016 "that they had begun building an underground wall along the 37-mile Gaza border . . . intended to thwart Hamas militants who have used tunnels to launch attacks"; the Hungarian Prime Minister Viktor Orban's statement on August 26, 2016 "that Hungary would build 'a more massive' structure on its border with Serbia . . . [to] reinforce an existing razor-wire fence, which was built to reduce the flow of migrants"; the Scandinavian country of Norway's announcement on August 24, 2016 "that it was erecting a 660-ft steel fence at its northern Skorskog border point with Russia to deter migrants from entering the country via the Arctic Circle".[68]

63 Sean Sullivan in "Donald Trump Jr. Sparks Outrage after Likening Syrian Refugees to Poisoned Skittles", available at www.chicagotribune.com/news/nationworld/politics/ct-donald-trump-jr-skittles-refugees-20160920-story.html (last visited on Wednesday, September 21, 2016), op. cit.

64 See J. Boima Rogers in "Nationalism Trumps Liberalism and Globalization", *The Guardian* (Lagos), Friday, December 2, 2016, p. 16.

65 See Anton Troianovski in "Merkel Says Germany Won't Stop Accepting Refugees, Muslims: Chancellor Disappointed by Her Party's Losses in Berlin State Election", available at www.wsj.com/articles/merkel-says-germany-wont-stop-accepting-refugees-muslims-1474288469 (last visited on Tuesday, September 20, 2016); see also "Merkel Admits Migrants Policy Mistakes", *The Nation* (Lagos), Tuesday, September 20, 2016, p. 45.

66 See Fred Aja Agwu (2016), *Nations among Nations* . . ., p. 433, op. cit.

67 See Tara John in "Barriers at the Borders", *Time* (New York), September 26, 2016, p. 8. Parentheses mine.

68 Ibid., p. 8.

There was also the resumption in March 2016 of the "construction of a 435-mile wall on Kenya's northeastern border with Somalia", which "authorities want to keep out al-Shabab militants who have launched deadly terrorist attacks in Kenya"; and the Ukrainian border with Russia where Ukraine began building a wall in 2014 "in an attempt to stem alleged flows of aid for pro-Russia forces in Ukraine", a wall less than 10% completed as of August 2015.[69] Thus, migration became thoroughly demonized because of the fear that it was spreading security and economic problems; and this triggered the pervasive worry and development of hard borders in many countries in reaction to the perceived "unfairness of immigration"[70] in their socio-economic lives and security.

Meanwhile, the privileged members of the international community do not seem to display a postmodern attitude or an even handedness in their response to the globalization of terrorism that the refugee flows orchestrate. For instance, whereas "the EU signed a multibillion-dollar deal with Turkey to stem the flow of refugees going to Europe", the East African nation of Kenya was clearly abandoned in the lurch with its refugee camp of Dadaab, a refugee complex that was set up by the United Nations High Commission for Refugees (UNHCR) in late 1991 and had over a quarter of a century played host to "hundreds of thousands of mostly Somali refugees and asylum seekers, effectively becoming one of Kenya's largest cities in which more people lived than in Newark, New Jersey (United States), all ona shoestring budget.[71]

After in 2015, "the UNHCR asked donors for $500 million for refugee programmes in Kenya and Somalia", "about $110 million was subsequently pledged, and only about $7.2 million" eventually came through, amounting to "only 1.4 percent of what was requested".[72] Thus, in the wake of the Dadaab refugee camp not getting the attention it required, and in addition to the fact that after "the [September] 2013 Westgate shopping mall siege that left more than 60 dead" and the April 2015 gunmen attack at Garissa University that left some 148 people dead,[73] the Kenyan authorities reckoned that the camp had become a breeding ground for terrorists (a hub for the militant al-Shabab—an al-Qaeda affiliate).[74] And after an apparent failed negotiated timeline with the United Nations for the reduction of Dadaab's population for more effective security,[75] they (the authorities in Nairobi) threatened to close it down and send the entire refugees back to Somalia in mass, irrespective of the potential dangers—rural Somalia still heavily infested with the al-Shabab, with all the

69 Ibid., pp. 8–9.

70 See Nana Adu Ampofo in "Brexit and the Black Atlantic", *New African*, July 2016, p. 6, op. cit.

71 See Krista Mahr in "Lost Refuge: Kenya Has Hosted Hundreds of Thousands of Refugees in the Past Two Decades. Now It Wants Them Out", *Newsweek*, August 5, 2016, p. 26.

72 Ibid., p. 27.

73 Ibid., p. 26. Brackets mine.

74 Loc. Cit.

75 Loc. Cit.

attendant risks of recruiting these returnees into its ranks and heightening the instability and insecurity in Somalia.[76]

Is Postmodernism an Antidote to Globalization and Terrorism?

It is in the character of the conservative advocates of globalization to flaunt its supposed gains in utter insensitivity to the inherent global complexities of the world, thus provoking the populist or anti-globalization forces (in both the state and non-state actors) that resist them. It was Snow, in his theory of war that asserts that war (just like an act of terrorism) is "a process of evolution" that is caused when the progressive movement of human molecules towards some form of betterment is unduly held back by forces of "stand pat-ism and vested interests".[77] This analogy can be applied in the struggle between the forces of globalization and the forces against globalization. In the contestations between the two forces, the progressives are presumably the populist forces that are anti-globalization whereas the forces of "stand pat-ism" can be likened to the protectors of globalization and all its vested interests.

Here, the angry populism inherent in anti-globalization clashes with the advocates of globalization; the former seeing themselves as progressives wanting to change the status quo, while the latter are perceived as the forces of "stand pat-ism" wanting to perpetuate the vested interests in globalization. Unfortunately, it is difficult to build a level playing ground in international relations because of its inherent asymmetric nature.[78] Yet, there is no discounting the fact that the world could be a better place (with all the international terrorism-inducing factors addressed or limited to a lesser degree) if the conduct of international relations can be shorn of a condescending and exploitative attitude inherent in modernism, that is, if international relations is imbued with the spirit of postmodernism, defined as tolerance of differences and a clear understanding that relative "frames of reference determine individual and societal perceptions of reality".[79]

76 Ibid., p. 27

77 See Fred Aja Agwu (2005), *United Nations System, State Practice and the Jurisprudence of the Use of Force* . . ., p. 34, op. cit; see also A. H. Snow (1913), "A Short History of War" (a book review), *AJIL*, Vol. 7, p. 427.

78 See Fred Aja Agwu (2016), *Nations among Nations* . . ., pp. 337–437, op. cit.

79 In his 2002 essay in the Military Review, George Washington of the U.S. Army drew a very lucid and interesting distinction between the realities in the pre-modern, modern, and the postmodern eras of human civilization. According to him, "in pre-modern era, most people were illiterate, which limited their access to information other than by word of mouth from authority figures"; an era in which "religious and political figures determined what was to be accepted by the masses as truth and reality"; and which "it did not occur to individuals that there could be any way but the "right way", the way being what their social leaders dictated". In the modern era, on the other hand, "modern thinkers accepted that people from other societies held different views", particularly because they "travelled to new places, saw new things and became enlightened to the fact that some societies were different from their own; . . . [unfortunately], they tend to find fault with those differences and believe that the only correct way to perceive the world is from their own societal perspective". But as distinct

Thus, while still focused on the national interest, the postmodern attitude accommodates international interests to the extent that it constructs international relations in manners that are cognizant of the material, ethno-religious, and cultural sensibilities of others. Unlike postmodernism; modernism—particularly in its modernization blackmail[80] and pretension to being suffused with universal truths—is held in thralldom by incurable preconceptions; and this is at the heart of the ethnocentrism and injustices it dispenses in the globalizing world. Contrarily, although liable to be slammed for its extreme permissiveness,[81] postmodernism reputedly eschews ethnocentrism and hostile policies like the "Morgenthau policy" of de-industrialization, impoverishment, and mass immiseration of others.[82] The "Morgenthau policy" under reference refers, not to Hans Joachim Morgenthau (February 17, 1904—July 19, 1980), one of the major 20th-century figures in the study of international politics, whose works belong to the tradition of realism in international-relations theory.[83]

It is rather that of Henry Morgenthau, Jr., who, as the United States Treasury Secretary (aided by his principal adviser on monetary matters and latter Assistant Secretary of the Treasury—the "articulate, mustachioed and nattily dressed" Dr. Harry Dexter White) practically upstaged, outwitted, or outsmarted the then Secretary of State, Cordell Hull,[84] to propose in a memorandum entitled *Suggested Post-Surrender Program for Germany*, that the Allied occupation of Germany following the end of the Second World War should aim at "measures to eliminate Germany's ability to wage war by eliminating its armament industry".[85]

Although some globalists associate globalization with post-industrialism and postmodernism,[86] postmodernist attitudes do not in many significant ways reflect in most dispositions of the "privileged" nations in the conduct of their relations

---

from the foregoing, "the postmodern era . . . tolerates differences and clearly understands that frames of reference determine individual and societal perceptions of reality"; see George Washington (2002), "Staffing the Post Modern Army", p. 28, op. cit.

80 See Fred Aja Agwu (2016), *Nations among Nations* . . ., pp. 109–114, op. cit.

81 Ibid., pp. 350–368, op. cit. On the issue of gender politics, for instance, postmodernism excessively aligns with neo-liberalism to orchestrate the commercialization or commoditization of the human body; in which, in the LGBT community, anybody can do anything with his or her body, such that one can by sex be female, but by gender male, giving rise to the existence of many trans men and women; see Jessi Hempel in "My Brother Evan Was Born Female. He Came Out as Transgender 16 Years Ago but Never Stopped Wanting to Have a Baby. This Spring He Gave Birth to His First Child", *Time* (New York), September 12–19, 2016, pp. 58–65.

82 See Fred Aja Agwu (2016), *Nations among Nations* . . ., pp. 253–256, op. cit.

83 See "Hans Morgenthau", available at https://en.wikipedia.org/wiki/Hans_Morgenthau (last visited on Tuesday, September 6, 2016).

84 See Anthony Kubek, "The Morgenthau Plan and the Problem of Policy Perversion", available at www.ihr.org/jhr/v09/v09p287_Kubek.htmlLLLL (last visited on Tuesday, September 6, 2016).

85 See "Hans Morgenthau", available at https://en.wikipedia.org/wiki/Hans_Morgenthau (last visited on Tuesday, September 6, 2016), op. cit.

86 See Dele Seteolu (2004), "Globalization . . .", p. 6,, op. cit.

with the less "privileged". For instance, the United States largely insists on its own values, especially the value of democratization and/or the implementation of the Washington Consensus, as a condition precedent.[87] This has been so much so that its intervention in Iraq, with the whole idea of the Arab Spring inclusive, is often argued to be a nation-building project—an attempt by Washington to make democracy "flourish in the lands where Islam prevails".[88] This in itself has been part of the reasons for the violent and terrorist resistance and attack on Americans by the Islamists, especially political Islam and Wahhabism aforementioned. But this nation-building project by the United States has always gone awry; for even when he was swept to power in Egypt through the so-called democratic process, President Mohammed Morsi of the Moslem Brotherhood Party (a party that has an anti-democracy antecedent) moved against the Egyptian Constitution, determined to abolish its democratic ethos.[89]

It must be emphasized that, going by George Washington's explications, whereas pre-modernism is intrinsically clueless because of ignorance; implicit in modernism is an ethnocentric behaviour, the sort (typically illustrated by the modernization theory) in which, although accepting that people from other societies have different views, "they tend to find fault with those differences and believe that the only correct way to perceive the world is from their own societal perspective":[90] hence the United States' insistence on the democratization of other societies and the unflinching determination by some groups in those societies to fight back, using the terrorist tactics. But unlike modernism, postmodernism is tolerant and cognizant of cultural relativity. Unfortunately, the postmodernist attitude does not perfuse international relations, owing ostensibly to the national interests of the exponents of globalization.

In recent times (especially since the Ronald Reagan/Margaret Thatcher years[91]), the West began the fostering of the "financialization" of economic activities, the transcendence of the service economy over agriculture, manufacturing, and productive activities; thus began the dawn of "Casino Capitalism".[92] This is even as some of the institutions of globalization (the International Monetary Fund, IMF, and the World Bank) with the declared objective of promoting global economic stability have apparently derailed or deviated into the propagation of financialization.[93] Meanwhile, this new objective of promoting the philosophy of capital market liberalization by the IMF, according to Joseph

87 See Fred Aja Agwu (2009), *National Interest, International Law* . . ., pp. 455–463, op. cit.
88 See Noah Feldman (2003), *After Jihad* . . ., p. 3, op. cit.
89 See Fred Aja Agwu (2016), *Nations among Nations* . . ., pp. 376–377, op. cit.
90 See George Washington (2002), "Staffing the Post Modern Army", p. 28, op. cit.
91 See Fred Aja Agwu (2009), *National Interest, International Law* . . ., pp. 515–519, op. cit; see also Rana Foroohar in "Saving Capitalism", *Time* (New York), May 23, 2016, pp. 24–25.
92 Fred Aja Agwu (2009), *National Interest, International Law* . . ., p. 516, op. cit; and Rana Foroohar, "Saving Capitalism", p. 25.
93 See Joseph E. Stiglitz (2003, 2002), *Globalization and Its Discontents* . . ., p. 230, op. cit.

Stiglitz, serves more of "the interests of the financial community than of global community".[94]

As an instrument of globalization, the IMF, in addition to the promotion of financialization, also apparently condones the sharp practices of all central banks and other public institutions that embark on the culture of secrecy, turning a blind eye and even defending "the secrecy of the offshore banking centers" in places like the Cayman Islands.[95] The "Panama Papers" that were released by a German newspaper on Monday, April 4, 2016, had revealed some of these offshore banking centers—which turned out to be "the biggest leak in the history of data journalism, publishing online, some 11.5 million documents from [a] Panamanian law firm, Mossack Fonseca".[96] These offshore banking centers that global financial institutions not only condone but sometimes defend do not only empower the rich at the expense of the poor and the state—the latter by facilitating "tax evasion, money laundering and other nefarious activities"—they have, since 9/11, been discovered to not only be deployed in the financing terrorism,[97] but also in creating conditions that make people to gravitate toward the terrorist malaise.

For these and other contradictions of globalization, many non-Western economies have been ruined as the developed nations that are driving globalization and its attendant institutions eschew postmodern attitudes in their dealings with others. Rather, their neo-liberal manipulations have tended to stoke the furnace of discontent that results in fierce violent contestations around many parts of the world, including, of course, in the oil-awash Middle East, a region in which many people are in deep poverty despite the petro-dollars coming to their leaders, and in which the epicenter of terrorism is located. The terrorist upsurge in the Middle East has since been worsened by the plummeting oil prices, which added to the anger of the "militant Islamic fundamentalists" that could no longer turn a blind eye to, in particular, the activities of the United States.[98]

It is in this context that the solution to terrorism in the Middle East must also require finding ways to carefully address such ancient angers in the region as the fallouts from the Sykes and Picot lines on the map of the Levant (without radically redrawing borders and risking the creation of more injustices and upheavals)[99] as well as addressing the tyrannies of globalization with the requisite postmodernist attitudes. In globalization as presently structured, the West eschews the

94 Loc. Cit.

95 Ibid., p. 228.

96 See John Alechenu, Sunday Aborisade, Eniola Akinkuotu, Adelani Adepegba and Oladimeji Ramon in "#PanamaPapers: Saraki, Ibori in Fresh Controversy over Secret Assets", *The Punch* (Lagos), Tuesday, April 5, 2016, p. 8, op. cit.

97 See Joseph E. Stiglitz (2003, 2002), *Globalization and Its Discontents* . . ., p. 228, op. cit.

98 See Craig Unger (2004), *House of Bush, House of Saud: The Hidden Relationship the World's Two Most Powerful Dynasties*, London, Gibson Square Books, p. 4.

99 See "The War within: Europe and America Made Mistakes, But the Misery of the Arab World Is Caused Mainly by Its Own Failures". . ., p. 7, op. cit.

virtue of postmodernism even in their societies; the same way they do in other societies. The U.S. President Obama adverted to this when he observed that although globalization and automation have created growth and prosperity and, thus, benefited those countries with skill, capital, and that are well resourced in these terms; yet, it has nonetheless not paid sufficient attention and, hence, created poverty and inequality, even in the Global North.[100]

It is for this reason that many people are reacting against globalization with both non-violent political measures (as in the Brexit vote) and the violent ones in extremism and terrorism. The West is, however, not alone in the tendency to continue to exhibit the defunct Cold War "Morgenthau policy" towards post-war Germany. China is also subtly into the Morgenthau policy, as in, according to U.S. President Barack Obama, when it fails to be sensitive, not just to free trade, but also to fair trade that would enable others (like African and fellow Asian countries) to build national capacity; or when it projects the Hans Joachim Morgenthau power (one of the exponents of political realism) by flexing its muscles, bullying, or imposing on the weaker states in the South China Sea, not just by building installations on the contested Island, but also disobeying the judgment of an international arbitral tribunal on the matter, apparently oblivious of the benefits of obeying international law.[101]

Just as in alliances like the Shanghai Cooperation Council (SCC; discussed shortly later) that reeks of divisiveness and cut-throat completions destructive of international solidarity or coalitions, thus, allowing terrorist organizations like the ISIS to feed fat on them, terrorism also feeds fat on poverty and inequality. But the United States itself, with all the vaunting about its soft power, is hardly or sparingly compliant with international law as, for instance, a way of projecting its postmodernist attitude in dealings with weaker nations. If soft power, according to Joseph Nye Jr., are primarily composed of a country's "culture, (in places where it is attractive to others), its political values (when it lives up to them at home and abroad), and its foreign policies (when they are seen as legitimate and having moral authority)",[102] then the election of Donald Trump is a complete antonym of American soft power.

Again, if it could be reckoned that China's bullying tactics in the South China sea can undercut its soft power—and that, as Joseph Nye asserted, Japan's soft power is undercut by its ethnocentric attitudes,[103] while Russia's soft power is undercut by President "Putin's revisionism", especially with the unattractiveness of the communist ideology, and with Russia flexing its muscles with its

100 U.S. President Barack Obama in Fareed Zakaria's Global Public Square (GPS) on Cable News Network (CNN), monitored in Lagos (Nigeria) on Monday, September 5, 2016, between 8pm and 9pm local time.

101 Loc. Cit; see also "A Ham-Fisted Hegemon: Despite Its Economic and Military Might, China Lacks the Finesse to Shape Asia to Its Liking", *The Economist*, September 24, 2016, p. 50.

102 See Joseph S. Nye, Jr. (2015), *Is American Century Over?* . . ., p. 59, op. cit.

103 Ibid., p. 30.

weak neighbours in Georgia in 2008, and in Ukraine in 2014, particularly with the annexation of Crimea[104]—then the U.S. soft power is equally undercut by the presidency of Donald Trump because the Trump persona emblematizes the standard American macho spirit (devoid of finesse), the largely American ethnocentrism and proclivity to dominate and exploit (seen in their dealing with the American-Indians) without caring about other nation's sensibilities. In short, it represents the bullish attitude of the American, a military culture that is allegedly rooted in the Appalachians South.[105]

On its part, China is blowing hot and cold at the same time in that Asian region it dominates as the only regional hegemon; it is intimidating and taking over territories in the South China Sea with its outrageous construction of artificial islands in some of the contested Islands in violation of the ruling of The Hague Tribunal; while at the same time projecting a diplomacy towards these neighbours that "is full of 'mutual respect', win-win relationships and common destiny", illustrated by the "One Belt, One Road initiative to create infrastructure tying Eurasia closer to China by land and sea".[106] This initiative by Beijing has since encouraged some of the unwary, like President Rodrigo Duterte of the Philippines, to begin talking tough against the United States, which is supposed to be an ally. And despite China's massive intervention in Africa at the level of assisting in the continent's infrastructural development in the globalizing world, sight must also not lost of the fact that, like the West, there are still some impediments in its trade policies with African countries (the "Rule of Origins", which a former Nigerian Ambassador has seriously rued[107]); and this is a dent on the imperative of not just free trade but also fair trade. China may now be affecting a postmodernist attitude towards Africa in some of its so-called infrastructural gifts, but sense must not be lost on the lessons of history, the fact that it is only doing this infrastructural intervention because it needs something from Africa in return.

The instruction in the foregoing narrative is that the absence of a postmodernist disposition in international relations (with the concomitant disinclination to amend the fractures in globalization and create a new international economic order that will enable the transcending of global socio-economic inequality and ideological schisms) has further diminished the capacity of many countries to experience economic renaissance and resultantly be seized with the appropriate national institutions that will enable them to forestall the conditions that lead to terrorism or tackle the malaise whenever it breaks out. This is why the backlash against globalization that has led to the resurgence of populism and its

104 Ibid., pp. 33, 36.

105 See Fred Aja Agwu (2011), *The Law of Armed Conflict and African Wars . . .*, p. 399, op. cit.

106 See "A Ham-Fisted Hegemon: Despite Its Economic and Military Might, China Lacks the Finesse to Shape Asia to Its Liking", p. 50, op. cit.

107 See Olusola Oladokun Sanu (2016), *Audacity on the Bound: A Diplomatic Odyssey*, Ibadan, Mosuro Publishers, p. 367.

concomitant ultra-nationalism and zero-sum attitudes to international relations is recognized as posing a threat to multilateralism and the ability to collectively solve the problem of terrorism in contemporary times.

Globalization: Weapon Against Terror in Spite of Itself

Globalization is a contradictory phenomenon. It may have contributed to the building of the present global wave of terrorist onslaught, but it is also paradoxically needed to solve the problem because of its obvious security benefits that are inherent in joint or collective actions; otherwise, a new wave of international terrorism-related problems will ensue. The spirit of benign (not malevolent) alliances that globalization can help create is very critical to waging a successful WoT. Unfortunately, in the prevailing wave of nationalism, ultra-nationalism, and populism, there are many tendencies towards anti-globalization. And it is in malevolent or adversarial alliances that anti-globalization is heavily manifesting. When it is supposedly bringing down borders, some adversarial alliances are at the same time increasingly (albeit sometimes inadvertently) therein built as nations become more suspicious of one another.

For instance, it was the emergence of the alliance that China created in the SCC that encouraged President Rodrigo Duterte of the Philippines to begin thumping his nose at the United States, his country's otherwise ally, boasting that, in his country's Asian region, "China is now in power . . .; and they have military superiority in the region".[108] Another instance was (although national security threats are not diminished but rather heightened by globalization) when the British momentarily suspended work on their nuclear reactor in Hinkley Point on account of national security concerns because of the Chinese involvement[109] an action that smacked of mistrust and an increasingly polarized world; even though the reverse ought to be the case for the sake of international peace and security. Despite the façade of the integration presented by globalization, the world is increasingly polarized by incidences like the United States' ambivalence to Europe's security and unity, which is exemplified by Washington's refusal to support Europe's Headline Goals security project.[110]

Washington's anti-European common security arrangement even infected the United Kingdom in the sense that despite Brexit in which the UK voted to leave the EU—yet, ahead of France and Germany's determination in 2016 to make a case for an increased European military cooperation at an informal talks in Bratislava, the Slovakian capital—the UK's Defence Secretary, Sir Michael Fallon, still expressed his country's opposition to the idea because it was capable

108 See "A Ham-Fisted Hegemon: Despite Its Economic and Military Might, China Lacks the Finesse to Shape Asia to Its Liking", p. 50, op. cit.

109 See "The World This Week", p. 5, op. cit.

110 See Fred Aja Agwu (2009), *National Interest, International Law* . . ., pp. 444–445, op. cit.

of undermining the NATO,[111] which is ostensibly Washington's own preference for Europe's security scheme. The UK insisted that it was not alone in this opposition to the creation of a European army that was begun earlier to confront or counter Russia's threat, warning that "simply duplicating or undermining NATO is the wrong way to do it".[112] Concerning European unity, Washington maintains an opposing (if not quixotic) attitude in the sense that, alongside the UK, it has, for 30 years, supported Turkey's accession to the EU talks knowing that "the larger and more diverse the EU was, the less it would represent a coherent challenge to the Anglo-American imperium"[113] because, according to Joseph Nye, a united Europe has a greater population and GDP, amongst other strengths, than the United States.[114]

But Turkey's dream of joining the EU was so publicly shattered by the British Prime Minister David Cameron's open denunciation of that prospect in the countdown to the Brexit vote in order to appease and dissuade the pro-Brexiters from their path; thus, apparently intensifying panic and the sense of global divisiveness that eventually forced Ankara to repair back to Russia—to look to the East by beginning dialogue with the SCC.[115] Comprising China, Russia, Kazakhstan, Kyrgyzstan, Tajikistan, and Uzbekistan (with Iran, Afghanistan, Belarus and Mongolia, Turkey, Sri Lanka, and Cambodia as observers or with a dialogue status), the SCC, by implication, "contains two thirds of the world's population, the biggest global economy by Purchasing Power Parity (China), and the world's second military power (Russia)".[116] The SCC has emerged as a counterpoise to the West's hegemony because it seeks to recreate "the famous Silk Road"—the "land-based trading system across Eurasia to the Middle East and Africa" that was "once the most lucrative international trading system, flowing from Beijing with terminus cities in different regional markets, including Damascus and the Mediterranean Venetian cities", but which had "lost its primacy when European seafarers opened up alternative sea routes to the East".[117]

Alliances of this nature increasingly compartmentalize the international system and fuel those competition and divergences of interests that militate against solidarity in the war on terror. In fact, an alignment or alliance that resuscitates the old silk road that is diametrically pitted in competition against the European seafarers/powers is redolent with the "Thucydides trap"—the phrase that was popularized by Professor Graham Allison of the Harvard Kennedy School and used to denote the possibility of "a rising power confronting a ruling power"—of China going to war with the United States of America in a manner reminiscent of the

111 See "UK to Oppose Plans to European Union Army", *The Guardian* (Lagos), Wednesday, September 28, 2016, p. 12.
112 Loc. Cit.
113 See Onyekachi Wambu in "The Old Silk Road and a New World Order", p. 98, op. cit.
114 See Joseph S. Nye, Jr. (2015), *Is American Century Over?* . . ., p. 24, op. cit.
115 See Onyekachi Wambu in "The Old Silk Road and a New World Order", p. 98, op. cit.
116 Loc. Cit.
117 Loc. Cit.

situation over 2,400 years ago when a rising Athens challenged Sparta in ancient Greece in order to enforce its entitlements in the new world order that Athens' rise occasioned.[118] But a rising China presenting the scare of this Thucydides trap appears to be downplayed by the reasoning that although there is the possibility of conflicts flaring in such geopolitical issues as the South China sea and North Korea, the United States is slowly integrating China in the post-World War I and II international system that it created and currently dominates.

Nothing illustrates this gradual integration of China better than the IMF's inclusion of the Chinese currency, the Yuan, in its basket of reserve currencies.[119] This is ostensibly an indication that Washington is open to the reform of the international system, and that it is receptive to China's ideas on the reform. Nevertheless, the compartmentalization of the international system and the scare of the "Thucydides trap" in alliances like the SCC are concrete sources of concern in the war on terror because the fact that a U.S. traditional ally like the Philippines (under President Rodrigo Duterte) is threatening to tilt toward China;[120] or that Turkey, an ally of the United States, maintains a dialogue or observer status with the SCC was not comforting at all at the point of the botched July 2016 coup in Turkey, given that one of the very first steps that President Erdogan took was to momentarily shut down (with everywhere abuzz with the conspiracy theory that the United States had covertly or overtly backed the coup) the Incirlik airbase in

118 The Athenian historian, Thucydides, explained that "it was the rise of Athens and the fear that this inspired in Sparta that made war inevitable"—the Peloponnesian war that ended 30 years later and left Sparta the nominal winner as "both states [Athens and Sparta] lay in ruin, leaving Greece vulnerable to the Persians". There was some inexorable "structural stress" that the rise of Athens had occasioned in the sense of causing "a rapid shift in the balance of power between [the] two rivals". This structural stress consisted of the rising power's (Athens) growing sense of entitlement, "sense of its importance, and demand for greater say and sway"; while on the other hand, the established power (Sparta) was gripped with "fear, insecurity, and determination to defend the status quo". Like today's China, wrote Thucydides in the fifth century B.C., Athens' position was clearly understandable as its clout had grown, "so too did its self-confidence, its consciousness of past injustices, its sensitivity to instances of disrespect, and its insistence that previous arrangements be revised to reflect new realities of power". And expectedly, "Sparta interpreted the Athenian posture as unreasonable, ungrateful, and threatening to the system it had established—and within which Athens had flourished". Although history had repeated itself in the Twentieth century when Germany challenged Britain (partly resulting in the First and Second World Wars), a repeat of that scenario with the rising China is considered unlikely and unwise, even though humanity has a capacity for supreme folly as could be seen in the agitation for the reform of the United Nations Security Council, in which the so-called emerging powers are demanding the power of the veto with the sense of entitlement analogous to the Athenians when they were challenging the established order under the Spartan hegemony; see Graham Allison, "The Thucydides Trap: Are the U.S. and China Headed for War?", available at www.theatlantic.com/international/archive/2015/09/united-states-china-war-thucydides-trap/406756/ (last visited on Wednesday, August 31, 2016). Parentheses mine.

119 See Fred Aja Agwu (2016), *Nations among Nations*. . ., p. 1060, op. cit.

120 See "A Ham-Fisted Hegemon: Despite Its Economic and Military Might, China Lacks the Finesse to Shape Asia to Its Liking", p. 50, op. cit.

Turkey from where the Americans were waging war on the ISIS,[121] even though the action might have presumably been for security reasons.

There are admittedly some serious dysfunctions in globalization, but there are equally some serious gains in the cosmopolitanism inherent in it (as opposed to parish-pump or local consciousness in isolationism), which can be exploited to fight terrorism at a global coalition scale. Ditching globalization would certainly not serve humanity because such an action will enable terrorism to blossom unencumbered. In other words, deserting globalization is unhelpful because it would apparently encourage the rest of the world to go back to the past, to ditch the spirit of internationalism, to retreat from cosmopolitanism (globalization), and consider re-embracing the forces of "aggressive nationalism" (as US President Obama put it in his address to the 71st UNGA[122]), populism, xenophobia and hate, instead of candidly fixing the problems with globalization by repairing the problems with, as *The Economist* put it, "protectionism and nativism"[123] in order to enable the creation of a greater inclusiveness.

So, the boon here for the apologists of globalization is that the phenomenon has come to stay and is clearly irreversible. Ultra-nationalism may have manifested itself in the Putinism in Russia;[124] the populism that led to the Brexit vote and the election of Donald Trump in the United States may be growing in Europe with increased visibility and the threat by right-wing parties to capture political power across many European countries;[125] yet all hopes are not lost for globalization. In fact, the centrist Italian Premier Matteo Renzi may have lost his constitutional referendum to the elation of the right-wing party that is anti-establishment, anti-globalization, and anti-the European Union;[126] but that was not the end of the story, or the end of the road for globalization.

As it were, "just when it seemed as if Europe's populist revolt couldn't be stopped", something like a dues ex machine intervention happened on December 4, 2016, when "Austria's Alexander Van der Bellen, a former Green Party leader who ran as an independent, defeated Norbert Hofer, his far-right counterpart, in the country's presidential election",[127] signaling that the populists, after all, were not having a field day across the entire countries of Europe.

121 See Jared Malsin in "Turkey's Long Night of the Soul", *Time* (New York), August 1, 2016, p. 7.

122 News monitored on CNN in Lagos (Nigeria) on Wednesday, September 21, 2016, at 7pm through 8pm local time, op. cit.

123 See "Why They're Wrong: Globalization Critics Say It Benefits Only the Elite. In Fact, a Less Open World Would Hurt the Poor Most of All", *The Economist*, October 1, 2016, p. 9, op. cit.

124 See Owen Matthews in "Putin Power", *Newsweek*, December 2, 2016, pp. 36–37.

125 See Matt McAllester in "New World Disorder: With Trumpism Advancing from the West and Putinism from the East, Can Europe's Centrists Survive the Hard-Right Onslaught?", *Newsweek*, December 2, 2016, pp. 28–31; see also Josh Lowe in "The Next Brexit", *Newsweek*, December 2, 2016, pp. 32–35.

126 See Gregorio Borgia in "Torn from Today's Headlines", *Newsweek*, December 16, 2016, p. 7.

127 See Leonhard Foeger in "A Broken Right Wing", *Newsweek*, December 16, 2016, p. 8.

Although this victory did not mean that the moderates in France, Germany, or the Netherlands were "safe in a post-Brexit world";[128] the victory, nonetheless, confirms that all may not have been lost by the proponents of globalization and multilateralism. In fact, immediately after Alexander Van der Bellen's victory, that of Emmanuel Macron followed suit on May 7, 2017 in France.[129] And again, Angela Merkel may have been dismissing the suggestion of her being the last "man" standing in the West in defence of the values of globalization as "grotesque, even almost absurd", but the truth is that the German Chancellor's announcement that she would stand for a fourth term in September 2017 still emits the confidence that despite the surge of populism across much of the Western world (in the United States and parts of Europe), the hard-right may not totally prevail at the end of the day.[130]

Given the extent to which capitalism has taken over the world, aided by the increasingly sophisticated but cheap technologies that are fueling its thirst for profit across international borders (even when it is taking people's jobs because of increased automation[131]), the world can only globalize rather than contract. This is why President Trump's "America first" mantra has apparently come a cropper (fall into ruin) immediately it confronted the reality of realpolitik, especially the consequences of abandoning America's treaty obligations to its allies in the West and the rest of the world in the United Nations. President Trump's "America first" mantra began to unravel immediately after he took office. The President who pretended to be only the President of the United States began acting like the President of the whole world: after the Syrian President Bashar Assad allegedly carried out a chemical bombing of his own citizens in Idlib, northern Syria, on April 4, 2017, killing at least 72 people, including children and women, Trump said that the attack "crosses many, many lines, beyond a red line".[132]

President Trump's response to Syrian President Assad's chemical weapon attack was to order the bombing of the Syrian air field from where the chemical attack was allegedly carried out.[133] And following North Korea's untrammeled nuclear weapons ambition, the Trump's Presidency declared an end to the "strategic patience" favoured by the Obama administration towards North Korea and authorized that an American flotilla, led by *USS Carl Vinson*, an American Armada, steam to the Korean Peninsula, while the American President also proceeded to authorize the deployment of a missile defence system, the Terminal

128 Loc. Cit.

129 See Ian Bremmer in "The Wave to Come: The Forces That Made Nationalism a Crisis in the West Will Go Global", *Time* (New York), May 22, 2017, pp. 18–21.

130 See Markus Schreiber in "Germany: Left Alone?", *Newsweek*, December 2, 2016, p. 8.

131 See "Why They're Wrong: Globalization Critics Say It Benefits Only the Elite. In Fact, a Less Open World Would Hurt the Poor Most of All", p. 9, op. cit

132 See *Time* (New York), April 17, 2017, p. 7.

133 See "Strategic Confusion: America Stokes Tensions on the Korean Peninsula, Then Tries to Lower Them Again", pp. 45–46, op. cit; see also Simon Schuster in "The Trump-Putin Reset Is Dead—But Don't Rule Out an Amicable Settlement", *Time* (New York), April 24, 2017, pp. 5–6.

High-Altitude Area Defence (THAAD) in South Korea.[134] Before then, President Trump had also authorized a punitive strike against Afghanistan with the biggest American non-nuclear bomb—the Massive Air Ordinance Blast (MAOB)—the "mother of all bombs", which was being used for the first time by any American President.[135]

President Trump had equally drawn "up plans to send more Special Forces to aid the AMISOM [the United Nations-sponsored African Union Mission in Somalia] troops and the Somali National Army as they battle the [al-Shabaab] militants".[136] In fact, in his first overseas trip on assumption of office, and despite his reiterating during his campaigns that "Islam hates us [America]" and embarking on his controversial Muslim ban, President Trump visited Saudi Arabia, the very bastion of Wahabbism—the Sunni sect of Islam that is allegedly sponsoring Islamic fundamentalism in the al-Qaeda and the ISIS.[137]

Also while in Riyadh (Saudi Arabia), President Trump, rather than insisting on his "America first" mantra, announced a foreign policy of "principled realism", in which he said that "we will make decisions based on real-world outcomes—not inflexible ideology. We will be guided by the lessons of experience, not the confines of rigid thinking. And wherever possible, we will seek gradual reforms—not sudden intervention".[138] This was a far-cry from the Trump on the campaign trails that promised to radically withdraw America from globalization. In fact, despite Donald Trump's consistent proclamation during his campaigns that in his first day in office, he would pull the United States out of the 12-nation Trans-Pacific Partnership (TPP)—which he later did in his first full day in office after inauguration on a Friday by signing an executive order the following Monday to withdraw the United States from the TPP.[139] And, despite the Japanese Prime Minister's (Shinzo Abe) skepticism that the Asian-Pacific trade deal would be meaningless without the United States, many of the participating nations like Canada, Japan, Vietnam, and Australia are still committed to the ratification of the pact.[140]

134 Ibid., p. 45.

135 Ibid., pp. 45–46; see also Owei Lakemfa in "War without End", p. 31, op. cit.

136 See Bevertone Kipchumba Some in "Kenya's al-Shabaab Paradox", p. 49. op. cit. Parentheses mine.

137 See "Trump Discards Campaign Baggage on First Overseas Trip", *Time* (New York), June 5, 2017, p. 11. The fact that Saudi Arabia is the sponsor of the ISIS was buttressed by the interlocutors in Fareed Zakaria's GPS programme on CNN, who maintained that rather than haranguing Saudi Arabia for this sponsor of terror, President Trump was deflecting attention by focusing on Iran, a Shiite Muslim nation that is itself fighting the Sunni extremists; GPS programme monitored in Lagos (Nigeria) on Sunday, May 28, 2017, between 8pm to 9pm local time, op. cit.

138 See "Trump Discards Campaign Baggage on First Overseas Trip", p. 11, op. cit.

139 See "Trump Signs Order Pulling US Out of Global Trade Deal: Cuts Funding for International Groups That Provide Abortion", *Vanguard* (Lagos), Tuesday, January 24, 2017, p. 44.

140 See "Trump's Pullout of TPP Opens Way for China", *The Guardian* (Lagos), Wednesday, November 23, 2016, p. 24.

And despite China's Han-centrism—the smug assumption that "to count as properly Chinese, you have in practice to belong to the Han people", otherwise, domestically, you are only but a second-class citizen[141]—and its ambivalence to globalization (especially as it does not permit China to recognize dual citizenship for its Han citizens[142]), it is still very keen at engaging the globalizing world. Although China was excluded from the TPP, the prospect of Trump pulling the United States out of it had triggered speculation that the remaining nations may amend the pact to include China, even as China itself had started pushing "its own version of an Asian-Pacific trade pact called the Regional Comprehensive Economic Partnership (RCEP), which notably excludes the United States" too.[143] In the United States, Donald Trump himself is facing fierce criticism for abandoning the free trade that is the tradition of the Republican Party. This is why, despite Brexit, Boris Johnson of the United Kingdom, the country's post-Brexit foreign Minister and himself a Brexiter, remarked that they would stress the importance of multilateralism to Trump, especially the importance of free trade and NATO.[144]

With all the victory songs by the forces of populism—the Trumpists and Brexiteers—Americans were to fight back in their "Not my President" protest in cities across the country, deprecating and describing the Trump victory as "Trumpocalypses".[145] In the same vein, the Brits were not leaving the EU without a fight that ultimately ended in the country's Supreme Court.[146] The Supreme Court ruled that "Parliament must vote on whether the government can start the Brexit process", implying that Prime Minister Theresa May would not trigger Article 50 of the Lisbon Treaty to begin talks with the EU until the MPs and Peers gave their backing.[147] This ruling held the apprehension that a vote in Parliament would see the Scottish First Minister, Nicola Sturgeon—since Scotland overwhelmingly voted for globalization or against Brexit—make good her threat to veto or block the Brexit.[148]

141 See "The New Nationalism: With His Call to Put 'America First', Donald Trump Is the Latest Recruit to a Dangerous Nationalism", p. 9, op. cit.

142 Ibid., pp. 20–22

143 See "Trump's Pullout of TPP Opens Way for China", *The Guardian* (Lagos), Wednesday, November 23, 2016, p. 24.

144 Loc. Cit.

145 See, amongst others, Adegoke in "Wole Soyinka Is Leaving the U.S. Because of Trumpocalypse", *The Guardian* (Lagos), Friday, November 18, 2016, p. 42; see also Vitoria Ojugbana and Merit Igumah in "Outrage, Shock as Americans Protest against Trump's Victory", *The Guardian* (Lagos), Friday, November 11, 2016, pp. 54–55; "Trump Bars Journalists from First Meeting with Obama", *The Guardian* (Lagos), Friday, November 11, 2016, p. 6; and Karl Vick in "The U.S. Continues to Come Apart in the Wake of a Divisive Election", *Time* (New York), November 28–December 5, 2016, p. 7, op. cit.

146 See "UK Govt. Loses Brexit Vote Appeal, Must Consult Parliament: Europe Reacts to Ruling", *Vanguard* (Lagos), Wednesday, January 25, 2017, p. 45.

147 Loc. Cit.

148 See "Nicola Sturgeon: Scotland Can Block Brexit", *The Nation* (Lagos), Monday, July 18, 2016, p. 39.

This was before the chequered political fortune of Prime Minister Theresa May in failing to win an outright majority in the snap national election of June 2017 equally triggered an apprehension that Brexit may never happen because not only was the Theresa May government too weakened to get a good exit deal from the EU, Britain's main political parties were too divided on the issue of Brexit.[149] So, like armed drones with their "blowback" effects, globalization may be partly congenial to the promotion of grievances that water the seeds of some terrorist organization, but some of its inherent institutions are paradoxically also congenial to the defeat of terror if the international community can find the requisite coalescence.

Can the Anti-Globalization in Populism Trump Anti-Terror Coalitions?

From the foregoing, it is clear that despite its many contradictions, globalization still harbours some potent weapons for fighting terrorism because of its ability to enable nations to cohere for collective actions. So, the answer to the question posed in the earlier rubric cannot be in the affirmative; that is, the sway of nationalism and anti-globalization inherent in populism cannot really torpedo the ability of the international community to collectively and effectively fight terror within multilateral frameworks. Be it in Africa (with the West African Lake Chad Basin nations' Multinational Joint Task Force, MJTF, fighting the Boko Haram); in Afghanistan (with the NATO force fighting the Taliban); in Iraq and Syria (with the U.S.-led coalition fighting the ISIS); in Yemen (with the Saudi-led coalition fight the Houthi rebel-terrorists); or in Southeast Asia (with "the Association of South East Asian Nations, ASEAN—the ASEAN Plus Three, APT, grouping and the ASEAN Regional Forum, ARF," fighting to prevent the al-Qaeda-linked pan-Asian terrorist organization, the Jemaah Islamiya, JI, from establishing bases in Southeast Asian countries[150]), the multilateral approach to the war on terror is a critical factor in its success.

As a matter of fact, the multilateral approach to the war on terror also goes beyond banding together to apply military power. Multilateralism is also required to curb terrorist funding, a multilateralism that involves cross-border international regulations or harmonization of laws to combat money laundering that enables terrorist financing.[151] Terrorist funding is not limited to money raised locally through such criminal activities as extortion and charity contributions, etc.; it also includes otherwise legitimate businesses or activities with international dimensions, like investments in international finance and telecommunications,

149 See "Brexit May Never Happen", *Vanguard* (Lagos), Monday, July 10, 2017, p. 39.
150 See Rosemary Foot (2005), "Collateral Damage: Human Rights Consequences of Counterterrorist Action in the Asia-Pacific" . . ., p. 414, op. cit.
151 See Jonathan M. Winer and Trifin J. Roule (2002), "Fighting Terrorist Finance", *Survival*, Vol. 44, No. 3, Autumn, The International Institute for Strategic Studies (IISS), p. 87.

and the purely illegitimate ones like narcotic trafficking;[152] all of which require some measure of multilateral collaborations to combat. So, unscrambling the jig-saw puzzle of what will ultimately become the future of multilateralism in the war on terror is very important because of U.S. President Trump's declaration that he would renegotiate all international obligations of his country that are loop-sided against Washington,[153] referring to NATO as obsolete and calling the organization's members spongers or freeloaders that must be made to pay up or lose the United States' "protection".

This is irrespective of the fact that this so-called protection is actually mutual in many ways, especially since the threats that led to the First and Second World Wars had demonstrated that an isolationist America risked inadvertently incubating a very hostile world or environment around itself that would come home, not only to hunt but also haunt it. From the perspective of realpolitik, therefore, it is inconceivable that, beyond the hustings, President Donald Trump will ever carry through his isolationist threats because as already stated earlier, the lure of geopolitical, strategic, and America's wider national security interests will not permit him to do so. Moreover, the logic of strength or power as an inherent determinant of the dynamics of international relations will never permit President Trump to embark on the policy of isolationism for the United States. An eternal verity in the logic of international relations from the perspective of power politics is that disproportion of power tempts attack, while balance or equilibrium of power (because it makes victory unlikely) is a deterrence to attack.[154]

It was that fear of German militarism that propelled the logic that ended the U.S. isolationism: the fact that the United States' protection of Germany and the rest of Europe, not just from themselves but also from communist Russia was "an elegant solution".[155] Nevertheless, the new international security realities of international terrorism, a nuclear weapons ambitious Iran, and a resurgent repressive and territorially ambitious Putin Russia,[156] certainly would not make isolationism an attractive global policy for the United States. Even for the obvious U.S. national security reasons, isolationism will be ill-advised. Hence, the President of the European Commission, Jean-Claude Juncker, warned that even "if the European Union would fail or decompose, or other members left, the U.S. would have a more difficult role to play in the world".[157] And one of President Trump's predecessors in office, the 43rd President of the United

152 Ibid., pp. 89–91.

153 See "What a Trump Presidency Means for Africa", a CNBC Africa's interview with Charles Stith and Steven Gruzd, *The Guardian* (Lagos), Friday, December 2, 2016, pp. 33–34, op. cit.

154 See John Spanier (1972), *Games Nations Play: Analyzing International Politics*, London, Thomas Nelson and Sons Ltd., p. 10.

155 Loc. Cit.

156 See Anna Neistat in "As Russia Becomes More Repressive, the Brave Spirit of the 1990s Still Endures", *Time* (New York), January 16, 2017, p. 17.

157 See Charlotte McDonald-Gibson in "The E.U.'s Chief Executive on Trump, Populism and Russia", *Time* (New York), February 27–March 6, 2017, p. 7.

States, George W. Bush, at this very time the European nations were becoming skittish that President Donald Trump may promote isolationist policies, warned against an "isolationist tendency" in the United States, which he described as dangerous to national security.[158]

So, it is obvious that whether consciously or unconsciously embarked upon, an American isolationism would certainly give room for the emergence of rogue regimes around the world, especially now that far-right movements are also gaining a crescendo in Europe and many parts of the world. Thus a far-right government may arise in Germany and begin to menace its neighbours, with the possibility of the dire consequence of history repeating itself. A Japan outside the nuclear protection of the United States may decide to re-arm with nuclear weapons. To protect itself from the erratic and unpredictable regime in North Korea (which growing nuclear programme would now continue to advance, completely untrammeled because of the absence in the global stage, of any form of pressure against it), South Korea may also develop its own nuclear arsenal. And in all of this, the world would surely become a more dangerous place.

The impossibility of President Trump dragging the United States back to an isolationist posture in the international system, or even introducing serious changes to much of his country's multilateral commitments, is underlined by the fact of America's iron-clad systemic responsibility to Europe (and, indeed, the rest of the world) under reference. It is also underlined by the fact that as far as American national interests are concerned, certain policies and the structures for their implementation have been institutionalized, leaving every denizen of the White House with only the peripherally option of tinkering with such policies with executive powers/orders, having been presented with a fait-accompli in the implementation of such policies until Congress approves a reversal.

President Trump may have successfully pulled the United States from the Paris agreement on climate change[159] because it was an executive agreement that did not need congressional approval. The President cannot pull the United States out of the United Nations because this involves a full-fledged treaty (not an executive agreement) that is subject to a congressional approval. This institutionalization and immutability of the United States' core geopolitical, geostrategic, and core national security interests (Africa's enormous natural resources, China's rise and rivalry, and the war on terror) is probably the basis for Africa's obdurate persistence on the radar of Washington's foreign policy calculation: if for no other reason, at least, because an ignored Africa will revert to America's nightmarish "ungoverned territory" that gives safe haven and incubates terrorists.

It is also because of this institutionalization of policy and the immutability of U.S. national security interests, especially at the level of cooperating in the war on

158 See Michael R. Blood of the Associated Press in "George W. Bush Warns against 'Isolationist Tendency' in US", www.yahoo.com/news/george-w-bush-warns-against-isolationist-tendency-us-041901539.html (last visited on Thursday, March 2, 2017).

159 President Trump announced his pulling the United States out of the Paris deal on climate change on Thursday, June 1, 2017; see *ThisDay* (Lagos), Friday, June 2, 2017, p. 1.

terror, that Washington's relations with a number of Asian countries got strengthened. This was manifest in (1) a thaw in a "decidedly frosty" relations with Malaysia and the enduring relationship with Indonesia, ("despite Jakarta's failure to bring to book those in its armed forces accused of widespread human rights abuses in East Timor and elsewhere") (2) the United States' "military and economic aid to the Uzbek government (despite Uzbekistan having one of the most egregious human rights records in the world); and (3) the United States' continued military and economic aid flow to Pakistan (designating it, like the Philippines, as a major non-NATO ally, and even inviting the then President Parvas Musharraf with great pomp and circumstance to Camp David, making Musharraf "the first South Asian leader ever to be invited to the US President's mountain retreat"—all these despite Pakistan's status as America's frenemy, with Washington regarding it as a virtual failing or 'rogue state'— with its fragile institutions and economy, a nuclear weapons capacity, and military dictatorship in charge").[160]

Meanwhile, the spirit of multilateralism that will see to it that the defeat of terrorism has continued to endure because the NATO and EU, for instance, have striven to unite their efforts, pull their own military weight, and, in a meeting in Brussels, at least, reassure the Trump administration that the European allies are prepared to spend more of their Gross Domestic Product annually on defence; and that NATO is alive to its responsibility to combat terrorism.[161] Interestingly, even if a paradox, President Trump said in his inaugural speech (as he vowed to put America first and make it great again) that "we [the United States] will seek friendship and goodwill with the nations of the world . . . [and] we will reinforce old alliances and form new ones and unite the civilized world against radical Islamic terrorism, which we will eradicate completely from the face of the earth".[162]

And despite President Trump attending the G7 summit in Brussels and haranguing America's NATO allies to pay their dues, he never pulled punches along the line of threats to exit the NATO security arrangement. If the U.S. President Trump (as one of the most powerful leaders that determine the rhythm or tempo of international coalescence)—in spite of his ultra-nationalist and anti-globalization rhetoric—has vowed to "unite the civilized world against radical Islamic terrorism", it is certainly not over for the multilateral approach to the war on terror. Not when President Trump himself declared that he was 100% behind NATO and even South Korea, the latter in the wake of North Korea's escalation of its "rush towards nuclear weapons and intercontinental missile" development.[163]

160 See Rosemary Foot (2005), "Collateral Vamage: Human Rights Consequences of Counterterrorist Action in the Asia-Pacific" . . ., pp. 414–415, op. cit.

161 See "NATO, EU Unite Amid Uncertainty Posed By Trump", *The Guardian* (Lagos), Wednesday, December 7, 2016, p. 40.

162 See "Full Text of President Donald Trump's Inauguration Speech", available at http://abcnews.go.com/Politics/full-text-president-donald-trumps-inauguration-speech/story?id=44915821 (last visited on Wednesday, January 25, 2017), op. cit. Parentheses mine.

163 See Wendy Sherman, Evans Revere, Chris Hill, Gregory F. Treverton, Victor Cha, and Kurt Campbell in "North Korea: How to Stop Kim Jong Un", *Time* (New York), April 3, 2017, pp. 29–32.

14 To Achieve a Successful WoT

Can the WoT be Won?

> The defining feature of the West's war against radical Islamic militants has been its constant shape—shifting; at times, it can seem like whack-a-mole—enemies are killed, others pop up. The fortunes of the opposition wax and—in the case of ISIS now—wane, as they figure out new ways to attack. ISIS, now degraded, as Obama vowed, will necessarily be in transition but perhaps no less lethal. Al-Qaeda is expanding, patiently, and still has ambitions for large-scale attacks in the West, at a time and place of its choosing. The war grinds on.
>
> (Bill Power et al, *Newsweek*, October 21, 2016, p. 33)

Indeed, the "war on terror" grinds on as Bill Power et al. said in the epigram; and it grinds on because of the intractability or resilience of terrorists. In early 2013 when he was winding down as the acting head of the CIA, Michael Morell told President Obama "who came to office wanting to end wars" that this was futile, insisting that "my children's generation and my grandchildren's generation will still be fighting this fight".[1] And so, as the United Nations Secretary-General, Antonio Guterres, declared when he took office on January 1, 2017 in the wake of the exit of Ban Ki-moon and was appealing for peace: in the war on terror, millions of people are caught up in conflicts and massive sufferings that have no end in sight.[2]

And specifically in Syria, Guterres declared that "civilians are pounded with deadly force; women, children and men are killed and injured, forced from their homes, dispossessed and destitute; even Hospitals and aid convoys are targeted. . . . No one wins these wars; rather, everyone loses".[3] These are pretty scary scenarios, painted at different occasions by Michael Morell and Antonio Guterres. And these scary scenarios can actually be possible, given that terrorism

1 See Bill Powell, Mahmoud Shikh Ibrahim, Jack Moore, and Mirren Gidda in "The New ISIS Crisis". . ., p. 33, op. cit.

2 See "Guterres Preaches Peace as He Takes over UN Sec-Gen Office", *The Nation* (Lagos), Monday, January 2, 2017, p. 45.

3 Loc. Cit.

and the war against it are unremitting; more so as "there are 20 million Arab Sunnis in the northern Middle East—350,000 military-age young men in Mosul alone—all asking [the United States], what are you doing'"?[4]

However, tremendous progress was made in 2016, through 2017, in the war on terror, at least, in the battle against the ISIS. In October/November 2016, the battle to retake Mosul after the liberation of many Sunni cities in Iraq held by the ISIS began.[5] By March 2017 (following the ISIS's loss of territories), Abu Bakr al-Baghdadi, the "Caliph" or leader of the ISIS who "declared himself the ruler of all Muslims from Mosul's Great Mosque after his forces swept through northern Iraq in 2014" had practically abandoned ship, leaving "operational commanders behind with diehard followers to fight the battle of Mosul" while "hiding out in the desert, focusing mainly on his own survival" and abandoning all modern gadgets of communication that could help the U.S. and Iraqi authorities locate him.[6] Caliph Abu Bakr al-Baghdadi had "abandoned the city [of Mosul] by far the largest population center his group has ever held".[7]

At the same time, the Syrian opposition forces, "backed by U.S. special operations forces" had "begun to surround Raqqa, cutting off supply lines and preparing the battlefield for an offensive likely to come" by next year.[8] The expectation was that the campaign to take Raqqa, the capital of ISIS, would be wrapped up by early 2017; in addition to the expectation that an aggressive cyber force would also be marshaled out against the terrorists in cyber sphere.[9] In fact, the prospects of routing the ISIS from their redoubtable territorial redoubts (including their presence in cyber sphere) was looking so good that pundits began drawing the attention of President Trump and other Western leaders to the need to "shift to defeating global terrorist strikes, tracking jihadist returnees to Europe and shutting down cybercriminal income streams" and operations in order to avoid "a major cyber event" comparable to the 9/11 attacks.[10]

Expectedly, by July 6, 2017, "all but the last alley ways of the Old City" of Mosul were back in the hands of the Iraqi government, while earlier on July 4, 2017, the American-led forces in Syria had breached the old city walls of the ISIS's capital in Raqqa.[11] By Sunday, July 9, 2017, the Iraqi Prime Minister Haider al-Abadi, had declared his government's victory over Mosul, living ISIS

4 See Bill Powell, Mahmoud Shikh Ibrahim, Jack Moore, and Mirren Gidda in "The New ISIS Crisis". . ., p. 32, op. cit.
5 See "Iraq PM Claims Mosul Victory", *Vanguard* (Lagos), Monday, July 10, 2017, p. 39.
6 See "ISIS Leader, Baghdadi, Abandons Mosul to Field Commanders, US, Iraqi Sources Say" . . ., p. 42, op. cit.
7 Loc. Cit. Brackets mine.
8 See Bill Powell, Mahmoud Shikh Ibrahim, Jack Moore, and Mirren Gidda in "The New ISIS Crisis". . ., p. 29, op. cit.
9 See Admiral James Stavridis in "The Foreign Policy Challenges That Will Fill up President Trump's Inbox", *Time* (New York), November 28–December 5, 2016, p. 16.
10 Loc. Cit.
11 See "Last Days of the Caliphate", *The Economist*, July 8, 2017, p. 27.

with only a sprinkle of presence in the rest of Iraq.[12] The victory over ISIS in Mosul and Raqqa was being proclaimed amid speculations that its leader, Abu Bakr al-Baghdadi, had been killed;[13] even though another report maintained that he was alive.[14] But although the taking of Mosul and Raqqa would be an ultimate humiliation for al-Baghdadi and the ISIS—"demonstrating that ISIS could not create and hold its 'Caliphate' indefinitely—it, nonetheless, does not mean it is defeated",[15] given its sprinkling presence in parts of Syria, Iraq, and other Middle East and African countries.

In fact, the spread of the ISIS to Southeast Asia (the Philippines) has made it trite knowledge that, "defeating Islamist insurgencies in battle is not the same as winning the war".[16] In Nigeria, even after the Buhari government had claimed victory over the Boko Haram because of the so-called seizure of its fortress at Sambisa Forest, the terror "group audaciously laid in ambush for the Nigerian National Petroleum Corporation crude oil exploration team to the lake Chad Basin, successfully slaughtering 18 soldiers, five University of Maiduguri members of staff and other civilians" and capturing and taking three Senior Lecturers hostage.[17] This and other campaigns of violence by the Boko Haram were to the chagrin of the United States and Transparency International.[18]

Not even the so-called "rubble-izing [of] Sunni cities"[19] can prevent this war from grinding on, given the resilience of ISIS, their capacity, after losing territory and their so-called Caliphate, to (like the al-Qaeda did) morph into a network that organizes terrorist attacks in distant Western countries.[20] This was in addition to the troubling news that cropped up at the cusp of the defeat of the ISIS in Mosul and Raqqa—that the terror group had spread to Southeast Asia, seizing the Philippine city of Marawi "whose mostly Muslim population of 202,000 people makes . . . the biggest Islamic community in what is otherwise an overwhelmingly Catholic country".[21] The ISIS in the Marawi city of Philippine is "what locals call Grupo ISIS, an ad hoc coalition of insurgent and kidnap-for-ransom militias that have pledged allegiance to ISIS leader Abu Bakr al-Baghdadi".[22]

12 See "Iraq PM Claims Mosul Victory", p. 39, op. cit; see also "Battle for Mosul: Iraq PM Abadi Formally Declares Victory", *ThisDay* (Lagos), Tuesday, July 11, 2017, p. 36.
13 See "ISIS Confirms Death of It's Leader, Al-Baghdadi", *Vanguard* (Lagos), Wednesday, July 12, 2017, p. 45.
14 See "ISIS Leader Alive, Sighted in Syria", *Vanguard* (Lagos), Tuesday, July 18, 2017, p. 44.
15 See Bill Powell, Mahmoud Shikh Ibrahim, Jack Moore, and Mirren Gidda in "The New ISIS Crisis". . ., p. 29, op. cit.
16 See "Mosul in Mindanao", *The Economist*, July 22, 2017, p. 45.
17 See "Boko Haram: De-Radicalization, a Misplaced Strategy", p. 20, op. cit.
18 See "Boko Haram: US, TI Reports Confirm FG's Deceit", p. 11, op. cit.
19 See Bill Powell, Mahmoud Shikh Ibrahim, Jack Moore, and Mirren Gidda in "The New ISIS Crisis". . ., p. 32, op. cit. Brackets mine.
20 Ibid., p. 30.
21 See Joseph Hincks in "A Deadly New Front for ISIS", *Time* (New York), July 3, 2017, p. 36.
22 Loc. Cit.

Besides, it has also been reported that the ISIS was beginning not to be much of a problem because the al-Qaeda had started "making a terrifying comeback, led by Osama bin Laden's son".[23] Obviously, the loss of territory or death/killing of a terrorist organization's leader is not tantamount to the defeat of the terrorism as the loss of territory (the "Caliphate") by the ISIS and the killing of Osama bin Laden have demonstrated. The increasing resilience of terrorists can be found in their capacity to embark on "digital insurgency",[24] in which they can create a "digital Caliphate" and use "digital madrassas" on the social media to spread hate and radicalize more militants,[25] which underscore the need to go beyond "geographic [or territorial] issues and amp up the . . . game on cyber security".[26] But the war on terrorism can be won if history does not repeat itself, if the very circumstances that led to the creation of both the al-Qaeda and ISIS are not re-enacted.[27] So, amongst other imperatives, the steps that are canvassed hereunder can be helpful in bringing terrorists to heel and to eventually winning the war against them.

Depoliticize, De-Stigmatize, and Leverage Exemplary Values

Despite its effectiveness in the series of attempts to pin pointedly target and take out terrorists in the midst of civilian habitations without incurring unacceptable collateral damage, the armed drone technology as a cutting-edge aerial instrument for combating terrorism has so far proved that reliance on its capability alone cannot win the global war on terror. This realization was what apparently dawned on Secretary Clinton in the heat of the 2016 United States Presidential election campaigns and led her in presenting her agenda or manifesto, to proffer a more comprehensive approach to defeating ISIS and ipso facto, winning the war on terrorism, declaring as it were that:

> We need to take out their strongholds in Iraq and Syria by intensifying the air campaign and stepping up our support for Arab and Kurdish forces on the ground. We need to keep pursuing diplomacy to end Syria's civil war and close Iraq's sectarian divide, because those conflicts are keeping ISIS alive. We need to lash up with our allies, and ensure our intelligence services are

23 See Ali Soufan in "Daddy Issues: Forget ISIS—Al-Qaeda Is Making a Terrifying Comeback, Led by Osama bin Laden's Son", *Newsweek*, June 30, 2017, pp. 12–17.

24 See Sinem Bilen-Onabanjo in "Digital Insurgency: For Governments, the Unguarded Voices on Social Media Are Now a Formidable Political Threat", *New African*, November 2016, pp. 26–27.

25 See "World-Wide Mullahs: The Rise of the Digital Madrassa", p. 46, op. cit.

26 See Admiral James Stavridis in "The Foreign Policy Challenges That Will Fill up President Trump's Inbox", p. 16, op. cit.

27 See Jonathan Broder in "Made in America? How the Origins of the Islamic State May Lie in Washington, D.C.", *Newsweek*, June 12 2015, published in a special *Newsweek* edition, "Killing ISIS: America's All-Out Assault on a Global Threat", 2016 (undated), pp. 22–25, op. cit.

> working hand-in-hand to dismantle the global network that supplies money, arms, propaganda and fighters to the terrorists. We need to win the battle in cyberspace. And of course we need to strengthen our defenses here at home. That—in a nutshell—is my plan for defeating ISIS.[28]

But it is also interesting to know that despite the entire hullabaloo that attends drone strikes, the U.S. President Barack Obama, throughout his Presidency, continued with the extensive use of this controversial weapon in his country's prosecution of the "war on terror".[29] In fact, President Obama never flinched from taking kinetic action against identified high value terrorist targets in the putative epicenter-frontlines of terror in Afghanistan, Pakistan, Syria, and Iraq; and using it also outside these epicenters, including places like Somalia, Libya, and other emergent theaters. And given his obsession with the use of force to get rid of the ISIS and other terrorist organizations, President Trump is definitely in no frame of mind to discontinue the use of armed drones. These drone strikes continued despite the mounting collateral damage that Washington's rigorous safety measures have consistently failed to successfully avoid. But the mounting casualties amongst the civilian population can best be explained by the fact that in this war, what the United States confronts is "battlespace" rather than battlefields, the former, "battlespace", deriving this name on account of the fact that the environment of engagement with the terrorists is highly contaminated with civilians that become unavoidably caught in the crosshairs.

Both the "war on terror" and the armed drones used in its prosecution by Washington are all controversial because of the numerous dilemma they present, especially to the law of armed conflict in general and international humanitarian law in particular. This dilemma also extends to the otherwise requirements of ethics and the exhibition of chivalry; not to talk of the frightening prospect of the emergence of automated and miniaturized armed drones. Ethics and chivalry are age-old values associated not just with the entire humanity but also highly expected of the United States because it is a great power as well as the leader of the "free" world. When, therefore, the view is expressed that in the fight against ISIS and other terrorist organizations, what the United States and the West writ-large are faced with is the dual responsibility of defending their citizen as well as their values,[30] this expression is actually hitting the nail on the head; it is pointing point blank on one of the major problems experienced in confronting or dealing with terrorists in the current "war on terror".

Thus, counter-terrorism through intense security tightening and the use of armed drones for targeted killings are actually pulling hard at the heart of

28 See "Hillary Clinton Speaks about National Security on Thursday in San Diego", available at www.marketwatch.com/story/text-of-hillary-clintons-speech-on-national-security-2016-06-02?siteid=rss&rss=1 (last visited on Friday, June 3, 2016), op. cit.

29 See Ian Bremmer in "The Risk Report: Debunking Trump's Foreign Policy", *Time* (New York), April 11, 2016, p. 12.

30 See "How to Fight Back . . .", p. 13, op. cit.

Western values. The U.S. President Obama acknowledged this much when he declared that because of the war on terror:

> . . . we strengthened our defenses—hardening targets, tightening transportation security and giving law enforcement new tools to prevent terror. Most of these changes were sound. Some caused inconvenience. But some, like expanded surveillance, raised difficult questions about the balance we strike between our interests in security and our values. . . . And in some cases; I believe we compromised our basic values—by using torture to interrogate our enemies, and detaining individuals in a way that ran counter to the rule of law.[31]

It is not just in using torture to interrogate, and in detaining in ways at variance with the rule of law, that the war on terror is at variance with Western values; much of the actions taken in the war also contradict or compromise the values of entire humanity, especially in the law regulating armed conflicts, an aspect of which is the place of targeting killings and unacceptable collateral damage in international humanitarian law. In other words, the confrontation with terrorism is tugging hard on all the entire gamut of values known to humanity in the conduct of armed conflict, from the more recent ethos of warfare as found in international conventions or treaties, to the medieval but cherished ethical and chivalrous values of yore. The war on terror is something that is continually feasted upon or taken advantage of by the "combatants", the terrorists themselves, the military authorities of the nation-state as well as the hardliners amongst politicians in many countries, particularly to create the divisive impression inherent in the notion of the war as a result of the clash of civilization.

But some of the cherished values in armed conflict are, nonetheless, not exclusively Western. They are actually the values of rational humanity; and one of these values is the capacity to show distinction or discrimination in favour of the innocent, including the capacity to resist tarring peoples and religions with the same brush and, thus, inadvertently giving credence to the proponents of the so-called theory of the clash of civilization in the "war on terror". As observed earlier in this book, the Millenarian conviction in modern international terrorism may be forcefully surging more than ever, and even transcendent; but as seen in the examples offered by the Palestinian resistance, the misbegotten policies of the Shiite-dominated government of President Al-Maliki in Iraq after the fall of Saddam Hussein, and the broken prebendal or patrimonial relationship between the Boko Haram sect and politicians in northeast Nigeria, imbibing the Millenarian conviction to commit acts of terror issues or results first and foremost, from the failings in material or socio-economic and political expectations.

31 See the "Full Transcript of President Obama's Speech on Counterterrorism Policy" at the National Defense University, Fort McNair, available at http://news.yahoo.com/full-transcript-president-obama-speech-counter-terrorism-policy-18 . . . (last visited on May 24, 2013), op. cit.

The implication of this is that terrorism, especially the heinous millenarian brand of it (in which groups like the ISIS not only attack people of other faiths but also attack Muslims that tend to be accommodating of Western values or culture) is not principally motivated by the clash of civilization or religion in itself; neither is the propensity for terror intrinsic in any people, ideology, race, or tribe. Curiously, although agentially,[32] it is also a critical component in the phenomenon of millenarian terrorism, the clash of civilization narrative tends to have preceded Osama bin Laden and his cohorts and, thus, sticks. In Africa, for instance, and "from a longer historical lens, the current [terrorist] insurgencies roughly coincide with what was once the southernmost expansion of the Arabic spread into the African continent, just below the line demarcating the Sahel"; thus, tending to re-pose the question: "are the Islamic insurgents operating on the premise of the long-held Arab expansionist ambitions in Africa?"[33] In other words, the theory of the clash of civilization in the explanation of contemporary terrorist predispositions tends to find credence in frontlines like Nigeria where "Islam and Christianity meet", with a "fault line [that] runs from east to west across the country roughly at the level of Jos . . . "[34]

Unfortunately, there are "similar fault lines in Sudan and Cote d'Ivoire";[35] and, indeed, other crisis and ultimate cultural-fault lines related civil wars (first in Chad and later in the Darfur region of Sudan) in many African countries that are tell-tale signs of this alleged Arab expansionist design on Africa, which, in addition to the invocation of the sense of clash of civilization, is also redolent of racism.[36] For this reason, "the concept of terrorism on the African continent has become for many, interchangeable with Islam", a situation that "is as true for the terrorist actors as it is for the managers of the African state and their allies";[37] these allies being the Western nations. But rather than being principally the function of a clash of civilization or religion, terrorism is, in addition, a function of failed material expectations, be it political, ideological, or economic materialism, on account of which no religion or people can be stereotyped.

Hence, if a nationalism-fiery young lecturer of the University of Nigeria, Nsukka, on a diplomatic mission for the defunct Christian-dominated Republic of Biafra, could be so persuaded by the pitiable plight of the people of war-ravaged

32 In northern Nigeria where the Boko Haram operates, failed prebendalism combines with the fact that Nigeria is one of the meeting points of two cultures (Islam and Western civilization) to enhance the theory of the clash of civilization in the incidence of terrorism; see Animasawun Gbemisola Abdul-Jelil (2016), Agential and structural explanations of radical Islamism in Northern Nigeria in the Fourth Republic" . . ., op. cit.

33 See Kalundi Serumaga in "Terrorism in Africa Is No Longer Somebody Else's War", p. 36, op. cit. Brackets mine.

34 See John Campbell (2011), *Nigeria: Dancing on the Brink* . . ., p. 41, op. cit.

35 Ibid., p. 42.

36 See Fred Aja Agwu (2009), *National Interest, International Law* . . ., pp. 420–424, op. cit.

37 See Kalundi Serumaga in "Terrorism in Africa Is No Longer Somebody Else's War", p. 36, op. cit.

secessionist enclave to want to ditch an airplane in an apparent fit or crave for suicidal terrorism;[38] and an Israeli nationalist like Menachem Begin could be a prime suspect in the blowing up of King David Hotel in Jerusalem during the struggle for the realization of the Jewish state of Israel,[39] then, His Eminence, Pope Francis, was right in his submission that "no religion is immune from forms of individual delusion or ideological extremism", and that "we must be especially attentive to every type of fundamentalism, whether religious or of any other kind".[40]

To be sure, terrorist attacks (both against the United States, within and outside the homeland, and other nations) did not begin with Islamic fundamentalists, the al-Qaeda and its associates. Before the activities of the al-Qaeda and its associates, there had been Timothy McVeigh who blew up the Alfred Murray Federal Building in Oklahoma;[41] there was also, in 1975, the shooting to death of the CIA's head of station in Athens, and the "fatal bomb explosion at New York's La Guardia airport";[42] just as elsewhere in Europe, there were other terrorist outrages—"by the Irish Republican Army in London, by the Palestinian Liberation Organization in Vienna, [and] by South Moluccan Separatists in the Netherlands".[43] Of course, the writer, Kalundi Serumaga aforementioned, in debunking the attribution of Islamic religious dynamics to terrorism, reminded that there was also terrorism in one of the earliest beheadings in recorded human history.

The beheading cited by Serumaga was the religious beheading of one Mukasa, the Katikkiro or native prime minister in the Kingdom of Buganda (in today's Uganda) who was "described by exasperated Christian Anglican missionaries as an 'inveterate pagan' and was thus dispatched [killed] during the religious civil wars in the 1890s that resulted in the formation of present-day Uganda".[44] Thus, modern-day terrorist tactics has a precursor in the fact that "many of the long-established mission stations in Buganda are built directly on top of destroyed native shrines".[45] And citing the firebombing of the German city of Dresden during the Second World War and the U.S.-led invasion of Iraq, "in which an estimated 650,000 civilians were killed, many by Uranium-enriched cluster bombs", Serumaga also reminded that "beheading aside, many of the methods now 'branded' Islamic, such as attacks on civilian sites, suicide bombings,

38 See Arthur Mbanefo (2015), *A Fulfilled Life of Service*, Ibadan, Bookcraft, p. 49.

39 See Kalundi Serumaga in "Terrorism in Africa Is No Longer Somebody Else's War", p. 37, op. cit.

40 See the "Full Text of Pope Francis' Speech to US Congress: Pope Takes His Case for Action on the Death Penalty, Climate Change and Immigration to US Congress in Historic Speech", available at www.aljazeera.com/news/2015/09/full-text-pope-francis-speech-congress-150924152204132.htmlSee (last visited on March 4, 2016), op. cit.

41 See Fred Aja Agwu (2013), *Themes and Perspectives . . .*, pp. 240, 258, op. cit.

42 See Niall Ferguson (2015), *Kissinger, 1923–1968: The Idealist*, Vol. 1, New York, Penguin Press, p. 38.

43 Ibid., pp. 37–38.

44 See Kalundi Serumaga in "Terrorism in Africa Is No Longer Somebody Else's War", p. 37, op. cit. Brackets mine.

45 Loc. Cit.

the destruction of cultural sites, conscription of children, taking of women as sex-slaves, and the like, have long been practices in many a theatre of conflict".[46] So, rather than the stereotyping, Pope Francis was of the conviction that "a delicate balance is required to combat violence perpetrated in the name of a religion, an ideology or an economic system, while also safeguarding religious freedom, intellectual freedom and individual freedom".[47]

Terrorism, especially the millenarian variety is a mixture of different types of causation. Even at the religious level, there are inter and intra-religious causes, like Christian/Muslim divisions and Sunni/Shiite divisions, divisions that are not along simple or fine lines and, thus, do not amount to a clash of civilizations, especially in the light of the intra-religious Sunni/Shiite hostilities. There are also economic and political dimensions to solving terror. It is particularly because of the economic and political causes of terror that the wind is taken off the sail of the cultural or religious motivation for terror, the said clash of civilization. As Bernard Lewis explains with respect to the anti-Americanism in the Middle East, as long as the American foreign involvement in the region is exclusively economic, "and as long as the rewards were more than adequate to sooth every grievance the alien presence could be borne"; but "with the fall in oil prices and the rise in population and expenditure, the rewards are no longer adequate; [and] the grievances have become more numerous and more vocal".[48]

Indeed, Osama bin Laden and his cohorts in the radical and terrorist Islamic movement noted the declining quality of life in the Arab world (vis-à-vis what obtains in the oil-rich Latin America countries) despite its oil wealth (itself a result of the plummeting oil prices) as one of their grouses and reasons for exhorting the Muslim world to make the United States and its allies the targets of violence.[49] This was a sharp contrast to when the oil trade boomed and the Saudis, especially the members of the royal family "became billionaires many times over", resulting in the "militant Islamic fundamentalists and the United States [turning] a blind eye to each other", a policy of "don't ask, don't tell", what Craig Unger said was instructed by the Koran's version of that policy which says, "ask not about things which, if made plain to you, may cause you trouble".[50]

Politically, the Iranian revolution that saw to the overthrow of the Shah, Saddam Hussein's ambitious coveting of Kuwait, and the Israel-Palestinian conflict have all "lent some plausibility to the cries of imperialism" that contributes the grievances of the terrorists.[51] For these, amongst other reasons, Kalundi Serumaga was

46 Ibid., pp. 36–37.

47 See the "Full Text of Pope Francis' Speech to US Congress: Pope Takes His Case for Action on the Death Penalty, Climate Change and Immigration to US Congress in Historic Speech", available at www.aljazeera.com/news/2015/09/full-text-pope-francis-speech-congress-150924152204132.htmlSee (last visited on March 4, 2016), op. cit.

48 See Bernard Lewis (2003), *The Crisis of Islam* . . ., p. xxxi, op. cit. Brackets mine.

49 See Fred Aja Agwu (2009), *National Interest, International Law* . . ., pp. 277–278, op. cit.

50 See Craig Unger (2004), *House of Bush, House of Saud*, p. 4, op. cit.

51 See Bernard Lewis (2003), *The Crisis of Islam* . . ., p. xxxi, op. cit.

inclined to compare the actions of the West in the Middle East that stirred up this wave of terrorist attacks against it to the European conquest of Africa, which he insists was a form of jihad in its own way; and that the enmity that the West has incurred with the Middle East jihadists is "sometimes well-deserved".[52] But this enmity is certainly not well-deserved; not when (even if the West were to be held responsible for the socio-economic and political woes in the Middle East) the victims of the terror attacks on the West are ordinary folks, not the architects of the offences that cause the grievances of the Middle East militants; and not when the West is not alone in suffering the terrorist threats, for Africa, on its part, as Serumaga acknowledged too, is also facing the threats from its own homegrown terrorists that have the active support of the Middle East militants.[53] As a matter of fact, it is also inappropriate, without prejudice to the Anglican missionaries' treatment of Mukasa (the Katikkiro of the Kingdom of Buganda) to characterize the Western missionaries' activities in Africa as a jihad in its own way, comparable to what the Middle East militants are doing at the moment.

It is also important to realize that combating terrorism of all varieties demands measures that go beyond military operations. It requires holistic measures that also include socio-cultural, economic, and political remedies. President Obama acknowledged this much in his counter-terrorism policy speech at the U.S. National Defense University when he declared that:

> . . . the next element of our strategy involves addressing the underlying grievances and conflicts that feed extremism, from North Africa to South Asia. As we have learned in the past decade, this is a vast and complex undertaking. We must be humble in our expectation that we can quickly resolve deep rooted problems like poverty and sectarian hatred . . . . But our security and values demand that we make efforts . . . . the peaceful realization of individual aspirations will serve as a rebuke to violent extremists . . . . we must help countries modernize economies, upgrade education, and encourage entrepreneurship—because American leadership has always been elevated by our ability to connect with people's hopes, and not simply their fears.[54]

This was the noble, uplifting and clearly inclusive view that President Barack Obama shared with respect to deploying America's supposed exemplary values to defeat terrorism. Unfortunately, President Trump, particularly during his election campaigns, did not seem to share in the use of those values to achieve

52 See Kalundi Serumaga in "Terrorism in Africa Is No Longer Somebody Else's War", p. 37, op. cit.

53 Ibid., pp. 34–35.

54 See the "Full Transcript of President Obama's Speech on Counterterrorism Policy" at the National Defense University, Fort McNair, available at http://news.yahoo.com/full-transcript-president-obama-speech-counter-terrorism-policy-18 . . . (last visited on May 24, 2013), op. cit.

the anti-terrorism objectives. With his stereotyping view of the Moslem faithful, Trump did not seem prepared to connect with the hopes and aspirations, or even douse the fears of the majority of moderate Muslims. Unlike President Barack Obama that believed that addressing socio-political and economic concerns can help tackle the menace of terrorism, President Trump, on the contrary, is a law and order person. In other words, he believes that merely rolling out laws and enforcing them can protect Americans from the scourge of terrorism. Listen to President Trump in his inauguration speech:

> We are protected and we will always be protected. We will be protected by the great men and women of our military and law enforcement and most importantly, we will be protected by God.[55]

Part of what President Trump did in pursuit of his law and order conviction as soon as he was sworn into office was to sign an executive order that cracks down on immigration; a border enforcement order that included plans "to hire 5,000 more US Customs and Border Protection agents used to apprehend people seeking to slip across the border; and to triple the number of US Immigration and Customs Enforcement agents used to arrest and deport immigrants living in the United States illegally".[56] Until the Trump executive order, "the Customs and Border Protection agency [had] struggled to meet its hiring mandate with a little more than 19,000 agents on the payroll, out of a congressionally mandated 21,000".[57] Unfortunately, the 9/11 terrorists never entered the United States illegally, and the American men and women in uniform did not protect the country on 9/11.

All of the American men and women in uniform, including the law enforcement officers, were caught unawares on 9/11, which is the most tragic and enduring character of terrorist strikes. All these outbursts from President Trump suggest his naivety in the understanding and handling of the terrorism challenge. And from Trump's suggestion that American Muslims should be profiled, through his advocacy (as a presidential candidate) that Muslims should be banned from entering the United States, to his executive order as the President of the United States to ban, especially, Muslim refugees from entering America, it is clear that he is implicitly (even if unwittingly) exaggerating the clash of civilization narrative, feeding extremism and not addressing some of the underlying grievances and fears that stoke the furnace of extremist behaviour and terrorism.

55 See "Full Text of President Donald Trump's Inauguration Speech", available at http://abcnews.go.com/Politics/full-text-president-donald-trumps-inauguration-speech/story?id=44915821 (last visited on Wednesday, January 25, 2017), op. cit.

56 See "Trump to Ban People from Syria, Six other Countries from Entering America", *Vanguard* (Lagos), Thursday, January 26, 2017, p. 38.

57 Loc. Cit.

Leverage a Collective/Coordinated Global Response

> When member states are divided, the U.N. cannot function properly. When Security Council members are united, they have been able to address the issues protecting international peace and security. I'm concerned about this growing trend of nationalism in many, many parts of the world. We are living on, after all, a very small planet. There is not much meaning at this time to the geopolitical borders or individual national regulations. We are going through such a rapid, transformative process of globalization that we have to act as one human being. We have to act as a global citizen.
>
> (Ban Ki-moon, former U.N. Secretary-General)[58]

The former United Nations Secretary-General, Ban Ki-moon's observation—made in 2016 as many countries in Europe and North America, beginning with Brexit and the election of President Trump in the United States, witnessed an unprecedented surge in nationalism and the rise of the ultra-right parties—underlines the importance of multilateral, collective, or coordinated response to the war on terror. This statement by Ban Ki-moon implicitly underlines the importance of globalization as the purveyor or bulwark of the global multilateral institutions that are critical for fighting terrorism. It, thus, equally underlines the imperative of curing globalization of its many ills in order to defeat the surge of nationalism (ultra-nationalism) and populism that are antithetical to globalization and the necessary coalescence to fight and defeat terrorism. Pope Francis added his voice to this need for a collective measure when, addressing some 50,000 faithful that gathered at St. Peter's Square in Rome for his traditional noon address on January 1, 2017 New Year, he urged "the Lord to sustain all men of goodwill to courageously roll up their sleeves to confront the plague of terrorism and this stain of blood that is covering the world with a shadow of fear and a sense of loss".[59]

There is therefore no doubt that any hope of success in the war on terror would require that the international community acts together through, in particular, the auspices of the United Nations, being the only planetary or most inclusive multilateral framework available to humanity at the moment. Going through the United Nations platform is a matter of necessity, not expediency because combating terrorism requires a global response that must set stock by (1) the cultivation of common global data bases, especially at the level of Interpol, (2) global intelligence sharing, (3) international borders securitization, and (4) the establishment of biometric identity scheme at a global level. In other words, to bolster or ensure the success of military operations in the war on terror, there must also be a complementary surge in communication and intelligence

58 Mr. Ban Ki-moon, former United Nations Secretary-General speaking with Elizabeth Dias "On Trump, Global Citizenship and the Future of Disarmament in His Departing Days from Office"; see *Time* (New York), December 26, 2016–January 2, 2017, p. 57.

59 See "Terrorism Casts Bloodstain over the World, Says Pope", *The Nation* (Lagos), January 2, 2017, p. 6, op. cit.

surveillance (amongst other related activities), standardization, coordination, and sharing amongst national and international security services.

Intelligence standardization requires a vigorous implementation of biometric identity cards across nations, a sort of international capacity building that would not discriminate against any nation, especially the most terror-infested or poor countries of Africa. The biometric identity scheme will facilitate a better tracking and identification of terrorists.[60] In the wake of the Brussels airport and metro attacks of late March 2016, serious suggestions were floated by analysts on the importance of installing computer software at airport lounges and other public places like metro stations, computer software that would advance behavioural profiling, such as the ability to detect the terrorists that are about to strike through their nervousness; even though this measure has a serious shortcoming because at the airports, for instance, innocent people who are nervous because they have a phobia for flying could be implicated.[61] As a matter of fact, instead of looking nervous or flustered, the security camera that captured the Brussels airport bombers shortly before their suicide mission was accomplished, showed them cool and well collected even though they were moments away from a sure or imminent death.

Nevertheless, this shortcoming should in no way deter this noble security tip. It was a task that Washington under the Obama administration was more focused on as it continued to discountenance any attempt by politicians like Donald Trump (and the terrorists themselves[62]) to use his anti-NATO[63] and anti-Muslim rhetoric to stereotype peoples and religions in the "war on terror".[64] But matters

60 See "Mali, B'Faso, Senegal, Cote d'Ivoire Raise Efforts to Fight Terror", *The Guardian* (Lagos), Friday, March 25, 2016, p. 18.

61 This suggestion came up in the programme, "Quest Means Business", hosted by Richard Quest on CNN, circa March/April 2016, the aftermath of the Brussels bombings.

62 Osama bin Laden and his co-travelers in the promotion of the clash of civilization in the war on terror tried and still try to cast the war in the mould of a struggle between Christian and Muslims, or between believers and infidels; see Bernard Lewis (2003), *The Crisis of Islam . . .*, pp. xvi–xxxii, op. cit.

63 See Ian Bremmer in "The Hollow Alliance: The Historic Concord between the U.S. and Europe Made the West Safe and Rich. Now, It's in Danger of Collapse", *Time* (New York), June 27, 2016, pp. 38–41.

64 Donald Trump, the Republican candidate who eventually won the U.S. 2016 presidential election, was controversial for his "trademark exhibitionist belligerence", his histrionics and bluster about his intention to embark on an "America first" foreign policy if elected President; vowing that although he would not scrap it, but that he would de-emphasize the North Atlantic Treaty Organization (NATO) because of its obsolesce; that some U.S. allies like Germany, Japan, and South Korea that outsource and depend on America for their security are free riders/loaders that would be meant to pay more of their bills or even acquire their own nuclear weapons; see Ian Bremmer in "Debunking Trump's Foreign Policy", p. 12, op. cit. Trump was also notorious for his anti-Muslim sentiments, having said that Muslims should be banned from entering the United States, that Islam as a religion was hostile to the United States and even the entire West; Trump also, in his campaign trails, pointedly (beyond the threshold of insinuations) accused President Obama of creating and being in sympathy with the ISIS; and that American Muslims should be profiled, a call he reiterated after the Orlando massacre; see Joe Klein in "After Orlando, Hillary Clinton Must Defang the Demagogue: And That's Harder Than It Looks", *Time* (New York), June 27, 2016, p. 25.

are not helped by the difficulty the United States as the pioneer (and still leading) nation in the deployment of armed drones is encountering in trying to protect itself from the cancerous threat of the terrorist malaise. Here, the United States is evidently threading between the devil and the deep blue sea because, in the absence of a defined legal and other necessary normative frameworks for the conduct of the war on terror (being not a traditional insurgency that is territorial and compels the observance of IHL as long as the armed forces are deployed) Washington is truly dealing with a murky situation. Although it has a responsibility as a pathfinder to define the norms, it is hardly ever possible for one nation to unilaterally delineate state practice in international law. And the ways of the terrorists themselves do not even permit for any refined or legal approach in dealing with them.

For instance, because much of contemporary terror attacks are suicidal (as the suicidal terrorist does not attack to return to base for another day), the United States, in self-defence, cannot implement the requirement of response to an armed attack; for after the event (the terrorist attack), Washington is left with nothing as the attacker must have blown himself in an ordinary vapour. All that Washington is left with is attributions to, at best, suspected sponsors, the link of which is sometimes very difficult to create. What to do? This is where the United States is compelled to resort to anticipatory or preemptive self-defence. And this is accomplished by using armed drones to take out the terrorists at the level of planning and mobilization, for the moment the terrorist fully accomplishes his or her plans and mobilizes with his or her suicide vest, an explosive-laden car, and any other form of IEDs, there will be no stopping him or her. It is in this preemptive self-defence that the use of armed drones to achieve "targeted killings" becomes unavoidable.

In conventional armed conflicts, even in the asymmetric traditional insurgency where the insurgents engage the state in pitched battles, they are entitled to the rights and privileges offered by the law of armed conflict; in which case "targeted killings" are forbidden; but in terrorist campaigns and the inevitable anti-terrorist responses ("war on terror") by the United States or any other country that may manufacture or acquire and deploy armed drones, this unusual asymmetry foists the inevitability of "targeted killings" in order that the victim state can protect itself and its citizens by pre-empting the enemy and forestalling the suicidal terrorist attacks. But like the drones in the hands of the United States for eliminating the masterminds of terror, terrorist campaigns are also an instrument at the disposal of modern or 21st-century insurgents like the ISIS, the Taliban, and the Boko Haram. Apart from the brazen secular terrorists that also operate as "lone wolves", these insurgent groups bear the responsibility for the terror attacks that prompted the United States to declare the "war on terror" after the 9/11 attacks by the al-Qaeda, the only congenital terrorist organization that has never been involved in regular insurgency, but has always dwelt on terrorist campaigns, enjoying vast sanctuaries in many sympathetic environments.

To defeat terrorism, the "regular" insurgents like ISIL (ISIS), the Taliban, Al-Shabab, and the Boko Haram must be defeated; and the generous sanctuaries or safe haven that the al-Qaeda and other terrorists enjoy in the territories of nation-states taken out. It was to facilitate this task that the ILC, after the Second World War, developed a framework, known as the "Draft Code of Offences Against the Peace and Security of Mankind", to be a guiding instrument for dealing with modern insurgents. It is under this Code that the nation-state can, acting with the requisite sense of proportionality and distinction, deal with insurgency and terrorism. It is under its protective embrace that the United States can leverage the armed drone technology to carry out both the "personality" and signature strikes", provided it is guided by the sense of humanity, enough to forestall unacceptable civilian casualties or collateral damage. To defeat terror, there is no alternative route other than the defeat of insurgency.

In addition, and especially as it concerns terrorist campaigns, the United Nations Security Council ought to by now have gone beyond the Code to develop a more creative and proactive way of dealing with these special categories of threats; at least to enable it to effectively preempt the arbitrary responses of the state with drone strikes; and, thus, avoid all the grisly human carnage that always goes with the failure of the capacity for precision by these drones. The implication of the international character of modern or contemporary terrorism is that it cannot be unilaterally and effectively defeated by a single country; but rather (especially as seen by the NATO and coalition of Arab forces the United States built against the Taliban and al-Qaeda in Afghanistan, and the ISIS in Iraq and Syria) through the collective effort of all or a significant international coalition.[65] It is not in doubt that the effectiveness of this collective action can best be assured at the level of the United Nations. But is it also doubtful that the United Nations Security Council can attain the requisite unanimity to act?

But the ability of the Security Council for unanimity is also very doubtful. The United Nations, as Ian Bremmer cynically put it, is "an organization led by five powerful countries interested mainly in thwarting one another's plans, and administered by functionaries obsessed with protocol and lacking in common sense".[66] In the Syrian conflict under reference, those who run the UN and who had brokered many failed peace deals had got their efforts stalled "because participating governments [especially between the US and Russia] can't agree on what a future Syria should look like".[67] Between the United States and Russia in particular, distrust runs deep on Syria. One of the instances of distrust between the two leading nuclear power nations in the United Nations Security Council manifested itself in the wake of a truce they negotiated in Geneva to take effect on Monday, September 12, 2016, and which would open a humanitarian corridor for the besieged rebel-held Aleppo.[68]

65 See Fred Aja Agwu (2013), *Themes and Perspectives* . . ., pp. 352–356, op. cit.

66 See Ian Bremmer, "Who Can Run the U.N.? Why the World Needs a Better Secretary-General", *Time* (New York), August 1, 2016, pp. 31–32.

67 Ibid., p. 32. Brackets mine.

68 See Jared Malsin in "Syria: A Fragile Ceasefire Raises Hopes for a Desperately Needed Peace", *Time* (New York), September 26, 2016, p. 13.

One of the conditions for the truce was that the United States would restrain the moderate opposition groups after separating them from the ISIS and other Islamic militants like the al-Nusra Front (a splinter group from the al-Qaeda), while Russia would restrain the Assad regime so that both countries (the United States and Russia) would at the success of the ceasefire, concentrate on the obliteration of the jihadists (the ISIS, the al-Nusra and other downright terrorist organizations). But barely six days after the agreed but tenuous ceasefire went into effect on Monday, September 12, 2016, it got endangered again on Saturday, September 17, after a reportedly inadvertent U.S.-led coalition airstrike in eastern Syria killed "no fewer than 62 Syrian troops . . . in Deir al-Zour", allegedly making it possible for the ISIS (after using the opportunity to "gain ground in the area around the Syrian airbase") to shoot down a Syrian warplane in the area.[69] However, a source on the British Broadcasting Corporation (BBC) hinted that Syria's rare admission that it lost an aircraft to ISIS was not only "intended to draw attention to the consequence of the U.S.-led air strike", but also to further the fantastic conspiracy theory it holds with Russia that the United States was covertly promoting the ISIS.[70]

This incident sparked "a bitter row between the U.S. and Russia at the United Nations Security Council" that Saturday night, igniting a fiery firework of verbal exchange between the envoys of the two countries in their separate meetings with the media that night at the United Nations headquarters in New York.[71] While in that bitter exchange, the U.S. envoy to the UN, Samantha Power, described an emergency Security Council meeting that Russia called a "stunt" that was "replete with moralism and grandstanding", a stunt "uniquely cynical and hypocritical"; her Russian counterpart (the Russian envoy to the UN), Vitaly Churkin, described Samantha Power's walking out of the Security Council in a huff (and, perhaps, the said inadvertent American airstrike against Syrian forces) as "an extraordinary display of American heavy-handedness" he had hitherto not seen in all his over four decades of international life.[72]

By the next day, Sunday, September 18, through Monday, September 19, 2016, the Geneva ceasefire agreement had irretrievably broken down as the Assad regime had resumed the shelling of Aleppo. Another opportunity to build trust and bridge the chasm between the United States and Russia on the Syrian civil war had been frittered away. Syria, once again, returned to active hostilities as another opportunity to evolve a united front against the ISIS and the al-Nusra had once more been lost. It was a testament to the strategic importance of the United States and Russia as power brokers that an end to this stalemate can only be determined by a concord between them. And it was also unfortunate that a

69 See "U.S. Air Attack Endangers Syria's Truce", *The Guardian* (Lagos), Monday, September 19, 2016, p. 11.

70 Loc. Cit.

71 Loc. Cit.

72 Loc. Cit. This development was also monitored from Lagos (Nigeria) on the Cable News Network (CNN) all through Sunday, September 18, 2016.

deterioration in the situation had continued even though there was an international coalition that was supported by some of the P. 5 members of the Security Council. Thus, the Syrian conflict basically plateaued because, apart from the fact that many of these permanent members of the Security Council were distracted by different "cresting waves of [domestic] challenges",[73] the United States and Russia as power brokers basically could not reach a consensus on the way forward.

Both Turkey and Syria were deeply involved in the Syrian conflict, with Turkey as a staunch opponent of the Assad regime, while Russia had deployed troops and its air force in support of the Syrian regime.[74] But because Turkey felt betrayed by the United States' response to the coup and, especially the continued sheltering of Gulen, it joined forces with Russia in Syria to the extent that both countries (Turkey and Russia) brokered a nationwide ceasefire between the moderate rebels and the Assad regime that reportedly took off on December 30, 2016, by midnight.[75] The United States was clearly not a party to that ceasefire; even though Russian President Putin wished that President-elect Trump, after taking office on January 20, 2017, would join the peace effort.[76] This was to heighten Russia's President Putin's relevance, not just in the Middle East in general but also in the Syrian civil war in particular; including heightening the blame on U.S. President Obama for his perceived retreat from Syria and description of the conflict as a trap to be avoided.[77] In that situation, it was felt that President Obama's retreat from Syria with the "smug prediction that Russia would be bogged down in a quagmire there had proved a historic misjudgment" because it moved "the world from a system where America often acted alone to defend its values, with a few countries like Britain riding shotgun, to one where the job of protecting international norms fell to all countries—because everyone benefited from the rules".[78]

Unfortunately, as argued by *The Economist*, President Obama's move was to prove a failed policy because America's step backward created a vacuum that, instead

73 Ian Bremmer wrote, for instance, that the United States, after the long and costly wars in Iraq and Afghanistan, was eager to "avoid any long-term commitment of troops and taxpayer dollars for the foreseeable future"; the UK and EU leaders were battling with the deluge of refugees and, later, Brexit, thus, unable to look abroad for new adventures; China's leaders were fully occupied by the complex, high-stakes domestic economic reform processes and, thus, were not interested in taking on unnecessary risks; and Russia was only prepared to act forcefully wherever President Vladimir Putin (as in Syria under reference) perceived the country's interest and national prestige to be at stake; see Ian Bremmer, "Who Can Run the U.N.? Why the World Needs a Better Secretary-General", pp. 31–32. Op. cit. Brackets mine.

74 See "Russian Ambassador Shot Dead in Gallery", *The Nation* (Lagos), Tuesday, December 20, 2016, p. 41.

75 See "Nationwide Ceasefire Agreed in Syria: ISIS, Affiliate Groups Exempted from Pact", *Vanguard* (Lagos), Friday, December 30, 2016, p. 52.

76 CNN Newsroom, monitored in Lagos (Nigeria), Monday, December 30, 2016, at 7am local time.

77 See "The Fall of Aleppo: Vladimir Putin's Victory, the West's Failure; and a Warning of What Happens When Interests Triumph over Values", *The Economist*, December 17, 2016, p. 11.

78 Loc. Cit.

of being filled by responsible countries that supported the status quo, had the likes of Russia and Iran that "see the promotion of Western values as an insidious plot to bring about regime change in Moscow and Tehran".[79] However, following the thaw in the diplomatic relations between Turkey and Russia; and the resultant fact that "Moscow and Ankara are now working closely together to evacuate citizens from Aleppo" after the regime's victory over the rebels—not discounting the December 30 ceasefire agreement aforementioned that would usher in peace talks in Kazakhstan within a month,[80] which Ankara and Moscow negotiated to the exclusion of Washington—many sympathizers of the rebels in Turkey who were enraged by the civilian casualties of the Russian bombings and the plight of the Syrian refugees became determined to undermine Ankara's dalliance with Moscow.[81]

In the United States, President Putin is considered "a Soviet man from head to toe" who "has always chafed at what he sees as U.S. post-Cold War triumphalism".[82] Hence, President Putin "never welcomed claims by Americans that the U.S. is indispensable and exceptional nation with a responsibility to promote Western values everywhere, including across Russia's neighborhood and inside Russia itself".[83] For these and other geopolitical reasons, President Putin draws deep-seated and variegated reactions that divide the political elite in the United States, both on Syria and on several other matters. For instance, "Hillary Clinton painted Russian President Vladimir Putin as an aggressive autocrat who threatens U.S. national security"; but Donald Trump "treated him as a strong and decisive leader with whom Washington could do business".[84] The implication of Trump's attitude to Putin is that "Trump isn't going to criticize Putin for building a Potemkin democracy at home"; and "his administration will see no value in challenging Russia's claim to Crimea or in going nose to nose over the broader question of Ukraine, an issue Putin cares deeply about", and "Trump isn't going to treat Putin like a thug and his country as a second-rate power".[85] However, the reality has been quite different since Trump took office as President, for his bombing of the Assad regime in the wake of the regime's alleged chemical weapon attack on rebel-held areas had been to the displeasure of President Putin.

But matters were not helped in the United States by the fact that "the American people did not want to get involved in the Syrian war; . . . and when Obama tried to lead them there, they told him [expletive] off".[86] In fact, "in 2013,

79 Loc. Cit.
80 See "Nationwide Ceasefire Agreed in Syria: ISIS, Affiliate Groups Exempted from Pact", p. 52, op. cit.
81 See "Russian Ambassador to Turkey Shot Dead in Ankara", p. 45, op. cit.
82 See Ian Bremmer in "Trump Will Thaw Chilly U.S.-Russia Relationship", p. 12, op. cit.
83 Loc. Cit.
84 Loc. Cit.
85 Loc. Cit.
86 See Jonathan Broder in "Made in America? How the Origins of the Islamic State May Lie in Washington, D.C.", published in a special *Newsweek* edition, "Killing ISIS: America's All-Out Assault on a Global Threat", 2016 (undated), p. 25, op. cit.

when Obama sought congressional authorization to bomb Syria after Assad used chemical weapons against civilians, the President was unable to summon more than 100 votes in both the House and Senate".[87] This was exactly why President Obama did nothing when his red lines were violated by Assad, having warned Assad that using chemical weapons in the conflict was crossing a red line, which would made his Washington to forcibly intervene.[88] The U.S. Secretary of State, John Kerry, was to later express his frustration at the inability of the Congress to support the use of force in Syria.[89]

But again, the situation was not helped by the fact that the then out-going Secretary-General of the United Nations, Ban Ki-moon, was "often accused of timidity and an eagerness to please the permanent members—the U.S. in particular",[90] thus, emerging as a stooge. The job of the United Nations Secretary-General entails walking a diplomatic minefield in which the incumbent must, in walking the tight rope, strive to strike an attitudinal balance; that is, by not being as defiant as a Dag Hammarskjold or as pliant as a Ban Ki-moon.[91] Being egregiously pliant toward any permanent member or showing bias towards all or any of the other permanent members can be very costly in the slippery terrain that is the United Nations Security Council; for as instructed by Kofi Annan, "any senior UN official who chooses to serve just one member of the permanent five members of the Council soon loses the support of the others".[92] In addition, "such an approach would undermine the Council's cohesion, hindering its ability to function as a decision-making body".[93]

Unfortunately, as Annan goes ahead to warn, once the credibility of any senior UN official (that allows himself or herself to be pliant towards or used by, say, the United States) "with the other members of the permanent five was shredded, the United States would then have little use for him, and they would

87 Loc. Cit.

88 See Fred Aja Agwu (2016), *Nations among Nations* . . ., pp. 736–751, op. cit.

89 John Kerry was heard over a hot microphone saying "I argued for use of force in Syria, and I've lost the argument. . . . I think force should not be used against people who defend their country—Syria but against jihadi terrorists and people who support them"; this story is available at www.liveleak.com/view?i=bfe_1475329637&comments=1 (last visited on Monday, November 7, 2016).

90 See Ian Bremmer, "Who Can Run the U.N.? Why the World Needs a Better Secretary-General", pp. 31–32. Op. cit.

91 As stated here, while the accusation against Ban Ki-moon was that of timidity and eagerness to please the West, Dag Hammarskjold, on the other hand, was known for defiance; even declaring in a cable on September 15, 1961, to Ralph Bunche (an American Envoy at the United Nations) that "it is better for the UN to lose the support of the US because it is faithful to law and principles than to survive as an agent whose activities are geared to political purposes never avowed or laid down by the major organs of the UN", see Henning Melber in "Lumumba, Hammarskjold and the Cold War in the Congo", *New African*, January 2017, p. 23, op. cit.

92 See Kofi Annan (2012), Interventions . . ., p. 322, op. cit.

93 Loc. Cit.

withdraw their support from him as well".[94] Meanwhile, although there were high hopes that Antonio Guterres as the successor to Ban Ki-moon would be objective and bring what Kofi Annan called "hard and painstaking work"[95] to bear on his responsibilities as the United Nations Secretary-General, he was clearly assuming office with a huge baggage: such as rising nationalism around the world, growing regional tensions in Asia and the Middle East, the simplification and decentralization of the UN's sprawling bureaucracy, the bridging of the gender-equality gap in UN appointments, the civil war in Syria, a feisty China, and a U.S. President Trump that was hostile to multilateralism, climate change and refugees, etc.[96]

However, it is expected that as the current Secretary-General of the United Nations, a successor to Ban Ki-moon that was considered too soft if not lackluster (and with his wealth of experience as the Portuguese former Prime Minister and the former United Nations High Commissioner for Refugees),[97] Antonio Guterres would show an improvement on the handling of the politics of the United Nations Security Council. Even if it is not expected that Guterres would be as defiant as Dag Hammarskjold, he would, at least, be expected to be instructed by the wisdom of one of his predecessors, Boutros Boutros-Ghali, that "the first priority of a Secretary-General . . . has to be the relationship between the United States and the United Nations",[98] being a country that, irrespective of being one of the major powers that founded the organization, is the chief (though sometimes reluctant) financer of the UN; but, yet paradoxically filled with UN-bashers, people that are highly suspicious and would prefer that the organization not be granted its well-deserved autonomy but should rather remain a stooge or lapdog of Washington.[99]

And obviously with the United States and Russia in mind, Guterres had tried from the outset to skillfully walk on this minefield when he told Christiane Amanpour while serving as the United Nations Commission for Refugees that the fighting in Syria was only going on because the belligerents were getting support from outsiders.[100] He spoke in euphemistic terms and had not tried to defiantly and pointedly apportion blames. Although the convergence of interests amongst the permanent members (especially the United States and Russia) rarely happens, but the United Nations needed a Secretary-General that would have as his or her primary responsibility, the enlistment of a personal charm and

94 Ibid., pp. 322–323.

95 Ibid., p. 322.

96 See "Spotlight: The World's New Diplomat in Chief", *Time* (New York), December 26, 2016–January 2, 2017, p. 9.

97 See "Portugal's Antonio Guterres Is Next UN Scribe", *The Guardian* (Lagos), Friday, October 7, 2016, pp. 1, 6.

98 See Boutros Boutros-Ghali (1999), *Unvanquished: A US-UN Saga*, London and New York, I.B. Tauris Publishers, p. 6.

99 Ibid., pp. 3–4; see also Fred Aja Agwu (2013), *Themes and Perspectives* . . ., pp. 180–181, op. cit.

100 Christiane Amanpour on CNN, monitored in Lagos (Nigeria), October 13, 2016, at 7pm local time.

some sort of activism to build bridges and enable the attainment of procedural objectives, if not an absolute unanimity among the permanent members of the Security Council in particular. Like in Bosnia where the United States and Russia attained a historic cooperation through "the unprecedented deployment of Russian troops . . . under American command as part of NATO-led peacekeeping force",[101] these two most important members of the UN Security Council must work together and try to get other members to cohere around them before the objective of world peace through the successful resolution of conflicts can be attained.

This unity of purpose at the Security Council would be the necessary prelude to the capacity of the organization to address substantive issues like the provision of "essential services and protections the world so badly needs".[102] But apart from the lack of consensus in the Security Council, there is also the problem of the ideological characterization that is often fastened to some of the insurgents that conduct terrorist campaigns. Although the two most powerful and assertive nations in the United Nations Security Council (Russia and the United States) are no strangers to the affliction of terrorism—Russia in its Dagestan region, and the United States in 9/11 and others attacks against its interests in the Middle East (Yemen) and Africa (the East African American embassy bombings)—they have largely remained divided on the question of how to deal with the ISIS and other insurgent groups in Syria. These national experiences with terrorism by both countries combine with the verdict of history to inform their disposition to terrorism.

For Russia, this verdict of history is embodied in what happened in Iraq and Libya. In Iraq, the dismantling of Saddam Hussein's regime resulted not in the establishment of democracy but in the sway of terrorist groups that have today coagulated and crystallized in the ISIS. In the height of the insurgency in Libya, Muammar Gaddafi warned the United States and its allies seeking to use the United Nations for humanitarian intervention that these insurgents (coming from its eastern city of Benghazi at that time) were nothing but terrorists. No heed was paid to him. After the overrunning of Gaddafi's regime and his death in the hands of those insurgents, his warning came to pass. Libya became completely taken over by terrorists, which resulted in an attack on the U.S. Consulate in Benghazi and the resultant death of the American Ambassador, Chris Stevens.[103] The fall of Gaddafi was also to lead to the diffusion of terrorism in the West African sub-region: from the *Ansar dine* in northern Mali, to the Boko Haram in Nigeria.[104]

101 See Richard Holbrooke (1998), *To End a War*, New York, The Modern Library, p. xvi.

102 See Ian Bremmer, "Who Can Run the U.N.? Why the World Needs a Better Secretary-General", p. 33, op. cit.

103 See pictures of Chris Stevens after the attack; *The Guardian* (Lagos), Thursday, September 13, 2012, back page.

104 See Fred Aja Agwu (2013), *Themes and Perspectives . . .*, pp. 360–361, 389–392, op. cit; see also Mohammed Abubakar and Kamal Tayo Oropo in "Buhari Links Terrorism in Africa to Gaddafi's Fall: Canvasses Special Committee to Stem Tide; Says 12,000 Killed, Displaced in Nigeria", *The Guardian* (Lagos), Sunday, November 29, 2015, p. 3.

But Washington had evidently not learned its lessons in Iraq and Libya as far as the liquidation of incumbents and creation of power vacuums are concerned;[105] not to talk about the eventual and disappointing manifestation of the rebels (insurgents) at the end of the day as ordinary terrorists, not genuine nationalists seeking for democratic change is concerned. It was probably for fear of a power vacuum that might lead to a total chaos comparable to the situation experienced in Iraq and Libya that in Syria, the United States was strongly advised to "focus on ISIS and leave Bashar alone", at least, temporarily.[106] And it was also apparently because of this verdict of history that Putin's Russia was hell bent in fostering Bashar Assad and saw nothing but terrorists beyond the Assad regime's forces.

Thus, the agendas of the United States and Russia vis-à-vis ISIS and Assad became difficult to be "perfectly aligned"[107] because the United States takes the ISIS as the only insurgency and terrorist group to be extirpated, believing that some of the "moderate" Sunni insurgents that are arraigned against Assad have a cause and should be supported. Thus, "Washington [is] providing increased support to moderate rebels in Syria while Moscow aids the dictator they are trying to unseat".[108] As it turned out, the agenda of the United States on Syria and ISIS turned out to be the agenda of the West writ-large; and instead of perfectly aligning this agenda with that of Russia, the two agendas literally collided when Turkey's missiles struck and downed a Russian fighter jet that allegedly strayed into Turkey's airspace while conducting bombings in Syria, putatively in an indiscriminate manner against both ISIS and the moderated rebels arraigned against Assad.[109]

The tense situation that arose from the downing of that Russian fighter jet did not only threaten to poison the relations between the two countries (Russia and Turkey), it also threatened to frustrate the overriding objective of countering ISIS in Syria and Iraq[110] as well as dent Russia's relations with the West, especially when the North Atlantic Treaty Organization (NATO) backed Turkey as its ally.[111] In a situation of this nature there was no Resolution raised in the United Nations Security Council to cavil or muster forces against the anti-Assad insurgents that would survive Washington's veto, except that such a Resolution was expressly targeted at the ISIS as was the case in the wake of ISIS' bombing of the Russian metro jet in Egypt's Sinai region.[112]

105 See Ian Bremmer in "Six Steps to Building an ISIS Strategy", *Time* (New York), December 14, 2015, p. 10, op. cit.

106 Loc. Cit.

107 Loc. Cit.

108 See Simon Shuster in "Putin's Syria Gamble", *Time* (New York), October 26, 2015, p. 25.

109 See "Russia and Turkey: No Room for Maneuver", *The Economist*, November 28, 2015, p. 15.

110 Loc. Cit.

111 Ibid., p. 16.

112 See David Von Drehle in "Beating ISIS: The War against the Terror Group Requires the Kind of Leadership That Has Gone Missing", p. 22, op. cit.

But in its approach, Russia, as opposed to the United States (and this is in Moscow's bid to foster Assad), tars all the anti-Assad forces with the same brush, implying that they are all terrorists that must be uprooted and done away with. Both Russia and Assad had claimed from the onset of the revolution in 2011 that all the rebels were terrorists, a claim that was then outrageous because at that initial stage, the uprising against the Syrian President was popular, given that it "saw Sunnis, marching cheerfully alongside Shias, Christians and Kurds" until President Assad destroyed the "peaceful resistance by using violence to radicalize his people".[113] With the fall of Eastern Aleppo meaning that the Assad government had taken over the entire strategic city, now driving the moderate rebels to Idlib province where the ISIS, the al-Qaeda, and the al-Nusra are all based, there is the probability that these moderate rebels would be contaminated by the terrorists and they would all now become terrorists, especially with the al-Nusra's known liaison with the moderate rebels in defence of Aleppo.

When Russia deployed its air power to devastating effect to ensure the fall of Aleppo, the city that was "the last Sunni Arab enclave" had "its 1,000-year-old Muslim heritage" turned to dust, with Russia's aircraft targeting its hospitals and schools; and its citizens shelled, bombed, starved, and gassed; so much so that the precarious fate of the tens of thousands that were crammed inside the ruins of where they were sheltering (not knowing whether a compromise truce would be reached to create a safe passage for their evacuation) became a metaphor for the international community's breach of their avowal to spare or protect the innocent from the ravages of war, but to also protect those that were directly targeted with genocidal intentions.[114] In fact, part of the reason that Russia is being enamoured of the terrorism bogey in Syria is in its determination to foster the Assad regime as a bulwark against Sunni fundamentalism that is fueling terrorism in its own Chechen region.[115]

The End Must Not Justify the Means

As a staunch ally of Syrian President Bashar al-Assad, it was in October 2015 that Russia began its coordinated airstrike campaign against the Assad regime's opposition in Syria that it regarded as "all terrorists" without any exception, culminating in its launching of rocket strikes on the ISIS from warships in the Caspian Sea; and with the 26 sea-based cruise missiles reportedly hitting and destroying 11 ISIS targets.[116] The United States and its allies had earlier begun their own arbitrary bombing campaigns against the ISIS without reference to the

113 See "The Fall of Aleppo: Vladimir Putin's Victory, the West's Failure; and a Warning of What Happens When Interests Triumph over Values", p. 11, op. cit.

114 Loc. Cit.

115 See Fred Aja Agwu (2016), *Nations among Nations*. . ., p. 744, op. cit.

116 See "Russia Launches Naval Bombardment against ISIS", *Vanguard* (Lagos), Thursday, October 8, 2015, p. 50.

United Nations procedures;[117] all because the United Nations Security Council cannot act, for its permanent members (Russia and the United States) could not cohere to act with a common purpose, will, or unanimity. This is part of the problem in dealing with some of the modern-day terrorists or insurgents. Everything is not just naked politics, it is focused exclusively on the national interest of the concerned permanent members of the United Nations Security Council, and this focus is without any meaningful sense of *noblese oblige* toward the much-rhapsodized principle of the responsibility to protect that the international community had collectively endorsed and sworn to uphold.

In this obsession about the national interest, Russia was apparently more culpable in Syria. As admitted by Leonid Kalashnikov, the first deputy chairman of the foreign affairs committee in Russia's lower house of parliament, the State Duma, although "Russia's air force did not distinguish between moderate rebel forces and the extremists of ISIS",[118] President Putin was still habouring the deeper design and waxing poetic about "a broad alliance against ISIS, one that would combine Russian and American airpower", the real calculation beyond the façade being that "the U.S. could hardly keep up its sanctions against Russia" in the wake of Russia's annexation of Crimea and support of the separatists in Eastern Ukraine if the two countries could successfully build a coalition or alliance in Syria.[119]

But President Obama was strongly opposed to this design because he believed that "from their [Russian] perspective, they're all [the entire opposition groups in Syria] terrorists", which according to him, is "a recipe for disaster, and it's one that I reject".[120] Yet, in persisting in his bombing of "the patchwork of rebel forces directly opposed to the Syrian regime—including those that have the support of the U.S. and its allies", Putin's key aim in Syria was reportedly "to convince the West that it cannot defeat ISIS without Russia's help"; that "as long as they don't back away from this [sanctions against Russia] [the West] will have a very hard time pacifying the storm of international terrorism".[121] So, as far as tackling this issue of terrorist insurgency (and its counterpart problem of international terrorism) in Syria is concerned, the United States and Russia are playing the Russian roulette, using the Machiavellian principle that the end justifies the means—that is, not being inhibited by any moral norm or scruples in the use of raw power (either directly or in disguise)—to achieve their various national interests in Syria. In the Machiavellian principle that the end justifies the means (as embodied in Chapter 18 of his controversial book, *The Prince*), the Prince is advised to be

117 See The US/Arab allies, which began their own airstrikes inside Syria a year earlier on Tuesday, September 23, 2014, comprised Saudi Arabia, the United Arab Emirates, Jordan, Bahrain, Qatar and, of course, the US itself; see "US, Arab Allies Launch Strikes on ISIS", *Vanguard* (Lagos), Wednesday, September 24, 2014, p. 16.

118 See Simon Shuster in "Putin's Syria Gamble", p. 25, op. cit.

119 Ibid., p. 24.

120 Ibid., p. 25. Brackets mine.

121 Ibid., p. 24. Brackets mine.

both man and beast (employ law and force as the occasion demands), to employ deceit and immorality, and to eschew discipline or the law if recourse to these "virtues" would limit or inhibit his power to control and ensure stability in his state.[122]

Applying the Machiavellian principle in international politics (in Syria and Iraq for instance), and as far as the war on terror is concerned, it does not matter to the United States and Russia that the recourse to this self-serving principle can sometimes be counterproductive. As observed by Fareed Zakaria,[123] it was clearly Washington's Machiavellian expediency that led it to put boots on the ground in Afghanistan and Iraq in search of the realization of the decidedly elusive Western democracy, but the result was chaos; it was also this Machiavellian tactic that guided this great global hegemon into the intermediate course of using the North Atlantic Treaty Organization (NATO) to pursue humanitarian intervention in Libya while eschewing the policy of putting boots on the ground, but the outcome was yet again total chaos; and it was the same obsession with the Machiavellian principle that propelled Washington to totally foreswear intervention or remain aloof in Syria, thus not putting boots on the ground and unfortunately making limited use of local forces, comprising only the anti-Assad rebels while Russia, still indulging in the same Machiavelli approach, was tugging in the opposite direction, resulting in the same chaotic situation as in Iraq and Libya.

It has been highly supportive of the war on terror, especially since 9/11; but Russia largely sees the insurgency in Iraq and Libya as an American problem; it also sees Syria as an arena for a test of will with the United States. In stressing this dilemma, *The Economist* was rightly of the view that:

> All attempts to bring peace to Syria have foundered on the question of what will happen to Mr. Assad. Russia, Iran and Mr. Assad himself view it as non-negotiable that he will remain in office throughout any transitional period leading to an election, in which he intends to be a candidate. For America, Sunni Arabs and the rebels, Mr. Assad's departure is an essential precondition for peace. They cannot abide the prospect of a man who gases civilians and deliberately bombs hospitals clinging to power.[124]

The missing like in all of this is the honest determination to transcend narrow national interests and embrace an all-inclusive or broad-based international agenda that will make confronting the insurgency and the war on terror more meaningful, effective, and rewarding; that is, a framework that will usher in a resounding defeat of international terrorism. But unfortunately, as seen earlier, the United States and Russia were seriously at odds over Syria, particularly over

122 See Niccolo Machiavelli (1961, trans. George Bull), *The Prince*, London, Penguin Books, pp. 56–58.

123 Fareed Zakaria in his Global Policy Square (GPS) on Cable News Network (CNN), monitored in Lagos, Nigeria, on Saturday, October 31, 2015, circa 8pm.

124 See "Syria's Ceasefire: A Risky Bargain". . ., p. 16, op. cit.

the fate of President Bashar Assad.[125] Although Russia is understandably afraid of a political vacuum in Syria that would eventually be occupied by terrorists, like Iraq and Libya, but Bashar Assad's departure is clearly key to any political resolution that will end the Syrian insurgency and its terrorist campaigns. To be opposed to by "as many as 70,000 moderate opposition fighters"[126] as is the case with President Assad, is surely a death knell for such a political regime.

Thus, Russia's President Putin's insistence on Assad's continued relevance in Syria, therefore, deserves a serious reconsideration. It is commonsensical that when one is digging a hole and one suddenly finds oneself inside that hole, wise counsel dictates that one stops the digging forthwith. This is the limits of any Machiavellian maneuvering or gymnastics. When the American Secretary of State, John Kerry, and his Russian counterpart, Sergei Lavrov, met on the sidelines at a meeting of the Organization for Security and Cooperation in Europe (OSCE), they actually recognized that it was these odds (the working at cross purposes with Machiavelli tactics) that had continued to militate against the defeat of Daesh (the derogatory name for ISIS), with John Kerry, while idealizing the possibility of the two countries transcending these odds, exclaiming as follows: "just imagine how quickly this scourge could be eliminated in a matter of literally months, if we were able to secure that kind of political resolution".[127] True to John Kerry's exclamation, it is amazing what the United States and Russia can achieve if they cooperate or join their efforts in fighting to subdue the ISIS.

A glimpse on what such a cooperation can achieve was seen in the Thursday, December 17, 2015 first-ever United Nations Security Council meeting of Finance Ministers in which the United States and Russia co-authored a Resolution that elevated ISIS to the same level as the al-Qaeda and targeted or sought to throttle its (the ISIS) financial network, sever its revenue from the sale of oil and antiquities, and extortion.[128] In the implementation of the Resolution, all these were to be achieved through asset freezes and arms embargo for companies, entities and individuals that were shown to be helping fund the ISIS.[129] In no time, and this was in early 2016 (the next year), these throttling financial measures added to the allied forces' attacks on ISIS oil wells to force the extremist organization "to cut its fighters' biweekly paychecks in half", culminating inevitably in its policy of "forced conscription and executions of deserters" recording increased cases.[130]

125 See "Airstrikes Alone Won't Defeat Islamic State, Kerry Warns", *The Guardian* (Lagos), Friday, December 4, 2015, p. 49.

126 Loc. Cit.

127 Loc. Cit.

128 See "UN Security Council Adopts Plan to Throttle ISIS Financial Network", available at www.irishtimes.com/news/world/us/un-security-council-adopts-plan-to-throttle-isis-financial-network-1.2470417 (last visited on Tuesday, February 23, 2016).

129 Loc. Cit.

130 See Mark Thompson in "War on ISIS Update: Two Steps Forward, One Step Back", p. 13, op. cit.

Al-Nusra: Do Away With the Al-Qaeda by Whatever Name Called

The al-Nusra, which changed its name from Jabhat al-Nusra to Jabhat Fatah al-Sham (JFS),[131] is the rebellious progeny of the al-Qaeda that has come to eclipse the parent organization after the death of its founder, Osama bin Laden.[132] Like the mainstream al-Qaeda that Osama bin Laden led—and even the ISIS that emerged from the ashes or ruin of the mainstream al-Qaeda that was dislodged from Afghanistan after 9/11—the al-Nusra is guided by the grand strategy that the co-founder (second-in-command) of the mainstream al-Qaeda, Ayman al-Zawahiri, had designed, and which stipulates that Muslims must have a "base in the heart of the Muslim world" from where they would cleave to the masses and galvanize other Muslims everywhere in the world to strike, not the local regimes but the United States and the West.[133] But unlike the ISIS that declared a Caliphate in 2014 from where it inspires jihadists everywhere in the world,[134] the al-Nusra—like its parent or mainstream body that Osama bin Laden led, even though its ultimate aim is the Caliphate—plans to declare an Islamic "emirate" that is one notch down from a Caliphate[135]—"a kind of protected territorial base on the borders of Europe that the international community would find very hard to root out".[136]

This is the extent to which the al-Nusra, like other terrorist organizations, is deeply pernicious and cannot be trusted or cultivated as an ally. But to make itself attractive to the masses amid the failing state of Syria in war, the al-Nusra began to perform political functions by practicing "the soft side of jihadism", functioning "as a quasi-government in areas where it is dominant" in Syria, paving roads, repairing electricity lines, pumping water and rebuilding damaged infrastructure, providing subsides for essential commodities like bread, running flour mills and bakeries, offering Islamic education, providing health care and ensuring that rents remain low for families displaced by the fighting, controlling the judicial system by settling disputes (thus, steering the locals toward its ideology), guaranteeing access to marriage certificates, access to property deeds, and forestalling looting, providing police functions, especially in marketplaces, amongst others.[137] So, although the al-Nusra and the ISIS share the same belief in the "jihad market",[138] especially against the United States, the West in general, and the Shiite Muslims, it differs substantially from the ISIS in so many contexts.

131 See "Syria's Ceasefire: A Risky Bargain". . ., p. 16, op. cit.
132 See "Al-Qaeda: The Other Jihadist State" . . ., p. 53, op. cit.
133 Loc. Cit.
134 Loc. Cit.
135 Loc. Cit.
136 Ibid., p. 54.
137 Loc. Cit.
138 See Bill Powell, Mahmoud Shikh Ibrahim, Jack Moore, and Mirren Gidda in "The New ISIS Crisis". . ., p. 32, op. cit.

Some of these contexts are as follows: whereas the ISIS took the fast lane to the realization of the Caliphate, the al-Nusra contented itself with an Islamic Emirate; whereas the ISIS "doubled down on its anti-Shia sectarianism and the management of savagery"—favouring "ostentatious brutality, the extermination of rivals and the imposition of strict sharia rules"—the "Jabhat al-Nusra, by contrast, seeks to win the respect of the brutalized and de-emphasize sharia strictures".[139] The consequence of this moderation (this lightening of the yoke for the people) is that the al-Nusra formed an alliance with the moderate opposition groups in Syria that are fighting Assad, focusing on the fight in Syria rather than the global jihad, and treating the establishment of the Caliphate as a long-term objective that will be realized when the conditions are propitious or ripe.[140]

In Syria, Shiites militias from Iraq had been deployed by the Iranians and Russia to fight Sunni rebel groups; thus, including not just the ISIS but also the al-Nusra (or Jabhat Fateh al-Sham) because of the latter's alliance with the moderate opposition hitherto defending the besieged city of Aleppo.[141] It was by joining forces with the moderate opposition to defend Aleppo, amongst other daring-do by the group that the al-Nusra "secured [their] place in the hearts and minds of the Syrian people".[142] So, in Syria, the importance of the al-Nusra has since grown in immensity. The group has remained highly invaluable. In fighting Assad, the al-Nusra had become a strategic and indispensible partner of the opposition, being to the moderate opposition fighting force in Syria what the Syrian jets and Russia were to the Assad regime.[143] In fact, al-Nusra's "cadre of suicide-bombers, known as *inghimasi*, was used with devastating effect to breach the Syrian regime's lines before rebel assaults"; thus, being "instrumental in breaking the siege of rebel-held Aleppo", a respite from siege though brief, earned the al-Nusra the gratitude of many in the city.[144]

The consequence of this invaluable asset that the Syrian rebels had found in the al-Nusra was that although the rebel groups kept the later botched September 10, 2016 ceasefire agreed upon in Geneva, few agreed with the condition that Russia demanded of the United States—that is, that the United States must make them to separate from the al-Nusra.[145] The rebel groups feared that should fighting resume (which eventually turned out to be the case)—as it did after the earlier abortive ceasefire in February 2016—Mr. Assad's forces would reclaim territory and the al-Nusra would no longer be there to help them out with its dare-devil suicide bombers.[146] So, many of the rebels felt that separating from or alienating

139 See "Al-Qaeda: The Other Jihadist State" . . ., pp. 53–54, op. cit.

140 Ibid., p. 54.

141 See Bill Powell, Mahmoud Shikh Ibrahim, Jack Moore, and Mirren Gidda in "The New ISIS Crisis". . ., p. 32, op. cit.

142 Loc. Cit.

143 See "Al-Qaeda: The Other Jihadist State" . . ., p. 54, op. cit

144 Loc. Cit.

145 Loc. Cit.

146 Loc. Cit.

the al-Nusra "would be like ripping a vital organ from the body of the revolution".[147] Although, as the U.S. Secretary of State, John Kerry, conceded, going after the al-Nusra was not a concession to anybody as, according to him, "it is profoundly in the interest of the United States to target al-Qaeda"; but for the very reason that the al-Nusra had "taken a central role in the fight against Bashar al-Assad's regime", Washington began pussy-footing toward the group; in fact, it can be said that the United States developed a cloven-hoof attitude toward it.[148]

The simple reason for the United States' apparent hesitation in separating the al-Nusra from the moderate rebel groups and going after the former was that it could risk "being seen as doing Mr. Assad's bidding";[149] that is, destroying one of Assad's most formidable enemies that could help defeat his regime on the battlefield. Thus, despite being an offshoot of the al-Qaeda that felled the twin towers (the World Trade Center in New York), but the fact that the al-Nusra demonstrated a "striking pragmatism" in Syria; the fact that the group demonstrated "prowess in fighting Mr. Assad" and even—upon changing its name in July 2016 to Jabhat Fatah al-Sham" (JFS)—declared that "it was severing its 'external' links with al-Qaeda", turning nationalistic and abjuring attacks on the West, some strands of thoughts in the United States began to suggest that some feelers should be put out to it.[150] These feelers would be tantamount to going into alliance with the al-Nusra. Unfortunately, dangerous alliances can be self-defeatist in the war on terror; and this, the East African nation of Kenya can tell better.

What complicated Kenya's fight against the al-Shabaab Islamists was that from the onset of its forces' invasion under the platform of AMISON, the country "allied itself with certain powerful clans to defeat the militants and set up a friendly administration in Southern Somalia".[151] The result was that this "unholy alliance" attracted resentment and backlash from the rival and excluded clan, thus, negating the benefit of the Kenyan invasion and precipitating the capacity of the al-Shabaab to stage more dare-devil raids, overrunning some AU camps, killing or capturing some of the peacekeepers despite the decimation of its leadership by U.S. missile strikes.[152] It was in this same way that the U.S. rapport with the al-Nusra, real or perceived, posed the danger of inhibiting the fight against the ISIS in Syria.

But the real problem was that given the extent to which the al-Nusra had blended into the opposition rebel groups, it was really very difficult for Washington to separate them from the moderate opposition rebels, which had cleaved or stuck with "the jihadists [al-Nusra] as long as they fear Mr. Assad may come

147 Loc. Cit.
148 Loc. Cit.
149 Loc. Cit.
150 See "Syria's Ceasefire: A Risky Bargain". . ., p. 16, op. cit.
151 See Bevertone Kipchumba Some in "Kenya's al-Shabaab Paradox", *New African*, June 2017, p. 51.
152 Loc. Cit.

back";[153] and the failure to abide by the terms of the ceasefire meant that the Geneva ceasefire agreement had no chance at all ab initio, prompting President Assad's resumption of the strafing of Aleppo with Russia when the September 10th ceasefire collapsed, and the inherent breaching of the red line that the United States had said Assad's use of chemical weapons would amount to.[154] In addition to gassing civilians and deliberately bombing hospitals, President Assad also deployed "barrel bombs and cluster munitions, destroying both hospitals and medical know-how in rebel-held territories" if not the entire Syria, which paved the way for basic "emergency room sanitation to decline back in decades, leading to the emergence of infectious diseases that were resistant to antibiotics, amongst other serious medical complications in the country".[155]

Many American red lines had been crossed in Syria apparently with Russia's collusion with the Assad regime in not allowing for consequences—a Russian collusion with Assad that may have equally encouraged Washington's reluctance to move decisively against the al-Nusra. On the other hand, President Assad got away with the violation of American red lines because the U.S. Congress refused to give President Obama the approval to use direct American force in Syria. It was in this context that the United States and the moderate opposition rebel groups might have felt that attacking the al-Nusra "would thus been seen as defending Syria's dictatorship", which was capable of inspiring or promoting more jihadism.[156] But the truth that the United States and the moderate opposition fighters in Syria ought to have been at home with was that whatever name called, the al-Nusra is still an integral part of al-Qaeda despite the change of name; [and that] the danger is that they are acquiring popular support [which] if it continues to grow then it could become a genuine mass movement . . . ; [and] with a large enough majority behind them, they could establish an emirate.[157]

And when the emirate is established (even though the al-Nusra has purportedly disavowed any intention to attack the West), the al-Nusra would certainly return to the original objective of the core or pristine al-Qaeda because the leopard can hardly shed its colour. With the emergence of President Donald Trump who had been critical of President Obama for using kid gloves against ISIS—and

153 See "Syria's Ceasefire: A Risky Bargain". . ., p. 16, op. cit.
Parentheses mine.

154 See Fred Aja Agwu (2016), *Nations among Nations* . . ., pp. 736–751, op. cit.

155 See Peter Schwartzstein in "Syria Superbugs: Bashar al-Assad's War in Syria Could Produce Something Far More Deadly Than ISIS; the End of Antibiotics", pp. 18–21, op. cit. However, there was also an argument by a UK government study that suggested that the antibiotic resistance, the antimicrobial resistance, could be blamed on "widespread drug use in agriculture, as farmers force-feed antibiotics to animals to fatten them up", ibid., p. 20.

156 See "Syria's Ceasefire: A Risky Bargain". . ., p. 16, op. cit.

157 See "Al-Qaeda: The Other Jihadist State" . . ., p. 54, op. cit.

with a Congress dominated by the Republicans after the November 8, 2016 elections—it is possible that the lawmakers may authorize a direct American force in Iraq if the ISIS survives the siege that has been laid on it since October 2016 by a combination of the Iraqi military, the Kurdish Persmerga, and the international coalition, which has significantly rolled back the territory of the Caliphate, taking Mosul and besieging its capital in the Syrian city of Raqqa.

But the snag here is that, based on his belief that U.S. confrontation with Russia "is pointless and that there is surely something to gain from toning down what might become a dangerous escalatory spiral in cyber conflict";[158] "Trump wants to destroy ISIS, preferably with Russian help",[159] which might unsettle American allies in Saudi Arabia and other countries that do not want anything to do with Russia and Iran, the latter of which were countries that allegedly prop up the Shiites in their confrontation with the Sunnis in the region. This is the delicate situation that is involved in the possibility of the United States contemplating working with Russia in the fight against the ISIS. It is a mutual distrust that had taken root over many years that dates back to the tumultuous ideological confrontation between the Western world led by the United States, and the defunct Soviet Union, which was succeeded by Russia. Overcoming this ancient mistrust is key to any convergence or global cooperation in contemporary times towards the solution of problems, be they in Syria, in Ukraine, and in the Korean Peninsula, amongst other crisis spots around the world.

Emphasize Counter-Terrorism Alongside Counter-Insurgency

It is trite knowledge that insurgency can only be defeated by counter-insurgency, and that counter-insurgency cannot defeat terrorism because terror is not territorial or amenable to pitched battles along unambiguous frontlines. However, it is only the defeat of insurgency by counter-insurgency that can deny insurgency the territory (aside from virtual or cyberspace) within which it can plan or incubate terror attacks. This in turn will pave the way for the implementation of counter-terrorism measures, part of which "involves addressing the underlying grievances and conflicts that feed extremism" that President Obama adverted to in his speech at the National Defense University quoted earlier above. It is the win-the-population strategy. Thus, a death knell on insurgency could be sounded and its life-line amongst the civilian population, especially by taking territories in places like Raqqa in Syria, Mosul in Iraq, or the Sambisa Forest in northeast Nigeria. This strategy creates a good turning point in the war on terror.

But even if the United States and Russia are to eventually transcend their odds over Syria, the overarching question would still remain: how can

158 See Ian Bremmer in "Trump Will Thaw Chilly U.S.-Russia Relationship", p. 12, op. cit.
159 Loc. Cit.

counter-insurgency destroy insurgency effectively enough to pave way for counter-terrorism measures? The point has been made that counter-insurgency measures that are exclusively grounded on airstrikes alone, including, of course, drone strikes, cannot defeat Daesh (the ISIS);[160] or, indeed, any other form of insurgency. In the wake of the Parish terror attacks that killed 130 people and left hundreds wounded, the United Kingdom joined France and the United States to ramp up airstrikes against the ISIS as the United States also reversed itself on the policy of no boots on the ground in Syria, but only deploying a paltry 50 U.S. Special Forces for purposes of coordinating on the ground with the U.S.-backed rebels.[161] Until the routing of the ISIS in Mosul and Raqqa, this was sheer tokenism. The refusal by the Obama administration to dispatch large numbers of U.S. troops to Syria or Iraq was dismissed by critics as an unacceptable "creeping incrementalism" that would not be enough to dislodge the ISIS from its self-proclaimed caliphate, especially when other actors like Russia were pulling from the opposite direction and "inadvertently" helping the ISIS to entrench itself as an enduring feature of the Middle East's landscape.[162] This is more so when (in some cases like Iraq where, under the tutelage of the U.S. military) "the Iraqi army remains a work in progress"; that is, not professionally fit enough to defeat the ISIS; neither is there a viable Arab force to do the job.[163]

Thus, "creeping incrementalism" is a flawed strategy on the part of the United States. This had resulted in the argument, matter-of-factly, that there must be boots on the ground, even if (for instance in Syria) these boots are not foreign (or Western), but rather local Syrian and Arab forces, particularly when there were already, "as many as 70,000 moderate opposition fighters in Syria ready to take on the Islamic State with the help of foreign airstrikes".[164] But the question is this: is it better to deal with the ISIS with local Syrian and Arab forces rather than Western, especially U.S. forces? Addressing this question requires the frank acknowledgement that there is always a problem of interoperability when multinational forces join hands to confront an insurgency, and that this problem is real.[165] Indeed, when the composition of any multinational force goes beyond the immediate socio-political, economic, and cultural environment to include forces from distant Western countries, this problem of interoperability is intensified or gets worse with some aggravated differences in professional parameters.[166]

And when these problems are combined with the ambiguous mandate or Rules of Engagement (ROE) for multinational forces confronting insurgencies

160 See "Airstrikes Alone Won't Defeat Islamic State, Kerry Warns", p. 49, op. cit.

161 Loc. Cit.

162 See Mark Thompson in "War on ISIS Update: Two Steps Forward, One Step Back", pp. 12–13, op. cit.

163 Ibid., p. 13.

164 See "Airstrikes Alone Won't Defeat Islamic State, Kerry Warns", p. 49.

165 See Giuseppe Caforio (2013), "Officer and Commander in Asymmetric Warfare Operations ", pp. 11–13, op. cit.

166 Ibid., pp. 17–18.

(rules of engagement written by politicians in their state capital or the cozy offices in international organizations, not by soldiers with field or operational experiences),[167] the unacceptable consequences will be better experienced than imagined. Yet, the overarching question remains that if boots must be put on the ground to defeat ISIS, there must be means, one way or the other, to also "put the boots on cyberspace" if possible. Who can take down the many ISIS radicalization and mobilization sites on the Internet? All these are the many problems that must be subdued before the defeat of any insurgency, particularly the ISIS. And the subdual of these problems must also be inclusive, as *The Economist* recommended, of the following: upholding or keeping intact all the West's liberal values; denying the insurgency its territory or "homeland" in Raqqa (Syria) and Mosul (Iraq), places that had once been a symbolic victory for extremism and insurgency; pacifying the "titanic struggle between Sunni and Shia Islam"; achieving a common cause against the ISIS for the United States and Russia; and getting the Middle East nations to live in peace, particularly if the regional powers stop fighting through their proxies.[168]

To advancing the cause of peace in the Middle East, an emphasis must be placed on such counter-terrorism political measures as healing the divisions between Arabs and Kurds as well as the deep rift between the Sunnis and the Shiites.[169] In the actualization of this objective, sight is not lost on the fact that the seemingly intractable Sunni/Shiite acrimony, in addition to Alawites and Kurdish question, can also be solved through "the creation of federal states in Syria and Iraq that gives Sunnis, Shias, Alawites and Kurds confidence that they can live together with decent representation in government", which "requires strengthening the administration in Baghdad" and "bringing an end to Syria's civil war".[170] Unfortunately, the battlefield equation in the Syrian civil war changed in February 2016 when "Russia's nearly five-month air war in Syria which has mostly targeted other rebel groups, not ISIS—strengthened the regime of President Bashar Assad".

But in the realization of the objective of bringing the Syrian civil war to a close, Ian Bremmer, for instance, reinforced this federalist option, advising, in addition, that political power vacuum must not be allowed in Syria; that the U.S. and Russia must close ranks or align forces, and if the alignment is difficult to achieve, at least, must not allow the collision of their differing agendas; that the ISIS must be denied funds; that the moderate opponents of Assad must be increasingly organized; that the Saudis must be roused from their complacency that had "allowed ISIS to become the best equipped and funded terrorist group in history"; and that both financial and political pressure must be piled to ensure

167 Loc. Cit.

168 See "How to Fight Back . . .", pp. 13, 14, op. cit.

169 See Mark Thompson in "War on ISIS Update: Two Steps Forward, One Step Back", p. 13, op. cit.

170 See "How to Fight Back . . .", p. 14, op. cit.

that Iraqi Sunnis have a stake in their country's future by establishing their place within the leadership in Baghdad"; for that is the only way that Sunni tribal leaders and those who follow them can turn on ISIS since "Shiite militia groups and the Shiite-dominated army will never fight to the death for Sunni cities".[171] These are tips that the United States, the leading power in the "war on terror" must take very seriously because, as the situation exists today, airstrikes, inclusive of drone strikes, alone cannot defeat the terrorist insurgents t; especially in their intractable and highly elusive terrorist campaigns.

171 See Ian Bremmer in "Six Steps to Building an ISIS Strategy", p. 10, op. cit.

Select Bibliography

Abdul-Jelil, A. G., "Agential and Structural Explanations of Radical Islamism in Northern Nigeria in the Fourth Republic" (2016), *Nigerian Army Journal*, Vol. 1, No. 1, February.

Achebe, C., *Things Fall Apart* (1958), London, Ibadan and Nairobi, Heinemann Educational Books.

Agwu, F. A., *From Rebellion, Insurgency to Belligerency: The Niger Delta Oil War in International Law* (2011), Ibadan, University Press Plc.

Agwu, F. A., *The Law of Armed Conflict and African Wars* (2011), Lagos, Ibadan, MacMillan Nigeria Publishers Limited.

Agwu, F. A., *National Interest, International Law and Our Shared Destiny* (2009), Ibadan, Spectrum Books Limited.

Agwu, F. A., *Nations among Nations: Uneven Statehood, Hegemony and Instrumentalism in International Relations* (2016), Ibadan, Heinemann Publishers Plc.

Agwu, F. A., *Themes and Perspectives on Africa's International Relations* (2013), Ibadan, University Press Plc.

Agwu, F. A., *United Nations System, State Practice and the Jurisprudence of the Use of Force* (2005), Lagos, Malthouse Press Limited.

Agwu, F. A., *World Peace through World Law: The Dilemma of the United Nations Security Council* (2007), Ibadan, University Press Plc.

Ake, C., *Social Science as Imperialism: The Theory of Political Development*, 2nd Edition (1979), Ibadan, Ibadan University Press.

Albright, M., *Madam Secretary: A Memoir* (2003), New York, Miramax Books.

Anderson, J., William, A., and Head, V., *War Crimes and Atrocities: Horrific Crimes Committed under the Guise of War* (2007), London, Fatura.

Annan, K., *Interventions: A Life in War and Peace* (2012), New York, The Penguin Press.

Archer, C., *International Organizations* (1983), London, George Allen & Unwin.

Aristotle, *Ethics* (1955, translated by J. A. K. Thomson), London, Penguin Books.

Bagudu, R., *Judging Annan* (2007), Bloomington, IN, Author House.

Barnett, T. P. M., *The Pentagon's New Map: War and Peace in the Twenty-First Century* (2004), New York, G. P. Putnam's Sons.

Barnhart, R. L., *The World Book Dictionary, Vol. One, A-K* (1974, ed.), Chicago, Doubleday & Company Inc.

Bond, J. E., *The Rules of Riot: Internal Conflicts and the Law of War* (1974), Princeton, NJ, Princeton University Press.

Bowett, D. W., *Self-Defence in International Law* (1958), Manchester, Manchester University Press.

Bush, G. W., *Decision Points* (2010), New York, Crown Publishers.

Byers, M., *War Law: Understanding International Law and Armed Conflict* (2005), New York, Grove Press.

Caforio, G., "Officer and Commander in Asymmetric Warfare Operations" (2013), *Journal of Defence Resources Management*, Vol. 4, No. 1(6).

Campbell, J., *Nigeria: Dancing on the Brink* (2011), New York, Rowman & Littlefield Publishers, Inc.

Carr, E. B., "Unmanned Aerial Vehicles: Examining the Safety, Security, Privacy and Regulatory Issues of Integration into U.S. Airspace" (undated), available at www.ncpa.org/pdfs/sp-Drones-long-paper.pdf (last visited on August 18, 2015).

Castaneda, J., *Legal Effects of United Nations Resolutions* (1969), New York, Columbian University Press.

Challis, D. S., "Counterinsurgency Success in Malaya" (1987), *Military Review*, No. 2, February.

Cheney, D., *In My Time: A Personal and Political Memoir* (2011), New York, Threshold Editions.

Clarke, R. A., *Against All Enemies: Inside America's War on Terror* (2004), New York, Free Press.

Clarke, R. A., *Sting of the Drone* (2014), New York, Thomas Dunne Books, St. Martin's Press.

Deeks, A., "New Battlefields/Old Laws: Shaping a Legal Environment for Counterinsurgency" (2011), *Proceedings of the Annual Meeting (American Society of International Law)*, Vol. 105, March 23–26.

Esposito, J. L. and Mogahed, D., *Who Speaks for Islam? What a Billion Muslims Really Think* (2007), New York, Gallup Press, Inc.

Estreicher, S., "Privileging Asymmetric Warfare (Part III)? The Intentional Killing of Civilians under International Humanitarian Law" (2012), *Chicago Journal of International Law*, Vol. 12, No. 2.

Eze, O. C., *Reciprocity in International Relations: Nigeria's Foreign Policy in Retrospect* (2010, ed.), Lagos, Nigerian Institute of International Affairs.

Feldman, N., *After Jihad: America and the Struggle for Islamic Democracy* (2003), New York, Farrar, Straus and Giroux.

Ferguson, N., *Kissinger, 1923–1968: The Idealist*, Volume 1 (2015), New York, Penguin Press.

Foot, R., "Collateral Damage: Human Rights Consequences of Counterterrorist Action in the Asia-Pacific" (2005), *International Affairs*, Vol. 81, No. 2, March.

Franke, V. C., *Terrorism and Peacekeeping: New Security Challenges* (2005, ed.), Westport, CT and London, Praeger.

Frunzeti, T., "Asymmetric, Unconventional and Hybrid Actions in 21st Century Warfare" (2013), *Strategic Impact*, No. 1.

Furtade, V., Page, R., and Scarcella, A., "Terrorism, Radicalization, Extremism, Authoritarianism and Fundamentalism: A Systematic Review of the Quality and Psychometric Properties of Assessments" (2016), *PLoS ONE*, DOI: 10.1371/journal.pone.0166947, December 21.

Galula, D., *Counter-Insurgency Warfare: Theory and Practice* (1964), New York and London, Frederick A. Praeger Publishers.

Gavshon, A. L., *The Last Days of Dag Hammarskjold* (1963), London, Barrie and Rockliff, with Pall Mall Press.

Gerges, F. A., *ISIS: A History* (2016), Princeton, NJ, Princeton University Press.

Ghali, B. B., *Unvanquished: A U.S.-U.N. Saga* (1999), London and New York, I.B. Tauris Publishers.

Gold, J., "Strengthening the Soft International Law of Exchange Arrangement" (1983), *AJIL*, Vol. 77.

Grant, M., *Cicero: On the Good Life* (1971, trans.), London, Penguin Books.

Grossman, L., "Middle Vision: Easily Accessible, Affordable Drones Are Giving us a New—Perhaps Temporary—Vantage on the World" (2014–2015), *Time* (New York), December 29, 2014–January 5, 2015.

Hallion, R. P., *Air Power Confronts an Unstable World* (1997, ed.), London and Washington, Brassey's.

Hayden, M. V., *Playing to the Edge: American Intelligence in the Age of Terror* (2016), New York, Penguin Press.

Heffelfinger, C. and Marquardt, E., *Terrorism & Political Islam: Origin, Ideologies, and Methods: A Counterterrorism Textbook*, 2nd Edition (undated, ed.), West Point, NY, Combating Terrorism Center, Department of Social Sciences, U.S. Military Academy.

Henkin, L., *How Nations Behave: Law and Foreign Policy* (1968), Washington, Praeger Publishers.

Herzog, R., "Dealing Death by Remote Control" (2015), *Newsweek* (London), April 17.

Holbrooke, R., *To End a War* (1998), New York, The Modern Library.

Horgan, J., "The Drones Come Home" (2013), *National Geographic*, March.

Ibrahim, R., *The Al-Qaeda Reader* (2007, ed.), New York, Broadway Books.

Jake Diliberto, J., "The New War Frontier: Understanding Modern Insurgency and the Syrian Civil War through the Iraq Insurgencies during 2006–2009", Paper for 2014 APSA Annual Conference (Unpublished).

Jeffrey, H. and Norwitz, J. H., *Pirates, Terrorists, and Warlords: The History, Influence, and Future of Armed Groups around the World* (2009, ed.), New York, Skyhorse Publishing.

Jennings, R. Y., "The Caroline and McLeod Cases" (1938), *AJIL*, Vol. 32.

Joffe, J., "Asymmetric Warfare: Since David Fought Goliath, the Weak Have Been Able to Vanquish the Strong" (2001), *Time* (New York), September 24.

Kalshoven, F., (1971), Belligerent Reprisals, Leyden, A. W. Sijthoff.

Kalshoven, F., *Constraints on the Waging of War* (1987), Geneva, International Committee of the Red Cross (ICRC).

Klare, M. T. and Kornbluh, P., *Low Intensity Warfare: Counterinsurgency, Proinsurgency and Antiterrorism in the Eighties* (1988), New York, Pantheon Books.

Knoops, G. J. A., "Legal, Political and Ethical Dimensions of Drone Warfare under International Law: A Preliminary Survey" (2012), *International Criminal Law Review*, Vol. 12.

Kuster, Jr., T. J., "Dealing with the Insurgency Spectre" (1987), *Military Review*, No. 2, February.

Lackey, D. P., *The Ethics of War and Peace* (1989), Englewood Cliffs, NJ, Prentice Hall.

Lauterpacht, H., "Revolutionary Activities by Private Persons against Foreign States" (1928), *AJIL*, Vol. 22.

Lee, M. C., *Africa's World Trade: Informal Economies and Globalization from Below* (2014), London, Zed Books.

Lewis, B., *The Crisis of Islam: Holy War and Unholy Terror* (2003), New York, The Modern Library.

Machiavelli, N., *The Prince* (1961, translated by G. Bull), London, Penguin Books.

Maclear, M., *Vietnam: The Ten Thousand Day War* (1981), England, Thames Methuen.

Macrine, S., "The Psychology of Radicalization" (2016), *The Counter Terrorist*, June/July.

Mamdani, M., *Good Muslim, Bad Muslim: America, the Cold War, and the Roots of Terror* (2004), New York, Pantheon Books, CODERIA Book Series.

Maria, B., "Current Issues of International Law in Regulating Counter-Insurgency and Counter-Terrorism" (2014), *AARMS*, Vol. 13, No. 4.

Maskaliunaite, A., "Exploring the Theories of Radicalism" (2015), *International Studies: Interdisciplinary Political and Cultural Journal*, Vol. 17, No. 1.

Mazrui, A. A., Bemath, A. S., and Adem, S., *The Politics of War and the Culture of Violence: North-South Essays* (2008, ed.), Trenton, NJ and Asmara, Eritrea, Africa World Press, Inc.

Mbanefo, A., *A Fulfilled Life of Service* (2015), Ibadan, Bookcraft.

McChrystal, S., *Team of Teams: New Rules of Engagement for a Complex World* (2015), New York, Portfolio/Penguin.

McClellan, S., *What Happened: Inside the Bush White House and Washington's Culture of Deception* (2008), New York, Public Affairs.

Meacham, J., *American Lion: Andrew Jackson in the White House* (2008), New York, Random House.

Nielsen, F. K., "The Lack of Uniformity in the Law and Practice of States with Regard to Merchant Vessels" (1919), *AJIL*, Vol. 13.

Nye, Jr., J. S., *Is the American Century Over?* (2015), Malden, MS, USA, Polity Press.

Oates, R. M., *Permanent Peace: How to Stop Terrorism and War—Now and Forever* (2002), Fairfield, IA, Institute of Science, Technology and Public Policy.

O'Brien, C. C., *On the Eve of the Millennium: The Future of Democracy through an Age of Unreason* (1994), New York, The Free Press.

Okadigbo, C., *Consciencism in African Political Philosophy (Nkrumah's Critique)* (1985), Enugu, Fourth Dimension Publishers.

Oppenheim, L., *International Law: A Treatise, Vol. II, Disputes, War and Neutrality*, 7th Edition (1952, edited by H. Lauterpacht), London, Longman.

Owen, M., *No Easy Day: The Autobiography of a Navy SEAL* (2012), New York, Dutton (A Member of Penguin Group, USA).

Patterson, R. B., *Dereliction of Duty: The Eyewitness Account of How Bill Clinton Compromised America's National Security* (2003), Washington, DC, Regnery Publishing Inc.

Piskulic, A., Zuzic, A., and Zekulic, V., "Support to Insurgency and Counter-Insurgency Operations" (2014), *AARMS*, Vol. 13, No. 1.

Proctor, P., *Longman Dictionary of Contemporary English*, Paper Edition (1978), London, Longman Group Limited.

Rashid, A., *Taliban: The Power of Militant Islam in Afghanistan and Beyond* (2000), London and New York, I.B. Tauris.

Ratnesar, R., "Life after Death: The Struggle against Jihadists Won't Be Won Just by Killing Their Leaders" (2007), *Time* (New York), May 28.

Rege, V., *Negotiating at the World Trade Organization: Lessons from the Commonwealth*, Volume 2, London, Commonwealth Secretariat.

Reisman, W. M., "Coercion and Self-Determination: Construing Charter Article 2(4)" (1984), *AJIL*, Vol. 78.

Reus-Smit, C., *The Politics of International Law* (2004, ed.), Cambridge, Cambridge University Press.

Rice, C., *No Higher Honour: A Memoir of My Years in Washington* (2011), New York, Crown Publishers.

Richards, A., "From Terrorism to 'Radicalization' to 'Extremism': Counterterrorism Imperative or Loss of Focus" (2015), *International Affairs*, Vol. 91, No. 2.

Robert, W. and Tucker, R. W., "Reprisals and Self-Defence: The Customary Law" (1972), *AJIL*, Vol. 66.

Robinson, J. A. and Acemoglu, D., *Why Nations Fail: The Origins of Power, Prosperity, and Poverty* (2012), New York, Crown Business.

Roggeveen, S., "Proliferation of Unmanned Aerial Vehicles: The Future of Drones" (2014), A Panelist Paper at the 2014 Council of Councils Annual Conference Panelist Papers, May 11–13.

Rosenzweig, P. and Carafano, J. J., *Winning the Long War: Lessons from the Cold War for Defeating Terrorism and Preserving Freedom*, Washington, DC, Heritage Books.

Roule, T. J. and Winer, J. M., "Fighting Terrorist Finance" (2002), *Survival*, Vol. 44, No. 3, Autumn, The International Institute for Strategic Studies (IISS).

Sadat, L. N., "The Legacy of the International Criminal Tribunal for Rwanda" (2012), Occasional Paper, Whitney R. Harris World Law Institute, Washington University in St. Louis, July.

Sanu, O. O., *Audacity on the Bound: A Diplomatic Odyssey* (2016), Ibadan, Mosuro Publishers.

Schachter, O., "The Legality of Pro-Democracy Invasion" (1984), *AJIL*, Vol. 78.

Schilling, W. R., *Nontraditional Warfare: Twenty-First Century Threats and Responses* (2002, ed.), Washington, DC, Brassey's, Inc.

Schmid, A. P., "Research on Radicalization: Topics and Themes" (2016), *Perspectives on Terrorism*, Vol. 10, No. 3, June.

Schwarzenberger, G., *The Inductive Approach to International Law* (1965), London, Stevens & Sons.

Sciolino, E., *Persian Mirrors: The Elusive Face of Iran* (2000), New York, The Free Press.

Seteolu, D., "Globalization: Challenges for the State in Africa" (2004), *Nigerian Forum*, Vol. 25, Nos. 1–2, January/February.

Sloane, R. D., "New Battlefields/Old Laws: Shaping a Legal Environment for Counterinsurgency" (2011), *Proceedings of the Annual Meeting (American Society of International Law)*, Vol. 105, March 23–26.

Small, S. C., "Small Arms and Asymmetric Threats" (2000), *Military Review*, No. 6, November/December.

Snow, A. H, "A Short History of War", (a book review), (1913), *AJIL*, Vol. 7.

Soyinka, W., *Climate of Fear: The Quest for Dignity in a Dehumanized World* (2004, 2005), New York, Random House.

Spanier, J., *Games Nations Play: Analyzing International Politics* (1972), London, Thomas Nelson and Sons Ltd.

Steiner, H. J. and Alston, P., *International Human Rights in Context, Law, Politics, Morals: Text and Materials*, 2nd Edition (2000), Oxford, Oxford University Press.

Stern, J., "Obama and Terrorism: Like It or Not, the War Goes On" (2015), *Foreign Affairs*, Vol. 94, No. 5, September/October.

Stiglitz, J. E., *Globalization and Its Discontents* (2002, 2003), New York and London, W. W. Norton & Company.

Stiglitz, J. E., *Making Globalization Work* (2006), London, Penguin Books.

Stone, J., *Legal Control of International Conflict: A Treatise on the Dynamics of Disputes and War-Law* (1954), Sydney, Maitland Publications Pty Ltd.

Thompson, M., "Can the Drones Be Stopped? As the US' Edge in Unmanned Aircraft Fades, a Scramble for Defenses" (2015), *Time* (New York), February 23–March 2.

Unger, C., *House of Bush, House of Saud: The Hidden Relationship between the World's Two Most Powerful Dynasties* (2004), London, Gibson Square Books.

Wagner, M., "Beyond the Drone Debate: Autonomy in Tomorrow's Battlespace" (2012), *Proceedings of the Annual Meeting (American Society of International Law)*, Vol. 106, March 28.

Warraich, A. N., "The Use of Drones: Legal Grey Area?" (2013), *Strategic Studies*, Vol. 38, No. 3/4, December.

Washington, G., "Staffing the Post Modern Army" (2002), *Military Review*, No. 6, November/December.

Weiss, M. and Hassan, H., *ISIS: Inside the Army of Terror* (2015), New York, Regan Arts.

Wilmshurst, E., Sliedgret, E. V., Heller, K. J., and Jones, R. W. D., "Milestones in International Criminal Justice: Recent Legal Controversies at the UN Yugoslav Tribunal" (2013), *International Law Summary*, Chatham House, October 16.
Woetzel, R. K., *The Nuremberg Trials in International Law, with a Postlude on the Eichmann Case* (1962), London, Stevens & Sons Limited.
Woods, N., "The Shifting Politics of Foreign Aid" (2005), *International Affairs*, Vol. 81, No. 2, March.
Woodward, B., *Plan of Attack* (2004), London and New York, Pocket Books.
Wright, Q., "Proposal for an International Criminal Court" (1952), *AJIL*, Vol. 46.
Yun, J., "Special Tribunal for Lebanon: A Tribunal of International Character Devoid of International Law" (2010), *Santa Clara Journal of International Law*, Vol. 7, No. 2.
Zakaria, F., *The Post-American World* (2008), London, Allen Lane.
Zenko, M., "Reforming U.S. Drone Strike Policies" (2013), Council on Foreign Relations, *Council Special Report No. 65*, January.

Index

For Product Safety Concerns and Information please contact our EU
representative GPSR@taylorandfrancis.com
Taylor & Francis Verlag GmbH, Kaufingerstraße 24, 80331 München, Germany

www.ingramcontent.com/pod-product-compliance
Ingram Content Group UK Ltd.
Pitfield, Milton Keynes, MK11 3LW, UK
UKHW022004180926
475701UK00003B/185

* 9 7 8 0 3 6 7 5 9 3 6 5 0 *